THE SOCIAL COSTS OF INDUSTRIAL GROWTH IN NORTHERN MEXICO

U.S.-Mexico Contemporary Perspectives Series, 22
CENTER FOR U.S.-MEXICAN STUDIES
UNIVERSITY OF CALIFORNIA, SAN DIEGO

Contributors

Diane Austin

Joe Bandy

Allen Blackman

Leonor Cedillo

James M. Cypher

María Eugenia de la O Martínez

Catalina Denman

Siobán Harlow

Alfredo Hualde

Alba Jaramillo

Michèle Kimpel Guzmán

Kathryn Kopinak

Edna Mendoza

Barbara J. Morehouse

Cirila Quintero Ramírez

María Eugenia Trejos

Robert Varady

THE SOCIAL COSTS OF INDUSTRIAL GROWTH IN NORTHERN MEXICO

Edited by

Kathryn Kopinak

LA JOLLA, CALIFORNIA

CENTER FOR U.S.-MEXICAN STUDIES, UCSD

Printed in the United States of America

Library of Congress Cataloging-in-Publication Data

The social costs of industrial growth in Northern Mexico / edited by
   Kathryn Kopinak.
     p. cm. – (U.S.-Mexico contemporary perspectives series ; 22)
   Includes bibliographical references.
   ISBN 1-878367-51-X (pbk).
     1. Industries—Social aspects—Mexico, North. 2. Offshore assembly
   industry—Mexico, North. 3. Mexico, North—Social conditions. 4.
   Mexico, North—Environmental conditions.
   I. Kopinak, Kathryn. II. Series

HD60.5.M482N677 2004
306.3'4'09721—dc22
                                                           2004057010

CONTENTS

1

Accounts Payable: An Introduction

Kathryn Kopinak

Both sides of the U.S.-Mexico border have been the destination for unprecedented numbers of incoming migrants and investors in the last forty years. North of the border, industries have restructured, moving from the "rustbelt" to the "sunbelt," setting up *maquiladora* industries along the international crossing. Firms have also relocated transcontinentally from Asia and Europe. Within Mexico, there has been a movement of firms northward, converting from production for domestic consumption to production for export, with the unemployed following in search of jobs. The magnitude of recent growth has been caused in large measure by the Mexican government's opening and liberalization of its economy during the 1980s and 1990s.

Legislation permitting maquiladora production, or production for export with taxes paid only on value added, was first introduced in the mid-1960s to provide jobs for braceros, Mexican male farmworkers who crossed the border annually to work. Slowly it became the economic base and motor of regional development for all of northern Mexico, and it is now the most successful export-industry model, not only throughout Mexico but also in the larger region that reaches to the Caribbean and Central America. This has made the U.S.-Mexico border a new "center" of the continent, recognized as one of the world's most successful export-processing regions, now planned to stretch as far as Panama.

There has been systematic, scientific research on Mexican maquiladora growth since the mid-1960s, when the Mexican government first passed legislation allowing foreign companies to import materials and equipment for processing duty-free and to export the products paying tax only on value added. Plants doing processing in Mexico have been called "in-bond" plants, export processors, and, most often, maquiladoras or simply maquilas. The subject of this book—the social costs of industrial growth—was a central part of the early maquiladora literature (Iglesias 1985; Fernández-Kelly 1983; Carrillo 1986). However, over the last decade there has been almost total silence on the issue. It last appeared in a debate between George Baker and Ellwyn Stoddard, published in the first two issues of the journal *Rio Bravo*, in 1991 and 1992.

Instead, research during the 1990s turned its focus to the arrival of a small number of large, capital-intensive plants that used advanced technology and hired more highly skilled labor in lean production processes—those called second- and third-generation maquilas (Carrillo and Hualde 1998).[1] First-generation plants, which were the norm from 1966 to the late 1970s, hired women to do simple assembly, especially in the garment and electronic sectors. Second-generation plants included more manufacturing, especially in the automotive and electronics sectors. A few third-generation plants emerging in the 1990s did some design and research as well. It was predicted that with greater investment due to free trade promotion under the North American Free Trade Agreement (NAFTA), second- and third-generation plants would become the new norm, stimulating greater production of supplies in Mexico, which on average had never comprised more than approximately 2 percent of all inputs. Unskilled assembly, in which little value was added, would supposedly no longer be done in Mexico by the majority of maquiladora industries, but would move to Central America and the Caribbean (Gereffi 1992). Researchers focusing on the "new maquila" (another name for second-generation plants) said that it was a "stereotype" to characterize export processing as dominated by simple assembly, and they argued that more advanced manufacturing work would bring the development of clusters, transfer of technology, and better-paid jobs.

Researchers' focus on the advantages of the "new maquila" is probably also part of the manifestation in the academy of the effects of the state-led opening of the Mexican economy to world markets. Although business

---

[1] Exceptions to this trend of ignoring the social costs of industrial growth during the 1990s were more likely to be published outside of Mexico. See, for example, Ganster and colleagues' work on childcare and family planning services in the maquiladora industry (Ganster and Hamson 1995).

groups paid lip service to the fact that workers' falling wages could hardly contribute much to the dynamism of the Mexican economy (Rodríguez 1997), the large research projects on maquiladora industries during the 1990s focused on topics more generally of interest to business. Carrillo and Santibáñez's 1993 study, *Rotación de personal en las maquiladoras de exportación en Tijuana*, represents the turning point of the literature in this direction. This is part of the Mexican version of the cult of management, whereby government—and the research institutions within its jurisdiction—were urged to become more like business, incorporating the values esteemed by the private sector (Mintzberg 1996: 83). Given that business is less concerned with social costs than is the larger society, it is not surprising that this research focus was abandoned during the 1990s. However, this leaves Mexico with a long way still to go to reach the goal of sustainable development, which Víctor Urquidi emphasizes has equity as a fundamental goal (1999: 32). If maquiladora industries are to contribute to sustainable development, their pay structures must facilitate greater equality in income, more employment security, and access to social benefits. Urquidi also notes that under sustainable development, people would suffer fewer disadvantages from the administrative acts of government and behaviors of business.

Jorge Alonso, Jorge Carrillo, and Óscar Contreras, well-known exponents of the advantages of second- and third-generation maquiladoras, began a recent article (2002) by noting that, though they see these industries as an opportunity for development, others see them as the origin of "social problems" such as deterioration in wages, employment, unions, and ecology—and with little positive offsetting impact on production. Unfortunately, these three authors fail to pursue such evenhandedness beyond the first few paragraphs, and the one citation they make in the first paragraph to a work on maquila-related social problems, a 2001 publication by Salas, is omitted from the bibliography. While this might be an editorial oversight, the one-sidedness of the remainder of the article is representative of a continuing and expanding blind spot in the research literature over the last decade.

This type of investigation tends to be strong on presentation of data, usually collected from interviews with managers and government sources. Unlike the early literature, it rarely includes interviews with workers and it consistently overlooks the social costs of maquiladora industrialization. For example, figure 3 in Alonso, Carrillo, and Contreras's article is a dramatic graphic illustration of how the 22 percent of autoparts maquiladoras that were domestically owned disappeared in the two years between 1997 and 1999, leaving this sector totally foreign-owned. Unfortunately, the authors highlight only the beneficial aspects of this development, stating, "The regional impact of maquiladora expansion goes much further than mere statistics about the concentration of plants and employment in certain locations. These agglomerations have generated diverse positive feedback effects, which are reflected not only in the scope of the firms but also in the localities in which these types of industries are specialized" (Alonso, Carrillo, and Contreras 2002: 51, 52).

There is no mention of why the Mexican-owned autoparts plants were closed or what happened to their employees. In the early 1990s, in fact, spokespersons for the Mexican autoparts industry had publicly protested the fact that Mexico's Trade Ministry (SECOFI) had ignored the stipulation that assemblers in Mexico had to use a specified proportion of domestically produced parts, as established under the 1989 Decree of the Development and Modernization of the Auto Industry (Kopinak 1996: 179, 180). The domestic autoparts producers urged strict application of the decree, arguing that they could have doubled their production between 1990 and 1995 had the decree been enforced. In the mid-1990s they called for this correction and for more assistance, predicting that their industries would disappear otherwise. They pleaded their case on the grounds that the domestic-owned autoparts producers paid more in wages, produced more products, and added more value in Mexico during 1989 and 1990 than the mostly foreign-owned autoparts maquilas, and hence they contributed more to the country. However, it appears that when the desires of foreign auto assemblers in Mexico differed from the public interest as defined by the Decree, the Trade Ministry was guided by foreign assemblers rather than national law.

ANOTHER INTERPRETATION OF THREE GENERATIONS OF MAQUILADORAS

There are well-known industrial leaders who believe that a first-generation maquiladora doing simple assembly, far from being a stereotype, remains the only sure bet for foreign industrial investors in Mexico. Alternative versions of the three-generation concept exist that do not focus on industrial upgrading. First-generation maquiladoras grew more in numbers and size than did "new" maquilas during the 1990s. This fact led some analysts to apply the three-generation concept to grandparents, parents, and children in the same family succeeding each other as employees in maquiladoras that serve as cost-reduction centers relying mainly on cheap wages.[2] Tacna International Corporation, a shelter company[3] in Baja California, titles its promotional pamphlet "Your Leader into Mexico's 'Maquiladora' Low-Cost Labor Arena" (see figure 1.1). Included inside the pamphlet are the following:

- "Low cost direct labor ... can save manufacturers up to $20,000 per direct labor employee per year" (figure 1.2).

- "The available labor force of approximately 800,000 is composed of third generation Maquiladora workers with the highest index of education in Mexico" (figure 1.3).

As Dale Fox, Tacna's vice president of business development, explained to participants in a recent tour of his Tijuana facilities, the savings of $20,000 per direct employee per year is in relation to the "fully loaded wage" in the electronics sector, which includes wages paid to employees as well as other costs such as telephone service, rent, electricity, and so on.

Putting Tacna's "three-generation" and "savings" arguments together, it is difficult not to suspect that savings to manufacturers have inhibited intergenerational upward mobility among workers, especially the low skilled, so that many among the current generation repeat the same kind of work as their parents and grandparents before them, at approximately the same real wage. Tacna's companies, which reduce costs to foreign firms by organizing and administering the low-skilled aspects of their production process in Mexico, are more the norm than are the advanced manufacturing plants of the second and third generation. They have shorter job ladders than maquiladoras doing more complete manufacturing, and thus they provide few "better" jobs to which workers might move up.

---

[2] Dale Fox, vice president of business development of the TACNA International Corporation, a shelter program, explained this version of the three-generation argument to participants in the Mexport Maquiladora Tour, in his shelter company in Tijuana on June 20, 2002. He also said that he started working in maquiladoras in Nogales, Sonora, in 1971, and that wages paid to direct workers were still the same in real terms.

[3] Shelter companies carry out a form of subcontracting in which a foreign company wishing to operate in Mexico supplies materials and components, while the shelter contracts with its own Mexican company to provide plant, labor, and administrative services. Shelter companies protect foreign companies from the necessity of legal involvement in Mexico.

Figure 1.1. Cover of Pamphlet for Tijuana Shelter Company

Coubès's (2001) work on the labor trajectories of Tijuana's low-wage workers, including self-employed workers and workers in services and maquilas, found that during these workers' childhood, more of their parents worked in agriculture than in any other economic sector. However, workers in maquiladoras were more likely (25 percent) than those employed in services (17 percent) and the self-employed (10 percent) to have had parents who had also worked in maquiladoras when today's generation of workers were children.[4] Moving from agricultural to maquiladora work may be considered getting ahead, but more investigation is needed to find out how much upward mobility occurs in families when two generations or more follow each other into the maquiladoras. In her longitudinal study of wages paid to maquiladora workers nationally, Susan Fleck (2001) has shown that the much-needed jobs that these industries supply do not provide for the growth of a middle class, something industrialization has done in more developed countries. Instead, this kind of job creation has been responsible for a decline in real wages.

Figure 1.2. First Page of Shelter Company Pamphlet

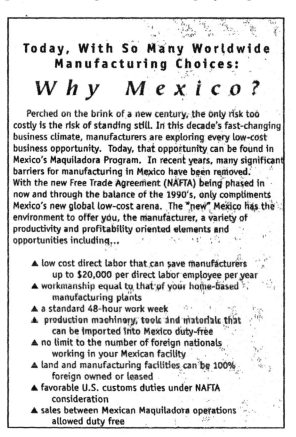

Today, With So Many Worldwide Manufacturing Choices:

W h y   M e x i c o ?

Perched on the brink of a new century, the only risk too costly is the risk of standing still. In this decade's fast-changing business climate, manufacturers are exploring every low-cost business opportunity. Today, that opportunity can be found in Mexico's Maquiladora Program. In recent years, many significant barriers for manufacturing in Mexico have been removed. With the new Free Trade Agreement (NAFTA) being phased in now and through the balance of the 1990's, only compliments Mexico's new global low-cost arena. The "new" Mexico has the environment to offer you, the manufacturer, a variety of productivity and profitability oriented elements and opportunities including...

▲ low cost direct labor that can save manufacturers up to $20,000 per direct labor employee per year
▲ workmanship equal to that of your home-based manufacturing plants
▲ a standard 48-hour work week
▲ production machinery, tools and materials that can be imported into Mexico duty-free
▲ no limit to the number of foreign nationals working in your Mexican facility
▲ land and manufacturing facilities can be 100% foreign owned or leased
▲ favorable U.S. customs duties under NAFTA consideration
▲ sales between Mexican Maquiladora operations allowed duty free

---

[4] There is an editing error in the lower right corner of Gráfica 1 of Coubès's (2001: 200) findings, whereby 25% is mistakenly given as 15%, as is clear from a close reading of the text. This was verified through communication with the author.

Figure 1.3. Final Page of Shelter Company Pamphlet

Who, What, Where, and the Simple Way It Works:

TACNA INTERNATIONAL CORPORATION was formed in 1984 to support foreign manufacturing companies who are seeking to improve their worldwide competitive position and looking to lower their manufacturing costs by setting up an offshore operation in Mexico. To help companies start and continue their operations in Mexico, TACNA services literally shelter you from the many time consuming obstacles, risks, and delays usually encountered when establishing and operating a foreign subsidiary. Our experienced administrative staff functions as the administrative arm of your Mexican subsidiary, bridging the cultural gap known as "the border". It is this ability to figurative eliminate the border and its inherent problems that allows TACNA to open the doors for US and other foreign firms to move significant manufacturing and processing operations into Mexico with no more difficulty than launching a new plant back home. After your start up, we continue to provide operational support, guidance, and administration for your plant and its manager. Our services include: Human Resources, US and Mexican Customs, Accounting, Finance, Payroll, Trucking, US & Mexican Brokerage, US Warehousing, and much more!

TACNA's "Cost Plus" Shelter Program allows our client total control and flexibility with the lowest possible cost exposure or liability in their Maquila operation. All Mexican operational expenses approved by the client are paid and passed through to the client at cost. There are no initial fees, assessments, or deposits required during the start-up process or for our daily services. For our complete Shelter Service Package, clients pay a modest fee times the total direct labor hours worked in Mexico.

Our Shelter Services are being offered throughout the Mexican State of Baja California in the cities of Tijuana, Tecate, Mexicali, Ensenada and others. Located in northwestern Mexico, Baja California is the primary center with the highest concentration of Maquiladora operations and complete infrastructure throughout all Mexico. Baja California has a population of nearly two million persons, 75% of whom are under the age of 35. The available labor force of approximately 800,000 is composed of third generation Maquiladora workers with the highest index of education in all of Mexico.

As Bamior and Jagerhorn argue in the conclusion to a study on the social costs of economic restructuring in ten Asian countries (1994: 70), highly skilled governance must simultaneously pursue economic growth, social development, and other desirable goals in order to avoid high social costs. Development must guarantee not only economic growth but also the popular exercise of rights such as those set out in the International Pact of

Economic, Social and Cultural Rights, signed in 1996: the right to equitable employment and to minimum living standards, including adequate nutrition, education, and enjoyment of mental and physical health (Roldan 2000). Researchers' lack of attention to social costs during the 1990s leaves the literature incomplete, biased, and unable to assess the extent to which industrial growth has or has not contributed to development.

Recent research, which once again includes such considerations, indicates that the general population in maquiladora cities and neighboring communities has disproportionately absorbed the social costs of industrial growth, especially in providing for such basic needs as housing, transportation, and education. One impact of the last decade's boom has been the transformation of border cities, with industry becoming the main economic base and organizer of urban structure. In Mexican maquiladora cities such as Ciudad Juárez, the supply of jobs attracted a large number of migrants, contributing greatly to population growth (Fuentes 2000: 36, 37). Promoters of industrial parks monopolized the best land, driving up prices and expelling the low-income population they employed to peripheral slums with no infrastructure.

Some observers in the United States argue that the government in Washington has forgotten the U.S. side of the border. The Senate Border Affairs Committee has expressed anger over the fact that southern municipalities in Texas, historically among the poorest in the country, pay the price of maquiladora expansion in terms of transportation problems and overcrowded schools, while the benefits go to the Midwest and Northeast in the form of profits for corporate headquarters and cheaper goods for consumers.[5]

Understanding the social costs of industrial growth has been made even more crucial by the spread of maquiladoras as the predominant form of industry throughout Mexico, Guatemala, Honduras, Nicaragua, and El Salvador, as well as the onset of the worst economic crisis in Mexican maquiladora history. The lower wages, poor working conditions, and unemployment inherent in industrial dispersion and crisis indicate that the question that Alonso, Carrillo, and Contreras pose at the beginning of their 2002 article—whether maquiladora industrialization leads to development or to social problems—is inappropriately framed. The issue is not, as Stoddard phrased it earlier (1987), whether the maquiladora industry is *either* a catalyst

---

[5] Pressure on fragile ecosystems has also been compounded by the expansion on the northern side of the border of military bases, tourism, and retirement communities.

or a calamity, but how, in fact, it is *both*. Framing the question in either/or terms inevitably leads to a one-sided view, which might be avoided by framing it as both/and.

The characteristics of the plants and communities most affected by industrial growth have changed greatly from the 1980s, the previous period with a focus on the social costs of industrial development on the border, making it impossible to generalize from earlier discussions. In their debate, Baker and Stoddard made very different predictions about the effects of NAFTA, the effects of maquiladoras on local community infrastructure, and the effects of maquiladoras on the environment (Stoddard 1992), all of which need to be reassessed in light of the immense changes that have occurred in the last decade. In some areas, such as the maquiladoras' effect on public health, there was little research to begin with, resulting in insufficient baseline data.

STRUCTURE OF THE BOOK

This book was planned as a first step in bringing together original studies that reconsider and update our knowledge about the social costs of industrial growth along the U.S.-Mexico border. As Mintzberg (1996: 82) argues, there is a need "to temper the influence that business values and currently popular Management [sic] thinking have on other sectors of society" and to work toward a new balance between the public, private, and other spheres of society. The articles are organized by threes and fours into three sections.

Section I deals with the consolidation of industry in key maquiladora centers along Mexico's northern border, where assembly plants first arose in the mid-1960s, and its spread southward. Alfredo Hualde's research on the Tijuana region indicates that even in this area, which has some of the most advanced manufacturing and design in electronics, labor markets are highly segmented, with most skilled jobs filled by men who advance through immense personal effort and investment, given the lack of industry or state support for their training. This chapter can be seen as an interesting response to Baker's (1989) earlier suggestion that one of the three major social costs associated with maquiladora industries was the Austin syndrome. By this he meant reliance on foreign experts from U.S. cities occupying the higher rungs of regional hierarchies and promising to bring capital, technology, jobs, and world-class manufacturing "know-how" to Mexico via maquiladoras. Baker argues that Mexicans can do more than sell real estate and cheap labor to foreign industrialists, and they should engage more actively in the design, manufacture, and export of Mexican products abroad. In the dozen years since his articulation of the Austin syndrome as a social cost of maquiladora growth, there has been tremendous effort within Mexico to upgrade the labor force and reap more benefits locally from maquilization. Hualde's essay is useful in assessing the degree to which the Austin syndrome is and is not being eradicated in the Tijuana region, as well as the costs of constructing an internationally competitive labor force.

The other two essays in the first section focus on the social costs that have been incurred as maquiladora industries have spread southward, becoming the predominant industrial form in Mexico. This type of industrialization is not an isolated phenomenon within the U.S.-Mexico border region; it has now become a prototype for restructuring the national Mexican and Central American economies. As the journalist Nancy Gibbs phrased it, "the border is everywhere" (2001: 23).

In fact, the growth of more-skilled jobs and the use of more-advanced technology in northern cities where some industrial consolidation has taken place are not usually the case elsewhere. María Eugenia de la O shows how the diffusion of maquiladoras southward into Mexico's interior has created three de facto internal borders, with women and people of color becoming more predominant and earning lower wages in the maquila labor force. Women's jobs, which are socially defined as less skilled, have expanded from Mexico's northern border to the interior, where there are higher levels of unemployment and poverty due to the closure of parastatal companies, the decline of agriculture, and so on. María Eugenia Trejos shows how maquiladoras incur even higher social costs in Central American countries, given the weakening of workers' organizations through civil war and state-led programs of economic restructuring. Research on Central American and southern Mexican maquiladoras is much newer, and Trejos's essay is important for predicting the potential social costs inherent in the Mexican government's plan to develop the area from Puebla to Panama.

One of the strengths of the early maquiladora literature was its careful attention to gender dynamics in different areas along the east-west expanse of the U.S.-Mexico border. When the proportion of men in the labor force increased in the 1990s, those constructing the "three-generation" perspective ceased to focus on how gender dynamics underlay the growth of industry. Taken together, the three essays in the first section of this book show how the varied gender segmentation of maquiladora labor forces in different places has made increasing inequality possible. They also show how north-south geographic forces have become stronger stimuli to the development of regional economies than east-west ones.

Baker (1989: 904, 905) emphasized two other major types of social costs incurred at Mexico's northern border besides the Austin syndrome: (1) the cleaning and conservation of the environment; and (2) adequate financing of physical and human infrastructure. Section II, on health and environmental costs, addresses these issues and moves to a more explicit focus on the community. A unifying thread of this section is the idea that full development must take into account not only the increase in trade and gross domestic product (GDP) but also the effect on the geographies and human populations that provide for such production.

The chapter by Siobán Harlow, Catalina Denman, and Leonor Cedillo is the first published survey of work on how employees of maquiladora industries and the larger society absorb the health costs of industrial growth. Despite the importance of maquiladoras for economic development, researchers have given little attention to the health impacts of such employment. This chapter throws some much-needed light on how changing occupational structures alter the health profile and health risks in Mexican communities. It also examines the implications for public health capacity and suggests several directions for future research.

Allen Blackman's chapter links environmental hazards to human health, focusing on air quality in Ciudad Juárez, which has been recognized as having one of the worst pollution problems on the border. His essay estimates how emissions from a sample of maquiladoras there affect morbidity and premature mortality. Health costs are an important form of social costs, given that the money deducted from workers' paychecks and paid by their employers for health care covers only part of the costs of services provided by the Mexican Social Security Institute (IMSS), with the rest coming out of general tax revenues. When workers are no longer employed in maquiladoras, they lose the right to use IMSS health care services (unless they get another formal job and are reenrolled), and they usually rely on the Health Ministry (SS), which is wholly supported by public funds.

The essay by Robert Varady and Barbara Morehouse compares two recently expanded twin-city areas along the Sonora-Arizona border in order to assess the environmental impact of the growth of communities based on maquiladora industries as well as mining, land development, and communal farming, particularly in regard to access to sufficient, usable water. The authors see the U.S.-Mexico border as a laboratory for studying the effects of development on water, since this resource is and will increasingly be of the greatest importance to the viability of other communities throughout Mexico. Infrastructural constraints on water quality and sanitation are examined, as well as the effects of industrial pollution. In each of their two study areas, these authors analyze institutions as well as stakeholder mobilization and public participation for developing policy and coping strategies.

Section III demonstrates how active Mexicans have been in efforts to reduce the burden they bear for social costs. It contains chapters on social organizations at three different levels of analysis, addressing environmental degradation, employee health and safety, benefits that support a better quality of life, and other important social issues. Taken together, the essays in this section reflect the heterogeneity of maquiladora cities and the complexity involved in strategizing how improvement might be achieved.

At the community level, Diane Austin, Edna Mendoza, Michèle Kimpel Guzmán, and Alba Jaramillo trace the emergence of a revegetation project in Ambos Nogales. They argue that such projects can arise via a new approach to partnering among maquiladoras, government agencies, educational institutions, nongovernmental organizations (NGOs), and residents. Responding to problems in air quality, these different private-sector and public-sector groups have helped make government-grown plants available for community and factory use. At least two maquiladoras have taken a leading role, along with educational institutions and community groups. This case study is an important example for the entire western end of the border for at least two reasons. Geographically, arid conditions have made revegetation difficult throughout the Sonoran Desert. In terms of political history and culture, the subordinated unions that exist in this area have contributed to strong anti-union sentiment, which makes it more likely for this form of partnering to succeed.

On the other hand, Cirila Quintero shows how a relatively successful union history in Matamoros has led to the development of maquila unions that are similar to traditional Mexican unions. They have won significant benefits for maquila workers in health, education, and housing; these achievements are particularly evident when compared to the failure of more subordinated unions in Ciudad Juárez. Joe Bandy's essay compares cross-border movements for social justice, analyzing why efforts to form a union independent of the system of Mexican union centrals succeeded in

Puebla but not in Baja California. The comparisons offered in these two chapters provide a good basis for a discussion of whether unions or social movement organizations are better for achieving greater equity and, within both, which strategies have worked. Readers might consider how these concrete examples could lead to solidarity between trade unions and social movements so that they are not competing for the participation of the same workers.

The concluding chapter, by James Cypher, is a reassessment of the economic viability of maquilization. It is important in showing how the economic model that Mexico followed from the 1980s onward has been based mainly on maquiladora industrialization, rather than on the more general idea of export-led development. Because maquiladora industries have become the predominant economic base, the social costs of maquilization can no longer be explained by the argument that the maquilas are a transition stage to a more modern economy. Cypher's essay shows how the social costs the maquilas incur are greatly expanded by their failure to add much value in Mexico or contribute to the tax base, with only some business groups within Mexico benefiting. Cypher also analyzes the opportunity cost associated with following this economic model rather than others, especially in terms of the lesser creation of jobs and weak purchasing power.

CONCEPTUALIZING SOCIAL COSTS IN THE CONTEXT OF MAQUILADORA INDUSTRIALIZATION

Definitions

The various authors in this book do not view the deterioration in wages, employment, unions, ecology, and so on that are associated with maquiladora industries as social problems. To take a social problems perspective is to assume that these phenomena are aberrant or that those suffering are at fault, leading to a "blame the victim" position. By starting with the analytic tool of social costs, researchers are more likely to understand how these phenomena are predictable outcomes of the kind of industrialization represented by maquilization—that is, that they are outcomes of a particular political economy.[6]

---

[6] Marchak defines political economy as "the study of power derived from or contingent on a system of property rights; the historical development of power relations; and the cultural and social embodiments of them" (1985: 673).

Social costs are commonly associated with private enterprise; this owes to individual firms' narrow accounting methods that calculate only the costs and profits for their own companies. "They plan for higher profits and expanded markets, but seldom plan to *reduce* social costs" (Feagin 1984: 123, emphasis in the original). From this perspective, social costs are considered to be "the negative consequences of private for-profit production, they are the costs which are not paid for by the individual firm; they are costs which are shifted onto other people, onto third parties including individuals and whole communities" (Feagin 1984: 122).

A related definition is the costs an entire society pays out of public funds. Baker (1989: 894n) set out an agenda for research on the social costs of Mexican maquila industries when he suggested studies that would show the total cost to finance all the public services that are needed for each hour worked in maquiladoras—that is, costs for public health, libraries, parks, housing, water, drainage, and so on.

Libraries may offer a way for researchers to evaluate the effectiveness of the various ways of provisioning services. The preference of President Vicente Fox, who served as CEO of Coca-Cola's Mexico division before entering politics, is to have the costs of social services supported as much as possible by the private sector. In a whirlwind visit to Tijuana in 2002, Fox presided in the same day over groundbreakings for a Toyota maquila that will manufacture truck beds at the eastern part of the city and a library that Toyota will build jointly with the government at the private Universidad Iberoamericana in the west-side neighborhood of Playas de Tijuana. In areas where maquiladora workers are better represented by trade unions, such as Matamoros, communities receive library services thanks to their unions' investment in such public services (see Quintero, this volume).

Peter Ward dedicated his 1999 book on self-constructed housing with the following words: "for *colonia* residents in Texas and Mexico, who with or without public-sector support have had to bear the brunt of the social costs of housing themselves." This is a powerful way of recognizing that, when public funds for essential services such as housing are insufficient or nonexistent and there is no support from the private sector or unions, social costs are often absorbed by individuals and families. Although he recognizes the resilience of those who construct their own housing and argues that Texas has a lot to learn from the Mexican side of the border on this issue, Ward is critical of the self-help house-building process because it is a manifestation of the "high rates of poverty and lack of development resources" (1999: 129). However, he also suggests that specific low-cost solutions to these "problem" situations are within the grasp of policymakers.

Other uses of the social costs concept may also be instructive. For example, in their study of inner-city African American communities, Durr, Lyons, and Cornwell (2000: 59) note, "social costs are successful disenfranchisement efforts, grounded in prejudice and discrimination, that are aimed at denying racial/ethnic minorities and women opportunities to participate in the larger social, cultural, and economic arenas of society." There are interesting parallels between how the concentration of African Americans in inner-city neighborhoods prevents their participation in the larger society and how the U.S.-Mexico border legally distances Mexican workers from their employers. Employees of Mexican maquiladora factories, most of which export their products to the United States, are not primarily disenfranchised in the same way as African Americans—that is, via racism and sexism. Although sexism and racism may operate to disadvantage Mexican workers in their workplaces, especially as maquiladoras move south, the obvious reason for these workers not having the same rights as U.S. workers is that they are not U.S. citizens. They are enfranchised in Mexico, which enshrines different labor laws in its Constitution, which in some cases (such as maternity leave for women) mandate better worker protection. Quintero's chapter in this volume shows how maquiladora workers' enjoyment of these legal rights depends on the kind of labor union that is legally responsible for representing them and how the majority have been deprived of the social rights of citizenship, not by racism or sexism, but by the subordinated character of these same unions.

Mexican maquiladora employees are in some ways more connected to the U.S. and world economies than inner-city African Americans, who may have fewer formal employment opportunities due to the restructuring of urban economies that has resulted in capital flight to suburban and greenfield sites. The maquila workers' separation from the parent companies of their maquiladora employers via the border, however, results in their occupation of a very similar location in the social stratification hierarchy. Erik Olin Wright (1995: 96) argues that both employed persons in the United States who earn poverty-level wages and Mexican maquiladora workers are part of the "working poor" because they are disempowered on the U.S. side by "a weak, fragmented, and relatively conservative labor movement" and on the Mexican side by "the absence of a solidaristic international labor movement."

Although the working poor must by necessity devise strategies at the household and community levels to help them cope, there are social costs involved nevertheless. Silvers argues, for example, that maquiladoras have increased the wages of low-income workers because they work very long hours (Silvers 2004). Thus poverty may have been reduced at the aggregate level, but it is the extra time worked daily that is responsible for this. As Harlow, Denman, and Cedillo indicate in their essay in this volume, long workdays can have negative health impacts and create stress both in and outside of the workplace. Combined with noise on the shopfloor and only a few short breaks for lunch and rest, co-workers can feel isolated from each other and unsupported by those with whom they spend most of their days.

In many regions where workers commute to work in maquiladoras, such as Aguascalientes garment factories (Bair: 2001) and the Coal Basin of Coahuila, long workdays are extended by a two-hour (roundtrip) commute, keeping workers away from their homes, families, and communities for an average of twelve hours each day. Contreras's (2001) survey found that Coahuila maquila workers considered the commute lost time, for which they believed their employer should compensate them in some way. They are compelled to take maquiladora jobs to survive because the better-paid mining jobs are disappearing. However, in the process they are marginalized and their communities are fragmented. They are not integrated into the larger labor force since they cannot participate in after-work activities, such as sports, unless they can find their own transportation. At home, they can only engage in family and community events on weekends.

Women's Disproportionate Burden of Industrial Growth's Social Costs

Moen argues that the social costs of development are borne more by women than men in both developing and developed societies, largely because, "Across time and space the pattern has remained the same: when a new technology is developed or introduced, men take over the work.... The consequence of technological displacement and social barriers is that compared to men, women have become less efficient workers because they are deprived of new knowledge, resources, and tools" (Moen 1981: 174–75). In Mexican maquiladoras, this technological displacement occurred as better jobs (as technicians and engineers, for example) in plants that did manufacturing as well as assembly were made available almost exclusively to men.

The gender analysis of social costs is a recurrent theme throughout this book. Alfredo Hualde argues that the emergence of highly skilled managerial work in the Tijuana area was based on a gendered polarization of the labor force. Harlow, Denman, and Cedillo point out how women's unique reproductive health needs are inadequately served by maquiladora industrialization due to managers' desire to avoid paying the costs of federally mandated maternity leave to pregnant women. De la O shows how the spread southward of jobs defined as low-skilled and favoring the employment of women, when overlaid on regional differences within Mexico, reinforced the inequality caused by such segmentation. For example, temporary employment agencies in Guadalajara and labor unions in Matamoros perform similar roles by recruiting, screening, and firing workers. However, in Guadalajara these organizations contribute greatly to job insecurity and inequality within the largely female labor force, whereas in Matamoros they do the opposite (Carrillo and Kopinak 1999). Near the end of this volume, Joe Bandy's analysis of cross-border solidarity movements shows how the heavy burden borne by women can be transformed into a strength by explicitly organizing around gender issues such as sexual harassment and the devaluation of women's work.

In the early literature, authors who stressed the benefits of maquiladora industrialization argued that Mexican women would be liberated via upward mobility within maquila factories over time. Instead, what can be seen after the boom of the 1990s is that labor force segmentation, which created gender inequality in the United States, Canada, and other places from which maquila production came, has been reproduced in Mexico. This gender segmentation arose—and continues—because women did not work in Mexican industry as a rule and the country has never had legislation mandating equal pay for equal work, affirmative action, or employment equity. Women still suffer more from ups and downs in the business cycle because they are segmented into jobs that use less advanced technology and, therefore, are less embedded in particular communities and can be moved to other regions relatively easily. Zúñiga and González (2002) reported that between June 2001 and April 2002, more than 149,300 workers lost maquiladora jobs; 121,000 of them were production workers. Sixty percent (73,000) were women, versus 40 percent (48,000) men. Job loss was due to the flight abroad of plants in the electronics, garment, and toy sectors, mainly to China due to its lower wages.

Not only do women suffer higher unemployment during periods of economic downturn, but they are also victimized in the social desperation that accompanies recession. Paterson (2002), for example, has suggested that the growing social instability in Ciudad Juárez caused by heavy job losses since 2000 has fostered domestic violence and other crimes against women. This surge in violence takes place in the municipality where 320 women have been brutally sexually assaulted and murdered since 1993; a significant number of them were maquiladora workers. Monárrez (2000: 114) argues that these heinous crimes are a signal of the thwarting of modernization in Ciudad Juárez and that they could occur and have remained unsolved because of the reproduction from times past of a culture permitting violence against women, which coexists with the newer culture of economic progress.

Social costs may also be paid by successive generations. Harlow, Denman, and Cedillo's public health perspective on the maquiladora labor force documents the overrepresentation of low birth weights among the babies born to women maquiladora workers. With the fall in real wages, families have had difficulty adequately supporting their children's formal education, resulting in their early departure from school to enter the labor force. In this volume, Cirila Quintero argues that while companies are required by law to provide scholarships, only the better unions at the eastern end of the border are able to ensure that this is anything more than window dressing. Alfredo Hualde shows how the majority of maquila workers in Tijuana have very low education levels.

Domestic Industries Shoulder the Tax Burden

Poorly paid as maquiladora jobs may be, they are arguably better than no jobs at all. High rates of unemployment have periodically plagued northern Mexico because of the maquiladora cities' economic dependence on foreign markets and the lack of diversification of their economies. Such a downturn began at the end of 2000, caused by recession in the U.S. and several Asian economies as well as other factors such as overvaluation of the peso and the Mexican government's lack of clarity on new tax legislation. While many Mexican jobs were also lost in 2001 in tourism,

> The most dramatic losses are in the manufacturing and assembly sectors, which INEGI says lost more than 6% of the work force, or about 226,000 jobs, to layoffs in 2001.[7] The loss

---

[7] Mexican labor law specifies that if an employer has insufficient work for the employees, the latter are to be fired and paid a certain period's wages as severance. The

> was especially evident in the states of Baja California and
> Chihuahua, and in particular the cities of Ciudad Juarez and
> Tijuana, home to thousands of maquiladora plants. Deputy
> economy secretary Rocio Ruiz said job loss in the maqui-
> ladora sector was accompanied by the relocation of dozens of
> operations to Central America and the Caribbean for the
> cheaper labor and lower production costs. The maquiladora
> industry experienced its worst year ever in 2001 (*SourceMex*
> 2002a).

While Wright pointed to the lack of protection by labor unions in explaining the class character of maquila workers as the working poor, there
are a host of other differences involved in living and working at the border
that are also fundamental to the social costs incurred by industrial and
population growth. Industries in the United States must often pay a "connection fee" to cover some infrastructure costs, whereas taxes that maquiladora plants pay in Mexico are applied only on value added in that country, which is mostly labor. Therefore, taxes are very low, and they are
collected by federal authorities more than state or municipal levels of government, and hence they contribute little to local improvements.

Within Mexico, domestically owned industries, which are mostly small
and midsize, have been disadvantaged compared to the few larger Mexican industries and non–Mexican-owned industries. Exports have become
the main form of economic growth in the last two decades, and access to
reduced tariffs on imports is crucial given that 84 percent of all exports are
made with temporary imports (Álvarez and Dussel 2001: 447). At the end
of 2000, Mexico passed new legislation, known by its Spanish acronym
PROSEC, which has been called a second, unilateral NAFTA because it
reduced tariffs on imports from NAFTA countries as well as from the rest
of the world. The effect is to make much less tax revenue available to the
Mexican federal government. Álvarez and Dussel also argue that while the
main winners are importers of merchandise from non-NAFTA countries,
the losers are domestic producers who make the same products as non-
Mexican producers, especially small Mexican companies that will not be
able to compete with lower-priced imports.

---

practice in other countries of temporarily laying off workers who may be called
back to work later does not legally exist in Mexico unless negotiated in specific
union contracts. Thus this quotation should say that 226,000 workers were fired in
2001.

Mexico's growing dependence on export processing for job creation has put it in an even more difficult situation since the economic downturn beginning in 2000. With companies downsizing and fleeing to Asia, the Mexican government has responded to the private sector's calls for relief by granting more tax breaks. In August 2002, Economic Minister Luis Ernesto Derbez announced that export-manufacturing companies no longer have to pay import taxes on 1,400 different products used mainly in electronics manufacturing. As reported in the *Maquila Portal Weekly Bulletin* (August 2002), a publication aimed at investors,

> The tax exemptions, which everyone hopes will bring employment rates back to their pre-recession levels, are to be implemented this month. Another desired effect of the program will be to convince those export manufacturers who are thinking about moving their operations to China, to stay in the good old Republic of Mexico. The possibility of eliminating the permanent establishment tax clause, which increases company tax burdens, is also being discussed.

Ernesto Ruffo, former governor of Baja California and current head of Mexico's Commission for Border Affairs, had stated early in his commission position that he planned to tax maquiladoras to help pay for infrastructure. However, given the deepening of the economic crisis and knowing that increased taxes might prompt companies to leave Mexico, Ruffo changed his position and stated that tariffs would not be raised (Treat and Kourous 2001)

New tax breaks for maquiladoras come at a time when the federal government has had to cut back spending, slashing budgets midterm. President Fox announced a reduction in the budget of more than 10 billion pesos (US$1.106 billion) in public expenditures in 2002. The reduction was justified by weak government revenues in the first quarter of the year due to lower oil income and reduced tax collections. Two billion pesos (US$221.2 million) of the reduction was taken from the PAFEF program created to allocate funds to state governments. Many of Mexico's governors said the reductions would force cutbacks in state programs for public safety, education, and health. "The PAFEF reduction no doubt will have a negative impact on our commitment to social programs in our states," noted Guerrero's Governor René Juárez (*SourceMex* 2002b). In the 2003 budget, opposition parties suggested that government funds be reduced for the bank rescue agency and increased for the PAFEF (*SourceMex* 2002c).

All three major political parties agreed, however, that foreign investors should not be "targeted" as new sources of tax revenue.

Mexico has developed a small dynamic export sector of foreign-owned companies that is polarized from the domestically owned economy (Dussel Peters 2000). Government efforts to support small and medium-sized domestic companies have fallen to a minimal level since 1988 (Dussel Peters 2001: 25). Legislation to reduce tariffs, such as PROSEC, widens the gap further. While all industries in Mexico benefit from existing infrastructure, the taxes spent to build it are paid mainly by Mexicans; many of them see this subsidizing of non-Mexican companies producing in Mexico as unfair. This translates more often into greater distrust of their government for facilitating such a situation than into negative sentiment toward foreign-owned maquiladoras, especially in times and areas of high unemployment.

Environmental Costs

As the *Report on Environmental Conditions and Natural Resources on Mexico's Northern Border* points out, maquiladoras have had both indirect and direct environmental impacts (ITESM and InfoMexus 2002: 63). They have affected the environment indirectly by acting as a magnet for migrants, causing high levels of growth in cities that host maquiladoras. In 1998, maquiladoras employed over a million people, 85.3 percent of whom lived in border states and 65.1 percent in fourteen border cities. Over a third (35 percent) were concentrated in only two cities: Ciudad Juárez and Tijuana. A full fifth lived in Ciudad Juárez. The budgets of border cities are very low and, as indicated above, maquiladoras contribute little to public funds via taxes, making little money available for infrastructure provision.

Maquiladora industries have also had a direct impact in their handling and discharge of hazardous waste. Mexico introduced new federal environmental legislation very similar to U.S. regulations in the late 1980s, but the country has few resources with which to enforce its laws. This allows maquiladoras, especially those abandoning hazardous waste in Mexico, "to use the border as a shield against legal action," according to the Commission for Environmental Cooperation (2002: 42). Companies can move production to Mexico in order to avoid paying environmental costs, not only because of the different sets of laws and vastly unequal amounts of public money available for enforcement on the two sides of the border, but also because border communities have historically been alienated from the central parts of their respective countries. They have less status and power, making it easier for violators of environmental law to act with impunity.

Tijuana, for example, has been plagued by a *leyenda negra* ("black legend") which since the 1930s, when the city's growth was based on the provision of entertainment services for U.S. nationals during Prohibition, has characterized it as a city of vice and violence. This tendency for Americans to see Mexico as a place where they can do things that would be illegal at home (Paz 1982) has the effect of "normalizing" bad environmental practices by justifying them in cultural terms. Likewise, what happens in twin cities such as Ambos Nogales is influenced by their place in the existing hierarchy of cities and regions. The character of these two cities as transshipment points positions them midway on the scale of importance, with places such as Tucson, Phoenix, and Los Angeles occupying more commanding rungs in the hierarchy (Kopinak 2002a).

Without continuing investment in environmental infrastructure, the negative environmental impact of industrial growth in border communities will make things even worse. According to Picou (1996: 213), "substantial sociological evidence exists to suggest that toxins in the environment contaminate more than air, water, or soil; they also damage the social fabric of a community, its neighborhoods, its families, and its residents' self-esteem. Environmental contamination, in short, is often both a biospheric and a sociological disaster." The effect of contamination in industrial, retirement, and tourist communities on the border is similar to the negative impact of technological accidents: residents perceive "that their community is a less desirable place to live, raise children, and (in general) have a happy life" (Picou 1996: 216–17). They also are increasingly aware of possible negative impacts in the future and express doubts about the sustainability of their communities.

Varady and Morehouse's chapter in this volume illustrates how more of the environmental costs are paid on the Mexican than the U.S. side of the border. Mining and maquiladora industries on the Mexican side use so much of the scarce water supply that the amount available for residential and community use is insufficient. Allen Blackman's modeling of air contamination in Ciudad Juárez (this volume) is an interesting analysis of how to cope with environmental costs. Although Blackman estimates that maquiladoras may not be responsible for the worst pollution in that city, he suggests that it may be less costly to achieve emissions reductions among maquiladora polluters than non-maquiladora polluters.

A question sometimes raised in discussions of social costs is what these costs would have been without maquiladora industries arising in northern Mexico and becoming the cornerstone of the economy. The question is often used erroneously to imply that Mexico would be unindustrialized and that the north, especially, would be without sufficient employment. However, as Lipietz has pointed out, Mexico is one of the old industrialized countries of the Third World (1995: 44). In the concluding chapter in this book, Cypher deals more fully with the costs and benefits of industrial regimes such as import-substitution industrialization and export-led development. Here, by way of introduction, it will only be noted that many researchers have shown that while exports have grown, wages and employment have fallen under the current regime.[8] A recent Americas Program policy brief (2002) is very straightforward on this point:

> The huge increase in bilateral trade stimulated by the North American Free Trade Agreement (NAFTA) brought greater economic expansion to the border region, but not prosperity or development. The region has absorbed a disproportionate share of negative impacts of that trade.

Northern Mexico was not devoid of commerce before the arrival of export-processing industries. States such as Coahuila and Tamaulipas had well-established ventures in coal mining and cotton. The social costs of those economies were smaller—and better offset by unions incorporated

---

[8] As maquiladoras boomed throughout the 1980s and domestically owned industries closed, some of Mexico's best industrial jobs, like those in the auto industry, moved from central Mexico to the northern border region and reappeared with characteristics that had previously been introduced in Mexico via the maquilas: lower pay, more women workers, a predominance of lower-skilled jobs, and less union protection for workers. Micheli (1994: 169) shows how wages were reduced by one-half or more through this form of restructuring in Ford, GM, Chrysler, Nissan, and Volkswagen plants which assembled finished products and manufactured large components such as motors (that is, "new" maquilas). While these reduced wages were higher than those paid in the traditional maquilas, which did simple assembly in electronics or garments, they were part of the downward pressure on wages felt throughout Mexico during the 1980s. Carlos Gutiérrez (1997), president of Mexico's National Chamber of the Manufacturing Industry (Canacintra), acknowledged that wages in the auto industry in Mexico had been reduced by half, as Micheli's research indicated. He explained that this was due to the lack of industrial policy that would help domestically owned companies link to the global economy. As the reference to Dussel's work earlier in this introduction shows, this has not yet happened.

into the ruling Institutional Revolutionary Party (PRI)—than is the case with maquiladoras. In younger cities like Tijuana and Ciudad Juárez, the economy was mainly tertiary, based on services. In Nogales, the economic base was agricultural exports. These earlier service and staple economies incurred social costs that could more easily be absorbed and transcended cross-generationally.

The problem with the industrial growth of the last forty years is that it has been of such great magnitude and speed that its host communities were not adequately prepared. As the previous subsection argued, cutbacks in public funds have not helped them catch up. Varady and Morehouse argue that one of the principal reasons for environmental degradation in the Arizona-Sonora border area is the lack of funding. And NAFTA-related programs such as Border XXI, which were supposed to assist in catch-up, have done little. Previously existing northern Mexican economies that have been eclipsed in importance by maquiladora growth, such as those based on services, did not produce waste products in such huge amounts or of such hazardous types as the maquiladoras (Kopinak 2002b; Kopinak and Barajas 2002). Until the maquiladoras arrived, there was little perception of a need for legislation to protect the environment, nor for thorough inspection of industries to assure their compliance.

Russo (1983) has argued that, over time, legislation in the United States has turned much of the cost of industrial pollution into business costs of the industries responsible for them. One option for those not wishing to pay such costs is moving to Mexico. A great deal of the furniture production that relocated from Southern California to the north of the Baja California peninsula transferred production so that companies would not have to comply with new, stricter environmental legislation in the United States. They could continue the very same production processes in Mexico and be in compliance with Mexican laws. Their new Mexican neighbors now must cope with contamination that Southern Californians would not.[9] Johnston

---

[9] Tom Barry (1994: 67) reported that in the case of the furniture maquila Muebles Finos Buenos in Tijuana, neighbors complain they can smell solvents which cause dizziness, sore throats, and nausea. Fine dust lacquer settles over nearby homes and vehicles. In the video "Borderline Cases: Environmental Matters at the United States–Mexico Border," directed by Lynn Corcoran (Bullfrog Films: 1997), Danny Finegood, the owner of the Tijuana furniture maquiladora Muebles Buenos Finos (called Fine Good Furniture in the United States), is shown explaining his company's move from Los Angeles to Tijuana to avoid strict Southern California laws which limited the amount of allowed contamination, making it necessary for the Los Angeles plant to stop production early in the workday if they hit the limit.

and Button argue that when companies produce in a less environmentally sound manner in Mexican maquiladoras than they do in their U.S. locations, they are practicing a form of environmental racism:

> Selective application of environmental protection measures constitutes a form of environmental racism. The victims in this case are, for the most part, poor Mexican women, whose health, lives, and reproductive success are threatened by maquiladora-generated pollution. These practices occur in a political context of government encouragement (if not outright support) by both the US and Mexico (Johnston and Button 1994: 210).

Neither did previous economies require so much energy. The Fox administration's 2002 cuts in subsidies for electrical power and the subsequent increase in energy costs for consumers have had an especially severe impact on low-income residents in many northern areas, such as Coahuila, Ciudad Juárez, Sonora, and the *municipios* of Baja California, leading to protests and complaints along the border (Nauman 2002; *SourceMex* 2002d). According to a recent Americas Program policy brief (2002):

> Mexican electricity demand is increasing nationally at 6.6% annually for a population that grew at an annual rate of 1.8% from 1995 to 2000. Much faster population growth in the border region (5.1% annually), coupled with an expanding middle class and strong dependence in the region on energy-intensive maquiladoras, translates into an even more rapid increase in electricity demand along the border probably closer to 15% per year.

Plans are in place to produce more power for local use and also for export, particularly to address the energy problems created by deregulation in California. Based on investigation by the Southwest Center for Environmental Research and Policy, the Americas Program report analyzes the rush to establish new energy-producing facilities in the border region and concludes that:

> While these new projects will help meet the energy demands in the border and elsewhere, they also pose the risk that the border region will suffer a disproportionate share of the environmental damage due to the location of a large number of

new facilities without proper evaluation of regional and transborder air quality impacts. The border faces the threat of becoming a pollution haven for energy production, absorbing significant environmental costs for other regions.

The specific populations that could be most negatively affected are Hispanics clustered in communities in southern San Diego County where the energy facilities will be built, as well as the Tijuana population due to the predominant direction of the airflow. Kamp (2001) argues that the reasons for locating the energy plants in the border region are questionable since natural gas is not a renewable resource, the plants will generate few jobs, and some will supply little or no electricity to local residents. However, if they are built in this area, the Americas Program report offers thirteen recommendations geared to prevent the costs being borne unduly by border communities. The recommendations are grouped into three areas: (1) increase cooperation and participation at a binational, regional level; (2) strengthen border environmental policies; and (3) build a sustainable economy. There is nothing inevitable about environmental degradation at the U.S.-Mexico border. It is socially constructed and can be prevented.

As industries move southward throughout Mexico and Central America to areas richer in natural resources, environmentally sound management and conservation of those resources is necessary if export processing is to provide a sustainable economic base. Another case of maquiladora industries' requirements for resources outpacing the demands of previous, more sustainable economies can be found in the Tehuacán Valley, supposedly the "Cradle of Corn in the Americas" (Ross 2002) and the "tortilla basket of Mexico's Altiplano." This valley was once famous for the purity of its water, and many bottled mineral waters sold in Mexico bear its name. Now only old men grow corn in the valley; the younger men have migrated to work in New York or are staying in the valley to labor in the maquiladoras, alongside the young women.

Three hundred clothing maquiladoras, many of which make jeans, are operating in the valley and threatening to contaminate the water supply. Twenty-five laundries wash a million pairs of jeans a week, using more water than is replaced and leaving the remainder too contaminated with toxic chemicals[10] to be used on farmland. Half of these laundries are illegal,

---

[10] The toxic chemicals include nonbiodegradable dyes, bleaches, acids, and other toxic agents used to produce stonewashed and chemically aged jeans, according to Ross (2002).

and thus probably not properly regulated. This example is noteworthy since, unlike the Sonora-Arizona border which Varady and Morehouse discuss in this volume, the Tehuacán Valley began its industrialization with a surfeit of good-quality water. Lack of environmental regulation, however, has created similar kinds of problems as in the north. If the modernization that is the goal of Mexico's Plan Puebla-Panamá is to be a genuine form of development, this kind of toxic contamination needs to be recognized as an unbearable social cost.

References

Alonso, Jorge, Jorge Carrillo, and Óscar Contreras. 2002. "Aprendizaje tecnológico en las maquiladoras de México," *Frontera Norte* 14: 43–82.

Álvarez, José Luis, and Enrique Dussel. 2001. "Causas y efectos de los programas de promoción sectorial en la economía mexicana," *Comercio Exterior*, May, pp. 446–56.

Americas Program, Interhemispheric Resource Center. 2002. "Energy Development on the U.S.-Mexico Border." Interhemispheric Resource Center, June 14, http://www.americaspolicy.org/briefs/2002/0206energy.html.

Bair, Jennifer. 2001. "Casos exitosos de pequeñas y medianas empresas en México: la industria del vestido en Aguascalientes." In *Claroscuros: integración exitosa de las pequeñas y medianas empresas en México*, edited by Enrique Dussel Peters. Mexico: Editorial Jus.

Baker, George. 1989. "Costos sociales e ingresos de la industria maquiladora," *Comercio Exterior* 39, no. 10: 893–906.

Bamior, Tariq, and Martina Jagerhorn. 1994. "Social Costs of Economic Restructuring: A Regional Overview." In *Social Costs of Economic Restructuring*. Development Papers, no. 15. Bangkok: United Nations Economic and Social Commission for Asia and the Pacific.

Barry Tom. 1994. *The Challenge of Cross-Border Environmentalism: The U.S.-Mexico Case*. Albuquerque, N.M.: Resource Center Press.

Carrillo, Jorge. 1986. "Maquiladoras: industrialización fronteriza y riesgos de trabajo: el caso de Baja California." In *Reestructuración industrial: maquiladoras en la frontera México–Estados Unidos*, edited by Jorge Carrillo. Mexico: Conaculta/El Colegio de la Frontera Norte.

Carrillo, Jorge, and Alfredo Hualde. 1998. "Third Generation Maquiladoras?" *Journal of Borderlands Studies* 13, no. 1: 79–97.

Carrillo, Jorge, and Kathryn Kopinak. 1999. "Condiciones de trabajo y relaciones laborales en la maquila." In *Cambios en las relaciones laborales: enfoque sectorial y regional*, vol. 1, edited by Enrique de la Garza and José Alfonso Bouzas. Mexico City: Universidad Nacional Autónoma de México.

Carrillo, Jorge, and Jorge Santibáñez. 1993. *Rotación de personal en las maquiladoras de exportación en Tijuana.* Tijuana: Secretaría de Trabajo y Previsión Social/El Colegio de la Frontera Norte.

Commission for Environmental Cooperation of North America. 2002. *Metales y Derivados Final Factual Record.* North American Environmental Law and Policy Series, vol. 8. Montreal: Yvon Blais.

Contreras, Camilo. 2001. "Geografía del mercado de trabajo en la cuenca carbonífera de Coahuila," *Frontera Norte* 13: 87–118.

Coubès, Marie-Laure. 2001. "Trayectorias laborales en Tijuana: ¿segmentación o continuidad entre sectores de empleo?" *Trabajo* 2, no. 4: 189–220.

Durr, Marlese, Thomas S. Lyons, and Katherine K. Cornwell. 2000. "Social Cost and Enterprise Development within Inner City African American Communities," *National Journal of Sociology* 12, no. 1: 57–77.

Dussel Peters, Enrique. 2000. *Polarizing Mexico: The Impact of Liberalization Strategy.* Boulder, Colo.: Lynne Rienner.

———. 2001. "Condiciones y retos de las pequeñas y medianas empresas en México: estudio de casos de vinculación de empresas exitosas y propuestas de política." In *Claroscuros: integración exitosa de las pequeñas y medianas empresas en México,* edited by Enrique Dussel Peters. Mexico City: Editorial Jus.

Feagin, Joe. 1984. "The Social Costs of Private Enterprise," *Research in Social Problems and Public Policy* 3: 115–50.

Fernández-Kelly, M. Patricia. 1983. *For We Are Sold, I and My People: Women and Industry in Mexico's Frontier.* Albany: State University of New York Press.

Fleck, Susan. 2001. "A Gender Perspective on Maquila Employment and Wages in Mexico." In *The Economics of Gender in Mexico: Work, Family, State, and Market,* edited by Elizabeth G. Katz and Maria C. Correia. Washington, D.C.: World Bank.

Fuentes, César. 2000. "Urban Function and Its Effect on Urban Structure: The Case of Ciudad Juárez, Chihuahua," *Journal of Borderlands Studies* 15, no. 2: 25–43.

Ganster, Paul, and Dana V. Hamson. 1995. *A Resource Guide for Child Care and Family Planning Services in the Maquiladora Industry.* San Diego: Institute for Regional Studies of the Californias, San Diego State University.

Gereffi, Gary. 1992. "Mexico's Maquiladora Industries and North American Integration." In *North America without Borders? Integrating Canada, the United States and Mexico,* edited by S.J. Randall with H. Konrad and S. Silverman. Calgary: University of Calgary Press.

Gibbs, Nancy. 2001. "The New Frontier. La Nueva Frontera. A Whole New World," *Time Magazine,* June 11, pp. 20–48.

Gutiérrez, Carlos. 1997. Presentation to the "Seminar on Incomes and Productivity," Commission for Labor Co-operation, Dallas, February 27–28.

Iglesias, Norma. 1985. *La flor más bella de la maquiladora*. Mexico: Secretaría de Educación Pública/Centro de Estudios Fronterizos del Norte de México.

ITESM and InfoMexus (Instituto Tecnológico y de Estudios Superiores de Monterrey and Instituto de Información Fronteriza México–Estados Unidos). 2002. *Report on Environmental Conditions and Natural Resources on Mexico's Northern Border*. Gila Resources Information Project (GRIP) and Interhemispheric Resource Center, http://americaspolicy.org/rep-envt.

Johnston, Barbara, and Greg Button. 1994. "Human Environmental Rights and the Multinational Corporation: Industrial Development in the Free Trade Zone." In *Who Pays the Price? The Sociocultural Context of Environmental Crisis*, edited by B.R. Johnston. Washington, D.C.: Island.

Kamp, Dick. 2001. "Powering up the Border: What's the Rush?" Americas Program Commentary. Interhemispheric Resource Center, September 5, http://www.americaspolicy.org/commentary/up010905.html.

Kopinak, Kathryn. 1996. *Desert Capitalism: Maquiladoras in North America's Western Industrial Corridor*. Tucson: University of Arizona Press.

———. 2002a. "Oportunidades desaprovechadas por las industrias maquiladoras en Nogales, Sonora." In *Globalización, trabajo y maquilas: las nuevas y viejas fronteras de la inversión transnacional en México*, edited by María Eugenia de la O and Cirila Quintero. Mexico City: Friedrich Ebert Foundation.

———. 2002b. "Environmental Implications of New Mexican Industrial Investment: The Rise of Asian Origin Maquiladoras as Generators of Hazardous Waste," *Asian Journal of Latin American Studies* 15, no. 1: 91–120.

Kopinak, Kathryn, and Ma. del Rocio Barajas. 2002. "Too Close for Comfort? The Proximity of Industrial Hazardous Wastes to Local Populations in Tijuana, Baja California," *Journal of Environment and Development* 11, no. 3: 215–46.

Lipietz, A. 1995. "De Toyota-City a la Ford-Hermosillo: la japonización de pacotilla," *Cotidiano* 67: 39–47.

Maquiladora Portal Weekly Bulletin. 2002. "Relief for Export Manufacturers," no. 122 (August 9), http://www.maquilaportal.com/cgi-bin/public/hist/hist/pl?Klein=2002-08-02&Klein2=4215&Klein3=AUGUST.

Marchak, Patricia. 1985. "Canadian Political Economy," *Canadian Review of Sociology and Anthropology* 22, no. 5: 673–709.

Micheli, Jordy. 1994. *Nueva manufactura, globalización y producción de automóviles en México*. Mexico City: Universidad Nacional Autónoma de México.

Mintzberg, Henry. 1996. "Managing Government, Governing Management," *Harvard Business Review*, May–June, pp. 75–83.

Moen, Elizabeth. 1981. "Women and Development." In *Women and the Social Costs of Economic Development: Two Colorado Case Studies*, edited by Elizabeth Moen, Elise Boulding, Jane Lillydahl, and Risa Palm. Boulder, Colo.: Westview.

Monárrez, Julia. 2000. "La cultura del feminicidio en Ciudad Juárez, 1993–1999," *Frontera Norte* 23: 87–118.

Nauman, Talli. 2002. "Rate-Hike War: Lights Are On but Nobody's Home," *The News Mexico*, http://www.thenewsmexico.com/noticia.asp?id=31351.

Paterson, Kent. 2002. "Downturn in Maquildora Industry, Local Economy Contribute to Increase in Crime and Violence in Ciudad Juarez," *SourceMex* 13, no. 33 (September 11).

Paz, Octavio. 1982. "Mexico and the United States: Positions and Counterpositions." In *Mexico Today*, edited by T.S. Montgomery. Philadelphia, Penn.: ISHI.

Picou, Steven. 1996. "Toxins in the Environment, Damage to the Community: Sociology and the Toxic Tort." In *Witnessing for Sociology: Sociologists in Court*, edited by Pamela Jenkins and Steve Kroll-Smith. Westport, Conn.: Praeger.

Rodríguez, Leticia. 1997. "Apertura de mercado sin sacrificio social: Coparmex," *El Financiero* 22 (September 18).

Roldán, Martha. 2000. *¿Globalización o mundialización? Teoría y práctica de procesos productivos y asimetrías de género*. Buenos Aires: Universidad Nacional de la Patagonia (SJB), Delegación Zonal Trelew, FLACSO, Eudeba.

Ross, John. 2002. "A Blue Curse on the Corn: Maquiladora Industry Making Corn Cradle Run Dry," *Latin America Press*, August 26. Reprinted in *SourceMex* 13, no. 41 (November 6).

Russo, George. 1983. "Industrial Pollution." In *Social Costs in Modern Society*, edited by John Ullman. Westport, Conn.: Quorum.

Silvers, Arthur. 2004. "Lower Income, Higher Income: Impact of the Maquiladoras on Both Sides of the Border." In *Challenged Borderlands: Transcending Political and Cultural Boundaries*, edited by Vera Pavlakovich-Kochi, Barbara J. Morehouse, and Doris Wastl-Walker. Aldershot, U.K.: Ashgate.

SourceMex. 2002a. "Study Shows Significant Growth in Informal Economy since Early 2001," vol. 13, no. 10 (March 13).

———. 2002b. "President Vicente Fox Announces 10 Billion-Peso Reduction in 2002 Budget Because of Weak Oil Revenues, Low Tax Collections," vol. 13, no. 13 (April 10).

———. 2002c. "President Vicente Fox Sends Austere 2003 Budget to Congress," vol. 13, no. 42 (November 13).

———. 2002d. "President Fox Sends Congress Formal Legislative Initiative to Reform Electrical-Power Sector," vol. 13, no. 35 (September 25).

Stoddard, Ellwyn. 1987. *Maquila: Assembly Plants in Northern Mexico*. El Paso: Texas Western Press.

———. 1992. "George Baker's 'Mexican Labor is Not Cheap': A Rejoinder and Critical Commentary," *Rio Bravo* 1, no. 2: 107–25.

Treat Jonathan, and George Kourous. 2001. "Border Czar Gives Progress Report," *Borderlines* 81, no. 9 (September 8).

Urquidi, Víctor. 1999. "Globalización, medio ambiente y desarrollo sustentable." In *Desarrollo sustentable, medio ambiente y población: a cinco años de Rio*, edited by Haydea Izazola. Zinacantepec, Mexico: El Colegio Mexiquense.

Ward, Peter M. 1999. *Colonias and Public Policy in Texas and Mexico: Urbanization by Stealth*. Austin: University of Texas Press.

Wright, Eric Olin. 1995. "The Class Analysis of Poverty," *International Journal of Health Services* 25, no. 1: 85–100.

Zúñiga, Juan, and Roberto González. 2002. "Se trasladaron a China y otros países que dan ventajas desleales: economía, BdeM e INEGI," *La Jornada*, July 17.

PART I

Maquilization as a Paradigmatic Form of Industrialization: Trans-regional Social Costs

2

Skills Segmentation and Social Polarization in Tijuana's Maquiladoras

ALFREDO HUALDE

INDUSTRIALIZATION ON MEXICO'S NORTHERN BORDER: AN OVERVIEW

In the 1960s economic activities along Mexico's northern border were largely limited to trade and services in Tijuana and Ciudad Juárez and agriculture in Matamoros. Late in the decade, however, a new economic activity appeared in some border municipalities as workshops began producing clothing and electronics for export. These workshops, known as maquiladoras, imported components from abroad for assembly in Mexico and then re-exported these materials, now as finished products, to the United States. From the beginning, these industries were protected by a legal structure coordinated by the Mexican and U.S. governments that exempted them from paying duty on materials imported for assembly in Mexico (González Aréchiga and Ramírez 1990; Hualde 1997) and which continued to evolve during the 1980s and 1990s to facilitate the transborder movement of goods.

Maquiladoras were expected to benefit populations on both sides of the border, creating employment in Mexico and providing inexpensive goods to the U.S. population thanks to the lower costs of production (labor, electricity, and so on) south of the border. Mexican maquiladoras closely resemble the export-processing zones of Central America, the Caribbean, and some Asian countries, with one key difference: Mexico and the United

States are joined by the world's longest border. Because the border cities' proximity to the United States facilitated operations and reduced transportation costs, what had begun as a relatively unplanned activity rapidly evolved during the mid-1980s as the maquiladora sector experienced skyrocketing growth.[1]

In the 1990s maquiladoras underwent significant changes as a result of restructuring in the international economy, as well as in response to regional dynamics in areas where maquiladoras are concentrated. In addition to plants that do simple assembly (sometimes called first-generation maquiladoras), border cities now house affiliates of major transnational corporations (TNCs)—Sony, Samsung, Philips, Hitachi, and U.S. and Japanese autoparts manufacturers—that are organizationally more complex and require more highly skilled workers for their production processes. These new maquiladoras are driving the emergence of local businesses— producers of packaging materials, human resources consultants, software developers, customs lawyers, and so on—and opening up the possibility of transforming the border into a site for a different kind of manufacturing process.

Local educational institutions and business groups welcomed these changes and hoped to institutionalize them, with border municipalities attracting technology-intensive investment while labor-intensive plants would tend to locate or invest in central and southern Mexico. This signaled a new perspective on the role of the maquiladoras. However, a series of events beginning in late 2000 put into question the possibility of upgrading in the maquiladoras:

- Economic recession in the United States sparked an employment crisis in the maquiladora sector. From October 2000 to early 2002, one-fifth of maquila jobs (a total of 200,000) were eliminated (INEGI 2002). In Ti-

---

[1] Politicians and scholars were initially critical of the maquiladoras, viewing the entry of foreign capital as incompatible with Mexico's import-substitution industrialization model. Academics also noted the poor treatment accorded the largely female workforce in the plants and the lack of linkages with local economies (Carrillo and Hernández 1985; Fernández-Kelly 1983; González Aréchiga and Ramírez 1990). Such criticisms have reappeared at key moments, as during negotiation of the North American Free Trade Agreement (NAFTA), when labor unions and environmental organizations in Canada and the United States based their opposition to the trade accord on the maquiladoras' working conditions and environmental impacts (Hualde 1997).

juana alone, some 40,000 jobs were lost, and the number of maquilas in this city dropped from 820 to 718 (see figures 2.1 and 2.2). [2]

- Asian-owned maquiladoras, which generate a significant number of jobs in Tijuana, threatened to leave the border region, claiming that NAFTA regulations penalize inputs imported from Asia and other third-party nations.[3]

- Export competitiveness was undermined by the increasing strength of the Mexican peso beginning in 2000 and up to the first half of 2002.

- Crime rates rose in some border cities, creating an atmosphere of insecurity that led some maquiladoras to consider relocating.

This chapter addresses the transformations that have taken place in the maquiladora sector in terms of the skill levels of the various grades of workers: production workers, technicians, and engineers (*ingenieros*). The main argument is that, although maquiladoras have created jobs that require some professional and technical skills, an important segment of production workers continues to do simple tasks (Hualde 2002a). Engineers and technicians represent a minor part of a labor market that is more broadly characterized by low educational and skill levels. The data indicate an increasingly polarized labor market: highly educated and professional workers were able to improve their incomes in the 1990s, in contrast to less educated workers, whose wages stagnated. Increasing differences between employee categories in the maquiladoras reinforce the inequality that was already present in Tijuana and other border municipalities, and can hinder the emergence of more competitive and fairer production systems.

The chapter is organized as follows: The first section below presents the dilemma regions face under globalization and their development options in light of theoretical developments in economic sociology and industrial geography. The second section describes the transformations in Tijuana's labor market in the 1990s. The third analyzes the skills developed by different categories of workers—production workers, technicians, and *ingenieros*—throughout their careers. The final section presents a series of conclusions related to the role of transnational corporations in knowledge

---

[2] César López, vice president of the Maquiladora Association in Tijuana, indicated that the number of registered plants had dropped to 644 (author interview, August 2002).

[3] The Mexican government tried to resolve this issue in the summer of 2002 by allowing duty-free importation in more than two hundred tariff categories.

Figure 2.1. Number of Maquiladoras in Tijuana, January 2001–January 2002

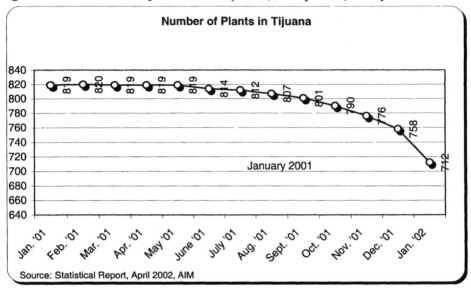

Figure 2.2. Number of Employees in Tijuana Maquiladoras, January 2001–January 2002

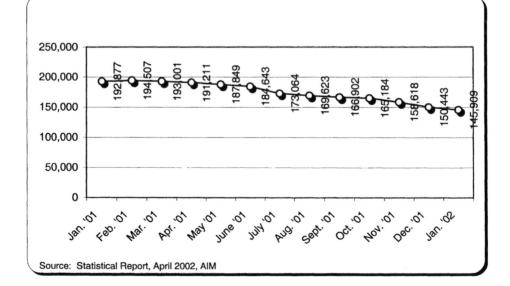

creation and the risks, limitations, and challenges facing regions as a consequence of the TNCs' contribution in this area.

REGIONS, GLOBALIZATION, AND TRANSNATIONAL CORPORATIONS

There is general consensus among scholars that, in this era of globalization, regions are gaining importance as centers of economic development. There is a dialectical movement in the configuration and transformation of the space-time axis (Giddens 2001), making it necessary to analyze the way in which remote locations can connect almost simultaneously through new information technologies and communication systems.

On the other hand, the region is thought of as a stakeholder endowed with the potential to direct its own development (Boscherini and Poma 2000; Benko and Lipietz 1994; Dini 1996; Florida 2000). Thus the region's reemergence under the "new regionalism" reflects existing differences, and its new role is based not on uniformity but on difference.

Mexico's northern border municipalities display some of the elements required for regional development: professionals are linked through networks, representatives of business associations work or have worked as maquiladora managers, and educational institutions have entered into agreements with key plants. However, an important part of the maquiladoras' dynamic is explained by global phenomena of a sectoral or commodity-oriented nature. Many large maquiladoras still depend on strategic decisions taken in Asia or the United States, and most specialized knowledge in the plants—though undoubtedly expanding—remains concentrated in the technical sectors, mainly among engineers and managers.

The northern border region's lack of an industrial tradition, in combination with a labor market composed largely of migrants from the interior of Mexico who have no industrial experience, has created a paradoxical situation in the maquiladora sector. On the one hand, cities with high concentrations of maquiladoras are deprived of the specialization that might give them a competitive edge in international markets. On the other hand, there is more latitude for establishing industries in a variety of subsectors and more diversity in industrial learning. Considering the characteristics of the maquiladora assembly process and the workforce, learning began at the ground level—building a labor force with basic technical, organizational, and social skills.[4]

---

[4] Managers see turnover and absenteeism, not workers' lack of knowledge, as the main problem in labor force management.

This means that Tijuana cannot be considered a knowledge society. Countries aim to become knowledge societies in order to lower unemployment levels and/or compete with low-wage industrializing countries. In these cases, there is broad support for education: the Left sees education as a means to improve equity and foster democracy, while the Right sees education as an investment that generates savings in social benefits over the long term (Crouch, Finegold, and Sako 1999: 4). The evolution toward a more intensive knowledge system would be socially desirable in the border region, but given current economic uncertainty, this goal would need to be concretized in specific policies.[5]

WORK, LABOR MARKET, AND TURNOVER

Tijuana's maquiladoras present two interrelated characteristics that differentiate them from those in other border municipalities: the importance of electronic plants and the presence of Asian-owned companies. According to Mexico's Trade Ministry (SECOFI), of the 1,025 maquiladoras in Baja California in 1998, 20 percent (203 plants) were in the electronics sector. Of these, 70 percent (143) were in Tijuana. Employment in the state's electronics sector in 1998 exceeded 55,000 jobs, approximately 70 percent of which (some 40,000) were in Tijuana.[6]

Economic recession in the United States and the events of September 11, 2001, put an abrupt end to the dramatic growth that the maquiladoras had experienced in the 1990s. Between October 2000 and the beginning of 2002, Mexico lost more than 200,000 maquila jobs, almost 20 percent of the total (see table 2.1). Over approximately this same period, Baja California had a net job loss of about 75,000, from 290,613 to 215,837 (http://dgcnesyp.inegi.gob.mx/cgi-win/bdi.exe). Approximately 50,000 of these positions were lost in Tijuana. Sony was among the plants hardest hit; it had to concentrate all of its operations, which until the late 1990s had been conducted at four plants, in a single location.

---

[5] Representatives of local business associations recommend attracting technology-intensive maquiladoras as a means of enhancing regional development. One proposal, the 2001–2006 Border Development Program, recommended promoting backward linkages and supports to small and midsize companies, ideas that had had been advanced by previous administrations.

[6] Other important subsectors in Baja California were plastics (7 percent of total employment) and wood products, textiles, and metal products (each of which accounted for about 6 percent of total employment).

Workers who were able to keep their jobs in the maquiladoras saw their hours reduced from 45 hours per week at the end of the 1990s to 43 hours a week in 2002. Meanwhile, the average workweek in the autoparts and electronics sectors overall fell to 39.3 hours (INEGI 2002).

Production workers represent about 80 percent of the maquiladora workforce nationwide. Technicians in these plants account for between 11 and 12 percent of all employed workers, and engineers and managers account for about 7 percent (Carrillo and de la O 2002). The employment structure in Tijuana's maquiladoras is similar to that found throughout Mexico. In 1993, there were 8,374 technicians in Tijuana maquiladoras. Five years later, that figure had more than doubled to 17,532. By July 2000, the number of technicians had increased to 21,009, representing approximately 11 percent of all employed personnel. Engineers increased even more: from 4,908 in 1993 to 11,053 in 1998 (INEGI 1999), and in July 2001 they numbered 13,524, or 7 percent of all employed personnel.

This labor market structure is characterized by acute gender differences. In 1998, slightly over half of production workers were women, compared with only 25 percent of technicians (4,531 of a total of 17,352 technicians; see Hualde 2001a: 65).

During the 2000–2001 economic crisis, key maquiladoras began to reconsider the sizable investments they were making in administrative and technical personnel, and some maquiladoras in Tijuana determined to reduce their numbers of these employees by about 15 percent to cut costs.[7]

Plant Characteristics and Employment

Employment structures vary widely among maquiladoras. In a representative sample of seventy-three Tijuana electronics plants, four had no technicians among their employees, but technicians accounted for 10 percent of employed workers at fifty-three of the plants (COLEF 2002).[8] Moreover, in eight of these plants, technicians composed more than 20 percent of personnel. The mode for engineering and administrative personnel is 10 percent. In seven plants, engineers accounted for more than 20 percent of

---

[7] Personal communication with a human resources manager who has fifteen years' experience in a Tijuana maquiladora.

[8] These data are drawn from a COLEF research project (2002) coordinated by the author and funded in part by the Consejo de Desarrollo Económico de Tijuana and the state Department of Education.

Table 2.1. Personnel Employed in Mexican Maquiladoras, by Job Category, 1994–2002

	Production Workers			Technicians	Administrative Employees	Total
	Men	Women	Subtotal			
1994	192,991	284,041	477,031	64,656	41,357	583,044
1995	217,557	314,172	531,729	71,098	45,436	648,263
1996	257,575	359,042	616,617	82,795	54,296	753,708
1997	312,457	422,892	735,349	103,855	64,324	903,528
1998	357,905	465,656	823,561	118,516	71,929	1,014,006
1999	408,432	514,444	922,876	138,246	82,119	1,143,240
2000[a]	466,004	574,073	1,040,077	152,622	92,308	1,285,007
2001	433,044	526,474	959,518	150,136	91,921	1,201,575
2002	386,314	462,526	848,840	137,555	85,315	1,071.710

Source: INEGI statistics on Mexico's maquiladora industries.

[a] Preliminary figures.

Table 2.2. Tijuana's Economically Active Population, by Education Level, 1990–2000 (percentages)

Education Level	1990	1992	1994	1996	1998	2000
No formal schooling	4.10%	3.30%	3.30%	3.70%	3.10%	4.00%
Primary school	32.20	34.00	33.40	32.70	33.60	31.30
Technical school	10.40	9.30	6.70	6.40	6.80	4.40
Junior high school	27.10	27.60	28.20	26.50	28.40	28.20
High school	13.10	13.10	15.30	16.10	14.70	16.60
College	12.30	12.30	13.00	14.60	13.40	15.20
Total	100.00	100.00	100.00	100.00	100.00	100.00
	(N = 291,739)	(N = 317,289)	(N =329,325)	(N = 387,863)	(N = 449,891)	(N =518,459)

Source: ENEU, second trimester.

the workforce, and in twenty-eight plants they formed just 5 percent or less of total employees.

Finally, in twenty plants, managers accounted for approximately 5 percent of total employment. Interestingly, eight plants claimed they had no managers or executive directors, sixteen plants had only one person in such a position, and another twelve plants had only two. In other words, half of the plants included in this study reported having a maximum of two people in managerial or directive positions.

To summarize, the percentage of production workers remains high on average, but between twelve and fifteen plants have important fractions of technicians, engineers, and administrative workers in relation to the total production workforce.

Educational and Occupational Structure

The data on Tijuana's labor market structure also reveal substantial educational inequality.[9] According to the National Survey of Urban Employment (ENEU), Tijuana's economically active population (EAP) in 2000 was as follows: 31.3 percent had a primary school education (*primaria*, grades 1–6); 28.2 percent had completed junior high school (*secundaria*, grades 7–9); and 16.6 percent had graduated high school (*preparatoria*, grades 10–12). College-educated professionals in technical and scientific fields (*ingenieros*) accounted for 15.2 percent of the working population, and technicians were 4.40 percent. Four percent of the EAP had no formal schooling (table 2.2).

When considering education level and economic activity, we find that employees in the maquiladoras have higher education levels on average than Tijuana's population as a whole. Among manufacturing workers (most of whom are employed in the maquiladoras), 36.4 percent—6 percent more than in the general population—have completed the equivalent of junior high school (table 2.3). However, the manufacturing labor force also includes a relatively high proportion of persons who have only completed primary school. By contrast, the percentage of manufacturing workers who attended a technical training school is slightly lower than the general population, and the percentage with professional training is much lower.

---

[9] These data are presented in Rodolfo Cruz's chapter in COLEF 2002.

Table 2.3. Distribution of Tijuana's Economically Active Population, by Economic Sector and Education Level, 2000 (percentages)

	No Formal Schooling	Primary School	Technical School	Junior High School	High School	Professional Training	Total
Manufacturing	3.50%	33.80%	3.90%	36.40%	14.60%	7.20%	100.00%
Construction industry	14.00	51.70	1.80	21.70	5.30	5.50	100.00
Distribution services	3.70	32.10	5.10	27.30	21.20	10.60	100.00
Producer services		11.00	6.50	12.00	20.00	50.30	100.00
Social service	0.90	5.40	8.00	8.20	14.50	63.00	100.00
Government	1.40	16.10	5.30	19.90	21.10	36.30	100.00
Personal services	4.90	41.90	3.80	31.60	12.90	4.90	100.00
Total	4.20	32.10	4.60	27.90	15.70	15.30	100.00
	(N = 19,946)	(N = 154,263)	(N = 21,836)	(N = 134,118)	(N = 75,277)	(N = 73,633)	(N = 480,250)

Source: ENEU, second trimester.

These data indicate that even though the number of professional and technical workers employed in maquiladoras increased in the 1990s, the manufacturing sector remains less professionalized than the local labor market as a whole. Looking at a broader context, in terms of industrial workers' education levels, Tijuana compares unfavorably with industrial cities in Mexico's interior (see table 2.4).[10]

Educational averages by economic sector in Tijuana—and elsewhere—indicate that manufacturing occupies an intermediate position, with schooling levels superior to those in the farming sector, construction, and personal services, but decidedly lower than those in producer services, government, and social services (table 2.4). The latter is the economic sector with the highest average educational attainment levels in all of the cities considered.

Finally, if we look at three occupation categories in manufacturing in these five cities—craftsmen/manufacturing workers, operators of continuous motion machines in fixed position, and foremen and supervisors—we find that average educational levels in Tijuana are generally lower than in Ciudad Juárez, Monterrey, Puebla, and Guadalajara (table 2.5).

Education and Wages

During the 1990s, monthly incomes for the Mexican population as a whole were pressed downward by currency devaluations and general economic crisis beginning in 1994. By the end of the 1990s, incomes had begun to recover, eventually approaching the levels that had prevailed at the beginning of the decade. However, the income gap has widened between college-educated workers and workers with lower levels of educational attainment. Only professionals with advanced studies were earning higher salaries at the end of the 1990s than at the beginning of the decade (table 2.6).

Workers' incomes also differ depending on the sector in which they are employed. For example, professionals in the manufacturing sector have higher average incomes than professionals employed in other economic sectors. On the contrary, technicians earn higher incomes in Tijuana's trade and services sectors than in the maquiladoras (table 2.7). These data are

---

[10] The ENEU data are for the manufacturing sector overall; however, because most manufacturing employment in border cities is in maquiladoras, the tendencies these data reveal are easily applicable to the maquila sector more narrowly.

Table 2.4. Average Years of Education of the EAP in Various Mexican Cities, by Economic Sector, 2000

Economic Sector	Tijuana	Ciudad Juárez	Monterrey	Puebla	Guadalajara
Farming and mining	6.07 years	5.59 years	9.47 years	5.94 years	9.18 years
Electricity generation and construction	6.95	7.06	7.98	7.53	7.71
Manufacturing[a]	8.02	8.22	9.97	9.32	8.87
Distribution services	8.84	8.67	10.03	9.45	9.07
Producer services	10.71	11.25	12.59	13.05	12.56
Social services	13.19	13.47	13.86	14.28	13.56
Personal services	7.56	7.62	8.27	7.85	7.89
Government	10.87	10.72	11.54	12.58	11.87
Total	8.58	8.62	10.21	9.95	9.58

Source: National Population and Housing Census, 2000.
[a] These data are for all manufacturing workers; in border cities, most manufacturing workers are employed in maquiladoras.

Table 2.5. Average Years of Education of the EAP in Various Mexican Cities, by Occupation, 1990–2000

Occupation	Tijuana	Ciudad Juárez	Monterrey	Puebla	Guadalajara
Craftsmen/manufacturing workers	7.08 years	8.59 years	7.89 years	7.48 years	7.53 years
Operators of continuous motion machines	7.26	6.33	8.82	8.27	8.11
Foremen and supervisors	9.57	10.53	12.08	12.56	11.54
Total	8.58	8.62	10.21	9.95	9.58

Source: National Population and Housing Census, 2000.

Table 2.6. Tijuana's Economically Active Population's Average Real Monthly Income, by Education Level, 1990–2000 (in pesos)

Education Level	1990	1992	1994	1996	1998	2000
No formal schooling	$1,120	$964	$854	$887	$944	$865
Primary school	1,574	1,212	1,086	860	1,110	1,087
Vocational school	1,589	1,599	1,297	1,036	1,265	1,348
Junior high school	1,313	1,184	1,132	895	1,154	1,147
High school	1,891	1,414	1,367	1,098	1,600	1,576
Superior professional	2,509	2,537	2,624	2,199	2,359	2,587
Not specified	1,462	1,750	NA	677	NA	836
Total	$1,627	$1,414	$1,334	$1,106	$1,359	$1,410

Source: ENEU, second trimester.

NA = not available.

Table 2.7. Economically Active Population's Average Real Monthly Income, by Education and Economic Sector, 1990–2000 (in pesos)

Schooling/Economic Sector	1990	1992	1994	1996	1998	2000
Technical Workers						
Manufacturing	1,480	1,558	1,197	964	981	1,220
Commerce	2,073	1,488	1,234	1,236	1,276	1,434
Services	1,371	1,542	1,439	953	1,300	1,422
Other economic sectors	1,803	2,314	1,246	1,068	1,920	1,068
Total	1,589	1,599	1,297	1,036	1,265	1,348
Professionals/Upper Management						
Manufacturing	2,719	2,777	2,358	2,327	2,427	2,622
Commerce	2,408	2,510	2,181	1,985	1,931	2,573
Services	2,294	2,411	2,769	2,121	2,150	2,586
Other economic sectors	3,347	2,844	2,837	2,830	3,301	2,566
Total						
Manufacturing	1,328	1,263	1,131	896	992	1,153
Commerce	1,992	1,400	1,320	1,202	1,253	1,496
Services	1,552	1,474	1,476	1,186	1,303	1,594
Other economic sectors	1,647	1,591	1,477	1,315	2,328	1,392
Total	1,627	1,414	1,334	1,106	1,359	1,410

Source: ENEU.

consistent with information about the professional trajectories of both oc-
cupations, to be discussed in a later section.

MAQUILADORA WORKERS' SKILLS AND CAREERS
Work on the Line

The information presented thus far offers a framework for examining some
general characteristics of Tijuana's labor market, drawing on research by
the author and others. Available information on workers' activities in Tijuana maquiladoras reveals that most work is manual, though some tasks
are carried out using instruments or machines (such as microscopes or
soldering tools) that require some limited technical knowledge.[11] These
kinds of activities predominate in maquiladoras that produce electric and
electronic products, medical instruments, and toys, sectors where employment has become increasingly concentrated. Other subsectors in Tijuana's maquiladora industries are clothing[12] and furniture and wood
products.

Work on the assembly line is not the only kind of work done in the
maquiladoras. There is also individualized work, where a single multi-
tasking (though not multi-skilled) operator carries out several operations at
a workstation. [13] It is doubtful, however, that this last type of work implies
greater technical complexity or is rewarded with a higher wage.[14] Since
firms aim to improve product quality, they have increased the number of
production workers dedicated to inspection, supervision, and quality control. Others do measurement tasks and even simple programming (Hualde
1999). The types of tasks assigned to production workers depend to a large
extent on the product involved.

In general, the operations done by production workers demand care,
concentration, and, in some cases, manual dexterity, traits that many man-

---

[11] The description of line workers' tasks comes from the author's observations in
some twenty-five plants in various sectors and from his interviews with workers
in 1996 and 2002. Other sources that address this topic include Kopinak 1996; de
la O 1994; Reygadas 2000; and Contreras 2000.

[12] Most textile maquiladoras in Baja California are located in Ensenada.

[13] These workers diversify their skills but do not gain new knowledge that could be
applied more generally.

[14] The pay scale for production workers in maquiladoras generally has five or six
levels. Workers move up in pay depending on performance and seniority. For
supervisors, range of responsibilities is also a factor.

agers claim are characteristic of women workers. Such gender images persist in Tijuana's maquiladoras, even though men now account for about half of production workers. These gender images are constructed and reproduced along two dimensions. On the one hand, they are part of a discourse among employers and managers that considers women to be better than men at performing certain kinds of work, including specific jobs on the assembly line. In skilled positions—supervisory jobs, industrial relations, engineering management, and so on—other qualities that are attributed to women (better communications and socializing skills) can also give them an advantage over men (Hualde 2001b).

On the other hand, it may be that the positive aspects linked to gender images selectively direct women to positions that are poorly paid (Abramo and Todaro 1998). For example, Susan Tiano (1994: 92) interviewed managers in apparel and electronics firms, first in 1982 and then in 1990, and found that the maquiladora managers' original preference for young, single, childless women had evolved from 1982 to 1990 into a preference for older women with children, whom they considered to be more responsible. In Nogales, Kathryn Kopinak (1996: 82–85) found that women were being excluded from technical positions. An analysis she conducted in the 1980s revealed that more than two-thirds of all job announcements naming a specific gender asked for women. This analysis and Kopinak's interviews with workers and managers in 1991 found, further, that 89 percent of the open positions that were specifically identified as jobs for women were unskilled jobs.

Kopinak's research also revealed that a higher proportion of men had jobs that could be defined as highly skilled or semi-skilled (25 percent) than was true among women (10 percent), largely because men received training that allowed them to move up the wage ladder, while women remained in low-skill jobs because managers saw them only as low-skilled workers (Carrillo and Kopinak 1999). The discourse about gender-differentiated workplace skills is not restricted to management; it is sometimes shared by the female employees themselves. That is why women workers take pride in a job well done even when their wage and labor conditions are relatively precarious.[15] Their satisfaction with their performance is reinforced when management accords them symbolic acknowledgements such as medals or awards.

---

[15] These observations come from interviews with workers in Tijuana.

The clean and well-lit facilities of today's large and modern companies undoubtedly represent an improvement over the workplaces of the past. Highly professional managers and supervisors trained in human relations humanize work in Tijuana's maquiladoras. Yet the positive aspects of maquila work coexist with less auspicious realities of work life. Hours of intense concentration on detailed tasks that offer no opportunity for creativity or autonomy produce tiredness and boredom, and may even lead to occupational injuries and disease (Kouros 1998; see also Harlow, Denman, and Cedillo, this volume); and some basic worker rights, such as collective bargaining, have not evolved significantly (see the chapter by Quintero, this volume).[16] Moreover, open questions remain regarding the pace of work in the maquiladoras, though there is a paucity of research on this topic. Have the maquiladoras increased the demand for speed on the job? If so, what are the impacts of a more intense work rhythm on the workers' well-being and income levels? These questions do not apply only to Tijuana; in France, for example, industries that employ highly skilled male workers and use just-in-time inventory control and other new techniques, show a higher level in work intensity (Hirata 1998: 9).

In sum, although maquiladoras demonstrate some advances over past workplace conditions, there is much room for improvement. Research in this area has found that most workers in Mexico's border cities display the proletarian characteristics of long-past generations. Their meager wages do not allow them to purchase anything beyond the basic goods essential to their survival (young, single women are an exception); a weak relationship with their firm; and a legal guarantee (collective bargaining agreement) that does little to ensure job stability or decent working conditions.

These three characteristics, which Castel (1995: 328) mentions in reference to the early stages of industrialization in France, help to introduce the issue that decisively conditions employment in Tijuana's maquiladoras: the sector's inherent instability, which derives from a number of considerations:

- These plants can, at any time, transfer their production processes to another country.

- New investments or mergers can bring a rapid change in processes and products.

---

[16] The Korean-owned Han Young maquiladora in Tijuana was the site of a labor conflict when workers attempted to create an independent union (Carrillo and Kopinak 1999; Bandy, this volume).

- Rapid turnover of management personnel is institutionalized in Asian-owned maquiladoras, where managers remain no more than three or four years before being transferred home, to a more desirable country, or to a plant where they will have greater responsibilities.

- Turnover among plant workers is very high, as discussed below.

With the notable exception of plants in Matamoros, border maquiladoras were characterized by high turnover rates at least until the 2000–2002 crisis (Canales 1995). Although several explanations have been offered for this phenomenon, some of the most important are related to employment conditions: long workdays, low pay, and conflict with supervisors. Others are linked to the profile of the labor force itself. For example, one would expect high turnover in a largely female workforce because women workers often must interrupt their work trajectory to care for children. Still other explanations seem to dominate Tijuana's labor market, including the high demand for labor, the characteristics of firms' productive cycles, and the nature of prevailing industrial relations. In Matamoros, where unions play a more active role, turnover has traditionally been lower.

Turnover has also been influenced by workers' expectations of quickly finding a job in another plant if they leave their current employment. Testing this hypothesis involves comparing turnover rates during a period of employment expansion with rates in a period of employment contraction. In the late 1990s, turnover in Tijuana was calculated at between 12 and 15 percent. In a survey of the electronics sector in 2001—when the crisis was generating its first impacts—turnover was 13.5 percent on average, though it rose as high as 21.3 percent in plants with fewer than one hundred employees (COLEF 2002: 7). In 2002, when the effects of the crisis were being fully felt, the turnover rate dropped to 3 percent.[17]

The various factors discussed above are not the only work and labor market characteristics that influence labor force turnover. Fluctuations in production also play a role. In some cases, such as the toy industry, production is seasonal, and firms in this sector take advantage of natural turnover to avoid having to fire workers, which would involve legally mandated severance pay. The same happens when firms experience sudden drops in production levels in nonseasonal productive cycles.

---

[17] Personal communication with a representative of the Industrial Relations Association of Tijuana (ARITAC).

Turnover should not, of course, be viewed as a tool for adjusting the size of the workforce, even though it can play that role quite well. High turnover rates in large firms imply additional expenditures for hiring and training new employees. Interestingly, high turnover rates may have less of an impact in plants that introduce more complex processes and operations. These plants tend to have a nucleus of stable workers devoted to these more complex jobs and a peripheral group of workers who rotate more frequently over time.

Turnover can also be understood as an expression of the lack of guarantees of stable employment or fluctuations in the size and age of the labor market. As the labor force ages, turnover may decrease. That is, highly vulnerable sectors of the labor market, such as single mothers, may, as they grow older, maintain a more stable relationship with certain firms. However, such instances of stability are typically based on personal relationships between the worker and management, and they fall outside any legal guarantees; that is, they are not protected under the workers' collective labor agreement with the company. This creates an emblematic sign of the times: "permanent temporary workers," who renew their contract over and over even though they can be fired at any time (Castel 1995). These workers are particularly vulnerable because most companies do not want to employ workers who are more than forty-five years old.

From the workers' perspective, turnover carries high social costs. Moving from job to job interrupts the worker's learning process and also prevents him or her from accumulating rights linked to seniority. Turnover as a permanent characteristic of the labor market stymies the creation of labor organizations. The instability in Tijuana's labor market hinders the creation of collective identities linked to a job, a company, or a career. However, as some authors have noted, moving between plants can also be part of workers' survival strategies as they try to gain better—though still not secure—employment.[18]

Some authors claim that workers' wages in maquiladoras that are large and internationally competitive—and hence are characterized by technological complexity—are kept artificially low. For example, Quintero Ramírez (2001) noted in a study of Deltrónicos, a large, high-tech plant in Mata-

---

[18] This observation points to insecurity as a subjective perception of risk. Such perceptions depend on a worker's age, family situation, and/or present employment conditions. To assume that subjective insecurity is uniform throughout the maquiladora sector is an oversimplification, although observable, "objective" security is largely absent from labor contracts (Standing 2000: 48–49).

moros, that wages for assembly workers are only slightly higher than in other maquiladoras. In their study of five plants in Chihuahua, Bensusán and Reygadas (2000) attribute low wage levels to the absence of institutions, trade unions, and labor officials that could support a closer correspondence between wages and productivity. These authors refer to maquiladora wages as "artificially depressed."

Technicians

Maquiladoras employ three kinds of technicians: engineers who have not yet completed their degree program; college-graduated technicians; and "empirical" technicians (Hualde 2001c). Maquiladoras require technicians specialized in electromechanics, electronics, and maintenance. To a lesser degree, they also need technicians with special training in machinery and production processes. Their main functions are the installation, maintenance, repair, and programming of equipment (COLEF 2002).[19]

The work and life trajectories of technical school graduates vary considerably. Many did advanced studies to increase their job opportunities. In a recent survey of 202 technicians in Tijuana and Mexicali, almost half of those who lacked a professional certificate were in the process of obtaining one; almost 80 percent of these were studying engineering. This suggests that the positions available to people who lack technical degrees often fail to meet the expectations of Tijuana's young people, who are studying to get the training they need to access better job options, even though the combination of work and school may mean workdays that begin at 6 a.m. and do not end until 10 p.m.[20]

Some technicians begin as operators in the maquiladoras and advance to higher positions after they complete their technical degree (Hualde 2002b). Importantly, the plants themselves have not anticipated a need for—or implemented—mechanisms for professional upgrading. Technicians wishing to continue their studies must individually negotiate with their employer to set a modified work schedule that allows them to take

---

[19] Surveys were carried out with technicians and engineers in Tijuana and Ciudad Juárez in 1993 and 1994, and with technicians in Tijuana and Mexicali in 2001. These surveys with personnel who had done advanced study and also demonstrated successful career trajectories aimed to identify: (1) the relationship between the studies and job positions, (2) the kinds of tasks these workers were assigned, (3) the coherence between education and professional path, and (4) the valuation and recognition given these workers in the maquiladoras.

[20] This observation derives from the author's fieldwork.

classes. Negotiating success depends on the relationship each employee has with management. Despite their efforts to improve their skill levels, it is not clear that graduates returning with technical certificates immediately receive a significant wage increase.[21] In a few cases, large maquiladoras offer training courses that can compensate technicians somewhat for their low wages.

Engineers

Engineers—whether they work as engineers or as managers—are clearly the group with the most solid and long-lasting careers in the maquiladoras. They also receive the most training. Training is the way in which plants try to close the gap between the knowledge acquired in school and the knowledge required in the plant. However, this does not mean that the poorest-performing professionals get the most supplemental training. Indeed, the opposite appears to be true. The maquiladoras offer most training opportunities to the engineers who show the best progress and the strongest interest, and who demonstrate a capacity to learn. Many of these workers ask the firm to send them to courses they have learned about on their own. In other words, the training to a certain extent is a result of the worker's initiative.

Of course, training is not the only means to acquire learning, and informal learning is essential in maquiladoras as well as in the world outside the factory. One worker expressed his perspective as follows:

> What I have learned is due to three factors: sharing with people who have more experience; the everyday problems that push us to use or create new problem-solving methods; and the basic methods we learned in school (author interview with a manufacturing engineer with four years of work experience).

Subsequent studies revealed a number of important characteristics among Mexican engineers employed in Tijuana and other northern border cities in Mexico (Hualde 1995, 2001a, 2001b):

---

[21] These are the results of ongoing research on industrial learning, employment, and worker training in the maquiladoras, funded by Mexico's National Council of Science and Technology (CONACYT, Reference Number 35049-S).

- Involvement in a variety of tasks—logistics, production, manufacturing, human resources management, process engineering, and even product design.

- Ascending professional trajectories that can reach the highest management levels, mainly in plants with North American capital (Contreras 2000). (Asian-owned plants reserve the highest positions for Asians.)

- Movement between plants aimed at maximizing learning. There are cases of local engineers being recruited by their company's U.S. headquarters after working in border municipalities.

- Training in the plants and at headquarters. Asian plants send some engineers—as well as some technicians and line workers—to train at their headquarters.

- A social network among engineers that supports the creation of flexible teams in different plants. This type of collective can be compared to "action communities" (Zarifian 2001).

A sense of community has grown up around the networks that connect maquiladoras to the educational sector, through which workers share their career-related objectives. This community of professional technical and scientific personnel linked through the maquiladoras anticipates two important limitations in their future. First, some of the engineers see a promising future only in plants that have gone beyond simple assembly. The second limitation is more subjective: engineers often plan to work in the maquiladoras for only fifteen years or so, at which point they feel that future advancement will not be possible. At this point, most intend to establish their own businesses. Women engineers note that maquiladoras are very stressful; in making heavy demands on their time, the maquiladoras make it very difficult for women to combine their professional work with caring for their family (Hualde 2001b).

FINAL REFLECTIONS

From the mid-1980s to 2000, Mexico's northern border municipalities experienced substantial growth due to the investment of U.S. and Asian (particularly Japanese) capital in electronics and autoparts production in these cities. The new plants differed in important ways from the maquiladoras of the 1970s, which had a very elementary organization, precarious work conditions, and poor facilities. Although these plants hired thousands of workers, technicians, engineers, and other professionals, their employment structure did not become statistically more professionalized, and the technicians and engineers tend to remain concentrated in a few big plants.

Maquiladora employees perform more than simple manual assembly tasks. But most of the tasks they carry out do not require the technical knowledge typical of a skilled worker, though they do require close attention and, occasionally, a bit of basic calculus. The need to maintain product quality is one of the considerations driving employee training, although the upgrading of tasks and additional worker training do not often bring parallel upgrades in wages or promotion structures. Working conditions are underpinned by weak legal frameworks; collective labor agreements allow substantial flexibility in the use of the workforce and give employers wide latitude in managing production processes. In some cases, workers have even been made members of a union without their knowledge. And when disputes arise, the courts have typically been slow in delivering a resolution (Quintero Ramírez 1997; Carrillo and Kopinak 1999).

Technicians mainly do maintenance and repair. Technicians who wish to gain additional knowledge generally must identify the learning opportunities themselves and then request permission from their boss, usually an engineer, to participate. Promotions are conditioned by each plant's organizational characteristics. In large plants, competition for promotion tends to be intense. Highly motivated technicians often study engineering, which they see as a good option for upward mobility.

At least until 2000, engineers generally had the most variety in their assigned tasks and the best possibilities for reaching well-paid positions, and many young graduates of local educational institutions are taking positions as manufacturing, materials, and quality managers. Asian owned and U.S.-owned plants typically send these new hires to their company headquarters to learn about new product characteristics. Two emerging areas appear to be quite promising in terms of employment options for professionals in the maquiladora sector: one is communications and information technology; the other involves recent developments in product design currently being tested in some plants.

The large educational gaps that remain between production workers—who generally have a primary or junior high school education—and professional employees in the maquiladoras are an obstacle to the collective learning that would bring substantial advantages to the border region. In a knowledge economy, there is a strong need for a common language and a common set of codes. Indeed, certain certification processes, such as ISO 9000, depend heavily on coordination and communication within the organization as a whole. A sizable educational gap between groups of employees reduces the possibilities for such communication and coordination.

Sorge (1987) and others have emphasized the need to reduce the educational disparities between production workers and engineers in labor markets. Although Nonaka and Takeuchi (1995: 151) focus on various levels of management, they also note that everyone in a company must create knowledge. The flow of information is a prerequisite for the creation of knowledge, so if maquiladoras want to create knowledge, they must implement a new structure, different from the hierarchical structure that currently exists in these plants (Von Krogh, Ichijo, and Nonaka 2000).

A United Nations Conference on Trade and Development (UNCTAD) report on the electronics sector in Mexico—mainly in Jalisco and on the border—and in Malaysia and Thailand concluded that Mexico, because of its proximity to the United States, will continue to be a regional center of electronics production in the future and, further, that if the technological capacities of the Mexican firms are strengthened, transnational companies manufacturing electronics in Mexico can grow to serve the Latin American market. The UNCTAD report also asserted that transnationals have great potential to develop human capital. Many foreign companies in developing countries pay higher salaries and invest more in training than do their domestic counterparts. They are more aware of future training needs and the need to develop new skills. They use state-of-the-art techniques in their training, and they train to the needs of the global market. However, this same report also noted the following:

> The host countries cannot depend on the transnational corporations (TNCs) to satisfy their extensive or emergent qualification necessities. The TNCs use the technologies that are appropriate for the local levels of education and train people in order to create efficient operators of such technologies, *but they do not tend to invest in creating the abilities needed for higher technological levels when these arise.* Such investments are generally more expensive and long term, and here is where the educational institutions have to satisfy these necessities. In other words, the improvement of the general level of qualification and ability as well as the provision of high level specialized training is something that the host countries must do for themselves. In fact, such upgrading must be used both to attract foreign direct investment of higher quality and to in-

duce the existing investors to turn to more complex activities (emphasis added).

Martinelli (2002: 9) also emphasizes that the TNCs have contradictory impacts in their host economies and societies. On one hand, TNCs introduce advanced technologies, organizational models, and corporate strategies, and they offer better wages than domestic companies. But they also exploit existing market fragmentation for labor and resources. Their production technologies, strategies, and structures may not be appropriate for local conditions, particularly in the least developed countries. Although some transnationals assume broader responsibilities with regard to their host communities, officials, workers, and consumers alike note that these companies enjoy power without responsibility. They are accountable only to their shareholders and not to all the other individuals and groups that their decisions affect.

Although learning can expand in all types of companies and regional contexts, Storper (1997) has noted at least two limiting factors. One is the taking-off point; that is, to optimize their learning gains, companies and regions must have attained a minimum level of capacity and competence. A second restriction lies in the fact that the management systems of some companies do not privilege learning, product quality as a growth strategy, or loyalty to their region. Instead, they focus closely on wage costs and an exit strategy they can implement if wage costs rise. Regions where these kinds of firms predominate tend to make fewer demands on companies entering the region and also on those already long established. The difference between the companies that are strong on learning and those that are not—"lean learners" who are prone to volatility—defines the new division between center and periphery.

In light of the preceding discussion, it is clear that cities like Tijuana need to evaluate the limitations that maquiladoras impose on learning, as well as the social costs that these limitations bring. Through the public education system, the Mexican population as a whole is carrying the economic weight of preparing a workforce for the maquiladoras, even though these plants complement their workers' public education with additional knowledge and contribute equipment to some schools.[22]

---

[22] Eight or ten large maquiladoras helped vocational schools in Tijuana acquire new machine tools valued at between US$40,000 and $60,000. Also, under an entailment agreement, maquiladoras pass their used computers to local schools.

Workers also share in the cost burden, in a number of ways: Production workers do not receive wage or benefit gains commensurate to upgrades in their professional trajectories. This is particularly true of women workers, who lack the social supports (daycare, transportation, and so on) that would allow them to work and also care for their homes and families. Technicians who pursue formal studies often get little recognition for their long days of study and work, and may see no improvement in their wages or position in the plant. And engineers, although rewarded with better wages and learning opportunities, hold jobs that are stressful and find their professional progress blocked as they approach their middle years.

In effect, the employment logic in the maquiladoras resembles the so-called Anglo-Saxon model described by Crouch, Finegold, and Sako:

> In both countries [Great Britain and the United States], the level of statutory labor protection being low, most employment security is provided by employers; they are concerned to provide this for employees whom they want to retain, which mainly means well-educated staff in whom the firm is therefore willing to invest a good deal of training. At the other end of the scale, a large number of low skilled workers can be employed and easily disposed of if they are not needed, with little attention to their training and with a frequent recourse to the external labor market (1999: 86).

References

Abramo, Laís, and Rosalba Todaro. 1998. "Género y trabajo en las decisiones empresariales," *Revista Latinoamericana de Estudios del Trabajo* 4, no. 7: 77–97.

Benko, Georges, and A. Lipietz. 1994. "De las redes de distritos a los distritos de redes." In *Las regiones que ganan*, edited by Georges Benko and Alain Lipietz. Valencia: Alfons el Magnanim.

Bensusán, G., and Luis Reygadas. 2000. "Relaciones laborales en Chihuahua: un caso de abatimiento artificial de los salaries," *Revista Mexicana de Sociología* 62, no. 2 (April–June): 29–57.

Boscherini, F., and L. Poma, eds. 2000. "Más allá de los distritos industriales: el nuevo concepto de territorio en el marco de la economía global." In *Territorio, conocimiento y competitividad de empresas*. Buenos Aires: Miño and Dávila.

Canales, Alejandro. 1995. "Condición de género y determinantes' sociodemográficos de la rotación de personal en la industria maquiladora de exportación." In *Mujeres, migración y maquila en la frontera norte*, edited by Soledad González, Olivia Ruiz, Laura Velasco, and Ofelia Woo. Tijuana: El Colegio de la Frontera Norte.

Carrillo, Jorge, and María Eugenia de la O. 2002. "Las dimensiones del trabajo en la industria maquiladora de exportación." Presented at the workshop "La Situación del Trabajo en México," Universidad Autómona Metropolitana, Mexico City.

Carrillo, Jorge, and Alberto Hernández. 1985. *Mujeres fronterizas en la industria maquiladora*. Mexico City: Consejo Nacional para la Cultura y las Artes.

Carrillo, Jorge, and Kathryn Kopinak. 1999. "Empleo y relaciones laborales: las maquiladoras en México." In *Cambios en las relaciones laborales*, edited by Enrique de la Garza and José Alfonso Bouzas. Mexico City: Universidad Nacional Autónoma de México.

Castel, Robert. 1995. *La metamorfosis de la cuestión social: una crónica del salariado*. Buenos Aires: Paidós.

COLEF (El Colegio de la Frontera Norte). 2002. "Hacia una articulación entre los perfiles educativos y las necesidades del desarrollo regional." Final research report.

Contreras, Óscar. 2000. *Empresas globales, actores locales: producción flexible y aprendizaje industrial en las maquiladoras*. Mexico City: El Colegio de México.

Crouch, Colin, David Finegold, and Mari Sako. 1999. *Are Skills the Answer? The Political Economy of Skill Creation in Advanced Industrial Countries*. New York: Oxford University Press.

De la O, María Eugenia. 1994. *Innovación tecnológico y clase obrera*. Mexico City: Miguel Ángel Porrúa/Universidad Autónoma Metropolitana–Iztapalapa.

Dini, M. 1996. "Políticas públicas para el desarrollo de redes de empresas: la experiencia chilena," *Revista Latinoamericana de Estudios del Trabajo* 2, no. 3: 131–57.

Fernández-Kelly, María Patricia. 1983. *For We Are Sold. I and My People*. New York: State University of New York Press.

Florida, Richard. 2000. "The Learning Region." In *Regional Innovation, Knowledge and Global Change*, edited by Zoltan Acs. London: Pinter.

Giddens, Anthony. 2001. "Dimensions of Globalization." In *The New Social Theory Reader*, edited by Steven Seidman and Jeffrey C. Alexander. London: Routledge.

González-Aréchiga, Bernardo, and J.C. Ramírez. 1990. *Subcontratación y empresas transnacionales*. Mexico: El Colegio de la Frontera Norte/Fundación Friedrich Ebert.

Hirata, E. 1998. "Reestructuracao productivo, trabalho e relacoes de genero," *Revista Latinoamericana de Estudios del Trabajo* 4, no. 7: 5–29.

Hualde, Alfredo. 1995. "Técnicos e ingenieros en la industria maquiladora fronteriza: su rol como agentes innovadores." In *El trabajo a fin de siglo*, edited by M. Gallart. Buenos Aires: Red Latinoamericana de Educación y Trabajo, CIID-CENEP.

———. 1997. "Las maquiladoras en México a fin de siglo." Cuaderno de Trabajo, Seminario Subregional Tripartito sobre Aspectos Sociales y Laborales de las Zonas Francas Industriales de Exportación. San José, Costa Rica: International Labour Organization.

———. 1999. "Saberes productivos y polarización en la frontera norte de México," *Sociología del Trabajo*, Siglo XXI, pp.59–87.

———. 2001a. "Del territorio a la empresa: conocimientos productivos entre los ingenieros del norte de México," *Región y Sociedad* 21 (January–July): 3–45.

———. 2001b. "Trayectorias profesionales femeninas en mercados de trabajo masculinos: las ingenieras en la industria maquiladora," *Revista Mexicana de Sociología* 63, no. 2 (April–June): 63–90.

———. 2001c. *Aprendizaje industrial en la frontera norte de México: la articulación entre el sistema educativo y el sistema productivo maquilador.* 2d ed. Mexico: Plaza y Valdez/El Colegio de la Frontera Norte.

———. 2002a. "Todos los rostros de la industrialización: precariedad y profesionalización en la maquiladora de Tijuana." In *Globalización, trabajo y las nuevas y viejas fronteras en México*, edited by María Eugenia de la O and Cirila Quintero Ramírez. Mexico: Fundación Friedrich Ebert/AFL-CIO/CIESAS.

———. 2002b. "Gestión del conocimiento en la maquiladora de Tijuana: trayectorias, redes y desencuentros," *Comercio Exterior* 52, no. 6: 538–50.

INEGI (Instituto Nacional de Estadística, Geografía e Informática). 1999. *Estadísticas de la industria maquiladora de exportación, 1999.* Mexico: INEGI.

———. 2002. *Estadísticas de la industria maquiladora de exportación, 2002.* Mexico: INEGI.

Kopinak, Kathryn. 1996. *Desert Capitalism: Assembly Plants in North America's Western Industrial Corridor.* Tucson: University of Arizona Press.

Kourous, George. 1998. "La salud y la seguridad laboral en las maquiladoras," *Borderlines* 47, vol. 6, no. 6 (August), www.zianet.com/irc/borderline.

Martinelli, A. 2002. "Markets, Governments, Communities and Global Governance." Address to the congress of the International Sociological Association, Brisbane, Australia.

Nonaka, Ikujiro, and Hirotaka Takeuchi. 1995. *The Knowledge-Creating Company.* New York: Oxford University Press.

Quintero Ramírez, Cirila. 1997. *Reestructuración sindical en la frontera norte: el caso de la industria maquiladora*. Tijuana: El Colegio de la Frontera Norte.

————. 2001. "Cambios productivos y condiciones laborales: la experiencia de Deltrónicos Operations-Delphi." In *Memoria del IX Encuentro de la Asociación de Historia Económica del Norte de México*. Mexico: Universidad Autónoma de Baja California Sur/Secretaría de Educación Pública/ Asociación de Historia Económica del Norte de México.

Reygadas, Luis. 2000. *Ensemblando cultura*. Barcelona: Gedisa.

Sorge, Arndt. 1987. "Implicaciones para el trabajo y la formación en la fábrica del futuro," *Sociología del Trabajo* 1: 175–87.

Standing, G. 2000. "La inseguridad laboral," *Revista Latinoamericana de Estudios del Trabajo* 11: 47–107.

Storper, Michael. 1997. *The Regional World: Territorial Development in a Global Economy*. New York: Guilford.

Tiano, Susan. 1994. *Patriarchy on the Line: Labor, Gender, and Ideology in the Mexican Maquila Industry*. Philadelphia, Penn.: Temple University Press.

Von Krogh, George, Kazuo Ichijo, and Ikujiro Nonaka. 2000. *Enabling Knowledge Creation*. New York: Oxford University Press.

Zarifian, Philippe. 2001. *Le modèle de la compétence*. Paris: Editions Liaisons.

3

Women in the Maquiladora Industry: Toward Understanding Gender and Regional Dynamics in Mexico

MARÍA EUGENIA DE LA O MARTÍNEZ

Women's participation in Mexico's maquiladora labor force offers a notable illustration of the dynamic that the globalized economy is imposing on regional economies. The easy mobility of export capital and the employment of a highly exploitable workforce have shaped a new geography of transnational production in Mexico that carries huge disadvantages and high social costs for many of the actors involved.

This situation particularly affects women workers, who have lost ground in the labor market via the structural degradation of their jobs. The downgrading of women's work has taken place despite a transformation over the past four decades in the industrial processes carried out in the maquiladoras, which brought some upgrading for other groups of workers (see Hualde, this volume). The subordinated character of women's work in these industries was identified in the early research literature of the 1960s and 1970s, which led much of the academic debate to focus on the type of work that these industries offered to women along Mexico's northern border.

In the 1980s, Mexico's economic crisis, in combination with the modernization of a significant number of maquiladoras, led to the occupational segregation of women in specific sectors such as garment and electronics production. By the 1990s, the impacts of flexible production methods on

---

Translation by Kathryn Kopinak and Sandra del Castillo.

women in a context of ongoing economic restructuring were obvious (Nisonoff 1999).

These varied considerations offered a window on women's incorporation into the maquiladora workforce over the course of nearly three decades, even though women's participation in maquiladora labor markets had not yet been linked to these industries' recent territorial expansion from the northern border into the center and south of Mexico. The industry's entry into new regions multiplied the area dedicated to export production and gave rise to a feminized and proletarianized periphery, thus demonstrating the strong links between the transnationalization of productive processes and women's industrial employment.

In order to explore this relationship, this chapter analyzes the articulation between maquiladoras' territorial mobility and the cyclic degradation of women's work. To this end, I identify three regions of maquiladora industrialization and three cycles of women's work in these industries. Among the latter are: (1) feminization of the labor force in the 1970s and 1980s along Mexico's northern border; (2) the de-feminization of the maquiladoras in the late 1980s and throughout the 1990s along the northern border and in key cities in the northeast and northwest; and (3) the re-feminization of maquila work in central and southern Mexico.

The first section of this chapter presents a brief overview of the relevant literature on women's employment in multinational corporations (MNCs), as well as core studies of women workers in Mexico's maquiladoras. The second section analyzes the process of territorial transformation in the maquila sector and its relationship with the cyclic nature of women's employment in this industry. The third section offers some interpretations of the importance of the feminization of work in the context of production-for-export models.

RESEARCH ON WOMEN IN MNCS AND MAQUILADORAS

Multinational corporations' employment of women workers in developing economies over the last forty years exemplifies one of the basic steps toward globalization. Most notably, linking less developed countries to the global economy spurred their implementation of structural adjustment policies and programs, opened local economies to foreign companies and capital, and undermined traditional sectors of the economy (Sassen 1998).

These outcomes brought enormous social costs for women and men in terms of job opportunities. Though foreign, export-producing firms did create employment, the new jobs came with no protections, and the workers who accepted them were virtually defenseless. This situation argues for a deeper understanding of the relationship between gender and economic globalization.

Recent decades have seen important advances in this area of study which allow the identification of at least three focal points for analysis (Sassen 1998). One involves the impacts over the 1960s and 1970s as a wave of foreign companies located some of their export-oriented production processes in countries previously characterized by production for the domestic market and subsistence economies. As modern capitalist corporations fractured local economies, working women assumed dual importance: as guarantors of the social and physical survival of the labor force, and as cheap labor for the transnationals (Boserup 1970; Deere 1976).

The second focus brings together studies of the impacts of the internationalization of manufacturing in nonindustrialized countries during the 1980s. This research analyzed the criteria that core countries followed when relocating production off-shore and the kinds of jobs that they created. In every case, company relocations depended on the massive mobilization of low-cost women workers, which drove a pattern of feminization of the industrial proletariat in poor countries. Ground-breaking studies were conducted of multinational production in the garment and electronics sectors, such as those by Linda Lim (1980), Helen Safa (1981), Patricia Fernández-Kelly (1990), and Saskia Sassen (1993). This line of research placed young women of the Third World at the center of the paradigm used to understand the mobility of transnational capital and work.

Later studies documented the transfer of abilities and character traits that women applied in the domestic sphere to the export-oriented plants established by the multinational corporations. Thus women's "docility and dexterity" were redefined as essential traits in the "meticulous and repetitive tasks" involved in assembly operations. In contrast, these same companies viewed their male workers as "lazy, demanding, and untrustworthy." In this sense, the cultural differences between gender groups provided the backdrop for explanations of the overwhelming predominance of women workers in the export industries of the Third World (Salzinger 1997).[1]

In recent years, poststructuralist feminists adopted this approach when discerning the uncritical and ahistorical formation of gender categories

---

[1] For more on this topic, see Sklair 1993; Standing 1989; Haraway 1985.

(Salzinger 1997; Scott 1988; Baron 1991), arguing the need to determine how gender characteristics are expressed in the workplace. An analysis of popular narratives revealed portrayals of women workers as "exploitable."[2]

Finally, the third analytic focus involves recent studies emphasizing the impacts of global capitalism in local societies. Sassen (2000) has contributed much on the role of global cities and the incorporation of women and migrants into foreign investment–driven activities. These new actors have now moved onto the global stage. As this new and populous class composed of women, youths, and migrants has moved into global cities, their presence has also signaled the decline of the traditional industrial workforce, known in other times as the "labor aristocracy."

This also highlights the emphasis of the new feminism,[3] which seeks to identify the cultural impacts that globalization exerts on prior traditions of women's work.[4] Some of the most relevant themes deal with migrant women and changing gender models, household formation in transnational communities, the composition of the domestic unit under conditions of economic globalization, new representations of gender in the workplace, and recent manifestations of international solidarity.

The role of women in the global economy has been at the crux of debates about industrialization processes for over four decades. The numerous studies on this topic went on to influence later research on women workers in export-processing zones (EPZs), of which Mexico's northern border region is a classic example in the developing world. Writings on the intensive maquiladora industrialization in this region can be divided into three groups depending on their analytical focus: (1) the internationalization of production in Mexico, the broad incorporation of women into the

---

[2] According to Salzinger (1997), a poststructuralist focus has permitted the construction of more precise definitions of hegemony and gender via linguistic analyses of the structuring of these concepts in the workplace and at specific cultural moments.

[3] Notable from this perspective is postmodern feminism's effort to integrate a critique of political economy with the position of the researcher vis-à-vis the object of study. For an example of this approach, see Lee 1998.

[4] One such effort is the work of Aihwa Ong (1987) on the feminization of transnational industries and the implications for the workers' struggle on the periphery. Ong found that local labor forces are composed of actors inexperienced in workplace relations who are now employed in high-technology sectors that coexist with native cultural systems and values. In these arenas, control over labor extends far beyond the workplace to affect the life of the community, which causes worker resistance to focus more on issues of gender, class, and local culture than on patterns of economic mobility.

maquiladoras, and the conditions under which they labor; (2) the articulation of the Mexican economic crisis with the restructuring of the maquiladora sector and the masculinization of the workforce; and (3) the social and cultural impacts of the flexibilization and globalization of the workforce.

Internationalized Production Promotes a Female Labor Force

A first set of studies looked at the internationalization of production in the 1970s and into the 1980s. Some early researchers noted that the maquiladoras' intensive use of women workers—a cheap and abundant labor force without prior experience with labor organizing—could be viewed by the industry as a kind of "comparative advantage" (Gambrill 1981; Carrillo and Hernández 1985; Fernández-Kelly 1990; Laison 1988).

Maquiladoras came to the northern border area at the end of the Bracero Program, and the expectation was that these new industries would create jobs for the former (male) braceros. When the maquiladora sector shunned this masculine labor supply and instead hired a highly feminized workforce all along the border, researchers began examining these firms' hiring policies and the gender discourse within the maquiladora sector. Some studies found that jobs in the maquilas liberated women from male-dominated households and brought new job opportunities to women. Others noted that the skilled and better-paid jobs in the maquiladoras were all going to male employees (Iglesias 1985; Arenal 1986; Tiano 1990).

All of these studies reflected the underlying issue of gender stereotyping in the allocation of maquiladora jobs and the social implications this has for women workers. Still other studies evaluated the kinds of jobs offered to women in the maquiladoras and looked at issues such as occupational health and job quality. They included case studies in key sectors and cities, as well as the first analyses of labor organizing in this sector (Murayama and Muñoz 1979; Fernández-Kelly 1990; Gambrill 1981; Carrillo and Hernández 1982, 1985; Barrera Bassols 1990; Barajas and Rodríguez 1992).

Together, these studies revealed new forms of exploitation of families unable to survive on a single income. The conditions that export-oriented industries along Mexico's northern border were able to impose on these workers extended beyond the factory to include in-migration from other regions of Mexico[5] and out-of-control urban growth, with the concomitant

---

[5] For more on this topic, see Seligson and Williams 1981; Catanzarite and Strober 1989; Tanori 1989. These authors examine the link between internal and interna-

result that border cities fell dramatically behind in their ability to provide urban services to their populations (Nisonoff 1999).

1980s Economic Crisis Leads to Greater Male Employment at the Border

The second approach taken in studies of women in the maquiladora sector fell within the framework of Mexico's economic crisis of the 1980s, a period marked by deep currency devaluations, rapidly falling real wages, the beginnings of economic liberalization, drastic cuts to social subsidies, privatization of state-owned companies, and, especially, export-promotion policies. One consequence of the crisis was widespread job losses, which changed the relationship between men's and women's paid work (Benería 1992). The sectors that traditionally absorbed the male labor force—agriculture and industries producing for the domestic market—proved unable to create new jobs. To offset the loss in household income, more and more women were entering the labor market, where they were welcomed by employers eager to take advantage of this cheap and easily replaceable workforce (Rendón 1993).

This tendency was accompanied by an increase in small-scale commerce and services carried out mostly by a male labor force, leading some authors to argue that there had been a "masculinization of commerce and services," mainly in Mexico City and Guadalajara (Rendón 1993). As a result of male workers' decreased employment opportunities in domestic industries and in moderately paid jobs in other sectors, they also sought jobs in maquiladoras in Mexico's large border cities, leading to a masculinization of the labor force in this sector (Catanzarite and Strober 1989).[6]

Researchers documented that the evolving definition of women's work was influenced by technological change and by the organization of work in the maquiladoras. The new profile revealed a set of technically skilled jobs that were being reserved for men, typically in the autoparts and electronics

---

tional migration and women's search for jobs in the maquiladoras. They identify two groups: the first migrates from the interior of Mexico to the border hoping to work in the maquiladoras, while the second undertakes a two-stage migration, working first in the maquiladoras and then, when they have accumulated sufficient resources, migrating internationally to join the U.S. labor market.

[6] An alternate explanation for the precipitous decline in women's workforce participation in the border cities beginning in 1985 is that these cities lost their ability to absorb labor as a result of the 1982 economic crisis. The crisis changed the composition of the labor force as more and more male workers were forced to compete with women for jobs in the maquiladoras (Cruz 1993).

sectors (Barajas and Rodríguez 1992). By the end of the 1980s, maquiladoras were hiring mostly men for technical jobs, inventory handling, maintenance, and operations. For the first time, women did not form the majority in the overall maquiladora workforce, although they remained the most numerous on the production line, reviving the debate about the gendering of maquiladora jobs (de la O 1995, 1996, 1997).

Later studies broadened our understanding of the dynamics of women's work in the maquiladoras by reviewing the kind of economic development prevailing in a region, the primary employment options, the degree of stability in maquila jobs, and predominant sociodemographic characteristics. These research efforts found that, at the beginning of the 1990s, men working in maquiladoras were relatively younger than the women workers. The fact that maquiladora jobs are generally neither stable nor long-term affects men and women equally, although men tend to look for better job opportunities. Finally, the life cycles of men and women differentially affect their integration and participation in the labor market in these industries (Canales 1996).

Women Workers Make Flexibilization Possible

The third analytic focus includes studies of the new maquiladoras' policies of flexible labor and production restructuring. This body of research examined the ways in which technological and organizational conditions affected women's labor force participation. Case studies in various border cities in northern Mexico found more flexible work schedules and new links between wages and productivity, although gender segmentation in terms of tasks and in opportunities for advancement persisted (Carrillo 1994; de la O 1997; Zúñiga 1999). These findings spurred a number of researchers to study the social meaning of gender in spaces dominated by the maquiladoras. In this literature, researchers tried to link economic globalization and feminist thinking by identifying several ways in which women were excluded, along with women's understanding of femininity, masculinity, and sexuality at a cultural level. The goal was to explain how the image of femininity operates in the workplace and makes possible the construction of a gender role in the context of globalization despite the increasing incorporation of men into the maquiladora industry (Salzinger 1997, 2001; Wright 2001).

In her studies of maquiladoras in Ciudad Juárez, Salzinger (1997) found that most of the workers on the line were women, while men were physically segregated in packing or maintenance activities. Further, methods for controlling workers relied on the women workers' higher visibility, such that the supervisor's authority allowed for the definition of jobs by gender and the sexualization of women's jobs.

In this sense, the body becomes a key space for understanding the role of gender in globalization, where the discourse surrounding women in the workplace encompasses not only gender but also issues of workplace discipline and control. These latter, as well as opportunities for advancement, can be engineered through manipulations of masculinity. This is true even given the variety of social contexts in which gender is represented, as these are lived, described, and imagined by these actors in their daily lives.

Melissa Wright (2001) focuses on the opposition between male supervisors and women line workers in the maquiladora industries and examines how the former take intimacy and the women's physical presence into account as they carry out their jobs.[7] The result is the construction of a third "body," without which the new world of work flexibility could not function. In her study on maquiladoras in Ciudad Juárez, she observed a mix of Fordist and flexible approaches to supervision of a predominantly female workforce doing assembly tasks. This supposedly unskilled workforce responds to representations of gender differences, like the differences between flexible and nonflexible workers.

This is an important point for the process of integrating women into the new maquiladoras given that the image these firms project is of a flexible workforce composed of male workers. Paradoxically, flexible supervision methods are only possible because of the demonstrated skills and abilities of the (women) workers being supervised, making women the element through which flexibility can be realized.

This overall body of research enables us to understand women's incorporation into the workforce during the early decades of maquiladora development, as well as the formation of a marginalized feminine proletariat in Mexico's northern border region. Nevertheless, these studies lacked a territorial approach that could take into account the maquiladoras' mobility to the rest of the country, identifying what appears to be a very large feminine proletariat in Mexico's economic and territorial periphery.

---

[7] Wright places her study midway between theoretical Marxist and poststructuralist feminist approaches given that both shed light on the subjective dynamics of the spaces of capital. A capitalism that encompasses employers and workers around the world is far from homogeneous, since the binary equation of capital and labor is nuanced in every location by identities of gender, race, and generation.

CYCLES OF FEMALE PARTICIPATION AND THE MAQUILADORAS' TERRITORIAL EXPANSION

When maquiladoras were first established along Mexico's northern border, they assembled a workforce that was predominantly young and female. Today, however, men make up a significant share of this workforce, although women still outnumber men in the maquiladora plants.[8] This confirms a gradual de-feminization of the maquila labor force since this industry's inception. It also uncovers how job markets operate in continuously evolving globalized productive sectors, hinting at the strong link between changes at the global and local levels and a restructuring of the labor force by gender.

More specifically, as these export-oriented assembly firms have extended across northern, central, and southern Mexico (see figure 3.1), they have stimulated the emergence of new patterns in the labor force, differentiated by gender and task specialization. A substantial number of maquiladoras have relocated away from the border, often to less urbanized areas, seeking to lower costs by hiring cheaper, usually female, workers. Nevertheless, a fraction of these industries, typically firms that incorporate more technology into their productive process, has turned toward a more sophisticated workforce, and a portion of this workforce is often male. Together, these two trends underscore the way in which geographic location affects the pool of workers (Fleck 2001).

We can identify at least three cycles in women's employment in the maquiladora industry in Mexico (see table 3.1):

- The first cycle—the 1970s and 1980s—saw a proliferation of poorly paid maquila jobs targeted specifically for women. At this point, the sector was largely confined to Mexico's northern border region, identified as the "traditional" maquiladora zone because of its historical and strategic importance in the growth of export-oriented assembly in Mexico.

- The second cycle involved the de-feminization of the maquila plants as these firms began hiring more male workers in the late 1980s and into the 1990s. This occurred in the traditional maquiladora zone but also

---

[8] According to preliminary data from Mexico's National Institute of Statistics, Geography, and Informatics (INEGI), in August 2002 there were 395,729 men and 468,941 women production workers in the maquiladoras, out of a total maquiladora workforce of 1,085,154. That is, women production workers accounted for 43.2 percent of total maquiladora employment, and male production workers for 36.4 percent of the total.

in new areas of maquila expansion somewhat removed from the border but still in northern Mexico.

- The third cycle, which began early in the 1990s, corresponds to the feminization of maquiladora jobs in newly emerging maquila zones in central and southern Mexico.

Table 3.1. Cycles of Maquila Expansion and Women's Labor Force Participation

Regions of Maquiladora Expansion	Cycles of Women's Labor Force Participation		
	Cycle 1 (1966–1980)	Cycle 2 (1980–1990)	Cycle 3 (1990–2000)
Traditional maquiladora zone (northern border)	Creation of female employment ⟶	De-feminization	De-feminization
Region of maquiladora expansion (northeast and northwest)	⟶	De-feminization	De-feminization
Emerging maquiladora region (north, west, and south)	⟶		New feminization of the workforce

Cycle One: The Creation of Women's Jobs in the Traditional Maquiladora Zone

The first maquiladoras were established in 1966 in the duty-free zone and border strip of northern Mexico[9]—in Tijuana and Mexicali, Baja California; Ciudad Juárez, Chihuahua; Matamoros, Tamaulipas; and Nogales, Sonora

---

[9] The duty-free zone includes all of the Baja California peninsula and the extreme northwestern part of Sonora. The border strip is an arbitrarily defined land belt along the entire the U.S.-Mexico border that extends south from the international line. For most of its length, it is 20 kilometers deep into Mexico; in 1987 the border strip in the area of Ciudad Juárez was increased to 70 kilometers in depth.

(see figure 3.1). At the time, some of these cities were witnessing a decline in their primary economic activities, such as cotton and tourism. Over time, with the introduction of the maquiladoras, these cities became important industrial centers, producing car harnesses, autoparts, and electronics.[10]

The transition from an agricultural and tourism economy to a maquiladora economy spurred a transformation in employment in these cities beginning in the late 1960s. This was especially notable in Matamoros, Ciudad Juárez, and Tijuana, with the large-scale incorporation of women into this industrial sector. For example, in 1975, for every 100 women hired by the maquiladoras in Ciudad Juárez, Matamoros, Tijuana, and Mexicali, there were fewer than 30 male hires. Nogales, with 63 men hired for every 100 women, was the sole exception to this pattern (see table 3.2). These numbers speak clearly to the feminization of the maquiladora workforce. Further evidence comes from nationwide data; in 1975, nearly 70 percent of all jobs created by the maquiladora industry throughout Mexico were held by women, nearly all of whom were line workers (see table 3.3).

With the onset of economic crisis in the early 1980s, industrial production for Mexico's domestic market stagnated. This occurred simultaneously with a gradual liberalization of the Mexican economy. In combination, these two forces brought about a sharp drop in real wages and an inability to generate a sufficient number of jobs for Mexican workers, especially in the country's northern and central regions. This forms the backdrop for the feminization of the manufacturing labor force that has been documented in the maquiladoras over this same period. Further, this female labor force, which was concentrated in the maquiladoras, was relatively absent from the non-maquila sectors and, therefore, less directly affected by economic restructuring (Pedrero, Rendón, and Barrón 1997: 191).

Thus the feminization of the labor force in the first cycle of maquiladora growth refers to a process that favored the incorporation of large numbers of women into these manufacturing jobs. Industrial jobs in Mexico during the country's import-substitution industrialization period had been largely a male domain countrywide; in contrast, employment in the new areas of export-driven industrialization, especially in the northern border region, was predominantly female and young. In 1980, women still occupied nearly 70 percent of all maquiladora jobs in the country (table 3.3).

---

[10] The electronics sector boomed after 1994 as Asian producers established subsidiaries in Mexico so that their products could enter the North American market under the terms of the North American Free Trade Agreement.

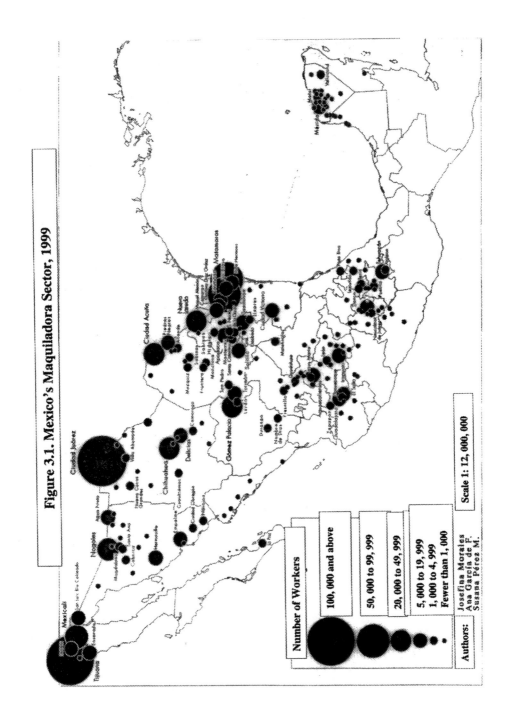

Figure 3.1. Mexico's Maquiladora Sector, 1999

Number of Workers

100,000 and above

50,000 to 99,999

20,000 to 49,999

5,000 to 19,999
1,000 to 4,999
Fewer than 1,000

Authors: Josefina Morales
Ana García de F.
Susana Pérez M.

Scale 1: 12,000,000

Table 3.2. Ratio of Male Maquiladora Employees per 100 Female Maquiladora Workers, by Region, 1975–2000

Maquiladora Zone	1975	1980	1985	1990	1995	2000
Traditional zone						
Tijuana	26.4	28.6	48.1	80.2	89.1	101.1
Ciudad Juárez	26.6	25.6	48.6	82.2	85.7	101.1
Mexicali	29.7	33.3	46.2	60.1	62.1	77.2
Nogales	63.1	67.8	84.9	107.4	96.1	99.8
Matamoros	20.2	21.5	35.9	44.4	45.7	62.9
Expansion zone						
Ciudad Acuña	24.5	20.7	59.4	85.3	130.6	143.6
Piedras Negras	9.0	30.2	27.7	87.7	92.8	107.6
Reynosa	9.2	26.1	37.1	61.3	68.4	83.9
Hermosillo				26.0	29.5	37.4
Emerging zone						
Puebla[a]						94.2
Lerdo						91.4
Torreón					51.3	86.5
Gómez Palacios						82.9
Mérida					35.8	69.7
México State and Federal District[a]					41.8	57.2
Aguascalientes[a]					34.2	49.9
San Luis Potosí[a]						53.0
Guanajuato[a]						35.4
Zacatecas[a]						33.1
Guadalajara and surrounding municipics				41.6	35.0	32.2

Sources: INEGI 1986, 1989, 2001.

[a] Statewide data.

Table 3.3. Male and Female Employment in the Maquiladoras, 1975–2000

	National Total, Production and Technical Workers	Number of Male Production Workers	Number of Female Production Workers	Male Workers as Percentage of Female Workers
1975	67,214	12,575	45,275	27.77%
1980	119,546	23,140	78,880	29.34%
1985	211,968	53,832	120,042	44.84%
1990	446,436	140,919	219,439	64.22%
1995	648,263	217,557	314,172	69.25%
2000	1,285,007	466,004	574,073	81.18%

Sources: INEGI, "Estadísticas económicas: industria maquiladora de exportación," August 1997 and May 2001.

In 1980, the ratio of 30 male production workers for every 100 female production workers continued to be the pattern in the traditional maquiladora region, especially in Tijuana, Ciudad Juárez, and Mexicali. However, Nogales and Matamoros present some interesting contrasts. In Nogales, the ratio was nearly 70 men for every 100 women employed as production workers in the maquiladoras, and in Matamoros, the feminization of the maquila workforce was even more marked than in the traditional maquila zone, with only 20 men employed for every 100 women (see table 3.2).

Despite a clear pattern of a largely female workforce in the maquiladoras during the first two decades of this industry's development in Mexico, this pattern was not homogenous across all subsectors within the industry. The highest proportions of women in the country's northern border municipalities in 1980 were found in firms producing electronics and textiles, where the ratio was approximately 20 male workers for every 100 women. In the autoparts sector, by contrast, there were 50 men for every 100 women workers (see table 3.4). These differences confirm a specialization by gender in certain job categories and subsectors within the maquiladora industry. This differentiation by gender reveals women's disadvantaged position in the local labor market, given that the traits attributed to women and the low status given to jobs that required these particular traits limited women's job options.

In the early decades of maquiladora development, it was not unusual to see widespread hiring of young women between 14 and 25 years of age because of their "quick hands" and "delicate movements." The labor conditions characteristic of the maquiladora industry overall confirmed that these women workers were being transformed into one more factor of production through the intense work pace, low pay, and lack of job stability that these women were willing to accept. Thus the hiring practices in the maquiladoras' early period reflect the forces that drove the industry in the beginning. One was a high demand for unskilled labor, which meshed the firms' low expectations in terms of the skills preparation of would-be employees with a population whose low education levels virtually compelled people to accept whatever job was available.

Cycle Two: De-Feminization in Traditional and Expansion Maquiladora Zones

The first hints of a de-feminization of the maquiladoras came in the late 1980s, as male workers gained share and women lost share in what had previously been an overwhelmingly female workforce. As noted above, this coincided with Mexico's economic crisis of 1982 and beyond, which brought declining real salaries and the closure of many private and state-owned businesses. The results included widespread layoffs, stagnation in local labor markets, and growth in the service sector. The crisis in local labor markets made it feasible to resuscitate maquila zones on the northern border that had failed to prosper in the 1960s, as happened in Reynosa, Tamaulipas. In other cities in northern and northeastern Mexico—such as Hermosillo—there was even a push to bring in new maquiladoras (see figure 3.1).[11]

In Piedras Negras and Reynosa, maquiladoras built in the 1960s only reached high production levels in the 1980s. In Piedras Negras, this was largely due to the restructuring of Mexico's coal-mining sector and the sale of state-owned power plants, which left much of the electricity-generation sector's workers without employment and ripe for hiring by the maquiladoras (Quintero 2002). A similar process occurred in Reynosa, where state-controlled companies that had been pumping natural gas were privatized, opening the way for maquiladoras to become the city's number

---

[11] This process coincided with a change in article 321 of Mexico's tariff code in October 1972, which permitted the establishment of maquiladoras anywhere in the country. By 1989, 5 percent of the maquiladoras in Mexico were located away from the northern border; by 1998, this figure was approaching 20 percent.

Table 3.4. Maquiladora Production Workers by Sector, Region, and Gender, 1980–2000

Industrial Sector/ Year	Border Region			Non-Border Regions		
	Men	Women	Male Employment as Percentage of Female Employment	Men	Women	Male Employment as Percentage of Female Employment
Electronics						
1980	9,369	43,024	21.8%	872	4,886	17.8%
1985	17,020	52,332	32.5	1,578	8,456	18.7
1990	39,729	74,703	53.2	4,911	13,919	35.3
1995	59,774	99,232	60.2	7,730	21,946	35.2
2000	113,774	153,737	74.0	25,158	54,473	46.2
Textiles						
1980	2,183	10,588	20.6	361	2,604	13.9
1985	2,985	9,854	30.3	701	4,738	14.8
1990	5,801	11,334	51.2	2,879	15,724	18.3
1995	8,650	15,721	55.0	16,191	45,939	35.2
2000	15,923	21,882	72.8	73,522	124,640	59.0
Autoparts						
1980	2,006	3,975	50.5	40	289	13.8
1985	14,746	16,309	90.4	724	2,010	36.0
1990	32,121	28,471	112.8	6,158	11,246	54.8
1995	44,895	38,690	116.0	10,212	16,062	63.6
2000	79,000	63,142	125.1	19,614		76.7

Sources: INEGI 1989, 2001.

one employer, most notably in electronics, furniture, and machine tools (Quintero 2002).

Unlike Piedras Negras and Reynosa, Ciudad Acuña and Hermosillo did not get their first maquiladoras until the late 1980s. However, by 2000 there were 56 maquiladoras in Ciudad Acuña, producing autoparts and machine tools and employing some 30,000 workers. In Hermosillo, meanwhile, a number of maquilas opened with connections to the Cemex and Ford corporations, as well as some clothing maquiladoras that planned to market to the United States and Canada under the terms of the North American Free Trade Agreement (NAFTA) (INEGI 2002).

This was the context in which the de-feminization of the maquiladora workforce took place. An early sign of this process was the fact that in 1985 women held only 57 percent of the jobs in the maquila sector nationwide. More male workers were being hired, and the ratio stood at about 45 men for every 100 women working in the same job category. This trend gained strength over the course of the 1990s, with the ratio rising to 60 men for every 100 female maquiladora workers Mexico-wide (see table 3.3).

The trend was evident in the traditional maquiladora zone as well. In Tijuana, Ciudad Juárez, and Mexicali in 1985, for example, there were some 50 male hires for every 100 women maquila workers. Nogales remained an exception, with 80 men for every 100 women, as did Matamoros (though in the opposite direction), with only 30 male workers for every 100 women (see table 3.2).

The shift from a predominantly female maquiladora workforce to one in which male workers came to represent an increasing share was collapsed in time in cities that had reactivated previously inactive maquiladoras. In Ciudad Acuña, for example, this shift happened in a decade or less; in the 1970s there were only 20 men for every 100 women in this city's maquiladora workforce, but by 1985 the ratio had gone to 60 men for every 100 women. Even so, a predominantly female workforce remained the rule in Piedras Negras and Reynosa as late as 1985, with 30 male workers for every 100 women (table 3.2).

Thus, as the maquiladoras spread throughout northern Mexico, the profile of new entrants into the workforces of these plants changed. On the one hand, plant managers began hiring more and more men as their perceptions about the feminine nature of the work changed and as the male labor force became more abundant and cheaper. On the other hand, industries that had traditionally hired a male labor force, such as autoparts producers, began to expand as a subsector within the maquiladora industry overall. The broad deindustrialization that preceded the expansion of maquiladoras into new areas of Mexico meant that newly unemployed individuals who had formerly worked in domestic market–oriented companies were now swelling the ranks of those seeking jobs in the maquiladoras, significantly altering the gender composition of regional labor markets.

Other factors were also at work, including technological diversification and an increase in the number of maquiladoras that preferred male workers for certain, more technical activities. One such case is plants in the autoparts sector, which from the first hired more male workers than did other types of maquiladoras. By 1985, the ratio of workers by gender in autoparts was 90 men for every 100 female workers. The electronics and textile industries in border cities also experienced an increase in their shares of male workers; in 1985 the ratios were 32 and 30 male workers, respectively, per 100 women (see table 3.4).

The impact of the extensive employment of male workers in the autoparts sector and the creeping de-feminization of maquiladoras producing electronics and textiles was amplified by the increasing number of maquiladoras in Mexico and their subcontracting arrangements. Under pressure from compact car imports from Japan and elsewhere, U.S. automakers seeking to reduce their costs relocated some production processes to Mexico; by the end of the 1980s, Ford Motor Company had established five autoparts maquiladoras in Mexico. Meanwhile, Japanese electronics firms stepped up their investments in electronics assembly plants in Mexico in a bid to remain globally competitive (Fleck 2001). This new wave of investment in technology-intensive processes produced two different images: the new autoparts plants, which hired large numbers of male workers, were huge, confirming that the increase in male employment in the autoparts sector is linked to this subsector's expansion. By contrast, the electronics firms remained fairly stable in terms of the number of employees.

By the 1990s, women as a proportion of the maquiladora workforce nationwide had dropped significantly; the national ratio stood at 64 men for every 100 women workers (see table 3.3). In northern border cities like Tijuana, Ciudad Juárez, and Nogales, the figures for male employment nearly doubled, to levels of 80 and even 100 male production workers for every 100 female production workers, virtually erasing the gender differentiation in these cities' labor forces. Mexicali and Matamoros also witnessed some de-feminization of the workforce, though to a much lesser degree, with a ratio of 60 and 44 male workers, respectively, per 100 women (table 3.2). A similar process took place in the region of maquiladora expansion. The maquila labor force in Ciudad Acuña in this period was 85 men per 100 women, and in Piedras Negras, the ratio was 87 to 100. Women continued to account for a larger share of the maquiladora workforce in Reynosa and especially in Hermosillo, where the ratio in 1990 was 26 male workers per 100 female workers (table 3.3).

It was during this same period that a clear pattern of sectoral specialization appeared, with a heavy concentration of autoparts and electronics maquiladoras on the northern border. In 2000 this region had 558 electronics plants and 175 autoparts manufacturers, which together employed nearly 500,000 workers (INEGI 1995, 2000). This regional industrial consolidation was particularly notable in cities that developed extensive industrial infrastructure, displayed a diverse range of productive processes, and had links to global production chains. They were located across the border from California or near the Houston-San Antonio-Dallas corridor in Texas.

The concentration of the autoparts sector correlated with the tendency toward more gender balance in the workforce, with companies hiring about the same numbers of men and women. This was not the case, however, for electronics or textile maquiladoras, which in 1990 continued to employ 50 men for every 100 women workers (table 3.4). A similar trend in workforce composition was visible in plants outside the border region, where the male/female ratio was 54:100 in autoparts, 35:100 in electronics, and 18:100 in textile maquiladoras (see table 3.4).

Reductions in the gender gap in the maquiladora workforce did not bring a parallel decrease in the differences between the tasks carried out by men and by women. Rather, what occurred was an overall deterioration in male workers' position in the national labor force and a concentration of women in the more traditional sectors such as electronics and garment manufacturing in plants located away from Mexico's northern border.

This gender imbalance is also visible in the distribution of technical jobs, with 300 men employed in such positions for every 100 females in equivalent jobs, both in the traditional maquiladora zones and in areas of maquila expansion. The most extreme cases are Reynosa, with 364 male technicians for every 100 female technical workers, and Hermosillo, with 186 male to 100 female technical workers in 2000 (see table 3.5).

Taken together, these differences illustrate gender segregation in the maquiladora industry by industrial branch, job category, and specific tasks. In terms of segregation by industrial branch, we have evidence of women's strong concentration in apparel and, to a lesser degree, electronics, reflecting the limited employment opportunities available to women in a context

Table 3.5. Technical Workers in the Maquiladoras by Region and Gender, 2000

Maquiladora Zone	Total of Technical Workers	Men	Women	Ratio of Male:Female Technical Workers
Traditional zone				
Nogales	4,716	3,562	1,154	309:100
Tijuana	20,985	15,671	5,314	295:100
Ciudad Juárez	30,005	22,327	7,678	291:100
Matamoros	7,064	5,221	1,843	283:100
Mexicali	7,983	5,667	2,316	245:100
Expansion zone				
Reynosa	8,794	6,899	1,895	364:100
Ciudad Acuña	4,623	3,419	1,204	284:100
Piedras Negras	2,040	1,423	617	231:100
Hermosillo	2,491	1,621	870	186:100
Emerging zone				
Guadalajara and surrounding muncipios	4,232	3,335	897	372:100
San Luis Potosí[a]	1,609	1,189	420	283:100
Torreón	5,615	3,930	1,686	233:100
Lerdo	468	319	149	214:100
Gómez Palacios	920	621	299	207:100
Mérida	3,892	2,269	1,623	140:100
Zacatecas[a]	642	357	285	125:100
Puebla[a]	3,170	2,011	1,664	121:100
México State and Federal District[a]	1,102	752	626	120:100
Guanajuato[a]	823	433	390	111:100
Aguascalientes	2,240	1,157	1,083	107:100

Source: INEGI, "Estadísticas de la industria maquiladora de exportación," May 2001.
[a] Statewide data.

of a prolonged process of de-feminization. Segregation by job category and task is confirmed by the overwhelming employment of women as line workers and their scant participation in technical or managerial positions. This differentiation inside the plants confines women workers to positions as line operators or group leaders.

Job segregation by gender in the maquiladoras is a key factor underlying the differences in men and women's income and work conditions. The fact that women are confined to low-income job categories and sectors, such as the textile industry, goes far toward explaining their 10.3 percent salary disadvantage vis-à-vis male employees in the maquiladoras (see table 3.6).

Table 3.6. Monthly Maquiladora Wage by Gender, 1997–1999 (pesos)

	Male Workers	Female Workers	Female Workers' Salary Disadvantage vis-à-vis Male Workers
1997	19,417	17,627	10.2%
1998	22,897	20,862	9.8%
1999	26,605	24,122	10.3%

Source: INEGI, "Estadísticas de la industria maquiladora de exportación," May 2001.

In sum, the de-feminization of employment in the maquiladoras reflects the impacts of declining job growth in the border region and a territorial distribution that located autoparts production on the border and garment assembly in non-border areas. This is reflected in wage levels, with machine tools and autoparts being the better-paying sectors, and garment manufacturing and food preparation those that pay poorly (Fleck 2001).

One could argue that the de-feminization of the maquiladoras is a function of labor supply. When this industry was first established on Mexico's northern border, there was a dramatic surge in women's employment as women were drawn to jobs in this sector. Nevertheless, in this second cycle of maquila development, the new jobs created in the sector went equally to men and women.

Cycle Three: New Feminization in Emerging Maquiladora Regions

The third cycle was one of a new feminization of labor in areas where maquiladoras have been recently introduced. The entry of the maquila industry into north-central, central, and western Mexico and the Yucatán Peninsula began in the 1990s (see figure 3.1). The industry developed very rapidly in this macroregion, with plants located in medium-size cities and rural areas.

Much of the investment for extending the maquiladora industry into these emerging areas was domestic or came in the form of co-investments between domestic and U.S. capital. Most of the cities where the new plants were sited were suffering a decline in their traditional economic base: leather goods and footwear, garment manufacture, machine tools, and cotton cultivation. The first of the new plants, in Guadalajara and Mérida, were established in the late 1980s, and they were soon followed by maquiladoras in Aguascalientes, Torreón, Gómez Palacios, and Lerdo. Other states that received maquiladoras were Puebla, Guanajuato, San Luis Potosí, Zacatecas, México, and the Federal District, where assembly-for-export plants were established in the 1990s.

Although the very first maquiladoras in Guadalajara were actually established in 1974, the industry did not take off until after the 1982 economic crisis, and this urban area only achieved the status of a maquiladora region in the 1990s, when the number of maquiladoras reached 41 plants with a combined workforce of over 6,000 producing apparel and electronics for the computer and telecommunications sectors. By 2000 the number of plants had climbed to 106, and workers numbered 28,907. The figures may be somewhat lower today because the downturn in the U.S. economy has caused some plant closures and employee layoffs.

Mérida and its surrounding urbanized area was the second location to be drawn into the maquiladora expansion. The local economy had been devastated when the introduction of synthetic fibers wiped out global demand for local henequen. A second blow came in 1992 when a constitutional reform to the nation's agrarian law allowed Mexican *ejidatarios* to sell their previously unalienable land rights. Unable to subsist on their landholdings, over 37,000 peasants exercised the option to sell and joined the ranks of the local labor force. In 1993, the state-owned CORDEMEX factory was privatized, and the area lost another major source of jobs (Morales, García de Fuentes, and Pérez 2002). The region's first maquiladora was built in 1982, but the real maquiladora boom began in 1997. Today Mérida is home to 126 maquiladoras; most are involved in apparel assembly, and a large portion of the workforce is Mayan.

The implementation of NAFTA in 1994 set the stage for the expansion of the maquiladora industry to move into north-central Mexico, beginning in Aguascalientes. Clothing imports entering Mexico under NAFTA wiped out the traditional local textile sector; its recovery was based on the introduction of apparel maquilas (Camacho 2002). By 1999 there were 87 maquiladoras in this region, with a workforce of 23,959 employed in garment manufacture. By January 2002, 36.3 percent of the jobs in this sector had disappeared, some because of the economic slump north of the border and some because of plant relocations to areas with lower labor costs, such as Central America (see Trejos, this volume).

Areas of particularly rapid maquiladora expansion beginning in the mid-1990s include Puebla and the states of Coahuila and Durango, in the Comarca Lagunera region. The economies of cities in the Laguna—Torreón, Gómez Palacios, and Lerdo—had long depended on the area's intensive cultivation of cotton. However, because of falling demand for this commodity, growers had begun scaling back production in the 1960s. The constitutional reforms to agrarian law, mentioned previously, further hastened the industry's decline (Van Dooren 2000).

This was the context in which the first maquiladoras were established in Lerdo, Gómez Palacios, and Torreón. They soon absorbed all of the urban labor force, and maquiladoras that entered the region later went to the region's rural areas, including the collectively managed ejidos. According to Mexico's National Chamber of Garment Producers (CANAIVES), there were more than 70,000 workers employed in 200 clothing maquiladoras in 1997; the figure could actually be twice as high if we take into account the various types of company registrations. In 2000 there were 72 plants in Torreón, 68 in Gómez Palacios, 14 in Lerdo, and 9 in other municipios in Durango; together they employed some 44,000 workers (INEGI 2001). The 2002 recession hit particularly hard in this region, which lost 45.4 percent of jobs in Durango and 11 percent in Coahuila.

The North American Free Trade Agreement also sparked the expansion of clothing maquiladoras in Puebla State. The maquiladoras resuscitated a local labor force devastated by the rural reform and declines in the local soft drink and poultry industries. By 1996, the state had 36 maquiladoras employing 12,000 workers. Four years later, these numbers had climbed to 106 plants and 38,000 workers (INEGI 2001). The maquiladora boom was most intense in Tehuacán, Teziutlán, Ajalpan, and Puebla City; but it was also felt in smaller towns and villages, such as Altepexi in Miahuatlán. In these latter cases, estimates suggest that approximately 80 percent of the workers were indigenous Nahuas, Mazatecs, and Mixtecs (Ramírez 2001). Puebla also suffered because of the economic slump in the United States, losing 20.6 percent of the state's maquiladora jobs by January 2002 (INEGI 2002). The current profile of maquiladoras in Puebla is characterized by two major trends: (1) many plants are leaving Puebla and relocating to Central America, Brazil, and Asia; and (2) the maquiladoras that remain are relying increasingly on homework in order to avoid paying taxes and legally mandated worker benefits.

The states of Guanajuato, San Luis Potosí, and Zacatecas in north-central Mexico and the Federal District and México State in the center constitute the remaining segments of the macroregion of maquiladora expansion. Maquiladoras employ 13,402 workers in 78 plants in Guanajuato; 11,403 workers in 19 plants in San Luis Potosí; and 5,903 workers in 19 plants in Zacatecas. The majority of maquiladoras in these states are located in midsize cities and rural areas.[12] Although maquiladoras are new arrivals in these states, they nevertheless felt the impacts of the recent economic crisis. Figures for January 2002 show job losses of about 15 percent, with Zacatecas and San Luis Potosí particularly hard-hit.

The Federal District and México State are the latest additions to the maquiladora sector, with, respectively, 29 plants with 2,286 workers, and 58 plants with 13,734 workers in 2000. Plants in the Federal District are widely distributed spatially and also differ substantially in terms of product. The situation is markedly different in México State, where plants are concentrated in industrial parks, and most are dedicated to apparel, machine tools, and furniture.

An analysis of the labor force in this third cycle of maquiladora evolution confirms an ongoing process of de-feminization, despite the existence of feminized enclaves in central and southern Mexico (table 3.1), and allows us to see in operation the demand for male and female workers in various productive sectors and regions. The typical maquiladora worker is no longer a woman. It is someone, male or female, in search of employment opportunities in a sector that is both flexible and expanding. The shift in the maquila labor force is evident in figures for the industry in 2000,

---

[12] Maquiladoras in Guanajuato State are located in Celaya, Irapuato, León, San Miguel de Allende, and Yuriria, as well as in smaller towns, including Purísima de Bustos and San Luis de la Paz. The maquiladoras in the state of San Luis Potosí are in Matehuala, Santa María del Río, and the capital city, San Luis Potosí. Maquilas in Zacatecas State are in La Calera and the city of Zacatecas, as well as the following smaller towns: Concepción del Oro, Fresnillo, Guadalupe, Jerez, Luis Moya, Morelos, and Ojo Caliente.

when the gender balance in maquiladoras nationwide was 81 male workers for every 100 women (table 3.3).

De-feminization has continued in the traditional maquiladora zone where, in 2000, line hires were about evenly divided between men and women. The same pattern is found in the maquiladora expansion area, though here we also find cities that retain a largely female workforce. For example, the gender ratio in Matamoros is 62:100, and in Hermosillo it is 37:100 (table 3.2).

The year 2000 marked a difficult milestone for the maquiladora sector. The terms of NAFTA spelled the gradual loss of the maquiladoras' privileged and protected status, at the same moment when the maquiladoras were reeling under the impacts of the economic crisis. In this same year, Baja California lost 23.1 percent of its maquiladora jobs; Chihuahua, 16.9 percent; and Tamaulipas, 10.6 percent. Apparel maquiladoras suffered most, and these are the same firms that employ the highest proportion of women (INEGI 2002).

The macroregion of recent maquiladora expansion—Mexico's north-central, central, and western regions and the Yucatán Peninsula—shows a complex pattern of female and male employment nuclei. For example, in cities in northern and central Mexico, such as Puebla, Torreón, Lerdo, and Gómez Palacios, new clothing maquiladoras employ a high proportion of male workers, approximately 80 to 90 for every 100 female workers (table 3.2). In contrast, in cities in the center-north and west and in Yucatán—including Guadalajara, Aguascalientes, and Mérida—maquiladoras have established a history of a workforce in which women outnumber male workers by 100 to between 30 and 60 (table 3.2). This tendency is also present in San Luis Potosí, Guanajuato, and Zacatecas, where there are fewer than 50 men for every 100 women workers. These contrasting patterns suggest a relationship between the entry of the maquiladora sector into Mexico's interior and an increasing feminization of employment opportunities.

The most feminized sectors are electronics and apparel produced in non-border maquiladoras, where the gender ratio among line workers in 2000 was between 46 and 59 men for every 100 female workers. At the other end of the spectrum are the autoparts maquiladoras, where the ratio in this same year was 76 men to 100 women (table 3.4). Of course, autoparts production has traditionally been identified as a male activity, and these employment ratios certainly reflect this fact. What may be interesting, then, is the large number of women doing jobs traditionally identified as men's work. The opposite has occurred in garment manufacture in Puebla and the cities of the Comarca Lagunera, where we find men assuming activities that were traditionally assigned to women, even to the point that traits identified as characteristic of women workers—docility and manual dexterity—are now applied to young male workers.

Paradoxically, the best opportunities for women aspiring to skilled positions are found in the emerging maquiladora zones. The male/female ratio among technical workers in 2000 was 10 women for every 10 to 14 men in Aguascalientes, Guanajuato, México State, the Federal District, Puebla, Zacatecas, and Mérida. One should keep in mind here that these same locations also tend to have lower numbers of positions for technical workers overall (see table 3.5).

There is also a regional difference in pay scales for technical workers. Salaries for technical workers are approximately the same along the border and in the cities that form part of the maquiladora expansion area. They are lower in the emerging region. In 1999, technical workers earned an average annual income of 96,761 pesos on the border and 74,283 pesos in the area of maquiladora expansion. Their counterparts in the emerging areas earned only 52,071 pesos annually on average (INEGI 2000), a detail that adds texture to this opportunity niche for female workers.

This body of evidence enables us to identify the territorial distribution of maquiladoras in Mexico and their impacts on the gender profiles of the labor force: higher participation rates for women in cities where the maquiladora industries are new arrivals, and relatively high male participation in areas of garment and electronics production for export. Men are increasingly in open competition with women for maquiladora jobs. Yet opportunities and outcomes remain unequal because of the structural conditions that the maquiladoras impose with regard to local hiring policies and a generalized deterioration in working conditions across Mexico.

CONCLUSION

This chapter analyzed the way in which the territorial mobility of the maquiladora sector affected the configuration of export-producing regions and patterns of women's employment. To this end, the discussion focused on the process of industrial mobility and the results of its expansion in three maquila regions in Mexico. Three cycles were identified in the territorial evolution of the maquiladora industry, along with their corresponding patterns of female employment. These cycles reflect the linkages that exist between the mobility of transnational capital and the availability and skill set of labor pools, factors that often work to the disadvantage of women.

To summarize, territorial mobility in the maquiladora industry has had structural impacts in at least three regions: (1) the traditional maquiladora region on Mexico's northern border, which includes the cities that pioneered in this area beginning in the 1960s; (2) the region of maquiladora expansion, which since the 1980s has encompassed cities in northern, northeastern, and northwestern Mexico; and (3) the emerging region, characterized by a proliferation of maquiladoras in north-central, western, and central Mexico, as well as the Yucatán Peninsula, since the 1990s.

The first region is noted for its specialization in electronics and auto-parts and the shift from a labor force first composed overwhelmingly of female workers to a workforce comprising men and women in approximately equal numbers. Maquiladoras locating in the second region entered local economies in the throes of deindustrialization, and these maquiladoras tended to hire higher numbers of male workers. The third, emerging, region has specialized in garment assembly and employed a workforce that comprises approximately equal numbers of male and female workers.

The territorial mobility of the maquiladoras also produced ascendant zones and disadvantaged interior regions, depending on the type of production in which each specialized—electronics and autoparts in the ascendant regions along the border and in northern Mexico, and apparel in the relatively disadvantaged interior.

Another feature of this industry's territorial mobility is the maquiladoras' link to regions in economic decline. These areas welcomed the maquiladoras as a strategy to create new jobs that would replace those lost when the former underpinnings of local development disappeared.

Although maquiladora employment increased overall in recent decades, the gender composition of the maquila workforce in different regions and time periods reflects patterns of cyclical change that disadvantage women in the labor force. When maquiladoras initiated operations on the northern border, they showed a strong preference for women workers, leading to a feminization of the local labor force. But over time, as maquila production became more specialized and as markets for some maquila products cooled because of the economic downturn, women workers found themselves relegated to more traditional and lower-paying maquiladora subsectors. This was followed by the entry of maquiladoras into the interior of Mexico, which saw a resurgence of feminization of the workforce but also narrower opportunity niches.

On balance, then, there was a gradual decrease in opportunities open to women in the maquila sector and a lengthy process of gender segmentation. The latter affected the employment opportunities for women and also their conditions of work. For example, women were made more vulnerable by new hiring schemes that offer jobs with fewer benefits, little chance of promotion, and no job security.

Given that maquila jobs are often the only jobs available in depressed local economies, we might expect these work conditions to extend to the remainder of the labor force. This is a strong argument for attending very closely to what is happening to the most vulnerable members of the labor force—women workers in the maquiladoras. We now see the disadvantaged conditions under which these women have long worked applying as well to Mexico's youths, male workers, and indigenous workers.

References

Arenal, Sandra. 1986. *Sangre jóven: las maquiladoras por dentro*. Mexico: Nuestro Tiempo.

Barajas, Rocío, and Carmen Rodríguez. 1992. "Mujer y trabajo en la industria maquiladora de exportación." Serie Documentos de Trabajo, no. 22. Mexico: Fundación Friedrich Ebert.

Baron, Ava. 1991. "Gender and Labor History: Learning from the Past, Looking to the Future." In *Work Engendered: Toward a New History of American Labor*, edited by Ava Baron. Ithaca, N.Y.: Cornell University Press.

Barrera Bassols, Delia. 1990. *Condiciones de trabajo en las maquiladoras en Ciudad Juárez: el punto de vista obrero*. Serie Antropología Social. Mexico: Instituto Nacional de Antropología e Historia.

Benería, Lourdes. 1992. "The Mexican Debt Crisis: Restructuring the Economy and the Household." In *Unequal Burden: Economic Crises, Persistent Poverty, and Women's Work*, edited by Lourdes Benería and Shelley Feldman. Boulder, Colo.: Westview.

Boserup, E. 1970. *Women's Role in Economic Development*. New York: St. Martin's Press.

Camacho, Fernando. 2002. "La industria maquiladora en Aguascalientes, 1990–1999." In *Globalización, trabajo y maquilas: las nuevas y viejas fronteras en México*, edited by María Eugenia de la O and Cirila Quintero. Mexico: Fundación Friedrich Ebert Stiftung/AFL-CIO/CIESAS.

Canales, Alejandro. 1996. "Mujer y trabajo en la frontera norte," *Revista Estudios Sociales* 6, no. 11 (January–June): 7–33.

Carrillo, Jorge. 1994. "Mujeres en la industria maquiladora de autopartes." In *Nuevos textos y renovados pretextos*, edited by Vania Salles and Elsie McPhail. Mexico City: El Colegio de México.

Carrillo Jorge, and Alberto Hernández. 1982. "Sindicatos y control obrero en las plantas maquiladoras fronterizas," *Investigación Económica* 161.

———. 1985. *Mujeres fronterizas en la industria maquiladora*. Colección Frontera. Mexico: Secretaría de Educación Pública/Centro de Estudios Fronterizos del Norte de México.

Catanzarite, Lisa M., and Mayra H. Strober. 1989. "Gender Recomposition of the Maquiladora Workforce in Ciudad Juárez." Presented at the meeting of the American Sociological Association, San Francisco, August.

Cruz, Rodolfo. 1993. "Algunos factores asociados a la participación femenina en los mercados de trabajo: ciudades de la frontera norte y áreas metropolitanas de México." Mimeo.

De la O, María Eugenia. 1995. "Maquila, mujer y cambios productivos: estudio de caso en la industria maquiladora de Ciudad Juárez." In *Mujeres, migración y maquila en la frontera norte*, edited by Soledad González Montes and Ofelia Woo. Mexico City: Programa Interdisciplinario de Estudios de la Mujer, El Colegio de México.

———. 1996. "Trayectorias femeninas en dos grupos ocupacionales de Tijuana y Baja California," *Revista Estudios Sociales* 6, no. 11 (January–June): 54–85.

———. 1997. "Y por eso se llaman maquilas. La configuración de las relaciones laborales en la modernización: cuatro estudios de plantas electrónicas en Ciudad Juárez, Chihuahua." PhD dissertation, El Colegio de México.

Deere, Carmen D. 1976. "Rural Women's Subsistence Production in the Capitalist Periphery," *Review of Radical Political Economy* 8: 9–17.

Fernández-Kelly, Patricia. 1990. "Chavalas de la Maquiladora: A Study of the Female Labor Force in Ciudad Juárez's Offshore Production plants." PhD dissertation, Rutgers University.

Fleck, Susan. 2001. "A Gender Perspective on Maquila Employment and Wages in Mexico." In *The Economics of Gender in Mexico: Work, Family, State, and Market*, edited by Elizabeth G. Katz and Maria C. Correira. Washington, D.C.: The World Bank.

Gambrill, Mónica Claire. 1981. "La fuerza de trabajo en las maquiladoras: resultados de una encuesta y algunas hipótesis interpretativas," *Lecturas del CEESTEM*.

Haraway, Donna. 1985. "A Manifesto for Cyborgs: Science, Technology, and Socialist Feminism in the 1980's," *Socialist Review* 15 (March–April): 65–107.

Iglesias, Norma. 1985. *La flor más bella de la maquiladora*. Tijuana: Centro de Estudios Fronterizos del Norte de México/Secretaría de Educación Pública.

INEGI (Instituto Nacional de Estadística, Geografía e Informática). 1986. "Estadísticas de la industria maquiladora de exportación, 1975–1985." Mexico: INEGI.

————. 1989. "Industria maquiladora de exportación, 1978–1988." Mexico: INEGI.

————. 1995. "Estadísticas económicas: industria maquiladora de exportación." Mexico: INEGI.

————. 2000. "Estadísticas económicas: industria maquiladora de exportación, marzo, abril, de 1998." Mexico: INEGI, May.

————. 2001. "Estadísticas económicas: industria maquiladora de exportación, 1995–2000." Mexico: INEGI.

————. 2002. "Industria maquiladora de exportación." Servicio de Información Estadística de Coyuntura (SIEC). At http://www.inegi.gob.mx/estadistica/espanol/economia/feconomia.html.

Laison, Silvia. 1988. "El impacto de la modernización en la mano de obra femenina: la mecanización en dos empresas productivas." In *Mujeres y sociedad: salario, hogar y acción social en el occidente de México*, edited by Luisa Gabayet and Patricia Arias. Guadalajara: CIESAS/El Colegio de Jalisco.

Lee, Ching Kwan. 1998. *Gender and the South China Miracle: Two Worlds of Factory Women*. Berkeley, University of California Press.

Lim, Linda. 1980. "Women Workers in Multinational Corporations: The Case of the Electronics Industry in Malaysia and Singapore." In *Transnational Enterprise: The Impact on Third World Societies and Cultures*, edited by Krishna Kumar.

Morales, Josefina, Ana García de Fuentes, and Susana Pérez. 2002. "Impacto regional de la maquila en la Península de Yucatán." In *Globalización, trabajo y maquilas: las nuevas y viejas fronteras en México*, edited by María Eugenia de la O and Cirila Quintero. Mexico: Fundación Friedrich Ebert Stiftung/AFL-CIO/CIESAS.

Murayama, María Guadalupe, and María Elena Muñoz. 1979. "Características de la mano de obra femenina en la industria maquiladora de exportación," *Cuadernos Agrarios* 9.

Nisonoff, Laurie. 1999. "Men, Women, and the Global Assembly Line." Mimeo. At http://wscenter.hampshire.edu/ford/nisonoff.html.

Ong, Aihwa. 1987. *Spirits of Resistance and Capitalist Discipline: Factory Women in Malaysia*. New York: State University of New York Press.

Pedrero, Mercedes, Teresa Rendón, and Antonieta Barrón. 1997. *Segregación ocupacional por género en México*. Cuernavaca: Universidad Nacional Autónoma de México/Centro Regional de Investigaciones Multidisciplinarias.

Quintero, Cirila. 2002. "La maquila en Matamoros: cambios y continuidades." In *Globalización, trabajo y maquilas: las nuevas y viejas fronteras en México*, edited by María Eugenia de la O and Cirila Quintero. Mexico: Fundación Friedrich Ebert Stiftung/AFL-CIO/CIESAS.

Ramírez, Jesús. 2001. "Explotación laboral en el paraíso maquiladora. Tehuacán: la capital de los jeans," *La Jornada*, July 29.

Rendón, Teresa. 1993. "El trabajo femenino en México: tendencias y cambios recientes," *El Cotidiano* 53 (March–April).

Safa, Helen. 1981. "Sunway Shops and Female Employment: The Search for Cheap Labor," *Signs* 7 (Winter): 418–33.

Salzinger, Leslie. 1997. "From High Heels to Swathed Bodies: Gender Meaning under Production in Mexico's Export-Processing Industry," *Feminist Studies* 23, no. 3 (Fall): 549–74.

———. 2001. "Making Fantasies Real: Producing Women and Men on the Maquila Shop Floor," *NACLA Report on the Americas* 34, no. 5 (March–April): 13–19.

Sassen, Saskia. 1993. *La movilidad del trabajo y del capital: un estudio sobre la corriente internacional de la inversión y del trabajo.* Madrid: Ministerio del Trabajo y Seguridad Social. 2000.

———. 1998. *Globalization and Its Discontents.* New York: New Press.

———. 2000. "Women's Burden: Counter-Geographies of Globalization and the Feminization of Survival," *Journal of International Affairs* 53, no. 2 (Spring): 503–24.

Seligson, Mitchell, and Edward J. Williams. 1982. *Maquiladoras and Migration: Workers in the Mexico–United States Border Industrialization Program.* Austin: Mexico-U.S. Border Program, University of Texas at Austin.

Sklair, Leslie. 1993. *Assembling for Development: The Maquila Industry in Mexico and the United States.* La Jolla: Center for U.S.-Mexican Studies, University of California, San Diego.

Standing, Guy. 1989. "Global Feminization through Flexible Labor," *World Development* 17 (July): 1077–95.

Tanori, Cruz Arcelia. 1989. *La mujer migrante y el empleo.* Colección Divulgación. Mexico City: Instituto Nacional de Antropología e Historia.

Tiano, Susan. 1990. "Maquiladora Women: A New Category of Workers?" In *Women Workers and Global Restructuring.* Ithaca, N.Y.: School of Industrial and Labor Relations, Cornell University.

Van Dooren, Robin. 2000. "Garment Production in the Rural Areas of the Laguna Region, Northern Mexico." Presented at the conference "Libre Comercio, Integración y el Futuro de la Industria Maquiladora," October 19–21, El Colegio de la Frontera Norte, Tijuana.

Wright, Melissa. 2001. "Desire and the Prosthetics of Supervision: A Case of Maquiladora Flexibility," *Cultural Anthropology* 16, no. 3 (August): 354–73.

Zúñiga, Mercedes E. 1999. *Cambio tecnológico y nuevas configuraciones del trabajo en las mujeres: un estudio de caso de una empresa de arneses para automóviles.* Cuadernos, No. 3. Mexico: El Colegio de Sonora.

4

Central American Development or Maquiladora Industry

MARÍA EUGENIA TREJOS

Maquiladora production, which spread throughout Central America beginning in the 1980s, has emerged as one of the region's principal sources of products for export. Apparel manufacture has been predominant, accounting for 63 percent of maquila production in Costa Rica (Barquero and López 2002: 13), 78 percent in El Salvador (Zamora 1999: 4), and 98 percent in Honduras and Nicaragua (Barquero and López 2002: 13). Although maquilas have been established in other industrial sectors in Costa Rica—for example, producing microelectronics, drugs, and medical equipment—clothing remains paramount, and the textile sector is also the leader in terms of labor conflicts and employment concentration (see table 4.1).

Although employment figures are only approximate (reflecting differences in the data sources), most countries in Central America have experienced rapid employment growth during the last twelve years. Costa Rica, where the maquila industry got an earlier start, is the exception, the pace of maquila industrialization there having slowed. In 1982, Costa Rica's maquiladoras employed some 5,600 workers; that figure had reached 46,100 by 1990 (OIT 1999: 65). By 2000 it was 49,300. For the Central American

This chapter is based on my research on work organization in the Central American garment industry. The full study has been reported in a doctoral dissertation for the Labor Studies Program of the Universidad Autónoma Metropolitana, Mexico.

I wish to thank Rocío Guadarrama for her pertinent suggestions and observations on this essay. Translation by Sandra del Castillo.

region as a whole, the Economic Commission for Latin America and the Caribbean (ECLAC/CEPAL) has estimated that three of every ten workers are employed in the maquiladoras (in Fernández n.d.1: 2).

Table 4.1. Employment in Central American Maquiladoras

Country	1990s	2000–2001	
		Data from the OIT Maquila Project[c]	Data from Barquero and López
Guatemala	59,343 (1993)[a]	100,000	93,300
Honduras	15,520 (1992)	126,000	106,530
El Salvador	12,301 (1994)[b]	90,000	84,023
Nicaragua	1,313 (1992)[b]	38,614	30,199
Costa Rica	46,100 (1990)	23,500	49,346
Total		378,114	363,398

Sources: For the 1990s, OIT 1996. For 2000–2001, Barquero and López 2002, which draws on data from the region's central banks; Fernández n.d.2, which draws on OIT country reports from the "Proyecto para mujeres trabajadoras de maquila en Centroamérica."

[a] Maquiladoras and garment export-processing zones producing apparel.

[b] Export-processing zones only.

[c] These numbers are assumed to reflect employment in clothing maquiladoras. However, some are higher than those in Barquero and López 2002, which appear to be more general. Costa Rica's data reflect the fact that there is an important sector in the maquila industry that is not clothing-related. For 2001 in Costa Rica and Honduras, employment tended to decline in the clothing maquiladoras, but in Costa Rica employment rose in other sectors.

For these various reasons, most research on maquiladoras in Central America has focused on the garment industry, as does the present work.[1] A comparison of maquiladora production and traditional clothing production reveals a double transformation. First, the target market for apparel produced in Central America has shifted from the regional market to the international market as local clothing manufactures became the region's principal export product. And second, whereas all phases of production—from design through sale of the final product—had previously taken place

---

[1] In Costa Rica, where other sectors have achieved relatively higher shares within the maquiladora industry as a whole, clothing was the second-most-important category in total exports in 2001.

within the region, under the maquila model certain stages of production are separated from the whole and concentrated in Central America.

We can identify three stages in the shift from local production for the regional market to maquila production for the world market. The first stage, from the beginning of the 1960s to the mid-1970s, witnessed a reduction in the relative importance of the garment industry within the framework of Central American integration as the focus shifted to intermediate products and machine tools in an effort to strengthen the region's weak industrial base. Clothing—which was protected by special protocols—saw its share of regional industrial production shrink (SIECA 1974). Despite the fact that this period was supposedly one of import-substitution industrialization (ISI), clothing production in Central America was highly dependent on imported inputs (CICR 1986), and production was insufficient to meet local demand, such that "internal demand made it necessary to import clothing from third countries" (SIECA 1974: 44).

In the second stage in this evolutionary shift—which took place from the mid-1970s to the mid-1980s—clothing manufacture regained its position, but now as a maquiladora industry and only in Costa Rica. Although other Central American countries took steps to attract clothing manufacturing plants, conditions of war in the region hindered the expansion of apparel maquilas to other countries. Only Costa Rica, with its peaceful electoral democracy and sociopolitical stability, met the conditions under which transnational clothing companies were willing to begin operations in the region, whether in their own plants or through subcontracting. In the first half of the 1980s, exports from Costa Rica were more than double those from any other country in Central America, although exports from Honduras and Guatemala grew at a faster rate during the last half of the decade. At about this same time, clothing imports to Central America began to decrease in volume, and for Costa Rica, clothing exports to the international market begin to rank among the country's principal export products (Fallas 1994: 12).

The third and last stage in the evolution of clothing manufacture in Central America, which began in the 1980s, gained strength in the 1990s, and continues to the present, included the spread of clothing maquiladoras to other countries in the region. Between the late 1980s and the early 1990s, peace agreements were signed in El Salvador and Guatemala, and Nicaragua's Sandinistas were defeated electorally. In 1984, the United States approved complementary measures to the Caribbean Basin Initiative, in which it permitted the duty-free import into the United States of some clothing items manufactured in Central America on condition that they were constructed of materials made in the United States and the fabric had been cut in the United States (Dussel 2001).[2] This political and diplomatic context encouraged investment and subcontracting by transnational corporations (TNCs) and sparked the spread of clothing maquilas throughout the region, to the point that each of the Central American countries ranks among the United States' top sources of clothing imports (Gereffi 2000).

Much of the foreign investment that entered Central America during this stage came from Asia (especially Taiwan and South Korea). Estimates by ECLAC (cited in Fernández n.d.1: 2) suggest that Asian investment accounted for between 43 and 45 percent of foreign investment in Nicaragua, Guatemala, and El Salvador during this period.[3] The investment profile in Honduras was more balanced, with 43 percent coming from the United States, 25 percent from Asia, and 25 percent from domestic investors; in Costa Rica investments were divided about equally between U.S. and domestic sources (Buitelaar 2000: 144). In contrast, the demand for the products was highly concentrated in the world's leading apparel market, the United States, where clothing manufactured in Central America has come to hold an important market share.

The analysis of this evolutionary shift in Central America's clothing industry and its significance for Central American development is divided into the following sections: a theoretical and methodological discussion of the hypotheses; the U.S. response to changes in the clothing market; a review of industry characteristics; international production chains in Central America's apparel industry; labor conditions in the region's plants; and, finally, a discussion of the importance of maquiladoras in the region's possible social and human development.

---

[2] The Caribbean Basin Initiative was promoted by the administration of President Ronald Reagan and later signed into law. It proposed liberalizing international trade in certain product areas (textiles were among the few that were excluded) for products coming from the countries of the Caribbean. The trade opening included technical and financial assistance to support greater U.S. investment in the region. In exchange, the "beneficiaries" had to meet certain conditions: be non-Communist, not have nationalized or expropriated U.S. property, and not have annulled any contracts involving U.S. citizens. In other words, it explicitly excluded Nicaragua and Cuba (CENPRO 1983).

[3] Because of the variety of sources from which they have been drawn, these data should be viewed with caution. What is very clear is that Asian investment has increased in recent years, even though some sources report a high proportion of domestic capital in El Salvador (Buitelaar 2000: 144).

A THEORETICAL-METHODOLOGICAL APPROACH TO CLOTHING MAQUILADORAS IN CENTRAL AMERICA

Authors generally agree that the process of industrial relocation that prompted the establishment of clothing maquiladoras in Central America was made possible by developments in the communications and transportation fields, as well as by the fragmentation of the productive process such that certain processes—the most technically demanding—are done in the core countries while labor-intensive processes are moved to countries on the periphery. Authors also tend to concur that these displacements are supported both by the governments where the transnationals locate their core operations and by the governments of the countries to which the labor-intensive production activities are relocated (see, among others, Fröbel, Heinrichs, and Kreye 1981; Bonacich and Waller 1994).

Differences emerge between authors, however, regarding the importance of this industrial growth in regional development. We can distinguish three positions. Some experts claim that it has positive—and essential—impacts in terms of employment creation, earnings, and advances in technological capabilities (Céspedes et al. 1983; R. Pérez 1991). A second group of observers sees some problems, such as poor vertical integration and the lack of national control over the market and the production process as a whole, as well as low wages and deteriorating working conditions (CEPAL 1997; Torres 1997; Calderón, Barquero, and Blanco 2001; Mortimore 1999; Fernández n.d.1). Of note, however, is the fact that these authors also believe these problems can potentially be addressed and resolved. And finally, the third position holds that this industrialization process is contained within the broader dynamic of capital expansion and therefore generates neither employment nor growth (Fröbel, Heinrichs, and Kreye 1981; Barajas 1989). The question that remains, then, is whether the expansion of the maquiladora industry forms part of social and human development in Central America—that is, whether, as a result of this industrial trend, the population is enjoying a better life materially and spiritually, individually and collectively, culturally and environmentally (ATBP/PODA-UNA 1994).

Given the notable importance of clothing maquiladoras in Central American industrial production, exports, and employment—as well as their importance in terms of imports to the United States—there is substantial merit in reviewing the broad range of studies conducted on this topic, including the wealth of materials that have resulted from the International Labour Organization's (ILO/OIT) project on improving the working and living conditions of maquiladora workers, in which I was involved as an external evaluator. I also include findings of various projects through which I have had direct contact with workers, union organizers, members of nongovernmental organizations, and managers of clothing maquiladoras, as well as the results of my dissertation research which are drawn from responses to a questionnaire on work organization presented to randomly selected clothing plant managers in El Salvador and Costa Rica.

THE U.S. RESPONSE TO A CHANGING CLOTHING MARKET

The United States' position in the world clothing market has undergone a series of changes beginning in the 1950s that have made it the world's largest clothing importer, with imports exceeding domestic production (Chacón 2000: table 1). However, much of the imported apparel is produced in plants controlled by TNCs whose headquarters are in the United States, reflecting the fact that the U.S. government, international institutions, and governments of other countries have all supported the expansion of the transnationals and their control over clothing manufacture and markets.

Beginning in the 1950s, when Japan increased its clothing exports to the United States, the U.S. government approved a number of measures to protect the U.S. textile industry and U.S. clothing manufacturers. For example, in 1957 the United States reached an agreement with Japan under which the latter country would limit its exports of cotton clothing. Later, when other Asian countries began to enter the clothing market, the U.S. government took additional steps to protect domestic manufacturers by favoring the domestic location of certain stages of the production process and the use of domestic inputs in production stages done off-shore. One such measure was clause 807 of the U.S. Tariff Code, approved in 1963, which limits the tariff on imported products assembled abroad to the value added in the country where assembly took place. This measure favored the geographical fragmentation of the production process and the placement abroad of only certain productive stages—basically assembly and finishing. Later agreements, including the 1974 Multifiber Arrangement (MFA), aimed to limit the volume of exports from certain countries.

On the other hand, beginning in 1971 the United Nations Industrial Development Organization (UNIDO) promoted the creation of duty-free zones, arguing in favor of supports for companies being affected by international competition and wage structures (Fröbel, Heinrichs, and Kreye 1981). Within these duty-free zones (also called export-processing zones, or

EPZs), countries construct infrastructure to support the establishment of export-oriented assembly plants, which operate "extraterritorially" and benefit from a series of special incentives.

And finally, the governments of countries receiving foreign investment to support selected phases of the production process implemented various measures designed to favor such investments. In the case of Central America, beginning in the 1970s various national governments passed laws to bolster export-oriented industrial production, primarily in assembly. These included tax exemptions (from income, export, and municipal taxes), free repatriation of capital by the foreign companies, export subsidies, the creation of duty-free zones, and, above all, the duty-free importation of all inputs to be assembled in national territory (OIT 1997; CEPAL 1998).

These varied measures have functioned as complements to the actions of transnational clothing producers, which pursue strategies designed to identify plants able to produce small lots and do complex sewing (Mody and Wheeler 1990); rationalize production through technological innovation or new production systems, especially in design and cutting (Taplin 1994); and/or break up the production process and diversify the geographical location of the various production phases. This last concern spurred a relocation of plants—both within the United States and from the United States to other countries—via subcontracting out some parts of production (Taplin 1994) or opening subsidiaries.

Thus the needs of U.S. clothing producers led to coordinated actions among governments (in the United States and abroad), international organizations such as UNIDO, and the companies themselves to protect U.S. production as much as possible and to relocate some stages of production in order to take advantage of resources in other countries when this was to the companies' benefit.

CHARACTERISTICS OF CENTRAL AMERICA'S APPAREL MAQUILAS

Within the framework outlined above, a new clothing industry appeared in Central America, displacing the traditional clothing industry which had been oriented to the regional market and included all phases of production. The maquiladoras, by contrast, are involved primarily in sewing and assembly, and their production is intended for export.

The new industry did not become the norm in Central America until the 1990s, coincident with the introduction of clothing maquiladoras in Yucatán. This Mexican state shares many characteristics with the countries of Central America. Yucatán and the Central American countries share a tradition of concentrating on a limited number of agricultural crops— henequen in Yucatán and coffee and bananas in Central America—and they have little in the way of industrial tradition. Both areas fit well with García de Fuentes and Morales's observations regarding Mexico's "abundant local labor supply, mostly campesino in origin, but with a tradition of wage labor" and the strong restrictions on labor organizing. In Yucatán this is owing to a lack of a union tradition (García de Fuentes and Morales 2000: 220). In Central America, we can add the blows delivered to organized labor by economic restructuring and the region's new political context. The absence of labor organizations has been turned into a "comparative advantage" that governments tout to attract foreign investment.

Costa Rica was the only Central American country that had an important maquila presence in the 1980s, thanks, as noted earlier, to its political stability in a region otherwise wracked by war. Nevertheless, by the 1990s neighboring countries were also exporting large volumes of clothing and gaining ground in the U.S. market.

The maquiladoras established in Central America display similarities and differences that merit study. They are examined below, by country, in order to find the most salient commonalities. Costa Rica is home to the region's oldest and smallest maquiladoras. Their investment is mostly domestic, and they have relatively little marketing power[4] in the international market. Garment production in Costa Rica has been losing market share because of "a failure to update assembly operations, except for the introduction of a few automated processes" (CEPAL 1998: 95), competition from "full package" plants being set up in other countries, and government policy that has privileged electronics maquiladoras. In the garment sector, plants have specialized in infant clothing, which is more complex to produce and is done in smaller lots (Buitelaar 2000; CEPAL 1998).

El Salvador follows Costa Rica in terms of the age of its maquiladoras, which are about fifteen years old on average. These plants are also the largest in Central America, with an average workforce of 1,300 individuals (in 1999). Here, as in Costa Rica, companies have limited marketing power in the international market (though more than is the case for Costa Rica) and domestic capital is very visible (Buitelaar 2000), although there has

---

[4] Buitelaar (2000) measures global marketing power based on: type of buyer (a single, constant buyer or several buyers); type of client (wholesale or retail); distribution channels (sales outlets near or distant from the factory); and market share in terms of price.

been a recent influx of investment from Asia. Maquiladoras in El Salvador also began to increase their range of activities to include cutting, embroidery, and serigraphy (Buitelaar 2000; Trejos 2004). The primary garment made for distribution in the international market is shirts, which are intermediate in terms of complexity (Calderón, Barquero, and Blanco 2001).

Guatemala's garment maquiladoras also have a history of about fifteen years on average, and their average number of employees is 750. Foreign investment, especially Asian capital, is predominant, and these plants, along with those in Nicaragua, have a higher—though still low—market power.[5] Several years ago, cutting was added to the operations done in these maquilas, and other production processes have been added more recently. Shirts are the most commonly produced garment, which, as noted earlier, are of medium complexity (Buitelaar 2000).

Maquiladoras in Honduras are a more recent development, with an average time in operation of about eleven years. Their average workforce numbers about 900 workers (in 1999), their primary tasks are sewing and finishing, and they have relatively little market power in the international market. Most of the products are simple garments such as T-shirts (Buitelaar 2000). The investment capital comes primarily from abroad, especially Asia and the United States (Gómez and Walker 1994).

The newest maquiladoras in Central America are in Nicaragua, and because they are a recent introduction they are also the fewest in number of any country in the region. They tend to be large—with workforces that average about 1,000 workers—and funded with Asian, especially Taiwanese, capital. They have the most market power. Nicaraguan maquilas also incorporate a broader range of production tasks than found elsewhere in Central America (Buitelaar 2000).[6]

In sum, the expansion of garment maquiladoras in Central America began in the late 1980s (except in Costa Rica, where maquiladoras were introduced earlier). These plants focus on a few basic tasks, not including anything much more sophisticated than cutting—that is, production stages that are generally low-tech and low-skill.[7] They are heavily dependent on

---

[5] In Buitelaar's measurements of global marketing power (see note 4), the maximum "score" is 1,500 points; maquiladoras in Guatemala range between 1,000 and 1,037 points.

[6] The maquiladoras reportedly doing "design work" that I encountered during my fieldwork were in fact only creating patterns based on information sent to them via computer. In very few cases were the maquiladoras involved in actual garment design.

[7] Later sections will discuss worker skills that are not socially recognized as such.

imported inputs, and their backward linkages to national firms are restricted to services such as communications, transportation, utilities, and property rentals. They have little power in the international market, though this tends to be somewhat stronger in plants with large Asian capital investment, as opposed to domestic funding, which reflects national investors' weak participation in marketing.

PRODUCTION CHAINS IN CENTRAL AMERICAN GARMENT MANUFACTURE

Maquiladoras are one link in chains of production. Although there is only limited discussion of the maquila concept, the most coherent definition is that offered by AVANCSO (1994) for the case of Guatemala. According to AVANCSO, a maquiladora carries out production activities for another party, with the contracting party "designing the products, planning the production processes, supplying the materials (at least the main raw material), and retaining ownership of the products." Maquiladoras are part of the new international division of labor, in which subcontractors do basic assembly tasks. Even when they carry out an entire production process,

> they have limited participation in the capital cycles managed
> by the contracting company, which involve, in addition to
> production, a preexisting conceptualization of processes, ac-
> quisition of the inputs to be turned into final products, and
> marketing of the final product, all of which remain under the
> control of the contracting firm. Maquiladoras fulfill the func-
> tion of direct producers, satellite firms through which the
> contracting firm, the indirect producer, extends its produc-
> tion lines (AVANCSO 1994: 2).

Thus the maquiladoras do not participate in the consumer market for their products. They contribute only a production capacity and labor force that remain indirectly subordinated to the logic of capital accumulation that is an extension of the contracting companies.

If we accept this as a workable definition of a maquiladora, then a plant is a maquiladora only if it is part of a chain of production as described by Gereffi (1995). In this section, I will identify the key characteristics found in plants in two Central American countries—El Salvador and Costa Rica—that form part of production chains, rather than similar plants that operate only within national territory (Trejos 2004).

- The initial links are established by transnational companies located outside the region that can function both as manufacturers and as brand marketers or retailers. The second level of linkages involves companies that have direct connections with the transnationals (such as subsidiaries and representatives) or indirect connections (such as subcontractors). The third level of linkages mostly includes domestic subcontracting companies.

- Plant size varies widely, and even companies at the third level can be large. This contrasts with the situation Reygadas (2001) found in Guatemala, where companies are smaller as one moves down the production chain.

- Contrary to findings reported by Gereffi (1995) and Reygadas (2001), the production chains we identified sometimes generate foreign direct investment through the representatives or subsidiaries of the buyer companies, as well as through some subcontractors.

- International production chains[8] are "buyer driven" since it is the transnational companies that control the process and make the decisions that define movement along the chain (Gereffi 2000).

- Control over the chain of production allows market pressures to be passed downward, to the point that some entrepreneurs asserted in interviews that they refuse to participate in international production chains because this structure gives them all the work but distributes all the profits elsewhere (Trejos and Daeren 2001).

- The most highly automated production stages are generally located in core countries like the United States, while stages that use the most direct labor, such as sewing, are placed in Central America, where the skills of the workforce are largely unrecognized[9] Even when a plant supposedly offers a "full package," this generally means that the plant is using designs provided by the contracting company/buyer, who

---

[8] I distinguish between national and international chains of production because I have identified production chains that produce only for the domestic market but which nevertheless demonstrate the same kinds of relations that are found in companies with links to the international market. This essay is concerned only with the latter.

[9] I refer to unrecognized skills because these workers do have dexterity and talents, such as those required for sewing, that are taught and learned in the home but are not recognized as formal skill training.

also controls product marketing, underscoring the lack of precision of this term.

• Production chains produce a segmented workforce that parallels the fragmentation of the production process. In Central America, the skills of the workforce go largely unrecognized, and these workers receive salaries far below those of workers in the country where the transnational buyer maintains its headquarters.[10]

• The companies that control production chains are generally unconcerned about working conditions given that the subcontracting formula obscures labor relations at the plants where products are assembled. The most extreme case was a manufacturer, a provider of products sold in U.S. warehouse stores, whose workforce consisted almost entirely of homeworkers. These workers are not subcontracted; they have a permanent relationship with their employer but there is no recognition of their labor rights.

WORKING CONDITIONS IN CENTRAL AMERICAN MAQUILAS

The Profile and Origins of the Labor Force

There is wide agreement among researchers that the overwhelming majority of workers in the maquiladoras are young,[11] unmarried women[12] with between six and eight years of formal education,[13] some illiterate (ASEPROLA 1995: 19), and without prior industrial work experience, except for previous work in the maquiladora sector (see, among others, J. Pérez 1994;

---

[10] This is not to ignore the presence of sweatshops or the discussion about whether the Third World has inserted itself into the First World via the migrant workers employed in clandestine and unregulated manufactories. Nevertheless, it remains the case that production stages that require higher skill levels are concentrated in the core countries.

[11] Maquiladoras in a few countries, most notably Honduras and Guatemala, hire minors, and plants in Guatemala employ indigenous workers (ASEPROLA 1995: 19).

[12] In El Salvador, half of the women employed in the maquiladoras are either married or in common law relationships (Cañas et al. 1998).

[13] Torres (1997: 29) found that the education level of maquila workers in Honduras is above the national average of 3.9 years of formal education. Thirty-three percent of maquila workers had completed middle school, 5 percent had received technical training, and 3 percent had done upper-level (non-university) studies. Formal education levels were higher among men (57 percent) than women (40 percent). In El Salvador, the majority of workers surveyed by ASEPROLA (1995: 19) were professional seamstresses.

MEC 1998; Martínez 1995; Fernández n.d.2). A substantial fraction (30 percent) are single mothers (Fernández n.d.2). Costa Rican maquiladoras have recently begun employing more men. Martínez (1995: 23) found that 74 percent of garment workers were women, and the International Labour Organization reported the female share of the workforce in garment manufacture at 62 percent (OIT 1996). However, Fernández (n.d.1: 10) notes that this trend toward some "masculinization" of the workforce may be reversing because women are more disciplined and more productive in the kinds of tasks done in the maquiladoras. There has been substantial migration of women to the rural areas of Guatemala, Honduras, and Nicaragua where maquilas have been established. In these cases we find, in addition to undesirable working conditions, new environmental, health, and urban problems that arise when municipalities are unprepared to deal with the population increase (Valverde, in Fernández n.d.3: 5).

It should come as no surprise, then, that there is an extensive literature on the high rates of employee turnover in maquiladoras. Explanations include the dynamics of the workers themselves as well as company policies. In the former category we find that factors such as low wages, poor working conditions, and family problems can prompt a worker to leave a job (OIT 1996). In the latter, we find "a broad discretionary and free worker-firing system" (OIT 1996: 33) which is encouraged by the ease with which companies can replace low-skilled workers and the presence of an abundant industrial reserve army (OIT 1996: 27). This regimen of dismissals and firings can take various forms. In some cases workers are dismissed for failing to meet predefined production levels, lack of company loyalty, absenteeism, pregnancy[14] (Martínez 1995: 42), illness, and suspected participation in labor organizing (Núñez 1999: 11). In other cases, firings follow set patterns, such as dismissals before workers complete their probationary period (Fernández 2001: 23–24) or at the end of the year in order to "avoid the additional costs that come with seniority, such as an increase in vacation days and payment of Christmas bonuses" (OIT 1996: 22). There is also a widespread practice that involves dismissals of part of the workforce to adapt to seasonal fluctuations in demand for clothing (OIT 1996: 22; Torres 1997: 30). And finally, entire workforces may be fired when a plant closes, a not-infrequent occurrence thanks to the ease with which transnationals can move their operations to another region or country.

---

[14] Obligatory pregnancy tests for women workers have been widely denounced; see, for example, CODEH in Lievens 1997.

Wages and Work Intensity

An analysis of wages in Central American maquiladoras involves considering both quantitative factors (wages, benefits, local living costs) and qualitative ones, such as work effort and intensity. The assumption is that the
wage paid is the minimum wage set in each country—although cases have
been found in which maquilas are paying workers less than the officially
mandated minimum (see AVANCSO 1994 for the case of Guatemala;
Cañas et al. 1998 for El Salvador). Even so, wages vary widely, as indicated
by the data in table 4.2. Even when maquiladora wages rise above national
minimums, they are still far below the average wage of $9.30 per hour that
is paid in the United States, the leading purchaser of clothing assembled in
Central America (OXFAM-Solidaridad, cited in MEC 1998).

Wages can also vary among plants depending on the source of their
investment capital, as Cañas and colleagues have shown for El Salvador,
and they can vary by gender given that in some countries men's wages are
higher than women's, as in, again, El Salvador (Cañas et al. 1998), although
ASEPROLA (1995) found no gender difference in wages in Central America. Finally and most importantly, in four of the countries of Central America, the wages paid in the maquiladoras do not cover the cost of a basic
food basket. Costa Rica is the exception; its maquila wage is 1.6 times the
cost of the food basket (Del Cid 1997).[15]

Other factors also lower the cost of the Central American labor force.
One is the progressive devaluation of the currency (OIT 1996: 36), especially in Costa Rica,[16] which translates into higher profits for companies
that pay wages in the local currency but receive U.S. dollars for the garments their Central American workers produce. There have also been
many worker complaints about companies' delayed payment of wages,
failure to pay legally mandated overtime and bonuses (CODEH in Lievens
1997), and evasion of full social security payments by, for example, stating
that workers earn less than they actually do (OIT 1996), a situation that is
made possible by the lack of adequate government oversight.

---

[15] The most extreme case is found in Nicaragua, where the maquila wage covers only
a third of the cost of the basic food basket.

[16] Costa Rica has a system of ongoing mini-devaluations. The colon drops in value
against the dollar by around 15 centavos daily.

Table 4.2. Minimum Daily Wage for Industrial Workers in Central America, by Country, 2002

Country	Minimum Daily Wage (US$)
Guatemala	3.60
Honduras	3.90
El Salvador	4.80
Nicaragua	1.70
Costa Rica	
Unskilled worker	7.90
Semiskilled worker	8.80

Source: Barquero and López 2002: 23.

To these factors, all of which "cheapen" the cost of Central American labor, we should add the formula by which wages are calculated. Two strategies are particularly noteworthy: piecework and production targets. A pieceworker is paid a set amount for each item, so a pieceworker's wage increases as does his or her daily output.[17] This exerts an inordinate amount of pressure on the worker to increase the rhythm of work. In this case, greater work intensity is the equivalent of a longer workday. Pieceworkers labor more in an hour than is the norm. Furthermore, their wage is not constant; it varies according to the worker's ability, drive, and health. In the case of production targets, workers are given a specific number of items that they are to complete during the workday. If they fail to achieve the goal during normal work hours, they are expected to continue working until they do. This extends the workday into overtime hours that are not recognized as such. Both regimens—piecework and production targets—translate into more work accomplished in a day of work—or, in other words, more profits for the company.

In addition to a set number of items to be completed during the workday, companies also set quality standards, leading many employees to point out the inherent contradiction between company demands for quantity *and* quality. In addition to the aforementioned pressures that extend the workday, maquilas often require more hours of work than allowed under national labor law, as, for example, by encouraging or even requir-

---

[17] A study of garment workers in El Salvador (OIT 1996: 34) found that pieceworkers sewing on collars worked 17 percent faster than the norm, and those sewing lapels worked 40 percent faster in order to offset a reduction in pay per piece.

ing employees to work overtime, often without advance notice. In extreme cases, employees have been required to work up to 24 consecutive hours (Núñez 1999; Martínez 1995; AVANCSO 1994; Cañas et al. 1998; OIT 1996).

These various factors produce a wide gap between garment workers' wages and clothing prices, as the following examples illustrate:

- A pair of jeans sewn in the Chentex factory in Nicaragua sells in the United States for $19.99 (246 córdobas). The amount paid to workers for producing this garment is 2.4 córdobas, or less than 1 percent of its selling price (Fernández n.d.1: 4).

- In El Salvador, a garment that sells for US$57 has a cost in wages paid to workers of about 58 cents, again about 1 percent of selling price (OIT 1996: 33).

Thus, among the factors that the ILO identifies as encouraging companies to invest in Central America are the intensity of work and the possibility of varying the size of the workforce as demand rises and falls (OIT 1996: 32). We can certainly add the low labor cost as a proportion of selling price. For their part, workers mention the lengthening of the workday and the increased work intensity. Buitelaar (2000) found that from 1993 to 1998 worker productivity and profits rose faster than wages, and in three countries—El Salvador, Nicaragua, and Costa Rica—wages actually declined. Although Buitelaar's productivity numbers most likely reflect the increase in work intensity, his research clearly reveals that rises in profits outpaced those in wages.

One possible interpretation here is that Central American maquiladoras are cost centers, where the need to reduce labor costs takes precedence over an interest in raising productivity. I would suggest that what we are seeing are not productivity increases but increases in the intensity of work, which is not the same as a simple decrease in costs. The International Labour Organization acknowledged this when it noted that remuneration mechanisms are based on an intensification of the rhythm of work, made easier by the lack of outside inspections and by the special treatment accorded to the maquiladoras even though such treatment contravenes labor law (OIT 1996: 32). Membreño and Guerrero (1994) combine these two arguments, noting that there has been very little technological upgrading but substantial increases in work intensity in Central American maquiladoras, with the lack of technology offset by low labor costs, in effect converting low wages into an "absolute comparative advantage."

Health and Work Environment

Although the factors that combine to create the work environment are acceptable in most maquiladoras, a significant portion of these plants do have problems in this area, and these often vary depending on the source of the investment capital.[18] Specific problems that have been noted include dampness, inadequate space, insufficient ventilation, and poor lighting (this last concern is only rarely mentioned). Other problems are linked to the machines and substances used in the work process, giving rise to complaints of excessive noise and vibration, as well as toxicity of the chemicals employed. Other issues include uncomfortable postures that both seated and standing workers must adopt for certain tasks, and the cadence of work, which can, depending on the pace and repetitiveness of the task, lead to musculoskeletal problems. And finally, there are problems tied to the cleanliness of the facilities, which signal a lack of respect for workers' basic dignity. These would include inadequate or unclean bathroom facilities and the lack of a dining area (Núñez 1999: 7; OIT 1996: 24; AVANCSO 1994; Cañas et al. 1998).

The impacts on the workers include respiratory ailments (caused by temperature changes or lint), varicose veins and muscle aches (because of awkward postures and repetitive movements), headaches (caused by noise and heavy lifting), and stress-related ailments such as depression, gastritis, and rashes (which can also be linked to chemical products). There have also been cases of gas poisoning (OIT 1996: 26–27; *Diario La Prensa*, cited in Núñez 1999; AVANCSO 1994; CODEH, in Lievens 1997).

Exacerbating this situation is the difficulty that workers report in obtaining permission to see a doctor and, even more difficult, in having their ailments recognized as work-related (ASEPROLA 1995: 25; personal observation). Work-related accidents are another consideration; they are particularly frequent in Nicaragua. In 1999 there were 1,716 accidents linked to the seventeen plants in Nicaragua's Las Mercedes export-processing zone; 377 of these occurred on the way to work; the remainder happened in the plants themselves (Núñez 2000: 16).

---

[18] AVANCSO (1994) found that five out of every twelve workers felt that their work environment was adequate. Cañas et al. (1998) found differences in El Salvador that they could trace to the source of investment capital, with the worst conditions existing in plants with Salvadoran or Korean capital. In these plants, about a third of the workers complained of problems with bathroom and dining facilities and with lighting. In nearly half of the plants, regardless of the source of capital, there were problems with ventilation.

The unacceptable physical conditions in the plants exist alongside other causes for complaint, such as the poor treatment that supervisors and foremen accord to the workers. This has been documented from the earliest days of maquila expansion into Central America.[19] Maltreatment can be verbal or psychological (Núñez 1999: 11) as well as physical, as documented by CODEH in Honduras, which found that in 40 percent of the cases analyzed, the worker had been subject to physical abuse, such as shoving, slapping, hitting, beating, and being forced to stand for extended periods in the hot sun (in Lievens 1997). ASEPROLA (1995) found cases in which workers had been shut up in cold rooms as punishment for failing to learn the Korean national anthem, in which pregnant women had miscarried as a result of being kicked by supervisors, and in which workers had been sexually harassed, which has also been documented by the ILO (OIT 1996), Martínez (1995), and Cañas et al. (1998). Even young girls have been subjected to this type of harassment (Cañas et al. 1998: 25). Such abuse causes feelings of humiliation, shame, and loss of a sense of self-worth in the women affected (ASEPROLA 1995), but it can also generate widespread conflict in the plants (AVANCSO 1994). In fact, it is one of the most frequently identified problems among workers in the region (Fernández n.d.2).

Gender Composition of the Workforce

As noted in previous sections, the majority of workers in the garment maquiladoras are women, even though women as a share of the maquila workforce has declined somewhat, as, for example, in Honduras, where it fell from 90 percent in 1990 to 69 percent in 1995 (Torres 1997: 28), and in Costa Rica, where the proportion of women in the maquiladora workforce fell to 62 percent. Among the factors accounting for employers' preference for women workers are the perceptions that they are more submissive and less likely to organize (López 1999: 3) and that they have greater manual dexterity, patience, focus, and self-discipline. Maquiladora managers see women as submissive, passive, and ignorant of their labor rights (OIT 1996: 36), knowledgeable about sewing and garment-making, docile, and dexterous. Moreover, they are willing to do detailed and repetitive tasks, accept low wages, and take a job of indefinite duration (Martínez 1995).

---

[19] I found only one source (J. Pérez 1996) reporting that workers were well treated. MEC (1998) reports some improvements in this area as a result of workers' actions, as well as passage of the Code of Ethics to be applied in Nicaragua's export-processing zone.

Women, for their part, report that they take jobs in the maquiladoras in order to satisfy their families' basic survival needs, which are threatened in this period of economic adjustment (Fernández n.d.3: 4). Many come from families that have little or no ability to accumulate savings; these are society's most vulnerable groups, and they have been hard-hit by structural adjustments in the economy. Their employment responds to the need to obtain family income (ASEPROLA 1995: 8), leading to the assertion that the maquiladoras have contributed to the proletarianization of the female labor force (OIT 1996: 30).

Nevertheless, women face specific kinds of barriers that hinder their access to jobs in the maquiladoras. One is age discrimination; the maquilas generally prefer to hire younger women. There is discrimination against women who are married or in a common law relationship, against women with children, and against pregnant women (Fernández n.d.3: 4). Even after joining the maquila workforce, women are often dismissed if they become ill or pregnant. Working mothers are also at a disadvantage because of the great difficulty arranging reliable childcare (Fernández n.d.2).

My research indicates that women hired to work in the maquiladoras are concentrated in the least physically demanding jobs and those that require skills that are generally not recognized as such, like sewing and cleaning. Male workers, in contrast, are found in more physically demanding jobs, as cutters and warehouse workers, and in machine maintenance, which requires formal training. Although sewing and cleaning are viewed as unskilled labor, they are not. The skills that these jobs require are simply not socially recognized. Sewing, for example, requires talent, aptitude, and dexterity that have been developed and passed from generation to generation of women within the household. But since this "training" occurs within the private family sphere, it is not seen as a learned skill.

In somewhat higher job categories—such as supervisor or quality controller—there is a more even mix of men and women, although some of the managers I interviewed noted that women also function better in these job categories because they are better at giving directions. Of course, these are very low positions in the overall command structure, and they provide more a sense of authority than any real power.

Labor Organizations and Worker Action Alternatives

Central America has a long tradition of suppressing labor unions. From the 1960s to the 1980s, regimes in most countries in the region attempted to crush all labor organizing, viewing labor unions as a direct line to guerrilla forces. However, a number of factors came together in the 1980s that encouraged unionization. The Sandinistas in Nicaragua and an upsurge of guerrilla/popular movements in other countries helped strengthen labor organizations that linked with other social movements and had a broad mobilizing capacity. The exception is Costa Rica, where companies, the government, and solidarity associations[20] developed a cooperative strategy in the 1980s to defeat unionism (author interview with union adviser Víctor Quesada, November 2002).

The signing of peace accords in El Salvador and Guatemala and the electoral defeat of the Sandinistas in Nicaragua plunged unionism into a new and deep crisis that combined internal and external problems. The former included divergent opinions about unionism's purpose, and the latter involved repression on the part of the companies, unimpeded by government (Quesada interview). In 2001, few unions remained in the maquila sector (see table 4.3).

Only in Honduras could one speak of unionization within the maquiladoras; there had been no guerrilla activity in Honduras, and this country's military-populist government of the 1970s had given its support to corporatist labor organizing (Quesada interview). Nevertheless, even here there were difficulties in unionizing the maquila labor force; in the 1990s, there were fifty-four labor unions in Honduras, and today there are only thirty-two.

In Costa Rica, in contrast, labor organizing has been concentrated primarily within the public sector since the mid-twentieth century; it managed to survive for some time in the banana plantations but was wiped out in this sector in the 1980s by the actions discussed above. There were seven unions in the garment industry in the 1970s (Barrantes et al. 1980); though this may seem few, the number is even lower today. In Guatemala, another country where maquila unionization has been notable for its relative absence, there were fourteen unions in the mid-1990s, compared with three today, and these three are struggling to obtain official recognition. In Nicaragua, there were thirteen unions active in eleven companies in 1999, just

---

[20] Solidarity associations are employer/employee organizations that operate like savings and loan associations, with monies set aside for severance payments and a worker savings fund. They have an important ideological component because, by uniting managers and workers across all employment categories in the company, they erase social distinctions. Additionally, they provide an alternative mechanism for resolving labor disputes directly with management.

as the maquiladoras were making their first foray into the country; today there are eight (Trejos and Daeren 2001).

Table 4.3. Number of Unions in Central American Maquiladoras, by Country, 2001

Country	Number of Maquila Unions
Guatemala	3[a]
Honduras	32[b]
El Salvador	4
Nicaragua	8
Costa Rica	1[c]

Sources: Trejos and Daeren 2001; Núñez 1999.

[a] These three unions are struggling to survive by including previous rank and file who have been dismissed from their jobs. Meanwhile, there is an ad hoc committee in one plant that serves as the workers' representative.

[b] The labor centrals report 32; the Labor Ministry reports 39 registered.

[c] This union is also struggling for its survival. There are another three unions that cover the entire private sector, without differentiating by subsector or company, and they have some affiliates within the maquiladoras.

Some problems identified as hindering the creation of unions within the maquiladoras include strong opposition from management (even though the companies themselves organize in strong associations; Fernández n.d.1: 4, 6); group or individual dismissals; plant closures; the assassination of a Guatemalan labor leader because of his "union activity" (López 1999: 5); the hiring of young workers who have little or no experience with organized labor; programs designed to predispose workers against organizing; hiring temporary workers; discrimination (assigning more difficult and poorly paid tasks to union activists); black lists; and support for solidarity associations. Moreover, labor ministries failed to provide adequate oversight; subcontracting can, by its very nature, mean that plants are widely dispersed, making inspection difficult. And industrial parks, where factories may be concentrated, can function to impede easy access to labor leaders and organizers (OIT 1996: 30–31; Torres 1997). Honduras went as far as to declare the maquiladoras "public interest entities" so that strikes would automatically be declared illegal (OIT 1996: 37).

Women face a particular set of barriers to union participation, as noted by Naranjo (2000):

- Gender roles. Unions do not take account of family problems that affect women disproportionately, such as the need to get permission from a male relative (husband, father, brother) to join the union, the heavy workload (combing domestic and workplace responsibilities), and obstacles to attending informal meetings.

- Political limitations. Women have difficulty rising to positions of authority within unions; they have little union consciousness or gender consciousness.

- Logistical or financial constraints. Women tend to lack control over their own budgets.

Interviews with workers also reveal that a large proportion of them do not know their labor rights and are fearful of being harassed or even fired if they join a union,[21] and they see little benefit in unionization (Fernández n.d.3: 11). The absence of unions

> favors various forms and degrees of labor rights violations, including failure to pay for overtime work, restricted access to health services, failure to allow workers time off for earned vacation and official holidays, underpayment of end-of-year bonuses, body searches that infringe on the workers' human dignity; ill-equipped bathroom and dining facilities, and authoritarianism in relations with the workforce. Three-way dialogue [among the company, union, and workers] is either nonexistent or a mere formality (Fernández n.d.1: 9).

Workers can address these kinds of abuses in a number of ways:

- Spontaneous collective responses that do not result in positive organizational outcomes (ASEPROLA 1995: 25). Despite numerous labor conflicts in Costa Rica, all efforts to form unions there have failed. The companies refused to accept collective negotiation, and they fired labor leaders and their associates or used a range of intimidation techniques to ensure that workers would not join the labor organization (Trejos and Mora n.d.).

---

[21] In this essay I deal only with the presence or absence of unions and leave the topic of union orientation—and its effectiveness in terms of producing worker benefits—for a later work.

- Continue to pressure for unionization, whether under traditional or redefined organizational forms. This has been attempted in Honduras, for example, where one union current has tried to create more participatory union structures, bring gender issues into the debate, redefine companies' responsibilities in the area of workers' health, and extend the union's action arena to cover issues outside the worksite (Trejos and Daeren 2001).

- International campaigns to support local labor organizing efforts. These can arise out of coordination between local unions and organizations in the United States to conduct simultaneous preparatory organizing work among maquila workers and to lay the foundation for pressuring for union recognition. Thus, when the union petitions for company recognition, there is an international campaign—involving consumer groups and nongovernmental organizations (NGOs)—ready to be launched in support of the petition (Quinteros 2001: 71).

International campaigns can also be used to press for other kinds of activities, such as:

- Independent monitoring. By coordinating their actions, local and international NGOs have successfully pressured for independent monitoring of workplaces. Monitoring is carried out by organizations that have no links to either the company or the union; they include NGOs, academic institutions, church groups, human rights organizations, and so on. These organizations do oversight to determine whether a company is meeting its obligations under federal labor law and the company's own code of conduct (Quinteros 2001).[22] Monitoring seems to have won a relatively permanent presence in El Salvador.[23]

- Actions by nongovernmental organizations, usually women's organizations. The various obstacles that have stymied unionization efforts in the maquiladoras have left an opening that is sometimes filled by NGOs that try to unify, oversee, and support workers in this sector. The most successful of these is the "María Elena Cuadra" Women's Movement in Nicaragua, which works with approximately six thou-

---

[22] Independent monitoring differs from other forms of company certification in that the overseeing organizations are not contracted by the companies and they are nonprofit.

[23] Unions are critical of independent monitoring, which they see as establishing participating organizations that form parallel structures to the unions.

sand workers (nearly 20 percent of the country's total maquila work-force). This organization won approval of an ethics code for companies operating in the Las Mercedes export-processing zone (the only such zone in Nicaragua), which has brought some improvement in working conditions (MEC 1999).

SOCIAL/HUMAN DEVELOPMENT OR MAQUILA INDUSTRY

From the foregoing discussion, it is clear that the maquiladoras that have been established in Central America, almost all of which are involved in garment production, respond not to the needs or dynamics of the countries of this region, but rather to the requirements of the sector's transnational corporations, most headquartered in the United States and a few centered in Asian countries. Their expansion into the region, which began in the 1980s but gained speed during the 1990s, resulted from the combined ef-forts of the U.S. and Central American governments, the United Nations Industrial Development Organization (UNIDO), and the transnationals themselves. The plants sited in Central America perform the less auto-mated phases of garment production, work that requires less skill (or skills that generally go unrecognized) and that forms part of a production proc-ess that is defined and controlled abroad. Production is highly dependent on imported inputs and technology, though the latter does little to support innovation or upgrading regionally. The prevailing arrangement is for workers to assemble pieces that arrive at the plant pre-cut into finished garments that are exported out of these Central American countries via distribution channels that are also under the control of the transnational firms. These companies' participation as links in production chains ensures that the transnational companies will retain complete control while at the same time allowing the TNCs to evade local labor responsibilities and to pass on to the local companies the pressure to increase output and improve product quality.

Local support comes only in the form of limited services, such as trans-portation, communications, and water, along with a labor force that is pre-dominantly young, female, poor, poorly educated, unskilled (or with un-recognized skills), and with no tradition of labor organizing. This profile, in a region marked by high levels of unemployment and informal em-ployment, fosters the existence of deficient working conditions, such as:

- Lack of job stability, owing to arbitrary and seasonal dismissals and to the ease with which workers move between companies.

- Excessive company control of the workforce, extending to compulsory pregnancy tests.

- A wage structure that is extremely depressed in comparison to wage levels in the United States, where the clothing produced in Central America is sold. These depressed wages do not even cover workers' most basic survival needs. The situation is exacerbated by the companies' ability to evade supplemental payments and by the way in which wages are calculated, putting inordinate pressure on workers to work faster and for longer hours in order to increase their incomes.

- Threats to workers' physical and mental health due to unsanitary working conditions and mistreatment that equate with a total lack of respect for their human dignity.

- The absence or near-absence of labor organizations (except in Honduras), owing primarily to an anti-union position on the part of the company and problems within the labor organizations themselves.

Does this industry portrait constitute a picture of development? As noted above, the various positions on this issue can be grouped into three perspectives, discussed below.

The Governmental Perspective

The first perspective is shared by the governments of Central America, their supporters, and the U.S. government. These actors affirm that maquiladoras are a response to the crisis in the Central American Common Market (CACM) and the small size of the Central American economies, which have forced these countries to face the "immediate and urgent need to seek new markets outside of Central America in order to increase exports and accelerate economic development" (Céspedes et al. 1983: 202). Proponents of this position also argue that the maquila industries "mitigate varied local problems such as unemployment, insufficient foreign currency reserves, and a negative balance of payments,... promote an image of competitiveness,... [and facilitate] technology transfers" (R. Pérez 1991: vi).

With regard to the arguments advanced by this first group of actors, the maquiladoras have indeed significantly increased the ranks of the employed. Nevertheless, unemployment rates have not fallen, except perhaps in Nicaragua, and they have actually risen in Guatemala and Costa Rica. One explanation for this situation is that increased maquila employment may coexist with decreased employment in other sectors as maquiladoras displace regional economic activities. Moreover, the labor force that is entering the maquiladoras is a new labor force. These young female workers did not form part of the labor force on which employment rates had been calculated, so their entry into maquila jobs will not necessarily reduce the figures on unemployment (AVANCSO 1994: 69). And even if there has been an increase in employment, the newly created jobs are far below an acceptable norm.

Moreover, foreign currency earnings generated by the maquiladoras do not remain in Central America. Local inputs are minimal, wages are rock bottom, and these companies pay no taxes. The transnationals capture the overwhelming share of profits. And finally, because these plants incorporate little or no innovation or technical expertise, they cannot be said to support technology transfer except in the most trivial sense of workers using technology that has been invented and applied in other countries.

Constraints on Technology Development, Vertical Integration, and Labor Issues

The second group perspective to emerge from an examination of maquiladoras as possible promoters of development encompasses both a focus on issues of technological development/vertical integration and a focus on labor issues. This group holds that the maquila construct has allowed foreign companies to use Central American countries to support the TNCs' own expansion (Torres 1997; Calderón, Barquero, and Blanco 2001; Chacón 2000). Further, these firms do not support vertical integration within these countries' industrial sectors because the regulatory structure within which the maquilas operate prohibits their use of local inputs (Mortimore 1999; Dussel 2001; Calderón, Barquero, and Blanco 2001). There is no research and development or innovation ongoing in the maquiladoras (CEPAL 1998), and market control remains firmly in the hands of the U.S. companies, with the support of their government (Calderón, Barquero, and Blanco. 2001). The governments of the Central American nations have little influence over the activities of the foreign companies that operate within their export-processing zones (Torres 1997).

Although this perspective identifies key problems in the maquiladora dynamic, its weaknesses are that it fails to identify the source of these problems and it concentrates on technical and material concerns, to the detriment of social considerations. What is objectionable in the maquiladora system is not a question of more domestic inputs or fewer regulations. It is a question of development that speaks to the participation of a range of social actors and satisfaction of their basic needs.

This perspective addresses the labor problems that have been identified in the maquiladoras, asserting that the female maquila worker, "on pain on starvation, must sell herself for any price and for any task" (Fröbel, Heinrichs, and Kreye 1981). In lieu of demonizing the maquilas, advocates of this second perspective outline mechanisms to support minimum labor standards in the maquila plants (no child labor, no coerced labor, the right to organize, no racial or gender discrimination, and so on). A weakness of this position is that it does not establish the linkages between working conditions in the maquiladoras and the expansion of transnational capital, the force responsible for creating this type of plant specifically so that TNCs can cast a veil over labor relations in the plants and take advantage of those conditions that allow the highest work intensity.

Maquiladoras as Part of the International Expansion of Capital

The third perspective on maquiladoras and development views these assembly plants as part of capital expansion, making it necessary to differentiate among all of the social actors involved in capitalist dynamics. Fröbel, Heinrichs, and Kreye (1981: 50) affirm that capital itself creates the conditions for its own valorization and accumulation, such as "an industrial reserve army, broad fragmentation of the production process, and efficient transportation and communications technologies." This movement has created a labor force and production centers, altering the old international division of labor between industrialized countries, on the one hand, and agricultural and extractive countries, on the other. The most advanced utilization of the industrial reserve army takes place in export-processing zones, which these authors define as sites "for the optimal utilization of the labor forces of underdeveloped countries for industrial production oriented to the world market" (Fröbel, Heinrichs, and Kreye 1981: 415), and which they identify as the most shameless and brutal form of exploitation among all industrial activities directed to the global market. Membreño and Guerrero (1994) add that maquiladoras do not contribute to the development process, the regional market, or the building of a national industrial sector.

This viewpoint enabled authors to identify distinctions *within* central countries between workers in high-tech, high-skill positions and those in lower-tech and lower-skill jobs, which gave rise to analyses of the displacement of garment production within the United States—from New

York to the Carolinas and eventually to Los Angeles—as firms sought a workforce that was cheaper and less likely to organize. The conditions in clandestine operations and sweatshops in the United States have led some observers to draw parallels, noting a convergence between these working conditions and those found in Third World countries (Blumenberg and Ong 1994); others suggest that this represents an insertion of the Third World into the First World (Loucky et al. 1994).

This analytic perspective, focused on capital movement, appears to offer a better understanding of the maquiladora dynamic. It allows us to distinguish between what is happening within countries and what is happening within international production chains. It also confirms that limited changes cannot lead to development or even sustained growth unless consideration is given to all of the actors involved (the owners of transnational corporations, plant owners in Central America, workers in different countries, government actors, and so on). An isolated improvement does not constitute a development process. For example, achieving better vertical integration or moving to "full package" manufacturing will not diminish the power of transnational firms nor lessen the veiled subordination of the laborers. Improvements in labor conditions (though a highly desirable goal) would not be sufficient to redefine the orientation of a process based on the intensification of work. Nor would the underlying sources of these processes be affected. That process can only occur if we begin to ask questions. Why apparel? Why electronics? What resources are being depleted? What needs do these products satisfy? Who is making the decisions?

In short, consideration must be given to the maquiladora industry's impacts on garment manufacturers that were already producing in Central America before the entry of the maquiladoras, businessmen whose purview is the domestic and regional market, regional governments and relationships among actors in the political arena, the workers in the maquila plants, regional consumers, and even the relationships between all of these groups and their counterparts in other Latin American countries. Development would have to take into account the needs of Central American consumers and workers: their material needs (a steady job with decent working conditions, food, livable housing, education, health care, and so on) and their emotional needs and realization of their potential (free time, opportunities for personal growth and development of their particular talents and creative abilities, healthy and harmonious relations with others, solidarity, and respect for their human rights and dignity). Development must also take into account the drains on current and possible future natural resources (land, fauna and flora, water, minerals) and the region's ability to provide these without jeopardizing its supply of nonrenewable resources or the regeneration of renewable ones.

This conceptualization far exceeds limited improvements in technology, design, or labor issues. Instead, it identifies development as a process by and for the impoverished peoples of Central America.

References

ASEPROLA. 1995. "Mujeres, maquila y organización sindical en Centroamérica y la República Dominicana." Research report. San José.

ATBF/PODA-UNA. 1994. "Hacia un desarrollo desde adentro y desde abajo." Heredia, Costa Rica: Asamblea de Trabajadores del Banco Popular. Mimeo.

AVANCSO (Asociación para el Avance de las Ciencias Sociales en Guatemala). 1994. "El significado de la maquila en Guatemala: elementos para su comprensión." Cuadernos de Investigación, no. 10. Guatemala: AVANCSO.

Barajas, María del Rocío. 1989. "Complejos industriales en el sur de Estados Unidos y su relación con la distribución espacial y el crecimiento de los centros maquiladores en el norte de México." In *Las maquiladoras: ajuste estructural y desarrollo regional*, edited by Bernardo González Aréchiga and Rocío Barajas. Mexico: El Colegio de la Frontera Norte/FES.

Barquero, Luvy, and Alfonso López. 2002. "Atractivos para la inversión extranjera directa en la región centroamericana y República Dominicana: mención especial a la actividad maquiladora." San José: Consejo Monetario Centroamericano. Mimeo.

Barrantes, Lizbeth, et al. 1980. "Algunas características del obrero textil y de confección del área metropolitana de San José-Costa Rica." Bachelor's thesis, Universidad de Costa Rica.

Blumenberg, Evelyn, and Paul Ong. 1994. "Labor Squeeze and Ethnic/Racial Recomposition in the U.S. Apparel Industry." In *Global Production: The Apparel Industry in the Pacific Rim*, edited by Edna Bonacich, Lucie Cheng, Norma Chinchilla, Nora Hamilton, and Paul Ong. Philadelphia, Penn.: Temple University Press.

Bonacich, Edna, and David Waller. 1994. "Mapping a Global Industry: Apparel Production in the Pacific Rim Triangle." In *Global Production: The Apparel Industry in the Pacific Rim*, edited by Edna Bonacich, Lucie Cheng, Norma Chinchilla, Nora Hamilton, and Paul Ong. Philadelphia, Penn.: Temple University Press.

Buitelaar, Rudolf. 2000. "América Central y República Dominicana: modernización y ajuste en la maquila de confección." In *Impacto del TLCAN en las exportaciones de prendas de vestir de los países de América Central y República*

Dominicana, edited by Rudolf Buitelaar˙ and Ennio Rodríguez. Mexico: CE-PAL/BID-INTAL.

Calderón, Claudia, Luvy Barquero, and Carlos Blanco. 2001. "Efectos de la maquila en el sector real y en la balanza de pagos de El Salvador." Preliminary draft. San Salvador: Banco Central de la Reserva/Secretaría Consejo Monetario Centroamericano. Photocopy.

Cañas, Mercedes, et al. 1998. *Los derechos humanos y la maquila en El Salvador.* San Salvador: Procuraduría Adjunta para la Defensa de los Derechos Humanos de la Mujer.

CENPRO (Centro de Promoción de Exportaciones e Inversiones). 1983. "Ley para la Recuperación Económica de la Cuenca del Caribe." Mimeo.

CEPAL (Comisión Económica para América Latina y el Caribe). 1997. "Maquila y transformación productiva en México y Centroamérica." Photocopy.

———. 1998. "Centroamérica, México y República Dominicana: maquila y transformación productiva." Photocopy.

Céspedes, Víctor Hugo, et al. 1983. *Costa Rica: crisis y empobrecimiento.* San José: Academia de Centroamérica.

Chacón, Francisco. 2000. "Comercio internacional de los textiles y el vestido: reestructuración global de las fuentes de oferta en EE.UU. durante la década de los años noventa." In *Impacto del TLCAN en las exportaciones de prendas de vestir de los países de América Central y República Dominicana*, edited by Rudolf Buitelaar and Ennio Rodríguez. Mexico: CEPAL/BID-INTAL.

CICR (Cámara de Industrias de Costa Rica). 1986. "Perfil del sector de hilado, textiles y confección de prendas."

Del Cid, Miguel. 1997. "Empleo y salarios en la maquila (hipótesis y evidencias empíricas)." Presented at the "Seminario Subregional Tripartito sobre Aspectos Laborales en las Zonas Francas Industriales," San José, Costa Rica, November.

Dussel, Enrique. 2001. "Un análisis de la competitividad de las exportaciones de prendas de vestir de Centroamérica utilizando los programas y la metodología CAN y MAGIC." Serie Estudios y Perspectivas, no. 1. Mexico. CEPAL, March.

Fallas, Helio, ed. 1994. *Evaluación de la competitividad en el Istmo Centroamericano: segmento confección de ropa de origen textil.* San José, Costa Rica: FEDEPRICAP/BID.

Fernández, Janina. 2001. "La maquila de vestuario y textil en América Central: informe analítico de la situación enero–junio 2001." Mimeo.

———. n.d.1. "La maquila textil crece en América Central: nuevas oportunidades, viejos problemas." Mimeo.

———. n.d.2. Documentos de archivos. Esquemas de charlas.

———. n.d.3. "La maquila de vestuario y textil en América Central." Presented at the "Seminario Tripartito sobre Libertad Sindical en Zonas Francas de Exportación, República Dominicana y Honduras."

Fröbel, Folker, Jürgen Heinrichs, and Otto Kreye 1981. *La nueva división internacional del trabajo: paro estructural en los países industrializados e industrialización de los países en desarrollo.* Mexico: Siglo Veintiuno.

García de Fuentes, Ana, and Josefina Morales. 2000. "La maquila en la Península de Yucatán." In *El eslabón industrial: cuatro imágenes de la maquila en México,* edited by Josefina Morales et al. Mexico: Nuestro Tiempo.

Gereffi, Gary. 1995. "Global Production Systems and Third World Development." In *Global Change, Regional Response: The New International Context of Development,* edited by Barbara Stallings. Cambridge: Cambridge University Press.

———. 2000. "La transformación de la industria de la indumentaria en América del Norte: el TLCAN ¿Una maldición o una bendición?" In *Impacto del TLCAN en las exportaciones de prendas de vestir de los países de América Central y República Dominicana,* edited by Rudolf Buitelaar and Ennio Rodríguez. Mexico: CEPAL/BID-INTAL.

Gómez, Rosibel, and Ian Walker. 1994. "La industria de maquila y la organización laboral: el caso de Honduras." In *Globalización y fuerza laboral en Centroamérica,* edited by Juan Pablo Pérez. San José, Costa Rica: Facultad Latinoamericana de Ciencias Sociales.

Lievens, Karen. 1997. *Las repúblicas maquiladoras: las zonas francas en Centroamérica.* Brussels: OXFAM-Solidaridad.

López, Carmen. 1999. "Informe de avance de Guatemala en OIT/Proyecto mejoramiento de las condiciones laborales y de vida de las trabajadoras de la maquila." Mimeo.

Loucky, James, Maria Soldatenko, Gregory Scott, and Edna Bonacich. 1994. "Immigrant Enterprise and Labor in the Los Angeles Garment Industry." In *Global Production: The Apparel Industry in the Pacific Rim,* edited by Edna Bonacich, Lucie Cheng, Norma Chinchilla, Nora Hamilton, and Paul Ong. Philadelphia, Penn.: Temple University Press.

Martínez, Ruth. 1995. "Impacto socioeconómico de las maquiladoras y zonas francas en Centroamérica." Final advisory report represented to the International Labour Organization, March.

MEC (Movimiento de Mujeres María Elena Cuadra). 1998. "Campaña Empleo sí ... pero con dignidad. Breve perfil de las zonas francas en Nicaragua." Informational brochure.

———. 1999. *Memoria 2do Coloquio "Empleo sí ... pero con dignidad."* Managua, Nicaragua, January.

Membreño, Roland, and Elsa Guerrero. 1994. *Maquila y organización sindical en Centroamérica.* Managua, Nicaragua: Centro de Estudios y Análisis Sociolaborales.

Mody, Ashoka, and David Wheeler. 1990. *Automation and World Competition: New Technologies, Industrial Location and Trade.* London: Macmillan.

Mortimore, Michael. 1999. "Industrialización a base de confecciones en la Cuenca del Caribe: ¿un tejido raído?" *Revista de la CEPAL* 67 (April).

Naranjo, Ana Victoria. 2000. *Participación sindical de la mujer en Centroamérica.* San José, Costa Rica: ASEPROLA.

Núñez, Carmen. 1999. "Informe de avance de Nicaragua en OIT/Proyecto Mejoramiento de las condiciones laborales y de vida de las trabajadoras de la maquila." Mimeo.

———. 2000. "Situación de las maquilas en Nicaragua: análisis de la coyuntura del primer semestre del 2000." In "Informe de avance de Nicaragua en OIT/Proyecto Mejoramiento de las condiciones laborales y de vida de las trabajadoras de la maquila." Mimeo.

OIT (Organización Internacional del Trabajo). 1996. *La situación sociolaboral en las zonas francas y empresas maquiladoras del Istmo Centroamericano y República Dominicana.* San José, Costa Rica: OIT/ACTRAV.

———. 1997. *La industria de la maquila en Centroamérica.* San José, Costa Rica: OIT/Oficina de Actividades para los Empleadores.

Pérez, Juan Pablo. 1996. *De la finca a la maquila: modernización capitalista y trabajo en Centroamérica.* San José, Costa Rica: Facultad Latinoamericana de Ciencias Sociales.

Pérez, Juan Pablo, ed. 1994. *Globalización y fuerza laboral en Centroamérica.* San José, Costa Rica: Facultad Latinoamericana de Ciencias Sociales.

Pérez, Robinson. 1991. "Efectos de la maquila en Costa Rica: énfasis en la industria textil." Master's thesis, Universidad de Costa Rica.

Quinteros, Carolina. 2001. "Organizaciones sociales y la lucha reivindicativa en torno a la maquila en Centroamérica en el 2000." In *Enhebrando el hilo: mujeres trabajadoras de la maquila en América Central. Contexto económico y social del empleo en la maquila textil y de vestuario,* edited by Janina Fernández. San José, Costa Rica: OIT/Embajada Real de los Países Bajos.

Reygadas, Luis. 2001. "Las maquiladoras de confección en Guatemala: un distrito industrial precario." Presented at the Congreso de la Asociación Latinoamericana de Sociología, Guatemala, October 29–November 2.

SIECA (Secretaría de Integración Económica Centroamericana). 1974. *El desarrollo integrado de Centroamérica en la presente década.* Vol. 4. Buenos Aires: BID/INTAL.

Taplin, Ian. 1994. "Strategic Reorientations of U.S. Apparel Firms." In *Commodity Chains and Global Capitalism,* edited by Gary Gereffi and Miguel Korzeniewicz. Westport, Conn.: Greenwood.

Torres, Olga E. 1997. *Honduras: la industria maquiladora.* Mexico: CEPAL.

Trejos, María Eugenia. 2004. "La organización del trabajo: el concepto y su movimiento. El caso de la industria de prendas de vestir in El Salvador y Costa Rica." PhD dissertation, Universidad Autónoma Metropolitana.

Trejos, María Eugenia, and Lieve Daeren. 2001. "Informe de evaluación externa del proyecto de OIT 'Redefinición de desarrollo según y para las mujeres trabajadoras del sector de la maquila en América Central: fortalecimiento de la presencia propositiva de las mujeres trabajadoras del sector de la maquila en los espacios de negociación local, nacional y subregional.'" ILO project "Mejoramiento de las condiciones laborales y de vida de las trabajadoras de la maquila." Mimeo.

Trejos, María Eugenia, and Minor Mora. n.d. "Entre la presión y el temor: condiciones laborales y organizativas en la industria costarricense." San José, Costa Rica: FES.

Zamora, Aracelly. 1999. "Informe de avance de El Salvador en OIT/Proyecto Mejoramiento de las condiciones laborales y de vida de las trabajadoras de la maquila." Mimeo.

PART II
Health and Environmental Costs

5

Occupational and Population Health Profiles: A Public Health Perspective on the Social Costs and Benefits of Export-led Development

SIOBÁN HARLOW, CATALINA DENMAN, AND LEONOR CEDILLO

In the last quarter of the twentieth century, Mexico underwent a dramatic economic, social, and political transformation, replacing a national policy of import substitution through national industrialization and self-subsistence agriculture, which had persisted until the 1970s, with a policy of economic restructuring. Economic restructuring has had complex effects on the society and numerous repercussions for the status and health of Mexico's population.

One of the early initiatives undertaken as these new policies began to emerge was the Border Industrialization Program (BIP), launched in 1965, which created the maquiladora export industries. The maquiladoras have been major and important actors in this social and economic transformation, providing jobs for migrants in search of work in Mexico's northern cities, creating an enormous shift in employment opportunities for women, and stimulating a restructuring of family dynamics. In the past two decades, maquila plants emerged as a leading source of economic growth and foreign exchange. Other authors have discussed these changes in national economic policy and their social repercussions, as well as the specific economic and social history of the growth of the maquiladora industry (see, for example, Brenner et al. 2000; Cravey 1998; Kamel and Hoffman 1999; Cypher, this volume). However, few authors have considered how the maquiladoras specifically, or export-led development more generally, have affected the health profile of the border region or of the men and women who labor in the maquila plants.

A central tenet of epidemiology and public health is that the health profile of a population is a reflection not only of their genes, their exposure to infectious or other noxious agents, and their access to health care, but also of their work activity, their work environment, and their patterns of social organization. The maquiladoras introduced large-scale changes in the occupational patterns and social organization of women and men in the northern border region of Mexico. One would expect to see concomitant changes in the health profile of the region and in the patterns and distribution of disease and disability of the population. Although an underlying premise of and justification for economic development activities is that they will improve the health and vital status of the population, economic development planning has not explicitly incorporated health promotion strategies, and the potential health implications of alternative development strategies have not been evaluated. Gains in health status are presumed to be a natural derivative of economic growth, and little consideration is given to evaluating the health infrastructure or surveillance needed to optimize the health benefits of economic growth or of development strategies. Amartya Sen, in *Development as Freedom* (Sen 1999), argues strongly for more explicit attention to effects of development strategies on poverty and the health status of a population, suggesting that these impacts are more legitimate indicators of successful development and not necessarily a direct function of income.[1]

The presumed health benefits associated with the emergence of and employment in the maquiladora industries in northern Mexico stem from the general health benefits of employment, including increased income and access to health insurance. Placed in context, these benefits must be evaluated relative to the diminishing opportunities in rural areas, including lack of jobs and credit for campesinos, decreasing crop prices, and increasing

---

[1] The United Nations Development Programme currently emphasizes the importance of social development, incorporating health indicators such as longevity and infant mortality along with gross national product (GNP), distribution of the GNP across the population (that is, inequality), education, and access to science and technology in their development ranking (UNDP 2002). However, the health indicators are limited and unlikely to expose potentially emergent epidemics such as diabetes, disability due to musculoskeletal injury, or mental illness, and consideration is rarely given to the question of how to optimize health benefits a priori in development planning.

poverty. The potential health costs are also multiple. Several authors have discussed the lack of planned investment in the housing and sanitation infrastructures necessary to accommodate the population growth secondary to the sudden and enormous increase in employment opportunities (see Varady and Morehouse, this volume). Other authors have drawn attention to the continuing failure to build an infrastructure capable of processing the industrial and toxic wastes generated by this emergent industry (Sánchez 1987, 1990). In this volume, Blackman discusses the negative health impacts of air pollution attributable to noncontained emissions from maquiladora factories. What has received considerably less attention is how employment in these industries may be expected to alter the health needs, disease, and disability status of the border populations.

Despite the importance of the maquiladora industries to economic development, research assessing the local or regional health implications of the emergence of or employment in maquiladora factories is scant. A framework for understanding the health status of maquiladora communities would need to incorporate both an understanding of the particular constellations of individual workers' lives within the context of maquiladora employment and community-level factors, while assigning responsibility to both the private and government sectors for providing necessary infrastructure and general environmental services. This chapter will argue further that, in addition to building a public health infrastructure, successful development requires evaluation of how changing occupational structures alter the health profile and health risks in a community and a concomitant reassessment of the public health sector's capacity to develop intervention strategies for optimizing health and preventing the emergence of new and unaddressed public health problems. It first reviews the standard indicators of vital health status, evaluating the extent to which regional economic growth has or has not led to general improvements in the health status of the population. It then evaluates the relatively scant occupational health literature in order to provide a more nuanced understanding of the potential social costs of maquiladoras from a public health perspective, suggesting areas in which more careful surveillance may be needed in order to prevent potential increases in disease and disability.

GROWTH AND DIVERSITY IN MAQUILADORA INDUSTRIES

Over its history, the trajectory of Mexican maquiladora industries has varied by region and time. Until recently, save for one decline in its growth rate in the late 1970s, this sector had grown continuously and exponentially in the number of plants as well as the number of employees (see table 5.1). Scholars who study the maquila phenomenon note that the maquiladora profile in each border city has unique characteristics reflecting particular regional histories, the amount of private and public support offered, and the internal and external articulation of the industry itself (de la O and Quintero 2000). For example, Tijuana, which has historically hosted a large number of small plants, is currently experiencing the relocation of many high-technology Japanese and Korean companies;[2] Ciudad Juárez has on average a larger number of employees per plant. Unionization also differs by region, reaching 100 percent in Matamoros. As Quintero's chapter in this volume shows, the type of union present can make an important difference in whether and how health benefits guaranteed to workers under the constitutionally enshrined federal labor law are implemented and distributed, and whether services superior to those legally required are available.

Table 5.1. Number of Plants and Jobs in Mexico's Maquiladora Sector, 1974–1999

Year	Number of Establishments	Number of Employed Personnel
1974	455	75,974
1980	620	119,546
1985	760	211,968
1990	1,703	446,436
1995	2,130	648,263
1999	3,297	1,140,528

Source: INEGI, *Estadísticas de la industria maquiladora de exportación*, 1974–1982, 1978–1988, 1989–1993, 1990–1994, 1995–1999.

The maquiladoras have also experienced a progressive change in the organization of production and in the products manufactured (Gereffi 1994). The maquiladoras of the 1960s and 1970s, which carried out simple assem-

---

[2] Beginning at the end of 2000, the number of industries and jobs began to decline and continues to do so. In Tijuana, many jobs were lost in Asian industries because of the Mexican government's lack of clarity over new taxes. Sony, previously employing 12,000 workers, closed three of its four plants and moved production to China. Meanwhile, Toyota is building a new plant that will employ large numbers of workers. The future investment profile remains uncertain.

bly processes, are being joined in some high-tech subsectors, such as auto-parts or precision tools, by a vertically integrated industry that includes more complex industrial processes. Initially, the maquiladoras were dominated by textiles and electronics, and the industry hired predominantly female workers and combined minimum wage with piecework, a situation that tends to sustain itself in the production of clothes, basic assembly of micro-components, and other types of light manufacturing (Gereffi 1994). In the early 1980s the importance of autoparts and furniture assembly, plastic products, leather, paper, and metalwork increased. As the maquiladora program attracted plants with more sophisticated autopart production processes and more advanced electronic components assembly, a substantial investment was made in new technology and a growing number of male workers were hired (Carrillo 1989). Since 1990, the electric/electronic and automobile industries have been the most important sectors (INEGI 1997). Thus a small new class of maquiladoras has emerged over time, characterized by higher productivity and applied technology, that incorporate complete manufacturing processes and not simply assembly.

Under the conditions negotiated in the North American Free Trade Agreement (NAFTA), the structure of the maquiladora industry continues to change. Labor-intensive assembly continues to dominate, but it coexists with plants using more sophisticated technological processes, more flexible job organization, and more highly trained employees (see Kopinak 1996; Contreras 2000). As Hualde and Cypher note in their chapters in this volume, it is unclear—in light of the current recession, the changing international panorama post–September 11, and the lack of clarity in the Mexican government—if this trend toward more sophisticated production is likely to continue or intensify as Mexico endeavors to retain its share of foreign direct investment in the global market. Because the more sophisticated production employs a relatively small number of more highly skilled, predominantly male workers, more research would be required to understand whether such changes in production patterns promote sustainable development and how they further alter the health profile of this population.

The demand for labor has also stimulated substantial migration to the border region, with the concomitant effect of creating considerable diversity in cultural practices and socioeconomic status within border populations. Several authors have argued for the need to distinguish between resources available to lifelong residents, longer-term migrants who have often resolved their housing and employment needs, and more recent arrivals whose existence is more precarious (see, for example, Ojeda 1999: 208;

González Block 1996). This heterogeneity in structure, product, and social integration has important implications for understanding the pattern and distribution of health status across Mexico's northern states. The local differences in state infrastructure investments, labor relations, population profiles, and organization of the maquiladora industries—as well as in the specific mix of manufacturing processes over time—would be expected to be reflected in differences in the incidence of specific health complaints or diseases across the region. A detailed analysis of the health implications of these macro-level differences or population heterogeneity across time and space has never yet been undertaken.

GENDERED EMPLOYMENT: A CENTRAL STRATEGY OF EXPORT-LED DEVELOPMENT

As has been true globally in foreign export-processing zones, another defining characteristic of the maquiladoras has been the high proportion of female employees. In some plants, particularly in the textile industry, the entire labor force has been composed of women (de la O 1995). Although the proportion of female employees is decreasing, the proportion of women employed in the maquiladoras remains significantly higher than the percentage of salaried female workers in industry nationally. In 1990, the proportion of maquiladora jobs occupied by women (61 percent; INEGI 1994) was significantly higher than the proportion of female workers in manufacturing industries nationally (20 percent; INEGI 1997) or than the proportion of women working in manufacturing in the United States (32 percent in 2001; U.S. Bureau of Labor Statistics 2001). Recent economic changes discussed by Hualde and Cypher in this volume are likely to spur additional transformations in the production process of these industries, with concomitant implications for the gender distribution of the workforce.

In 1950 women accounted for only 13 percent of the economically active population in Mexico (INEGI 1994), but by 2000 they constituted more than one-third of the economically active population (35 percent; INEGI 1997). Historically, women have worked for wages primarily in agriculture, domestic service, street vending, and clerical positions. Prior to the establishment of the maquiladoras in Mexico, there were few industrial employment opportunities for women, and those were limited to a few industrialized urban areas. Nationally, female employment continues to be concentrated in agriculture and the service sector, although in certain regions of Mexico the maquiladoras have become a leading source of employment for women. Since 1980, as the maquiladora industries have become a more dominant economic force and more technologically sophisticated, the proportion of women in the workforce has declined. However, women have also participated in this technological change, particularly in the electronics maquilas and the automotive industries (Carrillo 1992; Barajas and Rodríguez 1990). Table 5.2 describes the absolute increase of women workers in the maquilas and the decrease in the female-to-male ratio of maquila employment from 1975 to 1999.

The reasons for preferential recruitment of women into the maquiladora industries have been discussed amply elsewhere (see the chapters compiled in González et al. 1995) and include both the ideology of women as a compliant labor force and their availability as surplus labor. Contracting companies articulate a preference for presupposed "sex-specific" characteristics, such as greater docility and willingness to be subjected to work norms, to follow instructions, to accept poorer working conditions and lower wages, to be less resistant to the setting of production standards, and to be less interested in supporting unions (González et al. 1995). This rationale is similar to that mentioned by managers at Japanese-owned export-processing plants in Malaysia, who describe the biological attributes of Asian women in terms of manual ability, better vision, passivity in accepting monotonous work, and better adaptation to factory conditions, including lower wages (Ong 1987: 152). Ideology aside, women have historically been seen as an important source of surplus labor, and their recruitment permitted rapid growth of a new industrial labor force. Concomitantly, economic factors including land privatization and the growth of agroindustry, as well as Mexico's economic restructuring and the crises of the 1980s and 1990s, have helped propel increased participation of women in the labor market generally and in the industrial labor market specifically. Today, more than half of all manufacturing workers in the maquilas are women.

The health and social implications of the rapid creation of a large new female labor force, as well as the substantial differences between the gender profiles of maquiladora workers and that of the manufacturing labor force nationally, encourage an explicit focus on gender when evaluating the impact of the maquiladora industries on development (Canales 1995; Cedillo 1999). This gender profile entails radically different dynamics in worker relationships and labor trajectories, social relationships, family relationships, and health practices (Fernández-Kelly 1983; Ong 1987; Cravey 1998; González de la Rocha 2000). Women have different needs and motives than male workers and less experience facing factory risks. They

Table 5.2. Employment in the Maquiladora Export Industries in Mexico, by Sex, 1975–1999[a]

Year	Women		Men		Total
	Number	Percent	Number	Percent	
1975	45,275	78.3	12,575	21.7	57,850
1980	78,880	77.3	23,140	22.7	102,020
1985	120,042	69.0	53,832	31.0	173,874
1990	219,439	60.9	140,919	39.1	360,358
1995	314,172	59.0	217,557	40.9	531,729
1999	515,164	55.9	406,458	44.1	921,622

Source: INEGI, *Estadísticas de la Industria Maquiladora de Exportación, 1974–1982, 1978–1988, 1989–1993, 1990–1994, 1995–1999.*
[a] Employment figures do not include technical and administrative jobs.

also have unique reproductive health needs and more experience in developing health care strategies. One ethnographic study (Denman 2001) of female electronics workers in Nogales found that women working in the maquiladoras used a diversity of strategies to care for their pregnancy and childbirth, including social security, medical services supplied by the factory, and private, alternative and ethno-medicine—all in combination with domestic self-care. Denman also found that female workers tolerate many disagreeable work conditions given that they are primarily motivated by the desire to improve education and living conditions for their own children. Notably, delayed use of reproductive health and prenatal services is one strategy workers reported using to avoid being fired.

The presence of substantial numbers of female employees has brought into high relief the strains between Mexico's progressive labor law, which provides model maternity leave benefits (guaranteeing paid maternity leave for 45 days before and 45 days after childbirth), and corporate policies that endeavor to minimize costs by seeking strategies to avoid hiring or retaining pregnant women. Furthermore, although female employment has dominated the maquiladora labor force since its inception, few of women's needs have been accommodated. Discrimination against pregnant women has prompted international campaigns (Hertel 2002). Availability of child care facilities in the plants or through the Mexican Social Security Institute (IMSS) is severely limited (Saint-Germain, Zapien, and Denman 1993: 80). Although research has demonstrated the health benefits of Mexico's antenatal leave policies (Ceron-Mireles, Harlow, and Sánchez-Carrillo 1996), an often overlooked cost of foreign direct investment is the overt or covert efforts of employers to weaken strong national reproductive health and maternity care policies. Denman's recent study in Nogales (Denman 2001) indicates that when pregnant women are retained, the maternity leave policy is generally respected, although opportunities for breastfeeding during the workday are limited to the larger factories where child care facilities are available.

Gendered employment also has critical implications for the salary structure of the industry, which reflects the lower status and earning power of women. As noted elsewhere in this volume (see Cypher's chapter), salaries are low in the maquiladora industries as compared to other Mexican manufacturing industries, although they are higher than the national minimum wage and have gained ground in the last decade. Within the industry, salaries for female workers are consistently lower than salaries for male workers. In Nogales in 1986, the average salary of female maquila workers was 83 percent of that of male workers (Denman 1991: 45). A study carried out in the state of Sonora, based on the state employment survey of 1980–1995, found that, for each economic sector and employment level, women have, on average, higher levels of schooling and yet receive lower wages (Grijalva 1996).

In addition to providing monetary income, employment also confers status, which for women can be particularly beneficial due to their devalued social position. The prestige factor of working in the maquiladoras has varied by social class, migrant status, and time, but increases in women's autonomy and self-esteem are potential social benefits of employment in the maquiladora industries, with consequent benefits for women's health (see González et al. 1995; Mummert 1996). For women from rural areas, remunerated work with a set salary, as can be found in maquiladoras, is highly desirable. For women from urban areas, however, a job in public service or commerce has generally been perceived as preferable to working in maquiladora industries. Nonetheless, García and de Oliveira (1994) report that only a small proportion of women view their job as a career; the rest, regardless of social class, perceive it as a source of support for their family. Prestige remains secondary when economic necessity becomes paramount. The prolonged economic crisis in Mexico, with consequent inflation and reduction in public spending, has led many women to adopt new or additional strategies for meeting their basic needs. Women who formerly preferred employment in the commerce and service sectors now prefer jobs in maquiladora industries because these jobs entail less spending on personal appearance—that is, clothes and cosmetics (unpublished interviews with maquila workers in Hermosillo; Cedillo 1999). The prestige benefits are also somewhat tempered by the maquiladora industry's sensitivity to economic fluctuations. Maquila workers frequently opt to supplement their income or to sustain it during periods of economic slowdown by working in the informal economy, including as commercial sex workers (de la O 1995).

In summary, any effort to understand the impact of the growth of the maquiladora industries on the health needs and health status of the population should take into account the complexity of the industry and the diversity of the border populations, while also considering the importance of an explicit analysis of gender and gender strategies in development. It would be naïve to assume that the employment opportunities generated by the growth of this industry have not been beneficial, but it is likewise naïve to assume that industrial development along the border region generally, and employment in the maquiladora factories specifically, has not also had adverse impacts on health. Unfortunately, the data compiled to date are limited in their ability to answer the questions we pose. However, in the next two sections we evaluate what we can understand, first, from vital statistics data and, second, from the limited scientific literature on working conditions and health risks in the maquilas.

VITAL STATUS INDICATORS OF HEALTH STATUS

Population vital statistics such as life expectancy and mortality are frequently used as indicators of a population's health status and as a measure of social development. Table 5.3 compares several common health status indicators for the northern border states to the Mexican average. In 2002, the population of each of the six border states was between 2.5 and 4 million, with five of the six states experiencing an annual growth rate at or above the Mexican average of 1.3 percent, despite their lower fertility. The highest rate of growth, 2.3 percent, occurred in Baja California, which between 1980 and 2000 experienced an average annual growth rate of 3.8 percent, compared with 1.9 percent for the country as a whole. The specific health profiles of the six border states, although similar in some aspects (such as fertility), differ substantially in others.

Although life expectancy is slightly higher and maternal mortality is generally lower than for Mexico as a whole, several mortality indicators suggest that improvements in health have not necessarily kept pace with economic growth, particularly in Baja California. Age-standardized mortality, infant mortality, and perinatal mortality were all notably higher in Baja California than in Mexico overall, as was age-standardized mortality and perinatal mortality in Chihuahua and age-standardized mortality and infant mortality in Sonora. Among women, breast cancer mortality is notably higher in four of the six border states. Of particular concern are some characteristics of the border population, such as the prevalence of obesity and diabetes, which portend the emergence of chronic disease epidemics. Although the National Nutrition Survey (Secretaría de Salud 1999) reported a strikingly high prevalence of obesity (22 percent) among the 12-to-49-year-old female population, the highest proportion was observed in the northern states (30 percent). This high prevalence of obesity places women at increased risk of developing diabetes, the fourth leading cause of death in Mexico since 1994 (Secretaría de Salud 2000). The same survey (Secretaría de Salud 1999) suggests that the prevalence of diabetes is rising; the

Table 5.3. Comparison of Population Health Status Indicators for Mexico and Representative Northern Border States

Indicator	Year	Mexico Total	Baja California	Chihuahua	Coahuila	Nuevo León	Sonora	Tamaulipas
Population (1000s)	1980	66,847	1,178	2,005	1,557	2,513	1,514	1,924
	1990	81,250	1,661	2,442	1,972	3,099	1,824	2,249
	2002	102,037	2,505	3,169	2,442	3,985	2,307	2,819
Annual population growth rate	1970–1980	3.2	3.0	2.1	3.3	3.9	3.1	2.7
	1980–1990	2.0	3.6	2.0	2.4	2.2	1.9	1.6
	1990–2000	1.9	4.2	2.3	1.6	2.2	2.0	2.1
Life expectancy at birth (years)	1980	56.2						
	1990	69.7						
	2002	76.0	76.9	76.3	76.8	77.3	76.6	76.1
Total fertility (age-standardized)	1980	4.9	3.6	4.0	4.3	4.7	4.2	4.6
	1990	3.4	2.4	2.6	2.6	2.5	2.8	2.7
	2002	2.3	2.0	2.1	2.2	2.0	2.0	2.0
Mortality rate per 1000 population	2000	6.2	7.3	7.1	6.4	6.1	6.6	6.0
Perinatal mortality per 1000 live births	1997	13.7	16.7	14.2	9.2	11.8	13.2	9.6

Infant mortality per 1000 live births	1980	39.9	31.0	42.8	30.7	29.7	34.3	26.3
	1990	23.9	27.5	25.8	16.2	17.3	25.3	16.2
	2002	13.8	18.1	13.7	8.5	11.3	14.7	10.1
Maternal mortality ratio per 100,000 live births	1980	95						
	1990	54						
	1997	47	19	49	21	24	30	34
Breast cancer per 100,000 women aged 20 years and over	1997	12.2	10.1	12.3	15.0	18.2	17.5	16.0
Cervical cancer per 100,000 women aged 20 years and over	1997	17.1	15.1	18.2	13.8	12.1	16.0	19.3

Sources: INEGI, Censo de Población y Vivienda; INEGI Web site, www.inegi.gob.mx; INEGI, ENADID 1997; INEGI and Dirección General de Estadística e Informática SSA; INEGI, Anuario Estadístico. Estados Unidos Mexicanos, 2000; INEGI, Estadísticas vitals, http://www.insp.mx/salud/37/374-1s.html.

researchers observed a prevalence of self-reported diabetes of 9 percent in reproductive-aged women as compared to a prevalence of 6 percent estimated in 1992 in the adult population (Phillips and Salmerón 1992). Studies in Mexico also find large regional differences in the prevalence of gestational diabetes, with a prevalence of 11 percent recently reported in an insured population in Chihuahua (Meza et al. 1995).

The growth of jobs in maquilas has led to an important increase in the population covered by social security. In 2001 the IMSS provided health coverage for 56 percent of the country's population, including all private-sector workers (31 percent of the economically active population), their families, and retirees (IMSS 2001; INEGI 2001). Between 1997 and 2001, almost half a million new workers were added as IMSS beneficiaries in the northern states (IMSS 1997–2001). Another useful statistic to compare population health can be derived from data on the utilization of health services—that is, the annual frequency of visits to a health care provider. The general morbidity rate, as measured by the number of visits to a physician per 100 workers per year, was 93.2 in Mexico City (Villegas et al. 1996), while the rate in two electronics factories in Matamoros was 246.3 and 247.4 visits per 100 workers, respectively (Márquez and Romero 1988). Although this difference cannot be directly compared because the former includes manufacturing and non-manufacturing workers and the data derive from different years, the rate in Matamoros was more than double the rate of workers in Mexico City.

Although a formal study of health trends in the border region relative to other regions in Mexico is warranted, the infant, perinatal, and total mortality data for the region do beg the question as to whether the growth of the maquiladora industries has led to an improvement in health status of the population relative to the country as a whole. The difference in general morbidity rates noted above also raises a flag. Both point to the need for an explicit assessment as to whether the health status of the border populations, particularly the employed population, has in fact improved during the last quarter-century relative to the country as a whole, given the overall trend toward improvement in health status and reduction of premature mortality in the nation.

HEALTH PROFILES OF THE MAQUILADORA WORKFORCE

Heretofore, evaluation of occupational impacts on women's health have not been a priority in public health research, especially in developing countries, where funding for such research remains virtually nonexistent. Despite the importance of these industries to economic development, health research in developing countries has seldom addressed the health implications of employment in industries that focus on export-led development. Nonetheless, since the early 1980s several sociological and ethnographic studies began to raise questions about the health implications of working in maquiladora factories.

The first published research on maquila workers' living and working conditions in various border cities appeared during the 1980s (Gambrill 1981; Fernández-Kelly 1983; Carrillo and Hernández 1985; Iglesias 1985; Arenal 1986). These anthropological and sociological studies included participant observation, sociodemographic surveys, and ethnographic studies, including in-depth individual interviews with women who worked in maquila factories. These authors pioneered the investigation of health and safety issues in the maquiladora industries, and their publications were the first to shed light on potential job hazards in this economic sector. For example, Carrillo and Hernández (1985: 137) described the "poor working conditions in the maquiladoras such as lack of ventilation and insufficient light, use of solder, microscopes, and toxic substances" in Ciudad Juárez, while Iglesias (1985: 53) catalogued the symptoms women attributed to their work in the maquilas, including "dizziness, headaches, fatigue, sneezing, coughing; eye inflammation, pain, and irritation; skin dryness, irritation, itching, and rashes; trouble breathing; menstrual irregularities, irritability, and insomnia, among others." Both Fernández-Kelly in Ciudad Juárez and Iglesias in Tijuana described the poor living conditions, including inadequate housing and a lack of basic services such as drinking water, sewerage, and transportation, as well as the difficult family relationships and conflictive family dynamics often experienced by the maquila workers (Fernández-Kelly 1983; Iglesias 1985).

Shortly afterward, the first studies appeared specifically designed to describe health and safety conditions in maquiladora industries. This research (Carrillo and Jasís 1983; Carrillo 1984; Carlesso and Rodríguez-García 1985; Márquez and Romero 1988; Torres Muñoz et al. 1991), from the northern Mexican cities of Tijuana, Matamoros, and Chihuahua, tallied a copious inventory of self-reported health problems among maquiladora workers, including general symptoms, injuries, and reproductive health problems such as menstrual cycle disturbances. A few of these studies described working conditions in the factories in great detail and began to hypothesize potential connections between the self-reported health problems they catalogued and the working conditions they observed (Márquez and Romero 1988; Carlesso and Rodríguez-García 1985). However, none of these studies quantitatively assessed whether exposures exceeded safe levels or whether actual associations between specific exposures and adverse health outcomes existed. Thus these early studies do not provide sufficient information to permit evaluation of the potential impact of maquiladora industries on the health profile of the population. Similarly, routinely collected data by health institutions, such as the IMSS and Mexico's Labor Ministry (STPS), are of little utility because of the well-known underreporting of occupational accidents and illnesses (Carrillo 1984). Furthermore, information on incidence in the maquiladora industry cannot be disaggregated from the rest of the manufacturing industry in those data sources.

Nonetheless, by the 1980s both of these bodies of literature had identified potential adverse health implications of the newly emergent maquiladora industry and clearly defined a public health research agenda. Unfortunately, the challenge articulated by these early investigators has not been met, and research on specific hazardous exposures, potential health risks, and adequacy of health and safety programs remains scant despite the size and importance of this industry in Mexico and worldwide. From a public health perspective, the available data are insufficient given that they do not clearly quantify the extent of exposure, the level and trends of specific health problems in the population over time, or the strength of the association between specific exposures and adverse health outcomes.

Over the subsequent two decades, only thirteen studies, whose results have been reported in eighteen publications, provide quantitative documentation on the health status of workers employed in the maquiladora industries.[3] These studies focus on evaluating working conditions, occupational hazards, and worker health and safety programs; general health symptoms; infant birth weight and, to a lesser extent, other reproductive health outcomes; accidents; and ergonomic risks and musculoskeletal complaints. Despite the fact that the industry is now more than thirty years old, this lack of research prohibits an evaluation of temporal trends in health risks among workers employed in the maquiladora industries and,

[3] These thirteen studies are reported in Hovell et al. 1988; Denman 1990, 1991; Eskenazi, Guendelman, and Elkin 1993; Guendelman and Jasís 1993; Jasís and Guendelman 1993; Balcázar, Denman, and Lara 1995; U.S. GAO 1993; Cedillo et al. 1997; Harlow et al. 1999; Mouré-Eraso et al. 1994, 1997; González Arroyo et al. 1996; Takoro et al. 1999; Guendelman, Samuels, and Ramírez 1998; Meservy et al. 1997; Cedillo 1999; and González Block 2001.

consequently, an evaluation of the implication of the growth of this industry for the health of its workers.

Over the same time period, communities along both sides of the U.S.-Mexico border have shown increasing concern with issues of environmental contamination and clusters of health problems, such as systemic lupus erythematosus, specific cancers and birth defects thought to be associated with the growth of the maquiladora industry, and the lack of infrastructure necessary to contain environmental and occupational health hazards. Around the time that NAFTA was being negotiated and enacted, the discussions of the disadvantages of growth in industrialization along the border were published in several health journals (Nickey 1992; Albrecht 1993; Skolnick 1995; Hotaling 1999). Unfortunately, except for neural tube defects, scientific investigations of these concerns remain infrequent. Some concrete examples of events that have led communities to be concerned are the Mallory children (Dwyer 1994), a cluster of mental retardation among children born to women workers in Mallory Capacitors in Matamoros, Tamaulipas (most likely associated with the use of solvents in the Duracell Battery–owned factory); clusters of lupus in Nogales, Arizona; neural tube defects in babies on the Texas-Mexico border (Hendricks, Simpson, and Larsen 1999); and issues of childhood lead poisoning and other problems related to toxic waste management—or mismanagement—in the border region. In the next several pages, we review and summarize the thirteen extant studies and relevant data on neural tube defects, assess the health implications of their findings, and make recommendations for future research.

Working Conditions, Occupational Hazards, and Worker Health and Safety Programs

In 1993 the first and most extensive evaluation of working conditions in maquila plants was commissioned by the U.S. General Accounting Office (GAO) in response to congressional concerns as the NAFTA side agreements were being negotiated. The goal of this evaluation was to assess the occupational safety and health work environment in the Mexican autoparts industry. A two-day survey at eight plants, which employed about 13 percent of Mexican autoparts workers, included review of written documentation about health and safety programs, discussion with plant managers and safety and health staff, walk-throughs of each plant, and ergonomic evaluation of specific workstations. Presence of ergonomic, safety, physical, and chemical hazards was assessed based on standards set by the U.S.

Occupational Safety and Health Administration (OSHA) (29 C.F.R. 1900) and on the professional judgment of the researchers. Thus hazards were evaluated based on the standards that were then operative in the U.S. plants of the parent companies. Notably, this study is one of only two to date that conducted an actual in-plant assessment.

Ergonomic, safety, physical, and chemical hazards common to light manufacturing and assembly were observed. Although some hazards were serious, with the potential to cause permanent or prolonged damage to the body, none was considered an imminent danger to workers' lives or health. Ergonomic hazards due to repetitive motion were the most frequently observed hazards, with most of the workers in all plants exposed to such risks. Machines without guards were the most frequently observed safety hazards, and, consequently, the most common injuries entered in plant records were contusions, lacerations, and hand injuries. Noise was the most prevalent physical hazard, with noise levels exceeding 90 decibels in six of the plants. Although workers were provided with ear plugs, they often did not use them or did not wear them properly. Seven of the eight plants had established health and safety programs, but few had hazard-specific programs, and programs in all plants were absent or inadequate in at least six of the ten critical areas. For example, none of the plants had ergonomic safety or training programs, although two were in the process of developing such a program. The U.S. parent companies were found to give health and safety guidance and limited technical support, but the evaluations and audits commonly used in the U.S. plants were not used in the Mexican plants.

Three subsequent studies used community-based surveys to interview workers about the frequency of potentially adverse working conditions and occupational hazards in maquiladora factories. González Arroyo et al. (1996) reported on a study that surveyed workers from two cities. Chemical exposures were reported by 42 percent of these workers, but only 27 percent of those who reported such exposures were able to list the generic names of the substances to which they were exposed, and 53 percent had not received Material Safety Data Sheets (MSDS)[4] for the chemicals they handled. One-quarter of the workers who operated machinery reported that the machines were unguarded. Forty percent of workers had received no training regarding hazards associated with their jobs. Thirty-eight per-

---

[4] MSDS are information sheets supplied by the manufacturer which describe known hazards and health risks as well as procedures required for safe use of the chemical.

cent reported noise so loud they had to shout to be heard. Additional hazards such as inadequate environmental control of pollutants, lack of exhaust ventilation in the soldering area, and lack of an emergency plan for chemical spills were identified through in-depth interviews with supervisors. An interesting aspect of this study was the effort made by the authors to evaluate compliance with Mexican regulations based on the workers' reports. These regulations require employers to provide warning labels and MSDS in Spanish, to provide training, to monitor airborne substances and noise and maintain exposures and noise levels below permissible exposure limits, and to provide personal protective equipment. The authors conclude that lack of compliance was likely in the areas of hazard communication, workplace monitoring, and training.

Cedillo et al. (1997) reported results of a pilot study among women working in maquiladoras in Tijuana. The prevalence of exposures differed little between women who worked in electronics plants and women who worked in other types of maquiladoras. Among physical factors, noise was the most prevalent exposure, with three-quarters reporting frequent or continuous exposure to noise. Exposure to heat, vibrations, and poor ventilation were also commonly reported, with about one-third of maquiladora workers reporting these exposures. Radiation exposure was infrequent but sufficient to be observable even in this relatively small sample of fewer than four hundred women (6–8 percent of women). About one-third of the maquiladora workers reported having at least some chemical exposure, with alcohols and other solvents being the most frequently reported substances, followed by chlorinated hydrocarbons in the electronics factories and glues in the other factories. Approximately one-fifth of the women were potentially exposed to soldering fumes based on their job title, but few women noted this potential exposure. Although most women who used chemicals reported receiving some safety training, more than 90 percent had had inadequate training. More than 80 percent of the maquiladora workers reported that they worked on production lines, with over 60 percent reporting that they worked in awkward postures.

Mouré-Eraso et al. (1997) conducted a community-based survey of maquiladora workers in Matamoros and Reynosa. About 45 percent reported exposure to gas or vapors, and a similar proportion reported exposure to dust during at least part of their shift, while 41 percent reported skin contact with chemicals. Physical hazards included noise, which was reported by two-thirds of the participants, and heat and vibration, reported by more than half of the workers. Exposure to ergonomic risks included performance of repetitive movements (76 percent), manual labor applying strength (44 percent), and heavy physical work (26 percent). More than half of the workers reported that their jobs required high visual demands, and 43 percent reported having to perform their duties in uncomfortable positions during at least part of the workday. Approximately half the workers had received health and safety training; 94 percent of these individuals considered their training to be adequate, and about 50 percent regularly used personal protective equipment. However, regarding the areas of training considered in the questionnaire, less than half of the workers had received training in all eight of them.

In summary, these four studies suggest the presence of safety, physical, and ergonomic hazards in maquiladoras consistent with the type of hazards that would be expected in production-line activities associated with light manufacturing and assembly activities. The studies consistently report lack of adequate protection, including machine guards, ventilation, and noise reduction, and the lack of adequate safety and training programs. Excessive noise over extended periods can increase the risk of hearing loss. Although chemical exposures have been a major concern ever since the maquiladora plants began to dot Mexico's northern border area, in many plants use of chemicals is limited. Nonetheless, the evidence suggests that when chemicals are present, workers are improperly exposed, and they lack information about the potential toxicity of these exposures. Exposure to dust was also noted; dust exposure can provoke respiratory ailments, including occupational asthma. Ergonomic risks were noted in all studies and are of particular concern because of the potential for causing long-term disabling injuries to young workers. In addition to ergonomic risks common to production-line processes, national surveys in the United States and Sweden have shown that such jobs, which are characterized by high demand and low control, are associated with psychosocial risks that may provoke stress-related illnesses such as hypertension (Karasek 1979; Karasek and Theorell 1990). Occupational factors that may also increase job-related stress for women working in the maquilas include the fact that most bosses and supervisors are men and sexual harassment may occur, that work schedules are fixed and not adaptable to family exigencies, and that day care centers are lacking.

Although these four studies are informative, the paucity of data makes it difficult to fully evaluate the nature of working conditions or the distribution of hazards in maquiladora industries. Notably, only one of the above studies (U.S. GAO 1993) focused on a single sector, providing an in-depth analysis based on in-plant observations. Similarly, only one study (U.S. GAO 1993) included quantitative exposure assessments in specific plants. Exposure surveillance in the maquiladoras has been spotty at best, and neither corporate nor government actors have shouldered the cost of the routine exposure evaluations necessary to ensure healthy work environments.

Health Status and Health Risks

GENERAL HEALTH STATUS, PHYSICAL SYMPTOMS, AND PSYCHOLOGICAL DISTRESS

A total of six studies have provided quantitative data on the presence of self-reported general health symptoms or psychological distress among workers in the maquiladora industries. However, only three of these studies provide comparable information on other occupational groups or analyze their findings by level of exposure to potentially noxious agents. Such comparative or dose-response data are critical to evaluating whether the health profile of maquiladora workers differs from that of the surrounding community and to establishing causal relationships with occupational exposures if it does. The earliest community-based quantitative study of the health status of maquila workers was published in 1988, more than two decades after the initiation of the maquiladoras (Hovell, Bush, and Barry 1988). A validated symptom questionnaire (the Health Status Index; Kaplan et al. 1976) was used to assess workers' health status across four symptom domains in a systematic community-based sample of maquiladora workers, non-maquiladora workers, and housewives not employed outside the home. The mean scores for mental health symptoms and gastrointestinal/urinary symptoms in the past month, respiratory complaints and musculoskeletal complaints, and falls in the past year were compared across occupational groups. Maquiladora workers were more likely to report musculoskeletal symptoms, difficulty breathing, and falls in the past year than the other occupational groups. As would be expected because of the healthy worker effect,[5] homemakers received the worst scores for six out of

[5] People who are sick or disabled are less likely to work; thus working populations tend to be healthier than the general population. Also, workers who have experienced negative health consequences from their job may be the most likely to terminate employment; thus current employees may be preferentially selected to be those who have not experienced adverse health consequences. This difference in the health status of the working and nonworking population is referred to as the "healthy worker effect." Failure to consider the healthy worker effect can lead to an underestimation of occupational risks. For this reason, when studying a work-

nine measured outcomes. However, none of the morbidity indicators differed significantly once differences in age, income, and education across the occupational groups were taken into account. This study is limited by the small sample size (n = 108), its cross-sectional design, and the failure to consider the possibility of a healthy worker effect. Though important because it was the first study that tried to quantitatively evaluate the health status of maquiladora workers and to compare the health profiles of maquiladora workers with workers in other industries and economic sectors, the study contributes little to our understanding of the relationship between the growth of the maquiladora industry and the health impacts of development. The study by González Arroyo et al. (1996), discussed above, also included a symptom checklist, asking workers to indicate whether they had experienced any of forty-five symptoms in the past six months, if they had any symptoms caused by their work, and if they had been injured on the job. Symptoms such as fatigue (45 percent), back pain (41 percent), headache (33 percent), upper airway irritation (23 percent), and pain in the wrist (24 percent) and upper extremities (20 percent) were common. Twenty-one percent of the respondents reported having symptoms caused by workplace exposure, while 19 percent reported suffering a job-related injury. Although the presence of health and safety concerns is documented, it is not possible to evaluate whether or how the experience of these workers differs from other Mexican industrial populations, as no comparison population was included in this study.

In 1993, Guendelman and Jasís published results of their somewhat larger and better-designed community-based, cross-sectional study of female workers in Tijuana. Four measures of health status—functional limitations, depressed mood, nervousness, and perceived stress—were examined. Functional impediments were defined as having at least one of fifteen physical symptoms in the last thirty days that impeded performance. However, the diverse range of symptoms—including backaches, stomachaches, ear problems—renders this construct relatively meaningless. Depressed mood was measured by the Center for Epidemiologic Studies–Depression scale (CES-D) (Radloff 1977). The prevalence of functional impediments (18–27 percent) and mean depressed mood scores did not differ significantly by occupational group, although women working in the electronics maquiladora reported the lowest prevalence and scores. Nerv-

---

ing population it is usually preferable to use other working populations as a comparison group, as opposed to nonworking populations.

ousness was reported most often by women working in the service sector and least often by women working in the maquiladoras. Perceived stress (Cohen and Williamson 1988) did not differ significantly by occupational group. The authors concluded that the health of maquila workers is no worse than that of other working women; however, except for depressed mood, the health outcomes were not well measured in this study. Also, the sample size in each occupational group was small (n = 120); and because only current workers were included in the sample, the healthy worker effect may not have been properly accounted for. Nonetheless, the finding that CES-D scores were lower among women employed in the maquiladora industries does provide some evidence in support of the hypothesis that these jobs increase women's autonomy and status, with consequent health benefits. Notably, household stressors, especially financial strain, proved a more important risk factor for having each of the measured outcomes than did occupational group. The primary contribution of this study is the data it provides on psychological health status, as opposed to general health status or specific morbidities.

A recent study (Cedillo 1999) designed to develop and adapt scales to measure psychosocial risk factors among female maquiladora workers also provides some information on potential psychosocial health risks. Instruments included Karasek's Job Content Questionnaire, a measure of occupational strain, and five scales assessing psychological stressors outside the job in the domains of housing, domestic responsibilities, conflictive relationships with family, conflictive relationships with friends, and spillover between work and home responsibilities (Karasek 1979). Job-related stressors accounted for 12.5 percent, 13.1 percent, and 12.9 percent of the variance in anger, fatigue, and CES-D scores, respectively, among workers in two maquiladora factories. As was seen by Guendelman and Jasís (1993), non-job stressors were also important determinants of the workers' psychological symptom profile, given that a similar proportion of the variance was explained by psychological stressors outside the job, including spillover between home and work responsibilities, conflictive relationships with family, and conflictive relationships with friends (12.5 percent of the variation in anger scores, 16.6 percent of the variation in fatigue, and 17.4 percent of the variation in CES-D scores).

A much more informative study is González Block's (1996) large representative survey of maquiladora workers living in Tijuana. Although no internal comparison group is included, the author compares his results to data from national health surveys and to state surveillance data and clinical surveys. Also, unlike previous studies which focused on health symptoms, this study evaluated the frequency of specific morbidities. The self-reported prevalence of hypertension, deafness, and asthma was higher among maquiladora workers than among industrial workers nationally based on data from the second National Health Survey. Notably, the prevalence of hypertension was 3.8 times higher, although maquiladora workers were less likely to smoke compared to the average Mexican urban female population. This study suggests that the health status of maquila workers may well be compromised when compared with the health experience of industrial workers nationally, and it provides direction as to the diseases and conditions that might warrant further evaluation. Although the findings regarding hypertension, deafness, and asthma are consistent with conditions one might expect to find associated with production-line processes and with exposures noted in the studies of working conditions discussed above (such as occupational strain, excessive noise, and exposure to dust and chemicals), this study included no information on specific physical, chemical, or psychosocial exposures.

In contrast to all previous studies, Mouré-Eraso et al. (1997), in their community-based study, ascertained information on both health symptoms and chemical and airborne exposures, enabling them to evaluate associations between reported symptoms and chemical exposures, and thus to quantify potential health risks of employment in the maquiladora industries. More than half of the participants in this study reported experiencing headache, unusual fatigue, and depression, while more than a third of the workers reported experiencing forgetfulness, chest pressure, stomach pain, dizziness, and numbness or tingling in the extremities. Self-reported nausea, stomach pain, and urinary and breathing problems were significantly associated with frequency of exposure to airborne contaminants, while breathing problems were associated with frequency of exposure to dust. Exposure to airborne organics—including solvents, glues, and gasoline—was associated with reports of fatigue, chest pressure, and tingling in the extremities. Although this study is limited by its cross-sectional nature, lack of clear time frames for reported symptoms, and lack of information on level of exposure, it does suggest a potential association between chemical exposures in the maquiladora industries and respiratory and neurological symptoms, findings that warrant further evaluation.

Though the data are limited, the types of health problems reported in these studies—musculoskeletal complaints, deafness, asthma and respiratory complaints, hypertension, and psychoneurological problems—are consistent with the types of exposures noted above (such as ergonomic risks, noise, dust and chemicals, stress, and psychological strain). These findings suggest that maquiladora workers may be suffering adverse health effects associated with their working conditions, but no substantive research program has been initiated to follow up on these preliminary results. Nonetheless, the studies provide the preliminary findings necessary to guide future research endeavors, and they suggest several areas that warrant additional information.

ADVERSE REPRODUCTIVE OUTCOMES

Three intriguing studies have suggested that women working in maquiladoras may be more likely than other women to give birth to low-birthweight babies. One of the earliest studies of the health consequences of working in maquiladoras was a study of medical records that Denman conducted in Nogales (Denman 1990). The frequency of low birth weight (LBW) was 2.8 times higher among maquila mothers as compared to other working women (14 versus 5 percent, respectively). Also of concern was the finding that while 52 percent of the LBW infants of maquiladora mothers were premature births, only 33 percent of the LBW infants of other workers were premature. In a follow-up study in which all women who gave birth in the IMSS hospital in Nogales during a six-month period were interviewed, Denman (1991) found that 9 percent of the infants of maquiladora workers, 3 percent of other workers' infants, and 10 percent of housewives' infants were low birth weight. Women employed in maquiladoras reported working longer hours (85 percent of maquila workers, versus 37 percent of other workers, worked over nine hours a day not including overtime, and maquila workers reported 11.4 overtime hours per week). When asked about potential toxic exposures, 67 percent of the maquiladora employed mothers reported having been exposed to solvents, paints, degreasers, solder fumes, and other substances, versus none of the service employees. Maquila-employed mothers identified uncomfortable postures during most of their shift as the most problematic for their pregnancy. Although this study again found a difference in the frequency of LBW, the sample size of other workers was small, no difference was observed between housewives and women employed in maquilas, and the study did not adjust for potential confounders such as number of children born to each woman.

Notably, however, Eskenazi, Guendelman, and Elkin (1993), in a small study following up on Denman's findings, reported that after adjustment for age, parity, education, and smoking status, infants of garment workers weighed 279 grams less than those of electronics workers, whose infants weighed 312 grams less than infants born to service-sector workers. The authors point out that occupation actually proved a better predictor of birth weight than other well-known risk factors such as parity and smoking. Taken together, these three studies raise concern about the potential implications of maquiladora industries for the reproductive health of border populations and for women working in the maquiladora industries. Unfortunately, these findings have not been investigated further, and no more definitive study has been forthcoming.

González Block's study (1996) reported some findings on birth weight that only partially support the results of Denman and Eskenazi, Guendelman, and Elkin. Among women who had recently been pregnant, 12 percent reported having given birth more than two weeks early, but only 4 percent reported having had a low-birth-weight (< 2500 grams) birth. This low-birth-weight frequency is considerably below that reported by Denman (1990, 1991) or in a study of workers in Mexico City (Ceron-Mireles, Harlow, and Sánchez-Carrillo 1996), all of which obtained information on birth weight from medical records. However, the self-reported frequency of preterm delivery is slightly higher than the one other study of this outcome among Mexican working women (Ceron-Mireles, Harlow, and Sánchez-Carrillo 1996). González Block's survey also provides information on a few other aspects of reproductive health. When gynecological conditions of pregnant women were evaluated, the prevalence of reported signs of vaginal, urethral, or cervical infection was 29 percent higher than that reported by national health institutions. Pregnant workers were less likely to leave their job because of health problems during pregnancy before they were eligible for maternity leave than were workers in Mexico City (18 percent versus up to 42 percent).

Although provocative, these findings regarding potentially adverse pregnancy outcomes require follow-up in more methodologically rigorous studies. Future studies should endeavor to tease out the precise etiology of the low-birth-weight births. In particular, Denman's (1991) finding that more of the low-birth-weight infants born to maquila mothers were also premature compared to the low-birth-weight infants born to other working mothers suggests that more studies are needed that focus on preterm birth. Findings that pregnant women working in maquilas had an increased frequency of reproductive tract infection (González Block 1996) and recent reports of an association between occupational strain and risk of preeclampsia (Landsbergis and Hatch 1996; Marcoux et al. 1999)[6] suggest two possible avenues for such research.

Birth defects are another area of reproductive health that requires more research attention. The cluster of children with mental retardation among mothers who worked at Mallory Capacitors in Matamoros (Dwyer 1994), although the focus of lawsuits, has never been satisfactorily investigated. In contrast, the finding of a cluster of six anencephalic infants in Cameron County, Texas, in 1991 has led to a concerted and sustained binational research effort. Hendricks, Simpson, and Larsen (1999) published the results of a surveillance project in fourteen Texas counties that actively identified all cases of neural tube defects (anencephaly, spina bifida, and encephalocele) between 1993 and 1995. This study documented that the frequency of neural tube defects was higher in the Texas border counties (17.1 per 10,000 live births) than in El Paso County (9.8 per 10,000) or other U.S. populations (9.3 per 10,000 in California and 11.3 in metropolitan Atlanta), with rates for Mexico-born Hispanic mothers being higher than rates for U.S.-born Hispanic mothers. Results of comparable studies in Mexico are just becoming available. A retrospective review of health records in Tijuana reported a rate of 12.2 cases of anencephaly per 10,000 births as compared with 6.4 per 10,000 in the Texas study (Quintana et al. n.d.). However, research to date has not been able to attribute a specific environmental or occupational cause for this elevation in risk. The increased risk of neural tube defects could well be related to micronutrient deficiencies in the diet or to an interaction between nutritional and environmental factors, and thus a consequence of women's socioeconomic vulnerability.

ACCIDENTS

Only one cross-sectional study (Balcázar, Denman, and Lara 1995) has quantified the risk of accidents in maquiladoras. In that study, 13 percent of workers reported having had an accident within the last six months while working in a maquila, and 18 percent had had a work-related illness. More than 40 percent of the accidents required at least one disability day. Accidents most frequently reported were injuries caused by machine operation and tool manipulation, as well as burns and eye damage related to

---

[6] Preeclampsia is a toxic condition of late pregnancy characterized by hypertension, edema, and protein in the urine that can progress to convulsions and is an important cause of maternal morbidity.

toxic substance exposures. The parts of the body most commonly affected were the hands and fingers. Having a doctor or nurse at the plant was associated with a reduced risk of having an accident. The incidence of accidents reported in this study was two times greater than the incidence reported by the IMSS in Nogales, suggesting that about half of the accidents reported at interviews had not been registered. The only other study to provide quantitative information on the prevalence of accidents (González Block 1996) reported a lower incidence. That study found that 5.3 percent of the workers suffered at least one accident per year, with half of those accidents occurring in the maquiladoras.

MUSCULOSKELETAL COMPLAINTS AND INJURIES

Given the known ergonomic hazards of assembly-line production (Armstrong 1986; Armstrong et al. 1993), a major focus of public health concern in maquiladora industries has been the potential for musculoskeletal injuries. As noted above, the earliest sociological and ethnographic studies suggested that women who worked in maquiladora industries may be experiencing neuromuscular problems, including chronic lumbago (Denman 1991; Iglesias 1985; Fernández-Kelly 1983). Subsequently, four studies have provided some information on the prevalence of musculoskeletal complaints. The U.S. GAO evaluation of occupational hazards in autoparts plants (1993) found, during interviews with workers in one of the larger plants, that 42 percent reported pain in their upper extremities, 37 percent in their hands and wrists, 30 percent in their lower limbs, 25 percent in their neck and shoulders, and 14 percent in their lower back.

Somewhat lower frequencies of musculoskeletal complaints were reported by participants in the community-based study of Mouré-Eraso et al. (1997), who worked in a variety of maquila factories. Specifically, 21 percent reported experiencing pain or numbness in their hands within the past year, 12 percent reported elbow or forearm pain, and 14 percent reported shoulder pain. The fact that over half of those experiencing pain reported that it diminished after being away from work for at least a week provides some evidence that the pain was caused by their work. In addition, these authors evaluated the association between the experience of pain and exposure to specific ergonomic risks. Shoulder pain and hand/wrist pain were about twice as frequent among respondents who worked all day in uncomfortable postures and whose work involved repetitive movements or forceful manual labor, as compared to workers with no such exposures.

Harlow et al. (1999) estimated the prevalence of musculoskeletal complaints and compared the risks of having a complaint by occupation. The frequency of aches or pain in the lower back in the past twelve months was 30 percent; in the upper back, 38 percent; in the neck/shoulder, 26 percent; and in the hand/wrist, 18 percent. In general, working outside the home increased the risk of having a musculoskeletal complaint, with maquila workers having a 40 to 90 percent increased risk compared with women who had not recently worked for pay outside the home. Compared to women who had other types of paid jobs, maquila workers had a 20 percent increased risk of reporting lower back, upper back, and shoulder/neck pain. Although this study did not evaluate specific ergonomic risks, it does consider the role of the women's living circumstances. Notably, the risk of having a musculoskeletal complaint was found to be associated with women's sociodemographic characteristics and living conditions. Women who were heads of household had twice the odds of upper back and neck/shoulder pain. Very low socioeconomic level, measured by years of educational instruction or housing quality, was associated with an increased risk of having lower back and hand/wrist pain. These latter findings illustrate the importance of economic development occurring in parallel with development of the socioeconomic infrastructure. The absence of adequate safeguards in the former can be compounded by risks associated with the lack of infrastructure, increasing the likelihood of adverse health outcomes.

Only one study to date has conducted a comprehensive evaluation of ergonomic risks and musculoskeletal disorders among women working in a specific maquiladora (Meservy et al. 1997). A standardized questionnaire was used to evaluate the presence of cumulative trauma disorders (CTD), and workers were also examined by a physician to identify tendonitis, ganglia, and carpal tunnel syndrome (CTS). Videotapes of workers were used to identify exposure to ergonomic risk factors, including postural severity, cycle time, frequency, force, and duration. The twelve-month prevalence of upper extremity CTD was 46 percent in women and 12 percent in men, while the point prevalence was 24 percent and 8 percent, respectively. Tendonitis was diagnosed in 12 percent and CTS in 4 percent of the workers examined. Highly repetitive movement, pinch grip, and awkward posture of the wrist were identified as important risk factors for the presence of CTD. The gender difference in the cumulative trauma disorders is notable and consistent with other findings in the literature that indicate an increased susceptibility among women (see Punnett and Herbert 2000).

In summary, studies of musculoskeletal complaints and disorders suggest a profile of disability that is, again, consistent with what might be expected in manufacturing facilities characterized by production-line processes. The failure to establish adequate surveillance systems for ergonomic risks and for musculoskeletal injuries is a clear failing. Injury has undoubtedly occurred, with long-term disability likely to occur in at least some proportion of these cases. Yet no reliable studies exist that measure the incidence or prevalence of such injuries, the prevalence of permanent disability, or the economic and social costs of permanently disabling injuries, costs that are borne by the individuals, their families, and the public-sector health and social security systems.

Health Benefits of Maquiladora Employment

As noted in the introductory section of this chapter, employment in maquiladora industries may also lead to health benefits, especially for women. Increased income, socialization, and autonomy may have positive health impacts through increases in women's status and self-esteem. The effect of women's working on risk of depression has received considerable attention in the health literature, with a consensus now developed that the positive mental health impacts of employment are highly dependent on women's social class, marital status, and presence of young children in the home. Although increases in employment opportunities for women are generally touted as a benefit of the maquiladoras, few studies have actually endeavored to test this assumption. Guendelman and Jasís's finding (1993) that CES-D scores, a measure of depressed mood, were lower among women employed in the maquiladora industries compared to other workers does provide some evidence in support of the hypothesis that these jobs increase women's autonomy and status, with consequent health benefits, but more empirical studies are needed. Other authors have discussed the importance of women's employment in Mexico more generally (González de la Rocha 2000; García 2000; García and de Oliveira 1994), highlighting not only that women's income is key for family survival but also that, through their employment, women often achieve increased independence from their male relatives (partner, father, brother). Such independence can sometimes prove to be a double-edged sword given that violence against women may be unleashed in response. Younger women in urban settings appear to gain more advantages than older women in rural areas, as do women with more education.

Another obvious benefit to employment is the health insurance and other benefits associated with workers' right to social security through the IMSS. Currently, however, IMSS is undergoing a serious financial crisis, which is reflected in an increasing number of patient complaints and decreased benefits. Women working in maquiladoras state a preference for using services in the private sector or other branches of the public sector (such as the Health Ministry) because of the long waits, poor quality of attention, and distrust of the quality of the medicines provided by the IMSS. Thus the value of access to the IMSS is declining, and this may reflect a long-term problem of underinvestment over the last two decades of industrial growth.

Health of Maquiladora Workers, Families, and Communities

In the above review we have focused on studies that evaluate the occupational environment and occupational risk factors for adverse health outcomes among maquiladora workers. However, as noted in various studies (Cedillo 1999; Denman 2001), a complete assessment of the health impacts of the emergent maquiladora industry must also consider the broader social and environmental consequences of the growth of this industry and evaluate their impact not only on the workers but also on the workers' families and the surrounding communities. Factors such as housing quality and sanitation (including air pollution and disposal of hazardous wastes), as well as social integration of the communities and changes in family structure, are all determinants of the health status of border communities and are consequentially affected by the rapid industrialization and subsequent population growth that has occurred in the absence of a simultaneous development of adequate urban infrastructure. From a public health standpoint, the vulnerability of residents in border cities is aggravated by the lack of municipal services, the lack of enforcement of occupational regulations, and the lack of adequate organization in most communities to negotiate for safe work conditions and better salaries to improve living standards.

In the border region, where most of the maquila industries originated, environmental problems continue to be a prime concern for local communities in both Mexico and the United States. Air pollution, water pollution and water availability, disposal of industrial waste, and monitoring and registration of pollution transfers, along with the absence of strong right-to-know programs, have been discussed extensively by other authors (see the chapters by Blackman and by Varady and Morehouse, this volume; Sánchez 1987, 1990; Mouré-Eraso et al. 1994). The contamination of aquifers and of the Río Bravo/Rio Grande, Río San Pedro, and Río Santa Cruz with heavy metals and other chemicals is a concern for the maintenance of both biological diversity and human health (Texas Center for Policy Studies 1994; Sánchez 1990).

The joint impact of domestic and workplace exposures deserves considerably more focus; little attention has heretofore been paid to the health costs of tension between these two spheres, particularly for women, or to the potential impact of alternative development strategies on exacerbating or reducing these tensions. Several of the studies discussed above noted the impact of exposures outside of work, particularly psychosocial and socioeconomic risks, on workers' health. Most of these studies only considered the domestic setting in very general terms, modeling material housing deficiencies, general financial strain, and (occasionally) issues of family conflict (Harlow et al. 1999; Guendelman and Jasís 1993). Only relatively recently has the importance of analyzing the domestic setting, particularly family relationships, as a key determinant of workers' health been considered. The level of stress-provoking family conflict reported by female maquila workers in Hermosillo is noteworthy, and Cedillo concludes that the impact of stress within the workplace on the health of these workers cannot be understood in isolation from the levels of stress outside the workplace (Cedillo 1999: 190). Denman (2001) has demonstrated the ways in which gender relations and gender identity help define how women negotiate their health care at work and at home.

When considering the impact of external stressors, the importance of economic restructuring and its complex effects on people's lives cannot be ignored. For example, the number of Mexicans living in extreme poverty rose between 1984 and 1992 from 6.7 to 8.8 million (Boltvinik 1995: 34), while the proportion of income controlled by the wealthiest 20 percent of the population increased from 51 percent in 1984 to 58 percent in 1994. Based on official estimates, "the minimum wage was halved between 1986 and 1996," while average wages also fell in real terms (García 2000: 267). A severe economic crisis in late 1994 led to a currency devaluation, heavy borrowing from international finance agencies, an increasing need for foreign currency, and, ultimately, inflation of over 50 percent, which reduced the living standards of the poor and the middle class. Families have developed coping strategies: taking additional jobs, working overtime, having more household members (including children) work, and reducing the amount and quality of food (González de la Rocha 2000: 19), all of which are likely to further strain families' health resources.

Historically, occupational health has been conceptualized through a lens that focused on male employment and on industries dominated by male workers. The lack of attention to occupational health issues in the export-led development industries undoubtedly reflects, in part, the tendency to ignore occupational issues relevant to women's health. As occupational health theory and methodology adapt to address the challenges of investigating the health of maquiladora workers, researchers will need to be cognizant of reframing our methods to include crucial considerations of family, communities, and gender relations.

PUBLIC POLICY: NORMS AND IMPLEMENTATION

Although an obvious benefit deriving from the increase in private-sector jobs stemming from the growth of maquiladora industries in the border region is the increase in the number and proportion of the population with access to social security and the consequent growth in the health care delivery infrastructure of the Mexican Social Security Institute, a serious lack of public health capacity for environmental and occupational health regulation, surveillance, and training remains, as does the lack of capacity to evaluate the health costs and benefits of this development strategy more broadly. Mexican occupational health and safety regulation follows procedures defined by the Mexican standard for all norms and regulations (the Ley Federal de Metrología y Normalización), with the Labor Ministry being the responsible government agency for both regulating and monitoring compliance with occupational standards. The Health Ministry also has a mandate to address health issues related to exposure to hazardous materials and environment pollutants at the workplace and to implement health prevention and surveillance activities. IMSS, as the health care institution in charge of medical care and pension programs for private-sector employees, is responsible for the diagnosis, treatment, and reporting of occupational diseases and injuries. Although this regulatory and health care infrastructure exists, the capacity for surveillance of occupational illness is limited and does not easily permit compilation of data for the maquiladora industries separately. Maquiladora industries are aggregated within manufacturing, and standard reporting systems do not provide statistics on occupational accident and illness cases that originate in these specific industries. Furthermore, the professional infrastructure capable of evaluating the health and safety of work environments is significantly under-resourced, while high turnover within the industry makes effective surveillance difficult.

IMSS data on occupational accidents and illnesses in general reflect crude incidence reports, with little or no public review and no regional analysis of these data undertaken in the border region. Incidents are underreported in this database because workers are required to file a claim before an incident will be recorded in the IMSS medical-legal database. Many companies have medical services that handle minor accidents that are not reported to the IMSS, and because employers' contribution rates are based on the companies' risk group classification, clear disincentives exist to reporting such cases. The study by Balcázar, Denman, and Lara (1995) noted the twofold difference in the incidence rate documented in their study compared with that reported by the IMSS. A large proportion of maquiladora plants have on-site medical services. For example, in the survey done by Mouré-Eraso et al. (1997), 90 percent of the workers interviewed said that their workplace had medical services. Thus many occupational accidents and illnesses may never be identified as work-related in official surveillance databases, with the underreporting of musculoskeletal disorders probably most acute.

For example, in 2001, of a total of 413,748 reported incidents in Mexico, 78 percent were occupational accidents; 21 percent were accidents en route to work, and 1.1 percent were work-related illnesses (IMSS 2001). Of the 5,520 reported illnesses, 47.8 percent (2,637 cases) involved hearing impairment; 20.8 percent (1,147 cases) involved respiratory effects due to chemical exposures; and 10.4 percent (574 cases) were pneumoconiosis due to silica or silicates. If we consider just the problem of occupational musculoskeletal disorders, a higher frequency of problems such as lumbago, carpal tunnel syndrome, tendonitis, and tendosinovitis would be expected nationally, as well as within maquiladoras specifically. The absence of musculoskeletal diseases in Mexican occupational statistics is notable, especially when compared to the number of cases in other countries such as the United States, where the number of repeated trauma cases has risen steadily from 23,800 cases in 1972 to 332,000 cases in 1994 (O'Neill 1999). Such deficiencies in the official surveillance systems highlight the need for proactive investigations of potential adverse health outcomes as new industries take root and grow as part of any economic development program.

Mexico currently is deficient in human resources capable of evaluating health and safety hazards, in the work environment and environmental hazards in the community, with a significant lack of capacity in areas such as ergonomics, industrial hygiene, occupational safety, and occupational medicine. The majority of occupational health professionals are physicians; no PhD program or research training program in occupational medicine exists. There are several certification programs for medical practitioners within the factories. Large plants, especially those owned by transnational corporations, have corporate training programs for industrial hygienists and environmental engineers. Academic institutions, however, offer only a limited number of continuing education programs in occupational medicine and fewer still in the area of occupational safety or industrial hygiene.

Given this lack of capacity, Mexico has experimented with voluntary programs for maintaining healthy working conditions and establishing good practices related to environmental pollutants management. To date, the experience within the certification program for clean industry suggests that such voluntary programs have had a good response from domestic manufacturers but not in the maquiladora industries. However, because maquiladoras are engaged in global manufacturing, interest in obtaining ISO certification is growing.[7] Global social pressure and regulation of commerce may play a key role in improving production practices and working conditions in these industries in the future.

Another potential social cost that requires more investigation is the long-term health costs of sick and disabled workers. Currently, when a worker becomes ill or disabled and leaves maquila employment, he or she also loses IMSS coverage, and subsequent health care costs are absorbed by the Health Ministry. Given that companies only contribute revenue to IMSS and not to the Health Ministry, the social costs of disability are most likely being subsidized by the Mexican government.

DISCUSSION AND CONCLUSIONS

The lack of research into maquiladoras' health impacts on workers and the surrounding communities in which they are located illustrates the extent to which globalization of best labor practices and public health lags behind the globalization of production and financial systems. When considered in

---

[7] ISO refers to a series of standards developed by the International Organization for Standardization, founded in 1947, to facilitate the international exchange of goods and services. ISO comes from the Greek "iso," which means equal.

the context of local employment alternatives and of the current economic crisis, maquiladora jobs clearly remain crucial alternatives to unemployment. However, it is also true that a systematic evaluation of the health costs and benefits of the growth of this industry has yet to occur. In this chapter, we have endeavored to highlight several issues that are crucial to evaluating the health status of maquiladora communities and to confronting the challenge posed by the question of how to ensure that economic development strategies are optimally designed to improve the population's health without inducing unacceptable risks in specific subpopulations. Such strategies must incorporate the capacity to monitor potential increases in specific adverse health outcomes caused by occupational or environmental exposures, as well as programs to alleviate consequent health problems of workers and their families. These issues include:

- the distinct gender composition of the maquiladora workforce compared to other industrial populations;

- the specific occupational environments of the maquiladora plants, characterized by production-line processes with often uncontrolled exposure to noise, ergonomic risks, dusts, and chemicals;

- the importance of integrating our understanding of occupational exposures with information on risks associated with the suboptimal living conditions of these workers; and

- the importance of understanding the interplay of occupational and domestic psychosocial stressors.

The above review also highlights our current inability to assess how the maquiladoras, as a development strategy, have had an impact on the health of the population. However, areas of potential concern arise even from this scant literature. The vital statistics data point to a pressing need to understand the contribution of the growth of maquiladoras to the infant and adult mortality profile of the border populations, as well as to the rising prevalence of obesity and diabetes. Several aspects of the organization of work and of working conditions within the maquila factories also require more scrutiny, including the impact of excessive noise on hearing loss, the association between ergonomic risks and musculoskeletal injuries, the relationship between psychosocial risks and hypertension, and whether maquila workers are at risk of adverse reproductive outcomes, among other potential concerns.

As might be expected given their predominance in the workforce, female workers have often been the focus of research on the health impact of the maquiladora industries; these studies often but not always exclude males. Although understandable given the historic gender differential in employment, more research clearly needs to be conducted on male workers, as well as on non–reproductive health issues for female workers. The fundamental problem highlighted by this review is the general paucity of scientific data on the health status of this key occupational and regional population. Clearly, a substantive effort must be made to conduct population-based studies. Both the health costs and actual benefits of this new form of global production will remain hidden unless resources are made available with which to conduct longitudinal studies to measure the incidence and prevalence of relevant morbidity in the border regions and of the occupational diseases and injuries most likely to be associated with the types of adverse working conditions most prevalent in the maquiladoras. To maximize Mexico's capacity to conduct such studies, international collaborative research and training programs will be needed, both to generate the necessary research and to increase the capacity of local management and the workers themselves to minimize exposures to workplace hazards. Such programs could be conducted as collaborative projects with labor organizations, companies, academic institutions, and governmental and nongovernmental organizations, although such programs should strive to incorporate Mexicans and other relevant actors more effectively.

More innovative questions about the broader cultural impact of the maquila form of production on health are also warranted. Although many authors have discussed the transformative impact of the maquila export industries on family relationships, few studies have sought to characterize the positive and negative health consequences of this transformation. For example, characteristics of work organization—production-line processes, limited breaks (generally two fifteen-minute breaks plus one thirty-minute lunch), and high turnover of employees—promote isolation more than socialization. Similarly, as women spend less time at home because of the demands of work and transportation, their chances to socialize with neighbors or fellow workers are diminished. Thus the often-touted Mexican social support structures may well be at risk, with potentially important ramifications for the health status of the population. González de la Rocha argues that the social support networks in Mexico have been weakened in recent years, and she cautions against assuming that this psychosocial resource is limitless (2000: 34). Given the gender profile of the maquila workforce, further efforts to integrate our understanding of the joint impact of exposures defined by the domestic space and the workplace are warranted. Few theoretical models or methodological approaches have been developed to evaluate these joint exposures or to determine how their interaction may differ by gender.

Despite the importance of understanding the particular constellations of individual workers' lives as a framework for understanding the health status of maquiladora communities, it is also vital to avoid a framework that overemphasizes individual responsibility. An important unresolved problem is how to focus public health attention on the particular context of maquiladora employment while not ignoring community-level factors and the responsibility of both the corporate and governmental sectors in providing necessary infrastructure and general environmental services. Macro-level studies are needed that focus on the broad question of health inequalities within the border region and in relation to countries providing investment capital. For example, a study of the proportion of corporate taxes directed toward urban infrastructure and living conditions in country of origin compared with country of destination would be most informative for this dialogue.

Finally, it must also be acknowledged that a focus on generating relevant data and subsequently developing health interventions through research is only one strategy for monitoring and improving the health status of communities such as the maquiladora communities in Mexico. National and international pressure continues to be necessary to ensure that transnational companies comply with domestic laws and regulations, international agreements, and corporate policies as strictly as they do in plants in their countries of origin. As has been highlighted by Mouré-Eraso et al. (1997), Mexico needs to develop and improve strategies for monitoring corporate policies and their implementation in the maquiladoras. As a first step it would be useful to assess whether the practices of those transnational corporations that have been certified by ISO or other regulatory systems differ from those of uncertified companies.[8] Wider public participation in the discussion and development of labor and development policy is also needed in Mexico. Development of systems that would allow con-

---

[8] Less than one percent of Mexican firms fulfill international quality standards, according to the Mexican Institute of Norms and Certification (*La Jornada*, June 6, 2001). Currently, efforts to conduct this type of monitoring are in an initial stage (see www.cepaa.org).

sumers to evaluate production conditions from "cradle to checkout" may serve as one model for promoting such participation.

More effective dialogues with domestic policymakers, development economists, and critical multilateral organizations are also necessary if improving the health status of Mexico's population is to assume a more central focus in the evaluation of economic development strategies. Of particular import to this discussion is the fact that Mexico received a recommendation from the World Bank in April 2001 to decrease many benefits currently mandated by Mexico's federal labor law.[9] Given that the weight of the World Bank and other multilateral agencies on Mexican national legislation and policies is substantial, research that demonstrates the importance of labor law in ensuring a beneficial impact of development on health is crucial.

The recent economic recession and the potential for increasing pressure on the Mexican maquiladora industries from the opening of trade with China crystallizes the importance of developing a better understanding of the health costs of development and of proactively developing appropriate health infrastructure during cycles of economic growth in order to ensure maintenance of the health of the population during periods of economic crisis. In 2001, more than 140,000 jobs were lost in the Mexican maquiladora industry due to the economic recession and the consequent decrease in the demand for products from the maquiladoras, marking the first time in nearly twenty years that maquiladora employment had declined. Unemployed maquiladora workers increase the pressure on the public health infrastructure, while those still employed struggle to maintain their jobs by accepting smaller bonuses, doing more overtime work, and living under more stressful conditions. The full implications for Mexico of this recession and the anticipated changes in the global economy remain unclear; but whatever the future course, an increased focus on reducing the health costs of development and optimizing the health benefits is needed.

Public health holds as a fundamental principle the notion that risks and benefits to health must be balanced within individuals exposed to potential health risks. Just as it is not ethical to conduct studies that pose substantial risks to participants for the benefit of other populations or future genera-

---

[9] This advice was included in the World Bank's recommendations for Mexico. In its report, the Bank noted that labor reform was sorely needed to promote more investment, make Mexico more competitive in the world market, and avoid increasing growth of the informal labor market. See Lafourcade, Giugale, and Nguyen 2001.

tions, so too should the benefits of development accrue to those individuals who are exposed to the risks of development. Arguments that the health costs of development can be ignored in the short term because economic development will eventually lead to improved health and well-being run counter to this fundamental principle of public health.

References

Albrecht, Laura J. 1993. "Troubling Waters: Sister Cities Struggle with Health Conditions on the U.S.-Mexico Border," *Texas Medicine* 89, no. 10: 24-25.

Arenal, Sandra. 1986. *Sangre joven: las maquiladoras por dentro.* Mexico City: Nuestro Tiempo.

Armstrong, Thomas J. 1986. "Ergonomics and Cumulative Trauma Disorders," *Hand Clinics* 2: 553–65.

Armstrong, Thomas J., Peter Buckle, J.H. Fine, M. Habberg, B. Jonsson, A. Kilbom, I.A.A. Kuorinka, B.A. Silverstein, G. Sjogaard, and E.R.A. Vilkari-Juntura. 1993. "A Conceptual Model for Work-Related Neck and Upper Limb Musculoskeletal Disorders," *Scandinavian Journal of Environmental Health* 19: 73–84.

Balcázar, Héctor, Catalina Denman, and Francisco Lara. 1995. "Factors Associated with Work-Related Accidents and Sickness among Maquiladora Workers: The Case of Nogales, Sonora, Mexico," *International Journal of Health Services* 25: 489–502.

Barajas, Rocío, and Carmen Rodríguez. 1990. "Las mujeres ante la reconversión productiva: el caso de la maquiladora electrónica." In *Subcontratación y empresas transnacionales: apertura y reestructuración en la maquiladora*, edited by Bernardo González-Aréchiga and José Carlos Ramírez. Tijuana: El Colegio de la Frontera Norte/Fundación Friedrich Ebert.

Boltvinik, Julio. 1995. "Evolución de la pobreza en México entre 1984 y 1992, según CEPAL-INEGI," *Sociológica* 10, no. 29: 11–40.

Brenner, J., J. Ross, J. Simmons, and S. Zaidi. 2000. "Neoliberal Trade and Investment and the Health of *Maquiladora* Workers on the U.S.-Mexico Border." In *Dying for Growth: Global Inequality and the Health of the Poor*, edited by J.Y. Kim, J.V. Millen, A. Irwin, and J. Gershman. Monroe, Maine: Common Courage Press.

Canales, Alejandro. 1995. "Condición de género y determinantes sociodemográficos de la rotación de personal en la industria maquiladora de exportación." In *Mujeres, migración y maquila en la frontera norte*, edited by S. González, O. Ruiz, L. Velasco, and O. Woo. Mexico City: El Colegio de México/El Colegio de la Frontera Norte.

Carlesso, Edite María, and Julia del Carmen Rodríguez-García. 1985. "Proceso laboral y desgaste obrero: caso maquila de procesamiento de mariscos en Matamoros." Master's thesis, Universidad Autónoma de México–Xochimilco.

Carrillo, Jorge V. 1984. "Maquiladoras: industrialización fronteriza y riesgos de trabajo. El caso de Baja California," *Economía: Teoría y Práctica* 6: 97–132.

———. 1989. "Transformaciones en la industria maquiladora de exportación." In *Maquiladoras: ajuste estructural y desarrollo regional*, edited by Bernardo González-Aréchiga and Rocío Barajas Escamilla. Tijuana: El Colegio de la Frontera Norte.

———. 1992. *Mujeres en la industria automotriz*. Cuadernos de COLEF, no. 1. Tijuana:: El Colegio de la Frontera Norte.

Carrillo, Jorge, and Alberto Hernández. 1985. *Mujeres fronterizas en la industria maquiladora*. Mexico: Secretaría de Educación Pública/Centro de Estudios Fronterizos del Norte de México.

Carrillo, Jorge V., and Mónica Jasís. 1983. *La salud y la mujer obrera en las plantas maquiladoras: el caso de Tijuana*. Tijuana: Centro de Estudios Fronterizos del Norte de México.

Cedillo, Leonor. 1999. "Psychosocial Risk Factors among Women Workers in the Maquiladora Industry in Mexico." PhD dissertation, University of Massachusetts.

Cedillo, Leonor, Siobán D. Harlow, Roberto Sánchez, and David Sánchez. 1997. "Establishing Priorities for Occupational Health Research among Women Working in the Maquiladora Industry," *International Journal of Occupational and Environmental Health* 3, no. 3: 221–30.

Ceron–Mireles, Prudencia, Siobán D. Harlow, and Constanza Ivette Sánchez-Carrillo. 1996. "The Risk of Prematurity and Small–for–Gestational–Age Birth in Mexico City: The Effects of Working Conditions and Antenatal Leave," *American Journal of Public Health* 86, no. 4: 825–31.

Cohen, S., and Gail Williamson. 1988. "Perceived Stress in a Probability Sample of the United States." In *The Social Psychology of Health*, edited by S. Spacapan and S. Oskamp. Beverly Hills, Calif.: Sage.

Contreras, Óscar F. 2000. *Empresas globales, actores locales: producción flexible y aprendizaje industrial en las maquiladoras*. Mexico City: El Colegio de México.

Cravey, Altha J. 1998. *Women and Work in Mexico's Maquiladoras*. Lanham, Md.: Rowman and Littlefield.

De la O, María Eugenia. 1995. "Maquila, mujer y cambios productivos: estudio de caso en la industria maquiladora de Ciudad Juárez." In *Mujeres, migración y maquila en la frontera norte*, edited by S. González, O. Ruiz, L. Velasco, and O. Woo. Mexico City: El Colegio de México/El Colegio de la Frontera Norte.

De la O, María Eugenia, and Cirila Quintero. 2000. "Las industrias maquiladoras en México: orígenes comunes, futuros distintos." Paper presented at the international conference "Free Trade, Integration and the Future of the Maquiladora Industry," El Colegio de la Frontera Norte, Tijuana, October 19–21.

Denman, Catalina A. 1990. "Industrialización y maternidad en el noroeste de México." Gaceta de El Colegio de Sonora, Cuadernos de Trabajo, no. 2. Hermosillo: El Colegio de Sonora.

———. 1991. "Las repercusiones de la industria maquiladora de exportación en la salud: el peso al nacer de hijos de obreras en Nogales." Serie Cuadernos de Trabajo, no. 2. Hermosillo: El Colegio de Sonora.

———. 2001. "Prácticas de atención al embarazo de madres-trabajadoras de una maquiladora en Nogales, Sonora, México." PhD dissertation, El Colegio de Michoacán.

Dwyer, Augusta. 1994. *On the Line: Life on the US-Mexican Border*. London: Latin American Bureau.

Eskenazi, Brenda, Sylvia Guendelman, and Eric P. Elkin. 1993. "A Preliminary Study of Reproductive Outcomes of Female Maquiladora Workers in Tijuana, Mexico," *American Journal of Industrial Medicine* 24: 667–76.

Fernández-Kelly, María Patricia. 1983. *For We Are Sold, I and My People*. Albany: State University of New York Press.

Gambrill, Mónica Claire. 1981. *La fuerza de trabajo en las maquiladoras: resultados de una encuesta y algunas hipótesis interpretativas*. Mexico City: Centro de Estudios Económicos y Sociales del Tercer Mundo.

García, Brígida. 2000. "Economic Restructuring, Women's Work, and Autonomy in Mexico." In *Women's Empowerment and Demographic Processes: Moving beyond Cairo*, edited by Harriet B. Presser and Gita Sen. New York: Oxford University Press.

García, Brígida, and Orlandina de Oliveira. 1994. *Trabajo femenino y vida familiar en México*. Mexico City: El Colegio de México.

Gereffi, Gary G. 1994. "Mexico's Maquiladoras in the Context of Economic Globalization." Paper presented at the workshop "The Maquiladoras in Mexico: Present and Future Prospects of Industrial Development," El Colegio de la Frontera Norte, Tijuana, May 23–25.

González, Soledad, Olivia Ruiz, Laura Velasco, and Ofelia Woo, eds. 1995. *Mujeres, migración y maquila en la frontera norte*. Mexico City: El Colegio de México/El Colegio de la Frontera Norte.

González Arroyo, Michele, Garrett Brown, Simone Brumis, Elizabeth Knight, and Timothy Takaro. 1996. "The CAFOR Survey of Maquiladora Workers on Occupational Health and Safety in Tijuana and Tecate, Mexico." Berkeley, Calif.: Maquiladora Health and Safety Support Network.

González Block, Miguel Ángel. 1996. "La salud reproductiva de las trabajadoras de la maquiladora de exportación en Tijuana, Baja California: diagnóstico para las políticas de salud." Research report presented to the Instituto Nacional de Salud Pública, El Colegio de la Frontera Norte, and Fundación Mexicana para la Salud.

————. 2001. "Salud reproductiva de las trabajadoras de la maquila de exportación en Tijuana: diagnóstico y retos para las políticas de salud." In *Encuentros y desencuentros en la salud reproductiva: políticas públicas, marcos normativos y actores sociales*, edited by J.G. Figueroa and C. Stern. Mexico City: El Colegio de México.

González de la Rocha, Mercedes. 2000. *Private Adjustments: Household Responses to the Erosion of Work.* New York: Bureau for Development Policy, Social Development and Poverty Elimination Division, United Nations Development Programme.

Grijalva, Gabriela. 1996. "Empleo femenino: análisis de la encuesta estatal de empleo en Sonora, 1995." Hermosillo: El Colegio de Sonora. Draft.

Guendelman, Sylvia, and Mónica Jasís. 1993. "The Health Consequences of Maquiladora Work: Women on the U.S.-Mexican Border," *American Journal of Public Health* 83: 37–44.

Guendelman, Sylvia, Steven Samuels, and Martha Ramírez. 1998. "Women Who Quit Maquiladora Work on the U.S.-Mexico Border: Assessing Health, Occupation, and Social Dimensions in Two Transnational Electronics Plants," *American Journal of Industrial Medicine* 33: 501–509.

Harlow, Siobán D., Leonor Cedillo, Jerod N. Scholten, David Sánchez, and Roberto Sánchez. 1999. "The Prevalence of Musculoskeletal Complaints among Women in Tijuana: Demographic and Occupational Risk Factors," *International Journal of Occupational and Environmental Health* 5: 267–75.

Hendricks, Katherine A., J. Scott Simpson, and Russell D. Larsen. 1999. "Neural Tube Defects along the Texas-Mexico Border, 1993–1995," *American Journal of Epidemiology* 149: 1119–27.

Hertel, Shareen. 2002. "Campaigns to Protect Human Rights in Mexico's Maquiladoras: Current Research Findings," *Institute of Latin American Studies Newsletter* (Columbia University) 1: 6–9.

Hotaling, A. Caroline. 1999. "Tackling Environmental Health Problems on the U.S.-Mexico Border: A Case Study," *Borderlines* 7, no 3: 1–4.

Hovell, Melbourne, Carol Sipan, Richard Hofstetter, Barbara DuBois, Andrew Krefft, John Conway, Mónica Jasís, and Hope L. Isaacs. 1988. "Occupational Health Risks for Mexican Women: The Case of the Maquiladora along the Mexican-United States Border," *International Journal of Health Services* 18: 617–27.

Iglesias, Norma. 1985. *La flor más bella de la maquiladora.* Mexico City: Secretaría de Educación Pública/Centro de Estudios Fronterizos del Norte de México.

IMSS (Instituto Mexicano del Seguro Social). 2001. *Memoria estadística, 2001. Salud en el trabajo.* Mexico City: IMSS.

INEGI (Instituto Nacional de Estadística, Geografía e Informática). 1994. *Estadísticas históricas de México.* Vol. 1. Aguascalientes: INEGI.

————. 1997. *Encuesta nacional de empleo urbano 1995.* Aguascalientes: INEGI.

————. 2001. *Encuesta nacional de empleo y seguridad social 2000.* Aguascalientes: INEGI.

Jasís, Mónica, and Sylvia Guendelman. 1993. "Maquiladoras y mujeres fronterizas: beneficio o daño a la salud obrera," *Salud Pública Mexicana* 35: 620–29.

Kamel, Rachael, and Anya Hoffman A., eds. 1999. *The Maquiladora Reader: Cross-Border Organizing since NAFTA.* Philadelphia, Penn.: American Friends Service Committee.

Kaplan, F.M., J.W. Bush, and Charles C. Berry. 1976. "Health Status: Types of Validity and the Index of Well Being," *Health Services Research* 2: 478–507.

Karasek, Robert A. 1979. "Job Demands and Job Decision Latitude, and Mental Strain: Implications for Job Redesign," *Administrative Science Quarterly* 24: 285–308.

Karasek, Robert A., and Töres Theorell. 1990. *Healthy Work: Stress, Productivity and the Reconstruction of Working Life.* New York: Basic Books.

Kopinak, Kathryn. 1996. *Desert Capitalism: Maquiladoras in North America's Western Industrial Corridor.* Tucson: University of Arizona Press.

Lafourcade, Oliver, Marcel Giugale, and Vinh H. Nguyen. 2001. *A Comprehensive Development Agenda for the New Era.* Washington, D.C.: World Bank.

Landsbergis, Paul. A., and M.C. Hatch. 1996. "Psychosocial Work Stress and Pregnancy-Induced Hypertension," *Epidemiology* 7, no. 4: 346–51.

Marcoux, Sylvie, Sylvie Bérubé, Chantal Brisson, and Myrto Mondor. 1999. "Job Strain and Pregnancy-Induced Hypertension," *Epidemiology* 10, no. 4: 376–82.

Márquez, Margarita, and Josefina Romero. 1988. "El desgaste de las obreras de la maquila eléctrico-electrónica," *Salud Problema* 14: 9–24.

Meservy, Darlene, Anthony Suruda, Donald Bloskwich, Jeffrey Lee, and Mark Dumas. 1997. "Ergonomic Risk Exposure and Upper-Extremity Cumulative Trauma Disorders in a Maquiladora Medical Devices Manufacturing Plant," *Journal of Occupational and Environmental Medicine* 39: 767–73.

Meza E., L. Barraza, G. Martínez, V. Fernández, E. Ramos-Jaquez, C. Cano-Vargas, A. Valdez-Torres, and R. Izaguirre. 1995. "Gestational Diabetes in a Mexican-US Border Population: Prevalence and Epidemiology," *Revista de Investigación Clínica* 47, no. 6: 433–38.

Mouré-Eraso, Rafael, Meg Wilcox, Laura Punnett, Leslie MacDonald, and Charles Levenstein. 1994. "Back to the Future: Sweatshop Conditions on the Mexico-U.S. Border. Part I. Community Health Impact of Maquiladora Activity," *American Journal of Industrial Medicine* 25: 311–24.

————. 1997. "Back to the Future: Sweatshop Conditions on the Mexico-U.S. Border. Part II. Occupational Health Impact of Maquiladora Industrial Activity," *American Journal of Industrial Medicine* 31: 587–99.

Mummert, Gail. 1996. "Cambios en la estructura y organización familiares en un contexto de emigración masculina y trabajo asalariado femenino: estudio de caso en un valle agrícola de Michoacán." In *Hogares, familias:*

desigualdad, conflicto, redes solidarias y parentales, edited by María de la Paz López. Mexico: INEGI/SOMEDE.

Nickey, Lawrence. 1992. "The US-Mexico Border: Environmental Squalor Threatens Public Health," *Internist* 35: 14–16.

———. 1999. "Curso de vida femenino y conceptualización social de la salud reproductiva." In *Género, familia y conceptualización de la salud reproductiva en México*, edited by N. Ojeda. Tijuana: El Colegio de la Frontera Norte.

O'Neill, Rory. 1999. *Europe under Strain: A Report on Trade Union Initiatives to Combat Workplace Musculoskeletal Disorders*. Brussels: European Trade Union Technical Bureau for Health and Safety.

Ong, Aihwa. 1987. *Spirits of Resistance and Capitalist Discipline: Factory Women in Malaysia*. Albany: State University of New York Press.

Phillips, Margaret, and Jorge Salmerón. 1992. "Diabetes in Mexico: A Serious and Growing Problem," *World Health Statistics Quarterly* (Rapport Trimestriel de Statistiques Sanitaires Mondiales) 45, no. 4: 338–46.

Punnett, Laura, and Robin Herbert. 2000. "Work-Related Musculoskeletal Disorders: Is There a Gender Differential, and If So, What Does It Mean?" In *Women and Health*, edited by Marlene B. Goldman and Maureen C. Hatch. San Diego, Calif.: Academic Press.

Quintana, Penelope JE, Maura Patricia García, Martha Ramírez-Zetina, Teresa Dodd-Butera, and Audrey Spindler. n.d. "Identification of Environmental and Nutritional Risk Factors for Anencephaly along the California/Baja California Border." Research Report, Border XXI Project EH98-1.

Radloff, Lenore Sawyer. 1977. "The CES-D Scale: A Self Report Depression Scale for Research in the General Population," *Applied Psychological Measurement* 1: 385–401.

Saint-Germain, Michelle, Jill de Zapién, and Catalina Denman. 1993. "Estrategias de atención a hijos de obreras de las plantas ensambladoras de la frontera," *Revista de El Colegio de Sonora* 5: 77–93.

Sánchez Roberto. 1987. "Contaminación de la industria fronteriza: riesgos para las salud y el medio ambiente." In *Las maquiladoras: ajuste estructural y desarrollo regional*, edited by Bernardo González-Aréchiga and Rocío Barajas Escamilla. Tijuana: El Colegio de la Frontera Norte/Fundación Friedrich Ebert.

———. 1990. "Hazardous Waste in the Maquiladora: The Case of Mexicali," *Natural Resources Journal* 30: 163–86.

Secretaría de Salud. 1999. *Encuesta Nacional de Nutrición, 1999*. Mexico City: Instituto Nacional de Salud Pública, Secretaría de Salud.

———. 2000. "Recursos y servicios del Sistema Nacional de Salud," *Salud Pública de México* 42, no. 6: 548.

Sen, Amartya. 1999. *Development as Freedom*. New York: Alfred A. Knopf.

Skolnick, Andrew A. 1995. "Along the US Southern Border, Pollution, Poverty, Ignorance and Greed Threaten Nation's Health," *Journal of the American Medical Association* 273: 1478–82.

Takaro, Timothy, Michelle González Arroyo, Garrett Brown, Simone Brumis, and Elizabeth Knight. 1999. "Community-based Survey of Maquiladora Workers in Tijuana and Tecate, Mexico," *International Journal of Occupational and Environmental Health* 5: 313–15.

Texas Center for Policy Studies. 1994. *Binational Study Regarding the Presence of Toxic Substances in the Rio Grande/Rio Bravo and Its Tributaries along the Boundary Portion between the United States and Mexico.* Austin, Tex.: International Boundary and Water Commission.

Torres Muñoz, M., P.C. Morales, C.M. Sías, and R.G. Villarreal. 1991. *Proceso de trabajo y salud en la industria maquiladora: el caso de una maquiladora textil.* Chihuahua: Facultad de Enfermería, Programa de Salud en el Trabajo, Universidad Autónoma de Chihuahua.

UNDP (United Nations Development Programme). 2002. *Annual Report.* New York: United Nations.

U.S. Bureau of Labor Statistics. 2001. *Current Population Survey.* BLS Web site, http://www.bls.gov.cps/cpsaat18.pdf, consulted August 2002.

U.S. GAO (U.S. Government Accounting Office). 1993. *U.S.-Mexico Trade: The Work Environment at Eight U.S.-Owned Maquiladora Auto Parts Plants.* Report to the Chairman, Committee on Commerce, Science, and Transportation, U.S. Senate.

Villegas, J., M. Noriega, S. Martínez, and S. Martínez. 1996. "Trabajo y salud en la industria maquiladora mexicana: una tendencia dominante en el neoliberalismo dominado." Master's thesis, Universidad Autónoma Metropolitana–Xochimilco.

World Bank. 1993. *World Development Report 1993: Investing in Health.* New York: Oxford University Press.

6

Maquiladoras, Air Pollution, and Human Health in Ciudad Juárez and El Paso

ALLEN BLACKMAN

Like most metropolitan areas on the U.S.-Mexico border, Paso del Norte—composed principally of Ciudad Juárez, Chihuahua, and El Paso, Texas—has experienced exceptionally rapid population and economic growth during the last several decades.[1] For example, between 1990 and 2000, Ciudad Juárez's population grew by about 50 percent (from 0.8 million to 1.2 million), while El Paso's population grew by about 16 percent (from 0.6 million to 0.7 million), rates approximately twice those for Mexico and the United States (Desarrollo Económico de Ciudad Juárez 2002; *Economist* 2001). The maquiladora industry is partly responsible for the region's growth. Ciudad Juárez is home to approximately 300 maquiladora plants employing over 250,000 workers, the largest maquiladora labor force on the border (Desarrollo Económico de Ciudad Juárez 2002).

Paso del Norte's growth has had serious environmental consequences, particularly for air quality. No other metropolitan area on the U.S.-Mexico border—and very few in North America—suffers from air pollution as severe as Paso del Norte's. Ciudad Juárez does not meet national ambient

Many thanks—but no blame—are due to Michael Batz, Joe Cook, Lisa Crooks, David Evans, Steven Newbold, Alejandra Palma, and Jhih-Shyang Shih for their expert assistance.

[1] Paso del Norte also includes southern Dona Aña County, New Mexico, which contains less than 2 percent of the metropolitan area's combined population.

air quality standards (Official Norms) for ozone, carbon monoxide, or particulate matter less than ten microns (PM10); and El Paso exceeds national ambient air quality standards for ozone, PM10, and carbon monoxide. An overwhelming body of evidence links such air pollution to respiratory and cardiovascular disease and to premature mortality (U.S. EPA 1999). In addition, air pollution damages visibility, materials, and agriculture. Surveys show that Paso del Norte's residents are more concerned about air pollution than any of the region's other environmental problems (Joint Advisory Committee 1999).

This chapter examines the link between Paso del Norte's air pollution and its maquiladoras. To what extent are maquiladoras responsible for this pollution? What impacts does it have on human health? Are the poor disproportionately affected? Unfortunately, little reliable publicly available data exist to answer these questions. This chapter takes a first step toward filling this gap by marshalling two types of evidence. First, we use a publicly available sector-level emissions inventory for Ciudad Juárez to determine the importance of all industrial facilities (including maquiladoras) as a source of air pollution. Second, we use original plant-level data on two maquiladoras to better understand the impacts of maquiladora air pollution on human health. Specifically, we use a series of computational models to estimate health damages attributable to air pollution from these plants, we compare these damages to estimates for non-maquiladora polluters, and we use regression analysis to determine whether the poor suffer disproportionately from maquiladora air pollution. Two important caveats are in order: The two maquiladora plants for which we estimate health damages were selected for idiosyncratic reasons, and therefore they may not be particularly representative. Also, our plant-level maquiladora emissions data are estimated, not measured. Hence care must be exercised in interpreting the results.

Nevertheless, the broad message of this analysis is fairly clear. Air pollution from maquiladoras has serious consequences for human health, including respiratory disease and premature mortality. However, maquiladoras are clearly not the leading causes of air pollution in Paso del Norte. Moreover, most maquiladoras are probably less important sources of dangerous air pollution than at least one notoriously polluting Mexican-owned industry. Finally, we find no evidence to suggest that maquiladora air pollution affects the poor disproportionately.

The remainder of the chapter is organized as follows. The next section presents sector-level emissions inventory data. The following section describes the sample plants and the models used to estimate health damages, and presents the results of the modeling exercise and the environmental justice analysis. The last section summarizes and concludes.

EVIDENCE FROM SECTOR-LEVEL EMISSIONS DATA

The best available emissions inventory for Ciudad Juárez is the 1996 National Information System for Fixed Sources (SNIFF) for the state of Chihuahua (Gobierno del Estado de Chihuahua et al. 1998). Unfortunately, these data are problematic. Although plant-level data exist, only data aggregated to the level of the industry subsectors are publicly available. Also, questions have been raised about the reliability of the data. Nevertheless, there is a general consensus that the SNIFF provides a good "back of the envelope" indication of the relative importance of different types of emissions sources.

The publicly available SNIFF data provide information on emissions of five different pollutants—particulate matter (PM), sulfur dioxide (SO_2), carbon monoxide (CO), nitrogen oxides (NOx), and hydrocarbons (HC)—from four different sectors—industry, services, transportation, and soils—and thirty-four subsectors. These data clearly show that industry is not a leading source of air pollution (see table 6.1). Industry only accounts for 17 percent of total SO_2 emissions, 5 percent of total NOx emissions, 3 percent of total hydrocarbon emissions, and less than 1 percent of total PM emissions.

A caveat is in order with regard to particulate matter. Although soil from wind erosion and unpaved roads is listed as the source of 96 percent of total PM emissions, this statistic may overstate this source's importance as a human health hazard. PM from soils is principally composed of large particulates that are relatively benign epidemiologically. Smaller particulates related to combustion are much more dangerous because they are inhaled deeply into the lungs (Cifuentes et al. 2000; Laden et al. 2000). But note that even if particulate matter from soil is excluded, industry is still a relatively minor source of PM emissions, accounting for just 14 percent of remaining emissions.

Even within the industry subsector, maquiladoras are not the leading source of two of the SNIFF air pollutants. Table 6.2 shows the contribution of various industrial subsectors and brick kilns to total emissions. (For reasons that are not clear, SNIFF categorizes brick making as a service activity, not an industrial activity.) Although the SNIFF data do not differentiate

Table 6.1. Sectoral Contribution to Air Pollution in Ciudad Juárez (percentages)

				Pollutant			
Sector	PM	SO$_2$	CO	NO$_x$	HC	All
Industry	0%	17%	0%	5%	3%	1%
Services	1	44	0	3	25	4
Transport	2	38	99	92	72	88
Soil: wind erosion	31	0	0	0	0	2
Soil: unpaved roads	65	0	0	0	0	5
All	100	100	100	100	100	100
Total (tons)	46,607	4,146	452,760	26,115	76,132	605,760

Source: Sistema Nacional de Información de Fuentes Fijas (SNIFF) 1996, as reported in Gobierno del Estado de Chihuahua et al. 1998.

between maquiladoras and non-maquiladoras, we can be certain that maquiladoras are not involved in brick making which, as discussed below, comprises small-scale Mexican family-owned firms.[2] Indeed, as table 6.2 shows, brick kilns are the leading source of both PM and SO_2.

EVIDENCE FROM A PLANT-LEVEL MODEL OF HEALTH DAMAGES

This section presents estimates of health damages from two maquiladoras and an indigenous Mexican industry. The first maquiladora is an American-owned gray-iron foundry that produces table bases for restaurant and hospitality industries. It employs about 140 workers and is located in an industrial park called Gema II in a densely populated central section of Ciudad Juárez (figure 6.1). The second maquiladora is a Belgian-owned chemical plant that mainly produces hydrofluoric acid. It employs about 150 workers and is located in the sparsely populated southern section of Ciudad Juárez (figure 6.1).

The indigenous Mexican industry is a collection of approximately 350 tiny family-owned brick kilns. The typical brick kiln is a ten-meter-square primitive adobe structure that holds 10,000 bricks, employs five or six people, and is fired two to three times a month with scrap wood, sawdust, and other rubbish (Blackman and Bannister 1997). The location of the traditional brick kilns exacerbates their adverse impact on human health. They are clustered in seven poor *colonias* (low-income residential neighborhoods) scattered throughout Ciudad Juárez (figure 6.1).[3]

Sample Selection

The two maquiladoras in our sample were selected on the basis of two criteria. First, they are reputed to be leading sources of some air pollutants. Second, we were able to gather the data needed to estimate their emissions. Some brief additional explanation may be helpful.

We began the process of selecting maquiladoras for this study with a list of approximately two dozen of the principal industrial sources of air

---

[2] We can also be certain that they are not involved in energy generation, which is a state-owned activity.

[3] The brick-making colonias are Anapra, División del Norte, Fronteriza Baja, Kilómetro 20, México 68, Satélite, and Waterfill. When brick makers squatted in these colonias twenty-five or thirty years ago, all were situated on the outskirts of the city. Today, however, most have been enveloped by urban sprawl.

Table 6.2. Contribution of Industrial Subsectors to Air Pollution in Ciudad Juárez (percentages)

Industrial Subsector	Pollutant					
	PM	SO$_2$	CO	NOx	HC	All
Energy generation	2%	12%	2%	6%	0%	4%
Chemicals	7	15	4	3	0	5
Metallic minerals	3	0	12	1	0	2
Nonmetallic minerals	1	0	3	3	0	1
Wood products	0	0	0	0	0	0
Food products	0	0	0	0	0	0
Clothing	1	1	8	1	7	4
Construction products, various	0	0	0	0	1	0
Printing	0	0	19	0	1	2
Metal products	1	0	1	11	1	2
Construction products, medium life	22	1	40	44	36	27
Construction products, long life	7	0	9	30	3	7
Graphic arts	0	0	0	0	11	5
Others	2	0	0	0	0	0
Subtotal	46	29	98	99	60	59
Brick kilns*	54	71	0	1	40	39
Total	100	100	100	100	100	100

Source: Sistema Nacional de Información de Fuentes Fijas (SNIFF) 1996, as reported in Gobierno del Estado de Chihuahua et al. 1998.

Notes: n/s = not significant; n/a = not applicable; *classified as service activity in SNIFF.

Figure 6.1. Population, Maquiladoras and Brick Kilns in Paso del Norte

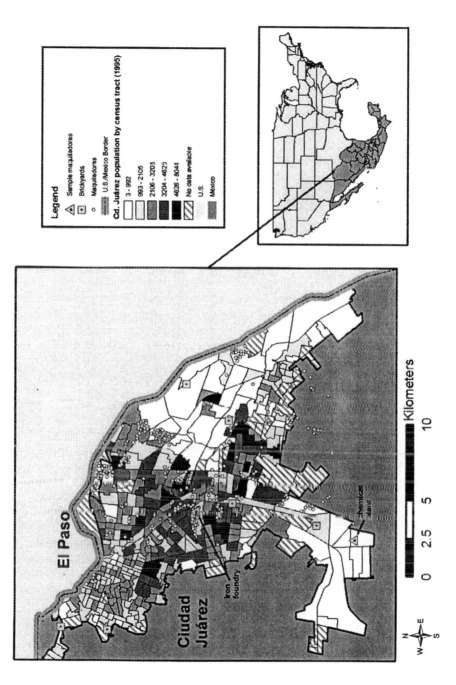

pollution. This list was compiled from informal information provided by local stakeholders. The next step was to estimate emissions for the plants on this list. We were not able to use existing plant-level SNIFF emissions data because, as noted above, these are not publicly available. Therefore, we relied upon U.S. Environmental Protection Agency (EPA) emissions factors—coefficients indicating emissions of various pollutants given detailed data on the scale of production, the type of technology, and the type of abatement equipment if any (U.S. EPA 1995). Based on engineering estimates and historical emissions data, these emissions factors are widely used by regulatory agencies around the world to estimate plant-level emissions. Unfortunately, the detailed plant-level data needed to estimate emissions using these factors are proprietary information and must be collected by interviewing plant personnel. We undertook a series of on-site and telephone interviews in the summer of 2001. Although most maquiladoras were unwilling to divulge detailed production information, the gray-iron foundry and the chemical plant described above were responsive.

Thus, because the two maquiladoras in our sample were selected from an informal list of the leading sources of air pollution in Paso del Norte, we can be fairly certain that they are more significant polluters than most other maquiladoras. However, among other leading sources of air pollution, these two plants are not necessarily representative since they were selected for idiosyncratic reasons.

Emissions and Abatement in Sample Plants

For reasons discussed below, we focus on only one type of pollutant: PM10. According to the U.S. Environmental Protection Agency (U.S. EPA 1995), the principal sources of PM10 emissions for iron foundries are, in order of magnitude: pouring and cooling of molten iron, handling of sand used to make molds, shaking sand from the molds, cleaning and finishing of cast iron, and operating an induction furnace. The bulk of the chemical plant's emissions come from the use of fluorspar, the principal material input into the manufacture of hydrofluoric acid. In particular, PM10 is emitted in drying, handling, and transferring fluorspar.

Unfortunately, information on the installation and use of pollution control equipment at our two sample plants is limited. While the two plants claim to use emissions abatement devices such as baghouses, regulatory inspection and monitoring data are not available, and there is no easy way to verify these claims. To account for this issue we present estimates of health damages given: (1) emissions that would result if the plants used no pollution control devices whatsoever, and (2) emissions that would result if they used all of the pollution control equipment that is standard in U.S. plants.[4] Given the claims of plant engineers and casual observation, the second scenario is probably more realistic than the first. Finally, we know from survey evidence that brick kilns typically employ no pollution control devices whatsoever (Blackman and Bannister 1997).

Methods

Although the plants in our sample emit a variety of pollutants, we have chosen to focus only on PM10 for several reasons. First, PM10 is generally thought to be responsible for a large proportion of the total noncarcinogenic adverse health impacts of air pollution (Pope et al. 1995). Also, data on the emissions of other types of air pollutants (such as toxics) from fixed sources are limited. Finally, the effects of PM10 on human health are relatively well understood.

We have also chosen to focus on only one category of adverse impacts of PM10: human morbidity and mortality. We do not consider the effects of PM10 on visibility, materials damages, or non-use values. Therefore, our estimates of the damages from industrial emissions may be thought of as a lower bound on the total value of the damages.

Estimating health damages from PM10 entails the sequential application of three models. First, we use an air dispersion model to estimate each source's contribution to annual average ambient levels of PM10 at several thousand receptor locations in Paso del Norte. Next, we use a health effects model to estimate the number of cases of human mortality and morbidity that result from this pollution each year. Finally, we use a valuation model to calculate the dollar values of these health impacts. This section briefly

---

[4] The "U.S.-level-of-control" scenario is constructed using the EPA's "Compilation of Air Pollutant Emission Factors (AP-42)" (U.S. EPA 1995). This document specifies what abatement equipment is typically used to control particulate emissions from different types of intra-plant emissions sources (such as boilers and transfer operations) at different types of plants, and also indicates the percent of particulate emissions eliminated. For example, according to the EPA, baghouses are used to control particulate emissions from induction furnaces at iron foundries, and they eliminate 80 percent of particulate emissions. Baghouses are the relevant control equipment for most of the intra-plant emissions sources at the iron foundry and chemical plant. Note, however, that fluorspar transfer operations are typically controlled by covers and additives to the fluorspar.

discusses each of these models. A more detailed description of the models is available in Blackman et al. 2000.

Air dispersion model. We use the EPA's Industrial Source Complex Short Term 3 (ISCST3) air dispersion model to estimate annual average concentrations of PM10 from our sample plants at a rectangular array of 5,546 receptor locations in the study area. ISCST3 uses data on emissions source characteristics (such as smokestack height, emissions velocity, and emissions temperature), local meteorology, and local topography to estimate annual concentrations of emissions in a defined study area. Where certain data on emissions source characteristics are confidential, we use publicly available data from U.S. facilities of the same type (U.S. EPA 2002).

Health effects model. To estimate exposure to the PM10 produced by our sample sources, we use population data at the survey unit level, that is, at the level of "basic geostatistical areas" (AGEBs) in Ciudad Juárez and census tracts in El Paso. We assign the inhabitants of each survey unit a distance-weighted average of PM10 concentrations predicted by the ISCST3 model at all model receptor points within 800 meters of the survey unit centroid. Next we estimate the health effects of this exposure using concentration-response (CR) coefficients reported in the epidemiological literature. CR coefficients indicate the expected change in the number of cases of some health endpoint due to a marginal change in the ambient concentration of a particular air pollutant. We model the nine different health endpoints: mortalities, respiratory hospital admissions, emergency room visits, adult respiratory symptom days, adult restricted activity days, asthma attacks, child chronic bronchitis, child chronic cough cases, and adult chronic bronchitis cases. We make the conventional assumption that these health effects are linear functions of PM10 exposure levels (see, for example, U.S. EPA 1999).

Valuation model. To estimate the monetary values of health damages, we use a combination of the following: (1) willingness to pay (WTP) figures from the economic literature, that is, a "benefits transfer" approach; (2) estimates of the value of work loss days based on average daily wages in Ciudad Juárez and El Paso; and (3) estimates of health care costs based on the value of work loss days. Since over three-quarters of the total estimated damages arise from mortality, by far the most important parameter in the valuation model is the value of a statistical life. We use a discrete distribution—US$1.9 million (33 percent), $3.8 million (34 percent), and $7.5 million (33 percent)—from Hagler Bailly, Inc. (1991). This distribution is relatively conservative. For example, the EPA used a mean value of $4.8 million per mortality avoided to assess the benefits of the Clean Air Act (see U.S. EPA 1999: appen. H-8). The parameters used to value respiratory hospital admissions and emergency room visits are estimates of medical costs associated with each endpoint. These estimates are based on workday-equivalent conversion factors taken from a study for Santiago, Chile (World Bank 1994). We also use conversion factors to estimate the value of child chronic cough.

Unfortunately, to our knowledge, direct estimates of Mexican WTP for reductions in the health endpoints considered in this chapter are not yet available. Therefore, we use WTP parameters (for adult respiratory symptom days, adult reduced activity days, asthma attacks, and chronic bronchitis) that are based on American studies. But given that average income adjusted for purchasing power parity is approximately four times higher in the United States than in Mexico, Mexican WTP may be lower than American WTP. Cultural factors may also cause WTP in the two countries to differ. To account for international differences in WTP, we use sensitivity analysis. For each health impact, we use three different values for Mexican WTP based on three different assumptions about the elasticity of WTP with respect to income, a parameter we will call E.[5] We assume alternatively that $E = 1$, $E = 0.33$, and $E = 0$. For example, $E = 0.33$ implies that if average per capita income adjusted for purchasing power parity is 10 percent lower in Ciudad Juárez than in El Paso, then WTP is 3.3 percent lower. An E between 0.2 and 0.5 is supported by some studies that look at differences in WTP across income groups (Alberini et al. 1997; Loehman et al. 1979). Thus the middle value of the discrete probability distribution we use to value premature mortality in Mexico is $3.80 million assuming $E = 0$, $2.42 million assuming $E = 0.33$, and $0.97 million assuming $E = 1$.

Finally, we use Monte Carlo analysis to account for uncertainty associated with the parameterization of our air dispersion, health impacts, and benefits valuation models. That is, where data on probability distributions are available, we treat model parameters as distributions and we use these

---

[5] The empirical foundations of this second-best approach to estimating international differences in WTP can be legitimately questioned. Evidence on the topic is sparse. Chestnut, Ostro, and Vichit-Vadakan (1999) find that median WTP to avoid respiratory symptoms is higher in Thailand than one would expect from U.S. studies. See also Alberini et al. 1997.

Table 6.3. Annual Health Damages Due to Estimated PM10 Emissions from Iron Foundry Maquiladora
(mean value of predicted number of cases)

Health Endpoint	No Controls			U.S.-Level Controls			Average
	Ciudad Juárez	El Paso	Total	Ciudad Juárez	El Paso	Total	Total
Mortality	1.44	0.15	1.59	0.09	0.01	0.10	0.85
Respiratory hospital admissions	26.69	2.14	28.83	1.58	0.15	1.73	15.28
Emergency room visits	61.70	4.93	66.63	3.66	0.36	4.02	35.33
Adult respiratory symptom days	38,970.00	3,520.00	42,490.00	2,319.00	253.10	2,572.10	22,531.05
Work loss days	327.20	26.17	353.37	19.42	1.88	21.30	187.34
Adult restricted activity days	14,320.00	1,145.00	15,465.00	849.90	82.46	932.36	8,198.68
Asthma attacks	4,350.00	347.80	4,697.80	258.10	25.04	283.14	2,490.47
Child chronic bronchitis	165.40	10.63	176.03	9.77	0.77	10.54	93.29
Child chronic cough	191.60	12.32	203.92	11.32	0.89	12.21	108.07
Adult chronic bronchitis	9.70	0.88	10.58	0.58	0.06	0.64	5.61

Source: Resources for the Future (RFF) model.

distributions to generate (95 percent) confidence intervals for model outputs. To make the tables easier to digest, however, we only report the means of these distributions here.

Health Damages Estimates

Tables 6.3 and 6.4 present the annual health damages attributable to PM10 emissions from the two sample maquiladoras. The tables present the number of cases for two different emissions control scenarios—absolutely no emissions controls and U.S.-level controls—as well as the average number of cases for these two scenarios. Table 6.5 presents the health damages attributable to PM10 emissions from brick kilns which, as noted above, are uncontrolled. Finally, table 6.6 gives the annual dollar value of all of these health damages.

We begin with two fairly obvious points. First, not surprisingly, for both of the maquiladoras, the health damages (whether measured in number of cases or in dollars) from uncontrolled emissions are considerably higher than for controlled emissions. For the iron foundry, damages are approximately seventeen times higher for uncontrolled emissions than for controlled emissions. For the chemical plant, they are approximately fifty times higher. Thus it bears emphasis that the magnitude of the health damages from maquiladora emissions depends critically on the level of emissions abatement.

Second, for both plants, health damages in Ciudad Juárez are far greater than in El Paso. For the iron foundry, health damages in Ciudad Juárez are about ten times greater than those in El Paso. For the chemical plant, health damages in Ciudad Juárez are just over three times greater than those in El Paso. The extent to which each plant's emissions affect Mexicans as opposed to Americans depends on the plant's location, local weather patterns and topography, and the plant's emissions characteristics.

But these two points are relatively minor. The main question addressed by our health damages modeling is: just how significant are health damages attributable to maquiladora emissions? On the face of it, the damages are quite serious. Even if we assume conservatively that emissions are controlled at U.S. levels, the iron foundry is responsible for four emergency room visits, thousands of adult respiratory symptom days, and hundreds of asthma attacks every year.

If we assume that the level of pollution control is the average between the "no controls" and "U.S.-level-of-controls" scenarios, health damages are far more serious. In this case, the iron foundry is responsible for one

Table 6.4. Annual Health Damages Due to Estimated PM10 Emissions from Chemical Plant Maquiladora
(mean value of predicted number of cases)

Health Endpoint	No Controls			U.S.-Level Controls			Average
	Ciudad Juárez	El Paso	Total	Ciudad Juárez	El Paso	Total	
Mortality	8.78	2.59	11.37	0.17	0.05	0.22	5.80
Respiratory hospital admissions	162.50	35.97	198.47	3.23	0.71	3.94	101.21
Emergency room visits	375.70	83.15	458.85	7.46	1.64	9.10	233.98
Adult respiratory symptom days	233,700.00	58,610.00	292,310.00	4,641.00	1,154.00	5,795.00	149,052.50
Work loss days	1,992.00	441.00	2,433.00	39.56	8.68	48.24	1,240.62
Adult restricted activity days	87,210.00	19,300.00	106,510.00	1,732.00	379.80	2,111.80	54,310.90
Asthma attacks	26,480.00	5,862.00	32,342.00	525.90	115.30	641.20	16,491.60
Child chronic bronchitis	1,030.00	183.70	1,213.70	20.45	3.61	24.06	618.88
Child chronic cough	1,194.00	212.90	1,406.90	23.69	4.18	27.87	717.39
Adult chronic bronchitis	58.19	14.59	72.78	1.16	0.29	1.45	37.12

Source: Resources for the Future (RFF) model.

premature mortality, fifteen respiratory hospital admission, thirty-five emergency room visits, tens of thousands of adult respiratory symptom days, and thousands of asthma attacks every year. The value of all such damages is approximately US$3 million each year. Assuming a similar level of pollution control, the chemical plant generates $22 million worth of health damages each year.

Table 6.5. Annual Health Damages Due to Estimated PM10 Emissions from Brick Kilns (mean value of predicted number of cases)

Health Endpoint	No Controls		
	Ciudad Juárez	El Paso	Total
Mortality	14.1	2.6	16.70
Respiratory hospital admissions	262	37	299.00
Emergency room visits	607	85	692.00
Adult respiratory symptom days	376,600	59,300	435,900
Work loss days	3,216	448	3,664.00
Adult restricted activity days	138,000	19,240	157,240.0
Asthma attacks	42,680	5,950	48,630.00
Child chronic bronchitis	1,637	184	1,821.00
Child chronic cough	1,878	211	2,089.00
Adult chronic bronchitis	93	15	108.00

Source: Resources for the Future (RFF) model.

While these figures may be alarming for those unfamiliar with the devastating health impacts of PM10 pollution, they are not particularly meaningful from a policy perspective. To allocate scarce resources available for pollution control efficiently, policymakers need to understand how health damages from maquiladoras compare to damages attributable to other sources. We have two types of data that allow us to compare the likely magnitude of damages across different types of sources.

First, recall that the SNIFF emissions inventory discussed above clearly indicates that industry is not the leading source of particulate emissions in Ciudad Juárez. Rather, the leading sources are vehicles, unpaved roads, and soil erosion (table 6.1). Moreover, even leaving aside vehicles and soils, it is brick kilns—not maquiladoras—that are the most important single industrial subsector in terms of air pollution (table 6.2). That is, brick kilns emit more particulate matter than all other industrial plants combined.

Table 6.6. Annual Value of Health Damages Due to PM10 Emissions (1999 US$; mean values)

Pollution Source	Ciudad Juárez			El Paso	Total
	(E = 0)	(E = 0.33)	(E = 1)		(E = 0.33)
Iron foundry maquiladora[a]	4,026,550	2,569,450	1,037,100	422,310	2,991,760
Chemical plant maquiladora[a]	23,594,350	15,058,150	6,078,300	6,765,600	21,823,750
Brick kilns	74,210,000	47,360,000	19,110,000	13,410,000	60,770,000

[a] average of "no controls" and "U.S.-level-controls" scenarios.

Note: E = the elasticity of WTP (willingness to pay) with respect to income adjusted for purchasing power parity.

Given that vehicles and brick kilns emit far more combustion-related fine particulates than maquiladoras, we can be fairly certain that they inflict far more severe health damages.

Furthermore, additional health damage modeling confirms that PM10 from brick kilns is more damaging than PM10 from our two sample maquiladoras. Table 6.5 shows that brick kiln PM10 is responsible for approximately 17 premature mortalities and 300 respiratory hospital admissions each year, while the two maquiladoras in our sample combined—assuming the level of pollution control is the average between the "no controls" and "U.S.-level-of-controls" scenarios—are responsible for 7 premature mortalities and 116 respiratory hospital admissions each year. Total monetized health damages from brick kiln PM10 emissions are $61 million, compared to $25 million for combined PM10 emissions from the two maquiladoras (table 6.6).

One of the principal reasons that brick kilns inflict such serious health damages is that they lack smokestacks. Therefore, emissions are not dispersed by wind and they mainly boost PM10 concentrations within a half kilometer of the kiln. Unfortunately, these areas are densely populated, low-income residential neighborhoods (Blackman et al. 2000).

Environmental Justice

Does maquiladora air pollution disproportionately affect the poor? The answer depends principally on whether the pollution the maquiladoras emit settles in poor areas. To address this issue, we have constructed a geographic information system (GIS) for Ciudad Juárez that includes data from our ISCST3 model on how PM10 from our sample maquiladoras disperses throughout the region. The GIS also contains Mexican census data on the location of poverty in the city. We exclude El Paso from this portion of the analysis because Mexicans are the principal victims of air pollution from the sources in our sample, and because differences in Mexican and U.S. census data greatly complicate the analysis.

Figure 6.2 presents the spatial distribution of poverty in Ciudad Juárez measured as the percentage of the labor force in each AGEB earning less than two times the minimum wage. It shows that the poorer sections of Ciudad Juárez are mostly in the southern and western parts of the city. Figures 6.3 and 6.4 map concentrations of PM10 attributable to uncontrolled emissions from the two sample maquiladoras. They show that PM10 emissions from the iron foundry are most heavily concentrated in

Figure 6.2. Poverty, Maquiladoras and Brick Kilns in Paso del Norte

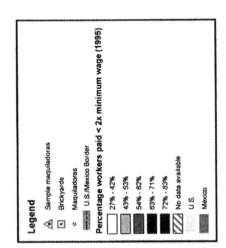

Legend

△ Sample maquiladoras
▣ Brickyards
○ Maquiladoras
━━ U.S./Mexico Border

Percentage workers paid < 2x minimum wage (1995)

☐ 27% - 42%
▨ 43% - 53%
▨ 54% - 62%
■ 63% - 71%
■ 72% - 83%
▨ No data available
☐ U.S.
▨ Mexico

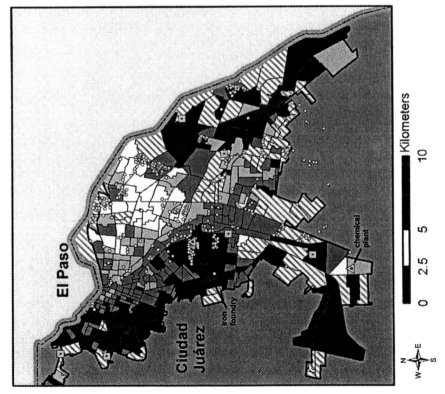

El Paso

Ciudad Juárez

iron foundry

chemical plant

N
W — E
S

0   2.5   5   10

Kilometers

Figure 6.3. Average Annual PM10 Concentrations Due to Iron Foundry Maquiladora Emissions (assuming no controls)

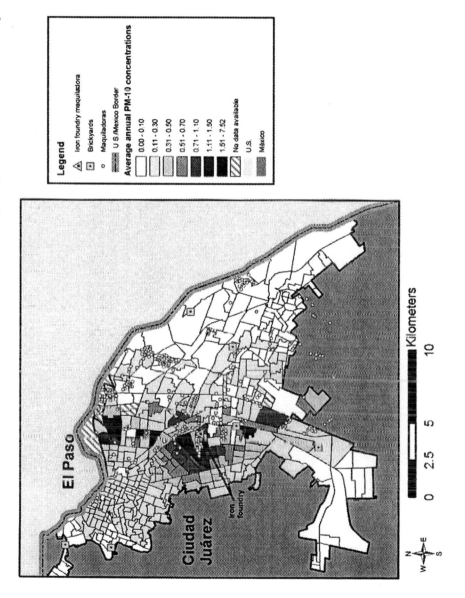

Figure 6.4. Average Annual PM10 Concentrations Due to Chemical Plant Maquiladora Emissions (assuming no controls)

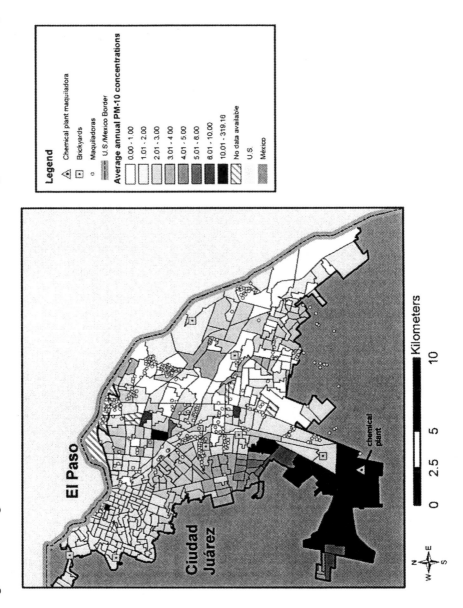

the northwest portion of the city, while PM10 emissions from the chemical plant are mostly concentrated in southwestern portions of the city. Both are relatively poor areas. Hence one might think that emissions from the two maquiladoras in our sample affect the poor disproportionately.

We use regression analysis to test whether this hypothesis is statistically valid. Taking AGEBs as our unit of analysis, we regress CONCEN-TRATION, the average annual PM10 concentration (in micrograms per cubic meter per year) attributable to an emissions source, onto POVERTY, the percentage of the labor force in each AGEB earning less than two times the minimum wage. Table 6.7 presents the regression results.

Table 6.7. Ordinary Least Squares Regression Results (dependent variable = CONCENTRATION [ug PM10/m³/year]; standard errors in parentheses)

Source	Controlled?	Constant	POVERTY
Iron foundry maquiladora	no	0.6379**	−0.5712†
		(0.1947)	(0.3289)
	yes	0.0195**	−0.0018
		(0.0074)	(0.0125)
Chemical plant maquiladora	no	12.2139*	−14.8264
		(5.5829)	(9.4306)
	yes	0.1602	−0.1642
		(0.0787)*	(0.1329)
Brick kilns	no	658.2924	2919.1870**
		(649.2084)	(1096.6330)

** significant at 1% level two-tailed test; * significant at 5% level two-tailed test; † significant at 10% level two-tailed test.

The regression results do not support the hypothesis that emissions from the two maquiladoras disproportionately affect the poor. The coefficient for POVERTY is only significantly different from zero in one of the four models: that for uncontrolled emissions from the iron foundry. However, the sign is negative. This implies that higher PM10 concentrations are typically found in wealthier AGEBs, not in poorer ones. Thus, overall we find no evidence that emissions from the two maquiladoras in our sample disproportionately affect the poor.

By contrast, for brick kilns, the coefficient on POVERTY is significant and positive, suggesting that brick kiln emissions do disproportionately affect the poor: higher PM10 concentrations are generally found in poorer AGEBs. This is undoubtedly because, as noted above, PM10 emissions from brick kilns mostly settle within a half-kilometer of the brickyards, areas that tend to be located in low-income residential neighborhoods (Blackman et al. 2000, and figure 6.2).

Note that the finding that the poor do not suffer disproportionately from maquiladora emissions does not appear to be driven by the idiosyncratic nature of our sample. As figure 6.1 illustrates, there is no obvious spatial correlation between the location of maquiladoras and the location of poverty in Ciudad Juárez.

CONCLUSION

We have used a limited data set—composed of a sector-level emissions inventory and original emissions data for a small sample of industrial facilities—to shed light on the links between maquiladoras, air pollution, and human health in Paso del Norte. We found that particulate emissions from maquiladoras undoubtedly have significant impacts on human health: collectively, these plants are probably responsible for dozens of cases of premature mortality and thousands of cases of respiratory disease each year.

However, particulate emissions generate health damages of similar magnitudes regardless of the source, and maquiladoras are clearly *not* the region's leading sources of particulates. That dubious distinction belongs to unpaved roads, vehicles, and brick kilns. Given that vehicles and brick kilns emit far more combustion-related fine particulates than do maquiladoras, we can be fairly certain that they inflict far more severe health damages. Finally, we found no evidence that health damages attributable to maquiladoras disproportionately affect the poor.

Do these results imply that policymakers and environmental advocates should not pressure maquiladoras to further control air pollution? Probably not. To use the scarce resources available for pollution control most efficiently, policymakers need to examine both the benefits and costs of pollution control. The evidence we have examined only suggests that the benefits of controlling emissions from maquiladoras are low relative to other sources. However, we have said nothing about the costs of pollution control.

Although an analysis of pollution control costs is outside the scope of this study—data on such costs are even more difficult to generate than data on emissions—a priori, there is good reason to suspect that control costs for maquiladoras are modest compared to other leading sources of fine particulate pollution. The reason is that control costs for brick kilns and vehicles are quite substantial when transactions and political costs are counted along with pecuniary costs. Complementary research has shown that the pecuniary costs of controlling emissions from all of the region's 350 brick kilns are reasonably low, on the order of US$20,000 to $200,000 per year (Blackman et al. 2000). However, the transactions costs incurred by regulators may be significant given the necessity of dealing with hundreds of firms that are tiny and informal. Moreover, the political costs of controlling brick kiln emissions would likely be quite high as well. Brick makers are among the most impoverished entrepreneurs in Paso del Norte—typically operating on profit margins of less than $100 per month—and, as a result, it has historically been difficult to muster support for stringent pollution control measures (Blackman and Bannister 1997). Put slightly differently, the political costs of enforcing the "polluter pays" principle in the brick-making sector may be substantial.

For similar reasons, the transactions and political costs of attempting to control emissions from mobile sources are likely to be quite high. Such sources are exceptionally numerous, and those that are the most polluting are typically owned by the poorest households. Moreover, the fact that so many of Paso del Norte's residents own cars implies that a sizable percentage of the region's residents have incentives to oppose drastic measures to control vehicle emissions.

Controlling air pollution from maquiladoras is likely to be straightforward by comparison. These sources are relatively large, limited in number, and decidedly not informal. Moreover, the owners' financial resources are relatively plentiful; at least, there is a perception that they have deep pockets. Thus transactions costs may be relatively low, and there is some hope that political costs may be low as well. The pecuniary costs of control will depend critically on whether the maquiladoras have already undertaken the pollution control investments required by law: the more investments have already been made, the more expensive it will be to further control emissions. Thus a key consideration in determining whether maquiladoras are an appropriate target for pollution control efforts is the extent to which they are complying with existing regulations. To the extent they are not, costs of control are likely to be relatively modest.

In conclusion, in this study we have tried to make use of sparse existing data, along with some limited original data, to shed light on maquiladora air pollution. As the above discussion suggests, further research on the benefits and costs of controlling emissions from a larger sample of emissions sources is needed. Such research would be greatly facilitated by the development and dissemination of a complete plant-level emissions inventory for the Paso del Norte air basin, along with plant-level data on abatement costs.

References

Alberini, A., M. Cropper, T. Fu, A. Krupnick, J. Liu, D. Shaw, and W. Harrington. 1997. "Valuing Health Effects of Air Pollution in Developing Countries: The Case of Taiwan," *Journal of Environmental Economics and Management* 34, no. 2: 107–26.

Blackman A., and G. J. Bannister. 1997. "Pollution Control in the Informal Sector: The Ciudad Juárez Brickmakers' Project," *Natural Resources Journal* 37, no. 4: 829–56.

Blackman, A., S. Newbold, J.-S. Shih, and J. Cook. 2000. "The Benefits and Costs of Informal Sector Pollution Control: Traditional Mexican Brick Kilns." Discussion Paper 00-46. Washington, D.C.: Resources for the Future.

Chestnut, L., B. Ostro, and N. Vischit-Vadakan. 1999. "Transferability of Air Pollution Control Health Benefits Estimates from the United States to Developing Countries: Evidence from the Bangkok Study," *American Journal of Agricultural Economics* 79, no. 5: 1630–35.

Cifuentes, L.A., J. Vega, K. Kopfer, and L.B. Lave. 2000. "Effect of the Fine Fraction of Particulate Matter versus the Coarse Mass and Other Pollutants on Daily Mortality in Santiago, Chile," *Journal of the Air and Waste Management Society* 50, no. 8: 1287–98.

Desarrollo Económico de Ciudad Juárez, A.C. 2002. "Estadísticas." http://www.desarrolloeconomico.org/eng/estal.htm.

Economist. 2001. "Between Here and There: Special Report on the US-Mexican Border," vol. 360 (July 7): 28–30.

Gobierno del Estado de Chihuahua, SEMARNAP, Gobierno Municipal de Juárez, and Delegación Federal de SEMARNAP Chihuahua. 1998. "Programa de Gestión de la Calidad del Aire de Ciudad Juárez 1998–2002." Mexico.

Programa de Gestión de la Calidad del Aire de Ciudad Juárez 1998–2002. Mexico.

Hagler Bailly, Inc. 1991. "Valuation of Other Externalities: Air Toxics, Water Consumption, Wastewater and Land Use." Unpublished report prepared for the New England Power Service Company, October.

Joint Advisory Committee for the Improvement of Air Quality in the Ciudad Juárez, Chihuahua / El Paso, Texas / Doña Ana County, New Mexico Air Basin. 1999. "Strategic Plan." http://air.utep.edu/bca/jac/jacsplan.html.

Laden, F., L.M. Neas, D.W. Dockery, and J. Schwartz. 2000. "Association of Fine Particulate Matter from Different Sources with Daily Mortality in Six U.S. Cities," *Environmental Health Perspectives* 108, no. 10: 941–47.

Loehman, E., S. Berg, A. Arroyo, R. Hedinger, J. Schwartz, M. Shaw, W. Fahien, V. De, R. Fishe, D. Rio, W. Rossley, and A. Green. 1979. "Distributional Analysis of Regional Benefits and Cost of Air Quality," *Journal of Environmental Economics and Management* 6, no. 3: 222–43.

Pope, D., M. Thun, M. Namboodiri, D. Dockery, J. Evans, F. Speizer, and C. Heath. 1995. "Particulate Air Pollution as a Predictor of Mortality in a Prospective Study of U.S. Adults," *American Journal of Respiratory Critical Care Medicine* 151, no. 3: 669–74.

U.S. EPA (U.S. Environmental Protection Agency). 1995. "Compilation of Air Pollutant Emission Factors (AP-42)." 5th ed. Vol. 1: "Stationary Point and Area Sources." Washington D.C.: EPA. http://www.epa.gov/ttn/chief/ap42/.

———. 1999. "The Benefits and Costs of the Clean Air Act 1990 to 2010." EPA-410-R-99-001. Washington, D.C.: EPA.

———. 2002. AIRS database. http://www.epa.gov.air/data/.

World Bank. 1994. "Chile: Managing Environmental Problems: Economic Analysis of Selected Issues." Washington, D.C.: Environmental and Urban Development Division, Country Department I, Latin America and the Caribbean Region, World Bank.

7

¿*Cuánto Cuesta?* Development and Water in Ambos Nogales and the Upper San Pedro Basin

ROBERT VARADY AND BARBARA J. MOREHOUSE

ISSUES AND CONTEXT

Development versus Environment: Roots of a Dialectic

In the United States and other industrialized parts of the world, until the 1960s economic development was generally perceived as a modernizing force that generated capital, wealth, and better living conditions. Of course, some of the costs of development were well known: unsafe or unhealthy conditions in the workplace, low wages, inequitable distribution of profits,

The authors are heavily indebted to the corpus of work that has preceded this study. This chapter draws heavily on previous work by the two authors and by Anne Browning-Aiken, a senior researcher at the University of Arizona's (UA) Udall Center for Studies in Public Policy. The authors are grateful for the help provided by Leah Stauber, a graduate research assistant at the Udall Center, and Robert Merideth, the Udall Center's assistant director. This effort could not have occurred without sustained support by several organizations: the Ford Foundation, the Morris K. Udall Foundation, the NSF-funded Sustainability of Semi-arid Hydrology and Riparian Areas (SAHRA) Project at the UA, the Holland-based Dialogue on Water and Climate, and the U.S. National Oceanic and Atmospheric Administration (NOAA). Finally, we note that our understanding of integrated water-management issues has benefited greatly from the global perspective added by participating in the UNESCO-based HELP (Hydrology for Environment, Life and Policy) and the DWC initiatives, both of which include the Upper San Pedro Basin.

and the disruptive consequences of boom-and-bust economic cycles. But the notion that industrial and urban growth were harming the natural environment and depleting finite resources was less well understood and appreciated.

The origins of environmental consciousness in Western societies are more than a century old. The pessimism of Thomas Malthus's treatise on population and food production (1798), utopian socialism of John Stuart Mill in *Political Economy* (1848), naturalism of Henry David Thoreau's *Walden* (1854), synthetical observations of George Perkins Marsh in *Man and Nature*, radical conservationism of John Muir, utilitarian forestry of Gifford Pinchot, and cynicism of Henrik Ibsen in his 1882 environmental play, *An Enemy of the People*, are often credited for yielding some of the earliest insights on the costs of unrestricted development. In the mid-1900s, forester and essayist Aldo Leopold, in his *Sand County Almanac* and other writings, was an influential interpreter and implementer of earlier ideas as well as an original theorist. This course of thinking arguably found full expression in Rachel Carson's 1962 classic, *Silent Spring*. In 1970, within a decade of that book's publication, passage of the National Environmental Protection Act, the creation of the U.S. Environmental Protection Agency (EPA), and the first large-scale mobilization of the public on Earth Day embodied this revisionism and firmly linked development and environmental quality (de Steiguer 1997).

Change, Vulnerability, and Risk: The U.S.-Mexico Border Region as a Laboratory

DEVELOPMENT AS A DRIVER OF CHANGE

Although many observers have seen the relationship of development and environment as an irreconcilable clash of values, a more nuanced interpretation is that development is a driver of environmental change—one of several such drivers. Such a view, which allows for inclusion of both natural and human causality, offers a useful way to analyze environmental impacts. This approach, an analogue of the scientific "state-pressure-response" mode of research, requires familiarity with the a priori physical and socioeconomic context and appreciation of the sources and nature of change. Only then can responses to stimuli be meaningfully evaluated (Kasperson, Kasperson, and Turner 1995). An especially useful feature of this technique is that it recognizes that each situation holds a unique capacity for vulnerability and risk.

In such a framework, given the extreme dependency on context, location is everything. But to be meaningful, case studies cannot be merely unique. They should exhibit characteristics and processes that can illuminate and inform situations elsewhere.

The area along the border separating the United States and Mexico (figure 7.1) offers numerous advantages for studying the tension between development and environment. First, since the 1942 initiation of the cross-border, labor-supplying Bracero Program, the region has been a cauldron of population growth fueled by manufacturing and trade and catalyzed by globalization. Second, the communities in which these changes have occurred lie in two countries with markedly disparate levels of economic prosperity and infrastructural capacity—or, put another way, this border is one of a few in the world that separate a developed and a developing nation.[1] Third, cultural, political, and business practices, on the one hand, and environmental sensibilities, on the other, are highly dissimilar and often incompatible, a factor that nearly always complicates the resolution of transnational environmental problems. Fourth, the physical environment of the region, which transcends the human-defined boundary, is arid to semiarid[2]—that is, it is water-short, vulnerable to climate variability, and prone to high-risk conditions. Fifth, by virtue of its sheer extension over 3,000 kilometers, the area is richly diverse and offers sites that show different types of development (commerce, industry, mining, agriculture, and urbanization) and various environmental responses (air and water quality, water availability, sanitation and public health, and natural habitat). Finally, in both the United States and Mexico, the phenomenon of public participation in environmental decision making has become more common and more significant (Liverman et al. 1999).

Why a Comparison?

The U.S.-Mexico border setting offers multiple opportunities to explore the environmental costs of aspects of development. To illustrate the variations that exist, this chapter compares two regions that are in close proximity to each other in the Arizona-Sonora portion of the border zone—Ambos Nogales and the Upper San Pedro River basin (figure 7.2).

---

[1] Although the North American Free Trade Agreement (NAFTA) has narrowed (halved, by some estimates) the economic gap between Mexico and the United States, Mexico's per-capita gross domestic product (GDP) remains just one-fourth that of its northern neighbor.

[2] Nearly everywhere, average annual rainfall is less than 300 mm.

Figure 7.1. U.S.-Mexico Border Region

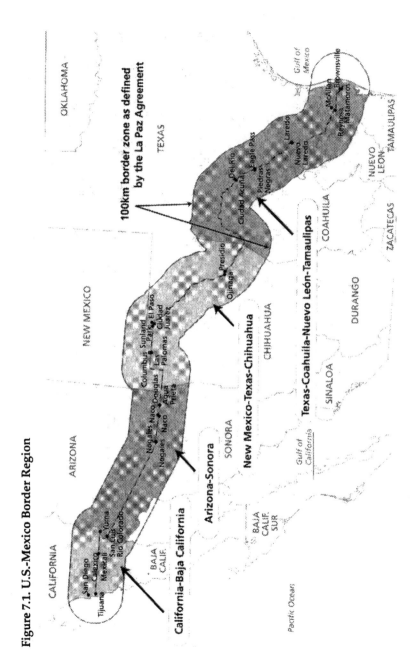

Source: U.S. EPA and SEMARNAT 2002.

**Figure 7.2. Arizona and Sonora, Showing Ambos Nogales
and the Upper San Pedro Basin**

Source: Adapted by the authors.

The first case, the metropolitan area encompassing Ambos Nogales—
literally "Both Nogaleses," the twin cities of Nogales, Arizona, and Nogales, Sonora—is an example of a fairly densely populated conurbation.
The two cities, with a combined population of about 200,000,[3] are characterized by a productive maquiladora sector, steady in-migration of laborers, substantial transboundary commerce, and considerable construction.
In particular, Nogales, Sonora, which has ten times as many inhabitants as
its cross-border neighbor, exhibits many of the problems found in other
U.S.-Mexico border cities. The most prevalent of these are poor access to
water and sanitation, susceptibility to chemical and biological contamination of water, worsening air quality, compromised public health, and insuf-

---

[3] Official census figures from 2000 placed the total at about 180,000 (Pick et al. 2002),
but most observers believe that the 164,000 figure for Nogales, Sonora, is an un-
derestimate.

ficient infrastructure. In short, Ambos Nogales typifies the primary and secondary effects of industrial growth and intense commerce on urban environment and health.

Just a hundred kilometers to the east, the binational Upper San Pedro River basin offers a sharp contrast to Ambos Nogales. Although there are two notable cities—Sierra Vista in Arizona and Cananea in Sonora—they are relatively small (populations of less than 40,000). As with Nogales, twin towns straddle the border—Naco, Sonora, and Naco, Arizona—but they are minuscule by comparison with Ambos Nogales, with a total population of fewer than 10,000 residents. Nor is this area dominated by maquilas. Rather, the two sides of the border feature very different economic drivers: land development and urban growth north of the border, and traditional mining and agriculture to the south. The consequences of development differ correspondingly. In the Arizona stretch of the basin, sustainable water use is the burning issue, with particular concern for protecting an important natural riparian strip along the San Pedro River. In Mexico, habitat protection is less of a priority. Instead, such fundamental issues as sufficient and safe drinking water for the mining town of Cananea and adequate water for *ejido* (communal) farmers in the basin are paramount.

The proximity of the two areas and the disparity in conditions and issues make for an effective and instructive comparison. Below, each of the case study areas is reviewed at some length, and the chapter closes by drawing some conclusions from the two instances. But first we discuss the concepts of sensitivity and vulnerability, two of the characteristics that enable us to distinguish between the impacts of development in the areas under consideration.

SENSITIVITY AND VULNERABILITY AS CONCEPTUAL FRAMEWORKS

Policymakers and managers have long recognized that significant water quantity and quality issues exist throughout the U.S.-Mexico border region (Utton 1984; Székely 1993; Mumme and Moore 1999; Sánchez 2002). The area's semiarid climate and concomitant scarcity of water pose challenges for water resources management even under the best of situations (Liverman et al. 1999). In both urban and rural areas, climatic conditions such as floods and droughts exacerbate these challenges. Typically, marginalized segments of local communities bear the greatest social costs. The concepts of sensitivity and vulnerability allow us to see how variations in the amount and quality of water may affect individuals and communities and, by extension, influence trends in the social costs of border development.

As developed within the climate-impacts research community, *sensitivity* refers to the extent to which humans or natural systems respond readily to physical or human-induced stressors. Thus, for example, surface water supplies—critical to sustaining populations in the semiarid U.S.-Mexico border region—may be very sensitive to variations in precipitation (that is, the amount of water flowing in a stream may vary relatively rapidly in response to changes in weather and climate), while some deep, confined groundwater supplies may be quite insensitive to such variations.

Vulnerability, by contrast, refers to potential or actual negative impacts imposed by external stressors. Again using the example of climatic variability, vulnerability of human and natural systems may be quite high in the event of local flash flooding or deep droughts. Additionally, vulnerability of communities includes an important social component: their relative wealth and resourcefulness. Cultures that rely on subsistence agriculture, for instance, barely survive during the best of times. When they are subjected to serious drought, they are far more vulnerable than societies whose income and sustenance derive from diversified strategies and benefit from access to markets. In general, it is virtually axiomatic that the poorer the community, the more vulnerable it is to variations from the norm. In the Arizona-Sonora border region, both sides are characterized by low income, inadequate infrastructure, a poor revenue base, and distance from loci of decision making. As a result, residents are often marginalized and therefore more susceptible to environmental stress (Ingram, Milich, and Varady 1994).

More specifically, drought conditions that started in the mid-1990s and persisted through 2002 have prompted intensive international negotiations to resolve issues over shortfalls in treaty-mandated delivery of water into the Río Grande/Río Bravo system (Kelly et al. 2002). U.S. interests in Texas have cited shortfalls in Mexico's deliveries through the Río Conchos as negative impacts on their water rights, while Mexico and Texas pressured New Mexico to assure deliveries at Elephant Butte Dam of waters from the upstream Rio Grande. Recognition that resolution of these issues would not occur immediately, but would depend on a return to higher precipitation patterns, highlights the extent to which—even in an era of hydraulic societies (Worster 1985)—water-management arrangements remain both sensitive and vulnerable to climatic stresses.

In Nogales, Sonora, these same drought conditions have prompted emergency delivery of water from Nogales, Arizona (Steller 2002). Long-standing cordial relations between the two neighboring cities and a history of sharing water and other resources in times of emergency provided a cultural framework that facilitated efforts to reduce the social costs of water scarcity (Ingram, Laney, and Gillilan 1995; Varady, Ingram, and Milich 1995). Illustrating the concepts of sensitivity and vulnerability, recurrent episodes of water shortages in Nogales, Sonora (such as in the summers of 1989 and 2002) are not merely a function of climatic conditions. Among the factors that play a role are insufficient water-delivery infrastructure, inequitable social and physical systems that favor wealthier households and businesses, and persistent lack of resources to keep up with rise in demand generated by the city's rapid population growth (Ingram, Laney, and Gillilan 1995).

In the Upper San Pedro River watershed, drought conditions also raised concerns about water supply and water quality, though not with the same immediacy as in Nogales. In this case, water quantity and quality are intimately related in that the amount of usable water depends directly on the quality of the water relative to its intended use. Thus social costs that arise from industrial impacts on local water resources remain a topic of considerable concern. Downstream in Arizona, issues of water quality and quantity linked with withdrawals for agricultural use remain hotly debated, particularly with regard to preservation of the riparian resources on both sides of the border. Extreme drought, such as that experienced from 2000 to 2002, serves to bring these issues even more to the forefront of local and regional discourse.

CONTRASTING CASES: AMBOS NOGALES AND THE UPPER SAN PEDRO BASIN

Ambos Nogales

PHYSICAL SETTING

Ambos Nogales—Nogales, Sonora, and Nogales, Arizona—is one of fourteen pairs of border cities recognized in the Border 2012 Plan, issued in mid-2002 (U.S. EPA and SEMARNAT 2002; see figure 7.1).[4] It is by far the largest of the three such pairs on the Arizona-Sonora border, these three pairs being the only ones situated in highlands. The two Nogaleses, at an elevation of 1,125 meters (3,690 feet), are within the Sonoran Desert life-

---

[4] The others are, from west to east: Tijuana–San Diego, Mexicali-Calexico, San Luis Río Colorado–Yuma, Naco-Naco, Agua Prieta–Douglas, Las Palomas–Columbus, Ciudad Juárez–El Paso, Ojinaga-Presidio, Ciudad Acuña–Del Rio, Piedras Negras–Eagle Pass, Nuevo Laredo–Laredo, Reynosa-McAllen, and Matamoros-Brownsville.

zone, in a narrow valley that stretches about 25 km north to south and is 0.8 km wide. Nogales, Sonora, especially, is dominated by populated hills to the west and east. The valley floor is bisected by the Nogales Wash, a small south-to-north tributary of the Santa Cruz River, which when it flows follows the general downward gradient into Arizona. The Santa Cruz continues northward until it merges with the Gila River, which eventually joins the Colorado River at Yuma.

The two communities lie in an area that is considered semiarid. Average annual rainfall is 430 mm (16 inches), but like all such relatively dry areas, the potential evaporation (the amount of water that would evaporate if it were present, or 2,280 mm per year) greatly exceeds actual rainfall. Normally there are two rainy seasons: one in winter and a more significant one in summer, with the monsoon, or *chubasco*, which provides about 60 percent of total annual precipitation and frequently causes serious flooding.

But despite the seeming predictability of the climate, a characteristic of semiarid zones is that both spatial and temporal (seasonal and annual) variability are high. The Nogales area is no exception, and the combination of unpredictability, steep hillsides, and human-induced changes to the landscape make the valley and its inhabitants especially prone to the effects of floods, particularly flash floods. At the other extreme, as already noted, droughts are frequent. Though they are less spectacular than flash floods, their effects linger over long periods and accumulate. Surface flows disappear during sustained periods of drought, adding pressure on the valley's already limited groundwater resources (Sellers, Hill, and Sanderson-Rae 1985; Ingram, Laney, and Gillilan 1995; Liverman et al. 1997).

Socioeconomic Setting

Assessing social costs of development—in the case of Nogales, primarily industrialization and associated commerce in individual border areas requires a foundation of basic socioeconomic trends. In terms of population, all the cities in the border zone have grown dramatically in the past century, especially since 1950 (figure 7.3). With the Mexican cities leading the way at twice the rate of U.S. cities since 1980, the total number of residents of the fourteen border-city pairs had risen from one million in 1950 to seven million by 2000 (Pick et al. 2002; Peach and Williams 2000). Ambos Nogales has followed this trend, with its population rising from under 20,000 in the 1940s to ten times that in 2000 (Pick et al. 2002). According to official census figures, in the 1990–2000 decade alone, Nogales, Sonora, grew from some 108,000 to 164,000 residents (figure 7.4).

Figure 7.3. Border Cities Population

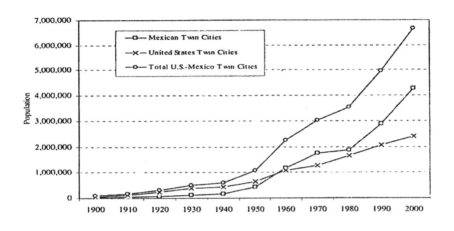

Source: Pick et al. 2002.

Much of the increase is attributable to in-migration. The maquila sector has grown markedly during the past several decades, and the assembly plants, manufacturing centers, and other facilities were unable to meet their employment needs relying exclusively on residents.[5] Thus, as in the other border twin cities, the gap was filled by workers moving north from elsewhere in Mexico. According to one set of projections, if recent migration rates hold, Nogales, Sonora, could be home to 297,000 residents by 2015 and 362,000 by 2020. Even under a low-growth scenario, the city could see some 190,000 residents by 2010 and 235,000 by 2020 (Peach and Williams 2000; Pick, Viswanathan, and Hettrick 2001).[6] The city has seen substantial border industrial development, and until the economic downturn of the post-"dot-com" collapse, it has hosted as many as eighty maqui-

---

[5] In that time the number of factories and of employees have quintupled, from approximately 500 and 100,000, respectively, to 2,500 and more than 500,000 (Lorey 1993).

[6] All of these projections are premised on the census figures which, as note 3 suggests, are considered by many as underestimates.

ladora plants. By 2002 that number had dropped to about sixty-five plants (figure 7.5), but these facilities still employed about 30,000 persons in mid-2002, or one in five workers (figure 7.6).[7]

Figure 7.4. The Population of Ambos Nogales

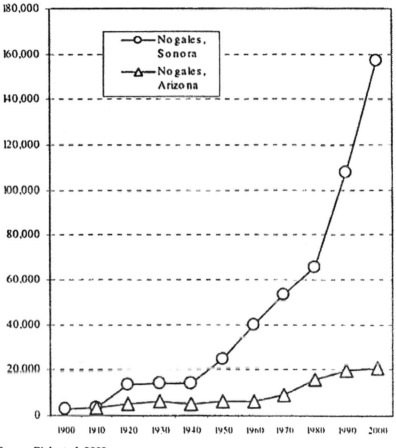

Source: Pick et al. 2002.

_____

[7] The number of employees was lower in 2002 than in the immediately preceding years, paralleling national and international economic trends (personal communication with V. Pavlakovich, December 4, 2002).

Figure 7.5. Number of Maquiladoras, 2002

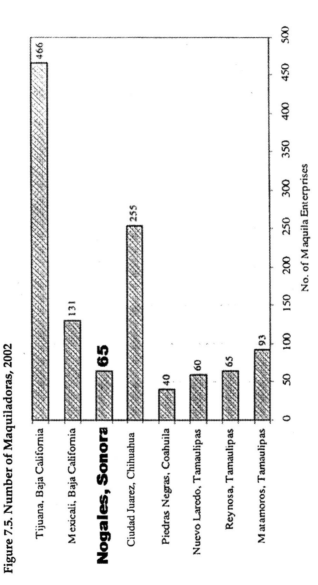

No. of Maquila Enterprises

Tijuana, Baja California — 466
Mexicali, Baja California — 131
Nogales, Sonora — **65**
Ciudad Juarez, Chihuahua — 255
Piedras Negras, Coahuila — 40
Nuevo Laredo, Tamaulipas — 60
Reynosa, Tamaulipas — 65
Matamoros, Tamaulipas — 93

Source: Pick et al. 2002.

Figure 7.6. Number of Maquila Workers, 2002

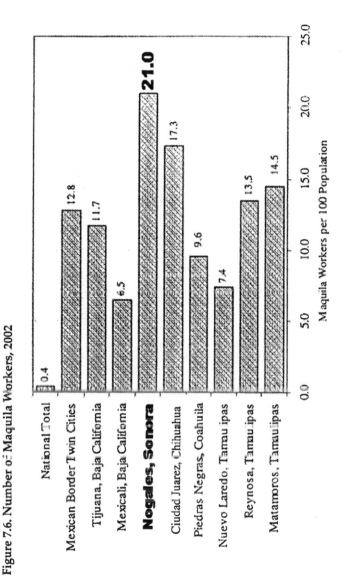

Source: Pick et al. 2002.

While the large increase in the number of inhabitants in Nogales, Sonora, has fueled the region's prosperity, it also has had numerous other impacts, both direct and indirect.[8] Many of the migrants settled in previously undeveloped parts of the city. These neighborhoods, most of them on steep hillsides, have been without the amenities usually provided by municipalities: paved streets, neighborhood schools, electricity, water, and sanitation. Without access to public services, the new residents have placed significant pressures on the natural resources of the area, particularly water. In addition, many migrant workers reside in substandard housing that is vulnerable to extremes of weather and is located near hazardous-materials sites. As a result, dwellers in unplanned settlements called *colonias* have been susceptible to water-borne and other contagious diseases, as well as to exposure to toxics and carcinogens (Varady, Romero Lankao, and Hankins 2001). Prevalence of illness has in turn strained the capacity of Nogales's public-health infrastructure. Other social and political problems have continued to plague colonias, including unemployment, inadequate child care, alcoholism and drug use, and lack of franchise and political voice.

In short, the 2001 report of the Good Neighbor Environmental Board noted that, largely due to the rise in the number of maquiladoras, "existing public infrastructures including water systems, sewage systems, and solid waste and wastewater treatment facilities have been unable to sustain the rapidly growing border populations" (GNEB 2001).

WATER ISSUES

Nogales was established as a sleepy, highland-desert trading outpost in 1859, shortly after the Gadsden Purchase. In the following 140 years, water occupied a dominant place in the development and evolution of the two Nogaleses. In particular, three major issues have been of concern to residents and officials: assurance of sufficient and secure quantities of water for domestic and commercial use; provision of safe, reliable drinking water; and possession of adequate sewage removal and wastewater-treatment capacity.

As Helen Ingram has written, "Water has the Midas touch. If a community has an ample, secure supply of water, it can grow and prosper" (1992). But as residents of Nogales have realized, the flip side of such opportunity is insecurity. The uncertainty brought by unreliable monsoons

---

[8] Víctor Urquidi provides a succinct overview of socioeconomic issues (2002).

and incomplete knowledge of available groundwater resources either dampens enthusiasm for development or entails unsustainable uses of nonrenewable resources.

QUANTITY

The Santa Cruz River, located just east of Nogales, supports some minor agricultural activity in Sonora as well as urban water uses for the city itself. The flows of the Santa Cruz and Nogales Wash, which are both intermittent (regular flows are present only in some stretches of the river) and ephemeral (the naturally flowing stretches dry up during dry conditions; other stretches flow only when precipitation occurs), are insufficient to fully meet all demands.

Beneath the surface flows of the Santa Cruz–Nogales Wash basin are sediments that include several groundwater galleries. While the extent and capacity of these aquifers are poorly known, they are being tapped on both sides of the border, at five different wellfields (figure 7.7).[9] What explorations have been done show that potential for new fields is lower in the more densely populated southern reaches of the valley than across the border in Arizona.

In view of the unpredictability, unreliability, and scarcity of water supplies, the cities of Nogales have diversified their sources for meeting their water needs. The communities are served by three major sources. The first is surface water and wells drilled into the alluvium of the Santa Cruz River; this source produces some 45 percent of the total supply. Hydrologists have determined that these aquifers are generally shallow and permeable. But while that means water can be more easily drawn from them, it also means that these water deposits are more vulnerable to climatic variations. In times of drought, such as those that have prevailed through most of the 1990s and into the early 2000s, these aquifers become easily depleted because of their shallowness and the high transmissivity of the alluvium.

The second source is wells drilled within the city limits, drawing from the Nogales Wash aquifer. The water from these wells accounts for about 15 percent of supply, and is handled as a reserve supply due to its poor quality: the primary input to this water source is fugitive flows from sew-

---

[9] The five wellheads are Mascareñas, Paredes, and Los Alisos in Sonora; and Santa Cruz and Potrero Canyon in Arizona.

erage and potable water pipes. Contamination from industrial activities is also a concern.

Figure 7.7. Ambos Nogales Water Basin

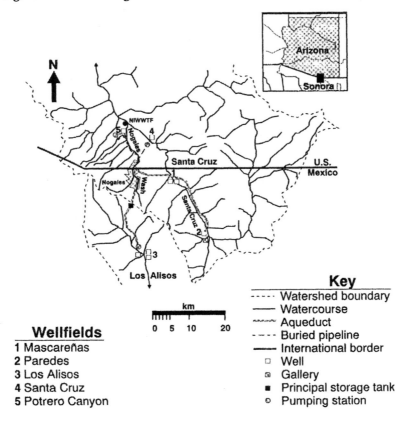

Source: Ingram, Laney, and Gillilan 1995.

The third source, which provides 40 percent of local supply, is wells drilled into the Los Alisos aquifer south of Nogales, Sonora (figure 7.7). This aquifer, which is located in the Río Magdalena watershed (not part of the Colorado River basin), is a fossil groundwater source that receives little if any recharge from precipitation. This source is viewed as being the most important source of future water for the Mexican city. Mexico's National Water Commission (CNA) has estimated that by 2015, Nogales, Sonora, will need an additional 14.3 million cubic meters (11,700 acre-feet) of water per year, to be developed from wellfields south of the city, between Agua Zarca and Cibutal.

Over the longer term, the Agua Caliente area, 44 km from the city, is viewed as an additional source. Delivery of water is primarily carried out by the Sonora State Water and Sewerage Commission (COAPAES). That agency supplies water to 64 percent of the residents in Nogales, Sonora, as well as 85 percent of the water used by residents in the surrounding area (Morehouse, Carter, and Sprouse 2000). In terms of delivery by type of use, 76 percent of water is delivered to domestic destinations, and the remaining 24 percent is delivered to industrial, service, and commercial users (Liverman et al. 1999). However, the steep terrain of some of the COAPAES service area poses challenges to achieving dependable water delivery. Only about 40 percent of the population receives water twenty-four hours a day; 36 percent receive water for shorter periods daily (Morehouse, Carter, and Sprouse 2000); and just 64 percent of city residents receive potable water (Liverman et al. 1999; U.S. EPA 1998). Between 74,400 and 128,000 people receive their water either through illegal connections (there are an estimated 3,000 illegal taps into the system, according to COAPAES) or water truck deliveries (Liverman et al. 1999; Morehouse, Carter, and Sprouse 2000). Overall, Nogales, Sonora, ranked third in 1996 among Mexican border cities in per-capita water use (ITESM 1999).

While the proliferation of maquiladoras has brought with it an influx of migrants who use water, residential use accounts for only a portion of the demand for water. Construction—of factories, houses, roads, and other infrastructure—is a large user of water, much of it for concrete. The manufacturing sector itself is a heavy consumer of water for processing, cleaning, washing, air conditioning, and other manufacturing-related tasks. Estimates of industrial use of water are difficult to come by, but with sixty-five plants operating and employing thirty thousand workers, it is clear that industry is a major consumer of valuable water. Finally, the commerce associated with industrial production also uses water. Thousands of trucks cross the border every day, moving manufactured goods and perishable commodities.[10] These vehicles require water for their radiators and their drivers.

---

[10] At Texas border crossings, the number of trucks more than tripled between 1995 and 2000; a similar trend certainly exists in Nogales (Sciara 2002).

QUALITY AND SANITATION

While the region's aridity and physiography pose the primary constraints to adequate water supplies, those features have less impact on the quality of the water. In Ambos Nogales, as in most intensely inhabited areas, human activity has been the major cause of deteriorating water quality. Several factors are easily identified, and they are the same ones that prevail in all the urban parts of the U.S.-Mexico border region. Population increase is by far the most important source of lowered water quality. In Nogales, the growth documented above has had several implications for water quality.

Infrastructural Constraints. Much of the water infrastructure dates from the early to mid-twentieth century, when many cities first emerged as viable urban centers. Water supply and sewer lines were constructed in those decades to accommodate very small populations. In Nogales, for example, the earliest water pumps were installed by a private company in 1896. Already by 1903, the water supply was determined to be inadequate. On the Arizona side, the city assumed responsibility by purchasing a private water company in 1911 and passed the first water system bond issue in 1920. It was only in 1946, however, that Nogales, Arizona, declared the city 100 percent sewered. South of the border, in Sonora, the Mexican government did not begin to construct a water delivery system until 1940, completing the work in 1949 (Sokota 1991; Varady and Gillilan 1993).

But even though the Nogaleses may have built their systems later than some of the older and larger twin cities, those systems are now five and six decades old. More significantly, they were constructed for cities that were much smaller in areal extent and population. The result—especially in Nogales, Sonora—is that for the past several decades, at an increasing pace, population has far outstripped the capacity of the water-delivery and sanitation systems. Thus, as the city expanded southward and into the surrounding hills (other areas were closed to expansion because of physical and political constraints), many parts of the community were not within the bounds of the original systems. In the unserved colonias, residents have either paid premiums to secure water or have compromised their health and that of their families by using unsafe sources. Further, even those areas that were covered by municipal supply and sewage lines long ago began overburdening the aged and deteriorating channels. In those instances, the combination of breakage and porosity of old pipes, poor maintenance, and infiltration of contaminants into water-supply lines has posed continuing public-health problems (Varady and Mack 1995).

Treatment of what sewage is collected is done entirely on the U.S. side of the border. By agreement between Mexico and the United States through the International Boundary and Water Commission (IBWC) and its Mexican counterpart, the Comisión Internacional de Límites y Agua (CILA), a single treatment plant has operated, north of the city of Nogales, Arizona, near Rio Rico (figure 7.7). The Nogales International Wastewater Treatment Plant (NIWTP) was constructed in 1951 and expanded twice, in 1967 and again in 1991. According to the terms of the binational arrangement, Mexico sends its raw sewage across the border for treatment and Arizona gets to keep the treated effluent. The treated water is used to sustain a riparian recreational area in the Santa Cruz River basin, a clear benefit for Arizona. But with drought-induced scarcity the norm for the past decade in Sonora, Mexico is conscious that it is relinquishing the rights to usable water. For decades, Mexico has considered building its own treatment plant south of the border. But because of the enormous cost of building a new facility and the added complication of a southward rise in elevation (the only possible sites for such a plant are south of town, entailing high pumping costs and the dangers of power outages), no such plant exists. Consequently, collected sewage is channeled up to 20 km, through the city of Nogales, Arizona, to the NIWTP (Ingram, Laney, and Gillilan 1995; Morehouse, Carter, and Sprouse 2000).

Industrial Pollution. We have already seen that the growth of the maquila sector and the concomitant rise in commerce and traffic have contributed to the area's unsustainable use of its limited water. Development also is responsible for an increase in environmental contamination that is exacerbated because of the inadequacy of resources applied to minimize, alleviate, or regulate pollution (Sánchez 2002).

The association between industrial production, environmental degradation, and human health is well established. In the border region, and in Nogales in particular, the chief sources of maquila-related contamination are: use of solvents, catalysts, pesticides, and other dangerous chemicals; generation of industrial wastes and by-products (solids, liquids, and gases); improper disposal techniques; and poor regulation of hazardous-materials handling, disposal, shipping, and accounting. The causes of concern are the destinations of the materials. Raw materials and production by-products are difficult to track and are not inventoried and monitored as strictly as necessary. The main weak points are the transportation and disposal processes. Without vigilant monitoring and accounting, chemicals are commonly disposed of improperly: into surface waters; directly into the ground, where they can contaminate aquifers; into containers, which are then illegally dumped or reused for storage; or into the air, as gases. Transborder shipments have proven especially difficult to track, as materials cross back and forth before and after processing. Identifying specific batches of substances through manifests has proven elusive, facilitating their disappearance and dissolution into the environment (Sánchez 1995; Varady and Mack 1995; Carter et al. 1996; Varady, Romero Lankao, and Hankins 2002).

The problems are worsened by serious institutional constraints. Each country features numerous jurisdictions, laws, rules, and bureaucracies that often work at cross-purposes. In the United States, the situation is complicated by the nation's multiple levels of government, with federal, state, county, and municipal agencies following different missions and priorities. Frequently, communication among responsible authorities breaks down; there are interagency rivalries; stakeholders disagree about strategies and goals; laws are contradictory or toothless; and funding is inadequate or misdirected.

In Mexico, the central government is paramount and applies national laws that are uniform. But the border is distant from the levers of power, and issues of importance to local residents are often ignored in the capital (Ingram, Milich, and Varady 1994). Financial resources—even if they were to be directed at border pollution—would be vastly insufficient. Additionally, most of the maquiladoras are foreign-owned (that is why they exist: to attract foreign capital). Strict enforcement of existing pollution statutes would present the Mexican government with the thorny problem of how to prosecute foreign nationals when a key national objective and the chief purpose of the North American Free Trade Agreement (NAFTA) is to attract more investment and promote economic development (Jacott, Reed, and Winfield 2002; Reinert and Roland-Holst 2002; Varady, Romero Lankao, and Hankins 2002).

Finally, there is the international boundary. The two governments and cultures have difficulty transcending this line on a variety of fronts, and nowhere is the barrier greater than on the issue of hazardous materials. Although the 1983 La Paz Accord addressed the issue and established a working group on hazardous materials, progress has been slow.[11] Ques-

---

[11] Still, these working groups have remained part of the binational landscape since 1983. They have been part of the successive border plans: the 1991 International

tions of provenance of toxics, verification of truck manifests, harmonization of laws and enforcement strategies, liability, insurance, institutional participation, and authority across the border have slowed efforts to reduce the presence of heavy metals, PCBs, and other contaminants in the environment (Jacott, Reed, and Winfield 2002).

POLICIES, COPING STRATEGIES, AND PROSPECTS

The changes caused by large social transformations such as the ones affecting cities in the U.S.-Mexico border region are extensive and pervasive. In the Ambos Nogales region, most environmental and water-related problems result from rapid industrialization, population growth, and rising commerce, mostly attributable to the inability of existing infrastructure and institutions to respond to the changes. Permanent water scarcity and climatic variability—coupled with the sheer magnitude and transnationality of the problems, cost of remediation, and insufficient financing—have obviated individual or purely local responses. Instead, decision makers, managers, community activists, and other residents have realized that solutions require large-scale, collective, ambitious, coordinated, institutional responses.

INSTITUTIONS

Until the advent of NAFTA in 1994, the institutional levers available were few and mostly inappropriate. The La Paz treaty provided a framework for U.S.-Mexico cooperation on environment, but little else. The 1991 Integrated Border Environmental Plan (IBEP) was a binational attempt to harness the treaty and arm it with specific actions. But suffering from lack of specificity, inadequate commitment, and few resources, IBEP failed to survive the first Bush administration, which ended in 1992 (Varady 1991).

The other principal instrument of water policymaking that preceded NAFTA is the mechanism of the International Boundary and Water Commission, working with its Mexican analogue, the Comisión Internacional de Límites y Agua. For more than a century, IBWC/CILA and the IBWC's precursor, the International Boundary Commission, have been the water-diplomacy agents of the U.S. and Mexican governments. The twin organizations have been responsible for regulating and facilitating navigation (when it existed); allocating water from the two main rivers, the Colorado

---

Border Environmental Plan, the Border XXI program, and, most recently, Border 2012 (U.S. EPA and SEMARNAT 2002).

and Rio Grande/Río Bravo; constructing and maintaining sewage treatment plants, dams, flood control, and hydroelectric facilities; and dealing with other issues relating to surface flows across or along the border. Via the superstructure of the 1944 water treaty between the two countries, IBWC and CILA have adopted a number of "minutes" that serve as amendments.

Over the years, IBWC/CILA developed a reputation as technocratic, top-down, secretive, and highly formal institutions that were slow to change and adapt (Ingram and White 1993). Until the mid-1990s, the advent of newer models of transboundary decision making that value openness, public participation, and environmental sustainability was largely overlooked by the IBWC and CILA (Milich and Varady 1999). In the Nogaleses, as elsewhere, as Francisco Lara-Valencia has observed, the "new regional scenario was clearly incompatible with an institutional framework that relied solely on the IBWC, in part because [of] the approach adopted by the Commission itself, but also in part because many of the new issues fell outside of its mandate" (Lara-Valencia 2002).

With the passage of NAFTA came a number of serious initiatives. The agreement itself included a negotiated side accord that created a trinational institution, the Commission for Environmental Cooperation (CEC), based in Montreal, Canada. The CEC was charged with assuring that trade did not adversely affect the North American environment. Through its policy-making board (the environmental ministers of the three nations), its secretariat, a three-country public advisory committee, and a series of charter articles, the CEC has sponsored research on trade-environment issues, responded to citizen-initiated complaints that environmental laws were being disregarded, and convened thematic conferences. The Commission lacks enforcement power and can only recommend courses of action to the governments of the three member nations. Further, the CEC is not focused on either of the two border regions (Canada-U.S. or U.S.-Mexico) but on the entire continent and coastal zones of North America. Because of this extensive purview, its limited budget, and its lack of power, the CEC's influence on the southern border as a whole or on particular twin cities such as Ambos Nogales has been minimal.[12]

In addition to the CEC, NAFTA parented a pair of institutions designed to address head-on the issue of inadequate environmental infrastructure.

---

[12] The next section will show, however, that in at least one region, the Upper San Pedro basin, CEC has effectively influenced public policy and mobilized stakeholders.

In early 1994, a parallel agreement between the presidents of the United States and Mexico established an environmental commission, the Border Environment Cooperation Commission (BECC), and a sister financing organization, the North American Development Bank (NADB). Unlike the CEC, these two institutions were chartered specifically to address problems in the U.S.-Mexico border region. And unlike the IBEP and its successor, Border XXI, the BECC and NADB were intended to improve water-related capacity, mostly by constructing new water delivery systems and sewage treatment plants. Their mission, as originally defined, was to remediate "problems of water pollution, wastewater treatment, municipal solid waste, and related matters."[13]

The BECC's role has been to identify areas of need, work with communities to generate technical proposals, provide technical assistance to improve the quality of those proposals; require that projects meet strict public-participation, transparency, and sustainability criteria; and certify worthy proposals. The NADB's task has been to secure low-interest loans to finance construction. The process, in place since early 1995, has been innovative but only modestly successful (Varady et al. 1997). BECC has certified dozens of important projects in poor communities on both sides of the border,[14] but financing by the bank has posed more of a challenge and has held up many of the approved projects. Resulting impatience on the part of residents and representatives of the two governments has led to some modifications to the original terms of the two institutions. In order to encourage more and quicker spending, the mandate was extended to include "all types of infrastructure projects," though still with a preference for water-related efforts. In addition, the border zone was expanded from its original width of 100 km to 300 km.

Until late 2002, Nogales had not been a notable beneficiary of the BECC-NADB process. Early on, Nogales, Sonora, submitted a proposal for an initial phase of a "Water Supply and Distribution Project," popularly known as the Acuaférico Project, at an estimated cost of US$39 million. The project, intended to benefit 215,000 residents, sought to solve the city's perpetual problems with water supply and distribution. Phase I was to rehabilitate the existing water lines, which currently leak some 40 percent of the water supply; construct 33 km of distribution lines; improve the efficiency of pumping; construct elevated water tanks; and substitute extraction wells. But although the project was submitted to the BECC in 1995,

---

[13] Chapter I, Article II, Section 2 of the BECC Charter (BECC/COCEF 2002).

[14] Sixty-seven were certified as of December 2002 (BECC/COCEF 2002).

the first year of the Commission's operation, it did not obtain NADB funding until November 2002, when the bank awarded a grant for $8.7 million from its Border Environment Infrastructure Fund. Construction of some of the first-phase parts is complete thanks to funding from the Mexican National Water Commission, but the construction of the plant itself had not started as of the end of 2002 (NADB 2002). A much smaller project, the "Comprehensive Solid Waste Project for Nogales, Sonora," is under development but not in progress. A third project that would have detected and repaired leaks was cancelled prior to certification.

Across the border in Arizona, the biggest undertaking attempted is a much-needed expansion of the NIWTP in Rio Rico, just outside Nogales. The US$46-million project would renovate and expand the plant (which would remain under the authority of the IBWC) and replace the international outfall interceptor and portions of the Nogales, Arizona, wastewater collection system. The upgrade of the NIWTP includes modifications to provide nitrogen removal in order to meet the required concentrations for protection of aquatic life and water-supply sources. The NIWTP expansion was certified in May 2000, but like the proposed water system expansion in Nogales, Sonora, it remains unfunded (BECC/COCEF 2002).[15] The two projects are linked, moreover, in that the U.S. Environmental Protection Agency does not want to release funds for the Acuaférico construction until the NIWTP issue is resolved.[16]

Meanwhile, shortly after the creation of the CEC, BECC, and NADB, the Clinton administration, working with Mexican President Ernesto Zedillo and Mexico's Environment Ministry (SEMARNAP), adopted a new plan called Border XXI. More specific and comprehensive than its progenitor, IBEP, Border XXI nevertheless failed to bring substantial new resources and, in particular, did not include provisions for investing in much-needed environmental infrastructure. Instead, the program identified major environmental and environmental-health issues, promoted the development of indicators, energized the technical working groups created by the La Paz agreement, and strengthened links and communication between the many projects and efforts already under way. Border XXI ended with the Clinton and Zedillo administrations in 2000 (U.S. EPA and SEMARNAT 2001). In cities like Ambos Nogales, it would be difficult to find concrete instances of actual, on-the-ground environmental improvements brought by Border XXI.

---

[15] The roadblock has been caused by a dispute between the city of Nogales, Arizona, and the IBWC.

[16] Personal correspondence with T.W. Sprouse, September 20, 2002.

STAKEHOLDER MOBILIZATION AND PUBLIC PARTICIPATION

The relative prosperity of the U.S. side of the border in comparison to the Mexican side is reflected in the pace of social mobilization in the two regions. In the United States, environmental activism is a tradition that is at least thirty years old. Environmental nongovernmental organizations (NGOs) wield considerable influence nationally, regionally, and locally. They are frequently well organized and reasonably well financed. Many are closely focused on single issues (such as, for example, wildlife protection, habitat preservation, safe drinking water assurance). In Mexico, by contrast, civil society has only recently begun to accommodate community-based groups and NGOs, both of which need government approval to operate. Few citizens can afford the time needed to volunteer or the money for dues or other revenue-generating fees. Until very recently, informal environmental NGO activity in Mexico as a whole, in the border region generally, and in Nogales, Sonora, specifically was elite-confined and therefore rare and generally ineffective.[17]

Accordingly, in Ambos Nogales the first signs of public reaction to the consequences of development surfaced in the early 1990s in Arizona. The most successful group has been Friends of the Santa Cruz River (FOSCR), which was formed in 1991 and has remained vital. Its chief interest has been to restore a portion of the Santa Cruz River to be used recreationally. FOSCR has been fortunate to benefit from a committed cadre of residents and, significantly, from the surpluses of treated effluent originating in Nogales, Sonora. By agreement with the city of Nogales, Arizona, and the IBWC, those surpluses are discharged directly into the stream and have allowed successful restoration of the riverine ecology. FOSCR remains active and interested in preventing Mexican interests from constructing a new sewage treatment facility south of the border, recognizing that such a development would halt the flow of Mexican water into the riparian channel.

In Sonora, although residents in Nogales would likely confirm that the actions of the new institutions have had little impact on actual conditions, they might agree that the BECC in particular has spawned greater public

---

[17] This was the conclusion of a 1991 panel on "The Needs of NGOs and Empowering NGOs to Participate Effectively," sponsored by the Ford Foundation in Guaymas, Sonora (Varady 1992). The situation has changed considerably since, and in the past four years there has been a sharp rise in environmental NGO activity in Mexico, as evidenced by the number of such organizations represented at the three Border Environmental Encuentros since 1998 (Liverman et al. 1999).

awareness and increased participation by stakeholders. The procedures leading to BECC certification of the Acuaférico Project had the effect of mobilizing a heretofore dormant community. A January 1996 public meeting of the BECC in Nogales, Sonora, drew some five hundred attendees, many of them highly motivated and deeply concerned with the future of the city's water. The meeting, which was strongly divided between supporters and opponents of the project, was perhaps the first major instance of environmental mobilization in the town. Even though construction has been stalled, the potential force of public voices has been let loose. According to María Carmen Lemos and Antonio Luna, the controversial certification process itself "has positively affected policymaking in the Ambos Nogales region" (Lemos and Luna 1999).

Back in Arizona, in 1999 the EPA and IBWC set up a Public Input Committee to secure community approval for BECC certification of the NIWTP. About thirty people attended the first public meeting in January 2000. Unusually, ten to fifteen of the attendees crossed from Mexico, many to speak out against undertaking any wastewater projects in Mexico until the stalled potable water system (the Acuaférico Project) was completed. Although the purpose of the session was to explain what was planned on the U.S. side, several of the Mexican citizens used the occasion to speak passionately against Mexico moving ahead with any new wastewater projects in Nogales, Sonora (personal correspondence with T.W. Sprouse, September 23, 2002).

In sum, stakeholder influence has been greater in Arizona than in Sonora. Additionally, because objectives have not converged sufficiently, there have been few examples of genuine cross-border NGO coalitions. But the chief impediment to progress in redressing the environmental effects of maquila growth and NAFTA-generated trade has been the inability of the designated institutions to secure financing and initiate construction. Public awareness has been awakened and is greater than at any time in the past, but bottom-up, community-based alliances thus far have been unable to break the impasse in alleviating water-related problems.

Upper San Pedro Watershed

The Upper San Pedro River basin provides a counterpoint to the Upper Santa Cruz watershed, which contains Ambos Nogales. Both watersheds are in desert highlands, and their rivers exhibit a number of similarities. They originate in Mexico and flow northward, merging with the Gila

River; traverse a mix of urban and rural landscapes; have portions that are protected, riparian zones; and feature serious water supply and quality problems. But the two regions within which the basins lie are fundamentally different culturally, demographically, and economically. In some ways, it can be said that the nearly perennial Upper San Pedro today resembles the now-dry Santa Cruz a century ago, the major difference being that development in the Upper San Pedro basin is on a very different trajectory than in the basin dominated by the Nogaleses. For this reason, the nature of salient water issues is substantially different in the San Pedro area than in Ambos Nogales.

PHYSICAL SETTING

The San Pedro River originates in Sonora, in the Sierra El Manzanal (figure 7.8). From its origins at 2,300 m in elevation, the stream flows northward past the urban areas of Cananea and Naco, Sonora. The stream then crosses the U.S.-Mexico border to flow past the Huachuca Mountains, between the nearby cities of Bisbee and Sierra Vista, Arizona. The river eventually reaches confluence with the Gila River in Winkelman, Arizona, about 300 km from its source (figure 7.2).

The Upper San Pedro basin (USPB) encompasses an area of approximately 6,400 km² (2,500 mi²), more than two-thirds of it in Mexico. It lies in a semiarid transition "basin-range" physiographic zone between the Sonoran and Chihuahuan deserts. There is considerable variation in topographic relief (from 900 m to 2,900 m) and in vegetation diversity. Annual precipitation ranges from 270 mm in the lowlands outside of Sierra Vista, Arizona, to as much as 750 mm in the mountains; the Cananea region receives an average of about 450 mm per year. Despite its general dryness, the area is sufficiently water-rich to support not only desert scrub but also extensive grasslands, oak woodland-savanna, mesquite *bosques* (woods), riparian forests, and coniferous forests (Vionnet and Maddock 1992; Liverman et al. 1997; Arias 2000). During the recent past, the upper basin has experienced significant land-cover change, from grasslands to mesquite. Between 1973 and 1986, this change resulted primarily from climate fluctuations, livestock grazing, and, more recently, rapid urbanization (Arias 2000; Kepner, Edmonds, and Watts 2002; Browning-Aiken, Varady, and Moreno 2002).

The river basin's most distinctive feature is its biodiversity. Birds—both native and migratory—are the chief faunal representatives of this diversity, and the river corridor is one of the last remaining international flyways

Figure 7.8. Upper San Pedro River System

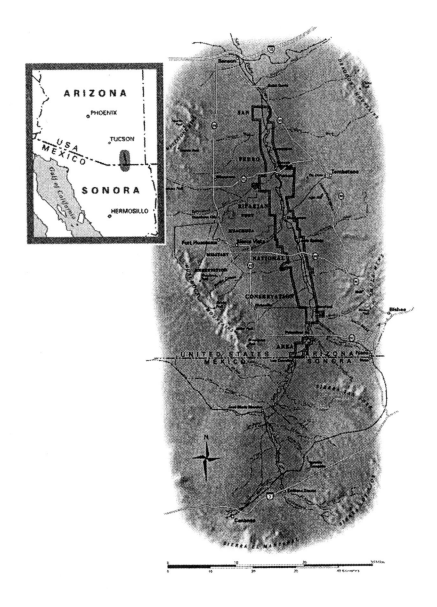

Source: CEC 1999.

connecting South America to Canada. Riparian vegetation also includes rare species, especially on the U.S. side, while the lands south of the border retain native semiarid grasslands that remain in good condition (Arias 2000). In 1988, in recognition of the value of the riparian corridor, a trade between the U.S. Bureau of Land Management and private owners created the nation's first protected river area (Glennon 2002). The resulting San Pedro Riparian National Conservation Area (SPRNCA) is a narrow, 19,000-hectare (47,700-acre) strip extending from the border to just south of the town of St. David (figure 7.8).[18] In spite of efforts by some Mexican environmental groups and U.S. pressure during the last years of the Clinton administration, Mexico has not designated for protection a comparable stretch of its portion of the river.

SOCIOECONOMIC SETTING

According to census figures, approximately 114,000 people live and work in seven incorporated towns and several unincorporated communities in the USPB. Population in the Mexican portion of the Upper San Pedro River basin is mainly concentrated in Cananea and Naco, Sonora. Cananea has 36,000 residents, about the same number as a decade ago. Closer to the border, Naco, Sonora, has approximately 5,300 residents, a figure that can grow to 7,000 if it includes transient workers waiting to cross into the United States. Its cross-border twin, Naco, Arizona, is much smaller, with no more than 1,000 residents.

Large-scale copper mining, which dates from the late nineteenth century, remains the predominant industrial activity in the Cananea area, and most residents depend economically on the mine. The facility was established by a U.S. citizen, William Greene, but is now operated by Mexicana de Cananea (owned by Grupo México). As is typical in boom-and-bust mining towns, the town's population and economy shrink and grow according to the price of copper and the policies of the mining company. In the outlying areas, ranching and agriculture are also strong components of the local economy. Approximately nine *ejidos*, or communal agricultural settlements, are dispersed across the Mexican portion of the basin. Unlike in Nogales, Sonora, and other Mexican border communities, maquiladoras are *not* a factor in the economies along this stretch of the international boundary.

---

[18] There is a small (3 km) gap beginning about 5 km north of the border (figure 7.8).

In the U.S. part of the basin, population is concentrated in Sierra Vista, a town with 40,000 residents, most of whom are retirees or are associated with the army base at Fort Huachucha. The military base is the area's economic engine, providing 40 percent of the jobs in the county and wielding proportionate political influence. Sierra Vista and its surrounding communities, furthermore, are very desirably situated, at about 2,900 m above sea level in a richly vegetated valley with year-round sunshine and relatively mild temperatures. As a result, military retirees and others are drawn to the area, causing a steep rise in the population, a trend mirroring that seen throughout the "Sunbelt" of the United States.[19] The growing number of residents has been accompanied by a boom in the real estate market, expansion of the city's boundaries, conversion of ranching and farming lands on the outskirts, and extensive land development and construction. The municipal and county governments have generally supported this expansion, seeing it as a stimulus for economic growth. Environmentalists and preservationists, on the other hand, have argued for limiting growth, seeing it as a threat to natural habitat and water sustainability (Emerson et al. 1998; CEC 1999; Varady, Moote, and Merideth 2000; Browning-Aiken, Varady, and Moreno 2002).

WATER ISSUES

As shown, the San Pedro region is sociodemographically distinct from the Nogales area. And instead of featuring two developed and populated urban zones on opposite sides of the border, the upper portion of the San Pedro basin has a series of moderately sized communities stretching across 100 km. Those characteristics, along with the markedly different nature of the driving forces of development in the two regions, assure contrasting sets of water-related issues. Further, the issues that are paramount north of the border are substantially different from those that concern Mexican residents from Naco to Cananea.

In binational settings such as those of Ambos Nogales and the USPB, local history clearly influences international dynamics. In order to appreciate U.S. and Mexican approaches to water issues, it is useful to see them in the context of disparate attitudes and meanings developed over time. On the U.S. side of the basin, the legacy of the frontier Fort Huachucha and an

---

[19] Six times as many residents lived in Sierra Vista in 2002 as in 1970, making it one of Arizona's fastest-growing cities. Arizona itself is the second-fastest-growing state.

associated "independent spirit" characterize many residents' reasons for living in the area. These perceptions affect views of resource use, transformation of the environment, and rights to private property. They help explain the pro-development orientation of some stakeholders.

In the Mexican portion, Cananea has its own reputation. It is known as a town that sparked the Mexican Revolution with its 1906 strike against the mine owner, William Greene, who once wanted to make Cananea part of the United States. A century-long tradition of social activism, previously channeled into labor-related causes, lately has begun addressing concerns over environment, water, and health. At the same time, among many Cananeans, fear of the mine's economic power and influence has dampened their impulse to speak out.

WATER AND CLIMATE

The highly variable nature of climatic conditions along the Arizona-Sonora border means that the amount of water available for use varies considerably at seasonal, annual, interannual, and decadal timescales. The gauging station at Palominas, 6.5 km north of the international boundary (figure 7.8), provides the best historical record for tracing streamflows for the 16 percent of the San Pedro watershed that lies within Mexico. Based on available records for the periods 1931–1933, 1936–1950, and 1951–1981, mean annual flow ranged from a low of 6.3 mm^3 to a high of 82.8 mm^3. Median annual flow for this time period was 20.8 mm^3. Periods of low flow, especially those lasting across multiple years, lead to reduced availability of water to meet demand, and they have the potential to generate serious equity issues, especially for individuals and enterprises that are on the margin even during "normal" times. Most threatened, however, is likely to be the capacity to preserve flows for riparian ecosystem protection unless alternative sources of water can be identified.

Drought conditions between 2000 and 2002 and a predicted continuing decline in water availability will certainly exacerbate increasing competition for water resources between productive sectors such as agriculture, industry, and domestic consumption (Magaña and Conde 2001). This situation has raised concerns about water supply and water quality, though perhaps not at the same high level of immediacy as in Nogales.

The social costs of extended drought are likely to be severe. Scientists suggest that global warming may bring even greater climate variability to this region, with both wet and dry periods being more severe and/or longer in duration. Yet current institutions, infrastructure, and policy tend not to take climatic and hydrologic variability into account sufficiently. Important challenges to averting or mitigating unacceptable social costs of development include identification of potential impacts of climate variability and change on local water supplies and devising policies to address such variability.[20] This, in turn, entrains the need for analysis of the actual and potential impacts of expansion of the mine, the implications of continued urban growth and development, and the need to understand the current and future roles played by agriculture and ranching in mitigating or exacerbating vulnerabilities to variability in water supply and quality for human uses and for support of the riverine landscape. For all these reasons, strengthening institutional arrangements to better plan for and cope with climate variability and change and water shortages is high on the list of priorities among stakeholders.

Addressing the above concerns requires efforts to link problem solving with the best available scientific information regarding interactions between climate and hydrology. In an area that features semiaridity, high vulnerability to climatic variability, rapid urban growth, traditional industry, agriculture, and important natural zones, a key issue is how to assign priorities to the various types of water use.[21]

MEXICAN ISSUES

The 36,000 residents of the *municipio* of Cananea rely primarily on the Río Sonora basin for their water; however, wells in the floodplain of the Upper San Pedro River produce about 2.4 million m³ (2,000 acre-feet) of water per year. The border community of Naco uses a minimal 0.37 million m³ (300 acre-feet) of San Pedro water each year; the same amount is consumed for domestic use in nearby rural areas (Liverman et al. 1997; Varady, Moote, and Merideth 2000).

Water-use patterns in the industrial, agricultural, and municipal sectors in the Sonoran sector of the Upper San Pedro set the framework for specific contests over water. In the process, serious issues arise regarding the na-

---

[20] Julia Carabias Lillo and Fernando Tudela Abad summarized potential vulnerabilities within Mexico to climatic change, including advancement of arid condition and desertification in the central and northern portions of the country, http://www.semarnap.bog.mx/quincenal/qui-53/historico.htm, accessed April 10, 2000.

[21] The CEC, in its Upper San Pedro River Initiative, cited coordinated, binational resource management as being essential for the protection of valued habitat in the basin and recognized the need for active engagement of diverse stakeholders in the region to achieve sustainable results (CEC 1999).

ture and intensity of social costs associated with different options available to cope with the lack of sufficient water of acceptable quality to meet all demands consistently and dependably. Because of the centrality of water to all aspects of society, this subject is of considerable interest within community discourse.

Located near the headwaters of the San Pedro River, Cananea would seem to have access to good-quality water. There, water quality and quantity are intimately related, in that the amount of usable water depends directly on the quality of the water relative to its intended use. Under conditions of water scarcity caused by overextraction and climate variability, groundwater and surface-water contamination diminish the quality of potable water supplies. Inadequate (Naco) or nonexistent (Cananea) wastewater treatment plants contribute to uncontrolled discharge of residual waters into the river. Unlined landfills introduce a variety of known and unknown substances that infiltrate into the aquifer. Moreover, the copper mine produces industrial waste that contaminates groundwater supplies via unlined and occasionally overflowing tailing dams (Moreno Vázquez 1991; Zavala 1987; Jamail and Ullery 1979). In 1998, with the approval of the municipalities of Cananea and Naco, Sonora, and the support of the IBWC and CILA, the University of Sonora and the Arizona Department of Environmental Quality tested water quality in the San Pedro River. Initial results indicated the presence of raw sewage and mining by-products, including arsenic, near the headwaters of the San Pedro and in wells close to Cananea (Da Viana 1998; Kamp 1999). This monitoring was reinitiated.

To gauge water-related perceptions of residents of Cananea and Naco, a team of Udall Center researchers conducted a survey in 2001. Consistent with actual water problems in the area, the survey showed that citizens primarily are concerned about two things: having enough water for everyday basic household needs such as drinking, cooking, and washing (92 percent), and assuring that the water they receive will not make them ill (89 percent). It is clear from the responses that most residents are not satisfied on either count: only 41 percent said they usually have enough water for bathing and drinking; 70 percent said they had heard of water-related illnesses in the community. Additionally, confirming the rise of environmental consciousness in Mexico, 84 percent of those responding were concerned about maintaining water in the rivers and springs, while 89 percent thought that pollution of the river, washes, and springs was very important (Moote and Gutiérrez 2001).[22] Given Mexico's shortage of financial resources and its economic development priorities, quick solutions to the expensive infrastructure problems are unlikely. In the long run, solutions will be found because assurance of public health is compelling to a nation that wants to raise the domestic standard of living. On the other hand, protection of natural areas will probably remain lower on the national agenda.

Much of the usage of San Pedro River water—surface water and groundwater—in Mexico is by the mine. Increased production of copper from extensive ore reserves in Mexico limits groundwater availability for municipal and agricultural uses in that region and compromises water conservation efforts. Expansion and modernization of the Cananea mine, from 1978 to 1986 and again between 1992 and 1997, increased water extraction from about 13 million m^3 in 1980 to about 20 million m^3 in 1990 (Browning-Aiken, Varady, and Moreno 2002).

U.S. ISSUES

"The 2,000–mile U.S.-Mexico border is the most environmentally degraded region in the U.S." (*State Legislatures* 1995). Strong statements such as this illustrate the visceral responses to habitat protection on the U.S. side of the border. In view of the polarization engendered by charged rhetoric by both environmentalists and advocates of development, agreement by those two camps on how to manage the river's scarce waters remains elusive. In Arizona, efforts to preserve sufficient water supplies to nourish highly valued natural areas, especially the riparian corridor, are raising the stakes considerably in contests over water. The social costs of asserting stronger regulation and management for conservation purposes are largely articulated in terms of loss of income associated with agricultural livelihood and urban/exurban development activities.

Although relations between U.S. and Mexican communities in the basin have been cordial and nonconfrontational, usage on the Mexican side of the border of waters from the San Pedro is a concern to some Arizona interests. While the river traverses a single watershed, experts disagree on the degree of connectivity between the subsurface waters of the sub-basin in the southern portion and the one to the north. While most hydrologists believe that pumping near Cananea does not reduce flows in the protected, U.S. portion of the stream, stakeholders in both camps remain skeptical.

---

[22] The sample sizes were between 245 and 270.

Those who are seeking to preserve SPRNCA worry that pumping by the mine degrades the riparian ecosystem by reducing flow and by introducing heavy metals and other mine-derived contaminants into the river. At the same time, the military base, builders, ranchers, and other pro-growth supporters resent having to conserve water when they think reduced supplies might be due to overpumping in Mexico. Not surprisingly, these concerns are mirrored south of the border, where communities commonly think that Sierra Vista wants Sonora to conserve basin water in order to promote more urban development north of the border.

The stakes are high, in no small part because the Upper San Pedro riparian area has been declared one of the world's "Last Great Places" by the Nature Conservancy and is a focus of considerable interest for environmentalists internationally. Julia Carabias, Mexico's environmental minister during the Zedillo administration, and Bruce Babbitt, secretary of the interior in the Clinton administration, carried the banner of riparian-area conservation in the Upper San Pedro into the international diplomatic arena. In 1999 they signed a memorandum of understanding stating that the two countries would work together to protect Mexico's part of the riparian corridor. The two successor governments have ignored that accord.

POLICIES, COPING STRATEGIES, AND PROSPECTS

Recognition of the deep differences in experience and resources between south and north have not deterred residents on both sides of the border from taking tentative steps toward finding common solutions for how to share the waters of the San Pedro. Whether the actors fully understand the implications of identifying mutually acceptable and viable water options for protecting one of the last intact riparian areas in the region, all the while addressing serious social needs in Mexico, remains unclear. What is clear is that any accord can only succeed if the social costs of development and industrial activity, and related impacts on local water supply and water quality, are taken into account.

INSTITUTIONS

The institutional resources available to communities in the region are of several types. First, there are traditional public-sector agencies charged with managing the water sector. In the United States this includes numerous agencies at the federal, state, county, and municipal levels. In Mexico the federal government, through the CNA, has the final word on water matters, though it delegates some authority to the state water agency (COAPAES in Sonora). As everywhere, the effectiveness of this mode is severely limited by overlapping and conflicting missions, poor communication, interjurisdictional squabbles, inability to operate across the international border, and low articulation with the needs of stakeholders.

Second are the pre- and post-NAFTA transboundary institutions: the IBWC/CILA, CEC, and BECC/NADB. The IBWC/CILA has had little involvement in the San Pedro region. Unlike the Nogaleses, the two Nacos do not have an international wastewater treatment plant. Nor has this generally sleepy portion of the border frequently come to the attention of the two commissions, which have devoted most of their efforts to major issues such as water-delivery commitments in the Colorado and Rio Grande/Río Bravo basins and sewage treatment in the large twin cities.

In contrast to the CEC's inactivity in Nogales, the Commission has played a significant role in the USPB. In 1998, at the initial behest of a citizen's petition filed under Article 14 of the Commission's charter, the CEC agreed to authorize a technical study of the effects of water withdrawals on the international bird flyway along the stream. Over the strenuous objections of some local officials, property rights advocates, and anti–United Nations activists[23] in Cochise County, Arizona, the CEC appointed a technical committee and charged it with assembling data and issuing a report.[24] Recognizing the importance of engaging the community, the CEC arranged for a concerted public-input process (Emerson et al. 1998). The resulting document, "Ribbon of Life" (CEC 1999), combined the findings of the authors and the comments and reactions of those who participated in the public airing of early draft versions of the report. The final report, which was endorsed by a binational advisory panel, appeared in 1999 and contained a number of recommendations. Arguably the most prescient and influential of these was the suggestion that multi-stakeholder watershed initiatives be created to help localize water decision making.

The BECC and NADB, like the CEC, have been active in the San Pedro region, though not on the scale of their involvement in Nogales or other major border cities. One of the first projects to be certified by the BECC was the US$1.6 million Integral Project for Water, Sewage, and Wastewater Treatment of Naco, Sonora. Through a combination of grants and loans from the CNA, EPA, and NADB, the project secured the necessary funds

---

[23] There were mischievous rumors afloat that the CEC was a United Nations agency intent on imposing "world rule" in this U.S. territory.

[24] This has been the CEC's only such investigation in the U.S.-Mexico border region.

and completed a first phase in late 1999. Rehabilitation and expansion of the treatment ponds began at that time and were scheduled to have been completed by 2002. A second proposed project to handle municipal solid waste, also in Naco, Sonora, is under consideration by the BECC but not yet certified. Cananea has submitted four proposals, two of which were canceled before action was taken. The other two—a $1-million construction of a sanitary landfill and a $10-million project to improve the water, sewer, and wastewater treatment system—were submitted in 1998 but have yet to be certified. In Arizona, Tombstone proposed in 1997 to improve its potable water and wastewater collection and treatment systems, but both requests are stalled in the development stage.

STAKEHOLDER MOBILIZATION AND PUBLIC PARTICIPATION

By far the most fruitful institutional resource has been the interest and commitment of the basin's stakeholders. As noted, issues surrounding water availability, quality, and use have been vital. In each country, they have drawn local interest for at least a decade. In Arizona, prior to the CEC's intervention, relations among interest groups were tense and unproductive. Opposing partisans found little in common, and attempts at compromise repeatedly broke down over deep conflicts in values. But beginning with the forums convened as part of the public-input process, dialogue became possible. In late 1999, an important binational conference called "Divided Waters–Common Ground," cosponsored by more than a dozen academic and government organizations, brought together many of the concerned parties. Meeting at venues in both countries, participants reviewed local history and scientific knowledge, discussed common problems, and considered policy options for resolving domestic and international aspects of the water problems facing the basin.

One of the outcomes of the "Divided Waters" event was the crystallization of a stakeholder group in Arizona. Earlier that year, a number of agency representatives had begun meeting informally with other stakeholders in Sierra Vista to talk about water management issues. Within a year, the group constituted itself into a formal watershed initiative called the Upper San Pedro Partnership (USPP). By 2002 the USPP had more than twenty members representing landowners, land- and water-use controllers, and resources agencies.[25] The Partnership has established a number of

---

[25] The USPP includes representatives of federal, state, county, and municipal government; two NGOs; a local conservation district; a state association of conservation districts; a ranching/water association; and a water supply firm.

committees to deal with information, technical issues, planning, and out-reach. They have received substantial resources from the state of Arizona and the federal government, and are developing a long-term water management plan for the U.S. portion of the Upper San Pedro watershed (USPP 2002). By 2002 the USPP had recognized the connectedness of the basin and began expressing interest in coordinating some of its work with Mexican counterparts.

While the USPP was forming and building its capacity, a similar "bottom-up" organization was emerging in Sonora. In Cananea and Naco a group of citizens that included educators, doctors, lawyers, mining engineers, farmers, ranchers, civil servants, and other citizens began meeting to talk about their shared environmental concerns. By mid-2000 the organization had named itself ARASA (Asociación Regional Ambiental de Sonora y Arizona, or the Arizona-Sonora Regional Environmental Association), significantly incorporating an explicitly binational outlook in its name. With assistance from a number of groups and individuals in the United States and with seed funding from two Mexican foundations, ARASA began meeting regularly and setting an agenda; it established a technical subcommittee to collect and interpret current research on the geohydrology of the basin and land-use changes (Varady and Browning-Aiken n.d.). In late 2002 the organization acquired office space in Cananea and hired a part-time coordinator.

In September 2002, members of ARASA met for the first time with members of the Upper San Pedro Partnership. Further meetings are scheduled, under the auspices of the Udall Center for Studies in Public Policy, under the terms of a project supported by the Dialogue on Water and Climate, a Holland-based international initiative. Joint discussions between the USPP, ARASA, and other stakeholders will consider binational strategies for managing water and incorporating climate information in decision making.

The parallel emergence of stakeholder associations in the two parts of the basin is noteworthy for several reasons. First, this development represents a genuine grassroots process that features a high degree of social mobilization in each country. This has occurred more or less spontaneously in response to a place-based sense of urgency. The reciprocal interest in binational coordination has occurred independently of formal diplomatic channels—highly unusual in a setting that has featured close adherence to national interests and tight control of the international border. These pioneering developments offer a promising model for addressing the environmental impacts of development.

CONCLUSIONS: SOCIAL COSTS AND ENVIRONMENTAL VIABILITY

Pivotal to resolving the dilemma of balancing very basic social well-being with ecological viability is the ability to enhance resilience to multiple stressors originating from both human and natural sources.[26] Adopting adaptive-management strategies such as in the San Pedro basin is one option. Such strategies would build iteratively on experiments designed to enhance the capacity of residents, managers, and decision makers to cope more effectively with the presence of multiple stressors, and would use varying combinations of scientific information, infrastructure development, and economic and political institutional strategies to achieve clearly articulated goals and objectives.

In both study areas, the aspirations, needs, and impacts of industrial, commercial, and residential development on the two sides of the border must be evaluated in the context of interactions among human and natural processes. These processes yield the kinds of fluctuations in water-quantity and water-quality issues that not only generate enormous social costs among marginalized populations but also cut across all sectors—both human and natural.

Contests over consumptive uses versus environmental sustainability will continue into the indefinite future. However, social and environmental costs need not continue to escalate. To rephrase the common mantra, "global change happens in local places." Put another way, the challenge at all levels is to find ways to work together to develop binational strategies that link national and international political and economic processes with place-based experiences.

The cases of development and water in Ambos Nogales and the Upper San Pedro basin illustrate two contrasting sets of circumstances. Though just 100 km apart, the two study areas offer useful and potentially extendable insights on a variety of approaches to coping with development-induced stress. .

---

[26] Resilience is defined here as the ability to withstand or recover from a shock or perturbation.

References

Arias, H.M. 2000. "International Groundwaters: The Upper San Pedro River Basin Case," *Natural Resources Journal* 40, no. 2: 199–221.

BECC/COCEF (Border Environment Cooperation Commission/Comisión de Cooperación Ecológica Fronteriza). 2002. BECC/COCEF homepage, http://www.cocef.org/englishbecc.html, December 2.

Browning-Aiken, A., R.G. Varady, and D. Moreno. 2002. "Binational Coalition-Building: A Case Study of Water-Resources Management in the Upper San Pedro Basin of Sonora-Arizona." Presented at the First International Symposium on Transboundary Waters Management, Monterrey, Mexico, November 19.

Carter, D.E., C. Peña, R.G. Varady, and W. Suk. 1996. "Health and Hazardous Waste Issues Related to the U.S.-Mexico Border," *Environmental Health Perspectives* 104, no. 6: 590–94.

CEC (Commission for Environmental Cooperation). 1999. *Ribbon of Life: An Agenda for Preserving Migratory Bird Habitat on the Upper San Pedro.* Montreal: CEC.

Da Viana, Virginia. 1998. "Hallan arsénico," *El Imparcial*, August 19.

De Steiguer, J.E. 1997. *The Age of Environmentalism.* Boston: WCB/McGraw-Hill.

Emerson, K., A. Moote, L. Evans, M. Brogden, A. Conley, S. Moodie, and R. Yarde. 1998. *Public Input Digest for the Upper San Pedro River Initiative.* Report to the Commission for Environmental Cooperation. Tucson: Udall Center for Studies in Public Policy, University of Arizona.

Glennon, R. 2002. "A River at Risk: The Upper San Pedro River in Arizona." In *Water Follies: Groundwater Pumping and the Fate of America's Fresh Waters*, edited by R. Glennon. Washington, D.C.: Island.

GNEB (Good Neighbor Environmental Board). 2001. *Fifth Report of the Good Neighbor Environmental Board to the President and Congress of the United States.* English and Spanish. Washington, D.C.: U.S. EPA.

Ingram, H. 1992. "United States/Mexico Water Management: An Ambos Nogales Example." In *Borders and Water: North American Water Issues.* Albuquerque, N.M.: International Transboundary Resources Center.

Ingram, H., N.K. Laney, and D.M. Gillilan. 1995. *Divided Waters: Bridging the U.S.-Mexico Border.* Tucson: University of Arizona Press.

Ingram, H., L. Milich, and R.G. Varady. 1994. "Managing Transboundary Resources: Lessons from Ambos Nogales," *Environment* 36, no. 4: 6–9, 28–38.

Ingram, H., and D.R. White. 1993. "International Boundary and Water Commission: An Institutional Mismatch for Resolving Transboundary Water Problems," *Natural Resources Journal* 33, no. 1: 153–75.

ITESM (Instituto Tecnológico y de Estudios Superiores de Monterrey). 1999. *Reporte del estado ambiental y de los recursos naturales en la frontera norte de México.* Mexico City: Instituto Nacional de Ecología, SEMARNAP.

Jacott, M., C. Reed, and M. Winfield. 2002. "The Generation and Management of Hazardous Wastes and Transboundary Hazardous Waste Shipments between Mexico, Canada and the United States, 1990–2000." In *The Environmental Effects of Free Trade: Papers Presented at the North American Symposium on Assessing the Linkages between Trade and Environment*. Montreal: Commission for Environmental Cooperation.

Jamail, M.H., and S.J. Ullery. 1979. "Pollution of the San Pedro River: Use Relations along the Sonoran Desert Borderlands." Arid Lands Resource Information Paper No. 14. Tucson, Ariz.

Kamp, Dick. 1999. *Northeast Sonora Water Project: Summary of the First Phase.* Bisbee, Ariz.: Border Ecology Project.

Kasperson, J.X., R.E. Kasperson, and B.L. Turner, II, eds. 1995. *Regions at Risk: Comparisons of Threatened Environments*. Tokyo: United Nations University Press.

Kelly, M.E., J. Pitt, C. Rincon (Environmental Defense), S. Cornelius (Sonoran Institute), M. Cohen (Pacific Institute), and K. Gillon (Defenders of Wildlife). 2002. Letter on U.S.-Mexico Border Issues to U.S. Secretary of State Colin Powell and U.S. Secretary of the Interior Gale Norton. November 21.

Kepner, W.G., C.M. Edmonds, and C.J. Watts. 2002. *Remote Sensing and Geographic Information Systems for Decision Analysis in Public Resource Administration: A Case Study of 25 Years of Landscape Change in a Southwestern Watershed*. Las Vegas, Nev.: U.S. Environmental Protection Agency.

Lara-Valencia, F. 2002. "Institutional Reform and Transboundary Cooperation for Environmental Planning along the United States–Mexican Border." PhD dissertation, University of Michigan.

Lemos, M.C. de M., and A. Luna. 1999. "Public Participation in the BECC: Lessons from the Acuaférico Project, Nogales, Sonora," *Journal of Borderlands Studies* 14, no. 1: 43–64.

Liverman, D., R. Merideth, A. Holdsworth, L. Cervera, and F. Lara. 1997. *An Assessment of the Water Resources in the San Pedro River and Santa Cruz River Basins, Arizona and Sonora*. Report to the Commission for Environmental Cooperation. Tucson: Latin American Area Center/Udall Center for Studies in Public Policy, University of Arizona.

Liverman, D., R.G. Varady, O. Chávez, and R. Sánchez. 1999. "Environmental Issues along the U.S.-Mexico Border: Drivers of Change and Responses of Citizens and Institutions," *Annual Review of Energy and the Environment* 24, no. 1: 607–43.

Lorey, D., ed. 1993. *United States–Mexico Border Statistics since 1900: 1990 Update*. Los Angeles: Latin American Center, University of California, Los Angeles.

Magaña, V.O., and C. Conde. 2001. "Climate Variability, Climate Change, and Its Impacts on the Freshwater Resources in the Border Region: A Case Study for Sonora, Mexico." Draft report. Mexico City: Universidad Nacional Autónoma de México.

Milich, L., and R.G. Varady. 1999. "Openness, Sustainability, and Public Participation: New Designs for Transboundary River-Basin Institutions," *Journal of Environment and Development* 8, no. 3: 258–306.

Moote, M.A., and M. Gutiérrez. 2001. *Views from the Upper San Pedro River Basin: Local Perceptions of Water Issues.* Tucson: Udall Center for Studies in Public Policy, University of Arizona.

Morehouse, B.J., R.H. Carter, and T.W. Sprouse. 2000. "The Implications of Sustained Drought for Transboundary Water Management in Nogales, Arizona, and Nogales, Sonora," *Natural Resources Journal* 40, no. 4: 783–817.

Moreno Vázquez, J.L. 1991. "El futuro de la problemática ambiental en Cananea y Nacozari." Paper presented at the Simposio de Historia y Antropología de Sonora, Instituto de Investigaciones Históricas, Universidad de Sonora, Hermosillo, February 23.

Mumme, S.P., and S.T. Moore. 1999. "Innovation Prospects in U.S.-Mexico Border Water Management: The IBWC and the BECC in Theoretical Perspective," *Environment and Planning C: Government and Policy* 17, no. 6: 753–72.

NADB (North American Development Bank). 2002. "North American Development Bank Signs a US$8.69 Million Grant to Finance Water Supply and Distribution Project in Nogales, Sonora." Press release, November 22.

Peach, J., and J. Williams. 2000. "Population and Economic Dynamics on the U.S.-Mexican Border: Past, Present, and Future." In *The U.S.-Mexican Border Environment: A Road Map to a Sustainable 2020*, edited by P. Ganster. San Diego, Calif.: San Diego State University Press.

Pick, J.B., N. Viswanathan, and J. Hettrick. 2001. "The U.S.-Mexican Borderlands Region: A Binational Spatial Analysis," *Social Science Journal* 38: 567–95.

Pick, J.B., N. Viswanathan, K. Tomita, and S. Keshavan. 2002. "Border Demographic Impacts on the Urban Environment and Sustainable Development of Imperial County, California, and Mexicali Municipio, Mexico." Final report to the California Urban Environmental and Research Center. Redlands, Calif.: University of Redlands.

Reinert, K.A., and D.W. Roland-Holst. 2002. "The Industrial Pollution Impacts of NAFTA: Some Preliminary Results." In *Both Sides of the Border: Transboundary Environmental Management Issues Facing Mexico and the United States*, edited by L. Fernández and R.T. Carson. Dordrecht, The Netherlands: Kluwer.

Sánchez, R.A. 1995. "Water Quality Problems in Nogales, Sonora," *Environmental Health Perspectives* 103, supplement 1: 93–97.

———. 2002. "Binational Cooperation and the Environment at the U.S.-Mexico Border: A Mexican Perspective." In *Both Sides of the Border: Transboundary Environmental Management Issues Facing Mexico and the United States*, edited by L. Fernández and R.T. Carson. Dordrecht, The Netherlands: Kluwer.

Sciara, G-C. 2002. "U.S. Transportation Responses to NAFTA: A Window on U.S.-Mexico Transport Issues." In *Both Sides of the Border: Transboundary En-*

vironmental Management Issues Facing Mexico and the United States, edited by L. Fernández and R.T. Carson. Dordrecht, The Netherlands: Kluwer.

Sellers, W.D., R.H. Hill, and M. Sanderson-Rae. 1985. *Arizona Climate*. Centennial ed. Tucson: University of Arizona Press.

Sokota, R.P. 1991. *Ambos Nogales, On the Border: A Chronology*. Tucson: Udall Center for Studies in Public Policy, University of Arizona.

State Legislatures. 1995. Vol. 25.

Steller, T. 2002. "The Gift of Water: Help from a Hose," *Arizona Daily Star*, July 10.

Székely, A. 1993. "How to Accommodate an Uncertain Future into Institutional Responsiveness and Planning: The Case of Mexico and the United States," *Natural Resources Journal* 33, no. 2 (special issue: Managing North American Transboundary Water Resources, Part 2): 397–403.

Urquidi, V. 2002. "Visión del ambiente, la población y la maquila en la frontera norte: ¿hacia el desarrollo sustentable?" Presented at the conference "La Población en el Norte de México," Tijuana, July 8–9.

U.S. EPA (U.S. Environmental Protection Agency). 1998. *The 1997 U.S.-Mexico Border Environmental Indicators Report: U.S.-Mexico Border XXI Program*. Washington, D.C.: U.S. EPA.

U.S. EPA and SEMARNAT (U.S. Environmental Protection Agency and Secretaría del Medio Ambiente y Recursos Naturales). 2001. *U.S.-Mexico Border XXI Program: Progress Report 1996–2000*. English version. Washington, D.C.: U.S. EPA.

———. 2002. *Border 2012: U.S.-Mexico Environmental Program* (English and Spanish). Washington, D.C., and Mexico City: U.S. EPA and SEMARNAT.

USPP (Upper San Pedro Partnership). 2002. *USPP Planning Activity: 2002 Progress Report*. Sierra Vista, Ariz.: USPP.

Utton. A.E. 1984. "An Assessment of the Management of U.S.-Mexican Water Resources: Anticipating the Year 2000." In *The U.S.-Mexico Border Region: Anticipating Resource Needs and Issues to the Year 2000*, edited by C. Sepúlveda and A.E. Utton. El Paso: Texas Western Press.

Varady, R.G. 1991. "Are EPA and Residents of the U.S.-Mexico Border Speaking the Same Language?" Testimony at Public Hearings on Integrated Border Environmental Plan (IBEP) by U.S. EPA and SEDUE. Nogales, Arizona, September 26.

Varady, R.G., ed. 1992. *The U.S.-Mexico Border Region under Stress: A Binational Symposium on Ideas for Future Research*. Proceedings of October 1991 symposium sponsored by the Ford Foundation in Guaymas, Mexico. Tucson: Udall Center for Studies in Public Policy, University of Arizona.

Varady, R.G., and A. Browning-Aiken. n.d. "The Birth of a Mexican Watershed Council in the San Pedro Basin in Sonora." In *Planeación y cooperación transfronteriza en la frontera México–Estados Unidos* (Transboundary Planning and

Cooperation in the U.S.-Mexico Border Region), edited by C. Fuentes and S. Peña. Forthcoming.

Varady, R.G., D. Colnic, R. Merideth, and T. Sprouse. 1997. "The U.S.-Mexico Border Environment Cooperation Commission: Collected Perspectives on the First Two Years," *Journal of Borderlands Studies* 11, no. 2: 89–119.

Varady, R.G., and D.M. Gillilan. 1993. "Transborder Urban Water Use: A Century of Cooperation and Competition in Nogales." Presented at the meeting of the Association of Borderlands Scholars, Corpus Christi, April 23.

Varady, R.G., H. Ingram, and L. Milich. 1995. "The Sonoran Pimería Alta: Shared Environmental Problems and Challenges," *Journal of the Southwest* 37, no. 1: 102–22.

Varady, R.G., and M.D. Mack. 1995. "Transboundary Water Resources and Public Health in the U.S.-Mexico Border Region," *Journal of Environmental Health* 57, no. 8: 8–14.

Varady, R.G., P. Romero Lankao, and K. Hankins. 2001. "Managing Hazardous Materials along the U.S.-Mexico Border," *Environment* 43, no. 10: 22–36.

———. 2002. "Whither Hazardous-Materials Management in the U.S.-Mexico Border Region?" In *Both Sides of the Border: Transboundary Environmental Management Issues Facing Mexico and the United States*, edited by L. Fernández and R.T. Carson. Dordrecht, The Netherlands: Kluwer.

Varady, R.G., M.A. Moote, and R. Merideth. 2000. "Water Allocation Options for the Upper San Pedro Basin: Assessing the Social and Institutional Landscape," *Natural Resources Journal* 40, no. 2: 223–35.

Vionnet, L.B., and T. Maddock, III. 1992. *Modeling of Groundwater Flow and Surface/Groundwater Interaction for the San Pedro River Basin: Mexican Border to Fairbank, Arizona*. HWR No. 92-010. Tucson: Department of Hydrology and Water Resources, University of Arizona.

Worster, Donald. 1985. *Nature's Economy: A History of Ecological Ideas*. New York: Cambridge University Press.

Zavala, E.V. 1987. "Minera de Cananea, SEDUE y el medio ambiente," *Comunicobre* 62, no. 5.

PART III

Efforts to Reduce and Offset the Social Costs of Maquilization

8

Partnering for a New Approach: Maquiladoras, Government Agencies, Educational Institutions, Nonprofit Organizations, and Residents in Ambos Nogales

DIANE AUSTIN, EDNA MENDOZA, MICHÈLE KIMPEL GUZMÁN, AND ALBA JARAMILLO

Increasingly the role of groups and teams as a catalyst for change in environmental management is becoming well accepted.... However, to foster a more collective approach to environmental management that is capable of transformational change, we have to do more than just work together on specific projects. Transformational change requires individuals and groups to develop the capacity to move beyond the completion of task-bounded activities. They must catalyse change within their immediate membership first, and spread that culture to others in their communities over the longer term.—Margaret Kilvington and Will Allen (Manaaki Whenua Landcare Research, at www.landcareresearch.co.nz/research/social/supporting_index.asp, September 26, 2002)

When we say 'building partnerships' we mean going beyond mere cooperation and into the realm of collaboration. The Community Partnerships initiative envisions all stakeholders in adult education—businesses, social service and workforce development agencies, libraries, local schools and colleges, faith-based organizations, community-based organizations, and more—developing a system to identify issues, share resources, and otherwise face challenges together.—Community Partnerships for Adult Learning (www.c-pal.net/build/, September 26, 2002)

Cross-sector collaboration today is required not only to tackle complex public problems that no one sector can handle alone, but also to better understand and redefine the relationships and strategies of [government, business, and nonprofit organizations].... Some of the most interesting and constructive collaborations are occurring in regions, where government, business, and non-profit leaders are working out practical ways of dealing with their common problems.—R. Scott Fosler (2002: 1, 6)

Of the many communities along the U.S.-Mexico border, those with ports of entry are identified as "sister" or "twin" cities. In Arizona-Sonora, there are three major communities of this type: San Luis, Arizona–San Luis Río Colorado, Sonora (Ambos San Luis); Nogales, Arizona–Nogales, Sonora (Ambos Nogales; see figure 8.1); and Douglas, Arizona–Agua Prieta, Sonora. These and other communities along the U.S.-Mexico border are chronically underfunded by their respective governments. On the U.S. side, federal and state distribution formulas count only U.S. residents and ignore the Mexican sister-city residents who seek goods and services in the United States—usually legally and legitimately. On the Mexican side, the population is consistently and dramatically undercounted. Even in good economic times, insufficient funding translates into inadequate infrastructure and services. During an economic downturn, such as has occurred in recent years, communities suffer from cuts in federal spending, reductions in local and state budgets, layoffs and wage decreases, and a decline in private philanthropy. The presence of an international border between communities marked by stark differences in income, population, and needs exacerbates the problem. Under these circumstances, the need for innovative solutions is tremendous.

The nature, scope, and persistence of environmental problems such as poor air quality and habitat degradation require multiple, simultaneous approaches. Given the general economic conditions in the border area, it is no surprise that neither market approaches, nor governmental regulations, nor voluntary changes have proven effective independently. Government officials, business managers, academic leaders, and private donors all have recognized and attempted to respond to this need. This chapter describes several programs for increasing collaboration among these sectors, focusing on the role and function of maquiladoras within them. It then explores how the development and rapid expansion of a specific initiative—the Ambos Nogales Revegetation Partnership—took advantage of the foundation of trust and cooperation they had laid.

Figure 8.1. Map of Ambos Nogales

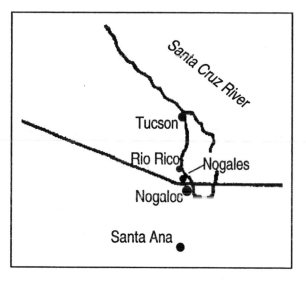

The maquiladora model has been widely criticized for its failure to ensure that adequate resources are made available for the development of physical infrastructure within the communities in which the maquiladoras locate. With the exception of labor organizing, sociopolitical infrastructure—the institutions and networks that bring people together to enable community development and functioning—has received less attention. This chapter addresses that gap and illustrates that the relationship between the maquiladora sector and social and environmental border conditions is neither permanent nor static.

The collaborative efforts described here have occurred within the unique border environment, where there is a regular flow of people, ideas, and materials. Nogales is a major border crossing for produce entering the United States and is the largest maquiladora city in Sonora (see Kopinak 1996). Until the 2000 economic downturn, the number of twin plants in Nogales and the other Arizona-Sonora border communities had climbed (see table 8.1). Now, though the maquiladora model of development has penetrated deep into Mexico, it has been challenged by closures and the relocation of some plants to Asia (Smith 2002; Zúñiga and González Amador 2002; www.maquilaportal.com) and has been deemed a failure by some (see, for example, Bendesky 2002). Recent layoffs along the border have been substantial and have led to increased uncertainty within all sectors. This chapter concludes, therefore, by reviewing the possible consequences of these changes for border collaborative efforts and discussing potential support for and barriers to the development of such efforts in interior Mexico.

Table 8.1. Numbers of Maquiladoras in Sonora's Border Cities

City	1999	2000	2001	2002	2003	2004
Nogales	104	109	109	73	79	81
Agua Prieta	32	33	34	21	21	20
San Luis Río Colorado	31	37	42	a	a	a

Source: Twin Plant News, June issue of each year.
a Beginning in 2002, San Luis is not differentiated from the rest of Sonora.

COLLABORATION AND TRUST

Cross-border collaboration on environmental issues has been one outcome of an evolutionary process within which the location and meaning of the border, the definition of problems, and the framing of solutions have shifted in both dramatic and subtle ways. These changes have been driven by national and international decisions and trends as well as by local events.

As the quotes at the beginning of this chapter indicate, individuals and groups within all sectors—government, business, nonprofits, and academia—have come to embrace collaboration as a requisite for addressing complex public issues. Calls for building partnerships respond to several problems: high levels of complexity, low levels of public confidence in institutions, and insufficient capacity within a single organization to go it alone. Numerous examples of successful collaboration have been published and guides for building and supporting groups disseminated (see table 8.2). Analysts have identified requisite capacities and stages of collaboration. Success is attributed to establishing and maintaining relationships of mutual benefit, identifying and working toward a common purpose, developing an effective group process, and demonstrating effectiveness through performance. At the same time, critics have expressed skepticism over such partnerships, especially when they involve groups with vast differences in size, resources, and power.

The long-term outcomes of collaborative relationships depend on both institutional arrangements and the commitments of individuals within the institutions. Individuals create partnerships. They utilize personal relationships (strong ties) to establish networks that then expand and set in place across disparate members the weak ties that enable interaction to occur (Granovetter 1973, 1982). Historically, institutions generally have been more stable than individuals. Yet today's business and political environment is characterized by rapid change both within institutions and of the institutions themselves. And even where institutionalized by formal agreements, partnerships flourish or wither according to the commitment and compatibility of their members.

For more than a century, since the U.S.-Mexico border was established in its current location, cross-border interaction has been variously promoted and stymied as different groups have migrated to the region (see Vélez-Ibáñez 1996; Staudt and Coronado 2002). Even along the border between Arizona and Sonora, binational collaboration is not uniform. Recently, stimulated first by the Border Industrialization Program (BIP) of the 1960s and then the rapid industrial growth of the 1980s, Mexican border cities have become highly populated. The nature and rate of that growth have influenced the level and tenor of interaction.

Nogales, Sonora's population is fifteen times larger than that of Nogales, Arizona (Davidson 2000: 10–11), and its industrial productivity is far greater (Arreola and Curtis 1993: 215). Still, Ambos Nogales are united by numerous factors. Many families have members on both sides of the border, individuals cross the border to work and go to school, and commerce is lively. Many of these relationships extend to Rio Rico, Arizona, a small community that borders Nogales, Arizona, on its north side, and to Tucson, 65 miles from the border. Unfortunately, uneven growth and heightened border security—a powerful trend with notable consequences even before September 11, 2001—have strained relationships and challenged cooperative efforts.

At the same time, air and water recognize no international boundaries. Exhaust from automobiles, dust from unpaved roads and parking lots, and

Table 8.2. Elements of Successful Collaboration

Source	Members	Elements of Successful Collaboration
Project TIES—Teaching for Inclusive and Effective Schools [Jackson-Madison County School District and Tennessee Developmental Disabilities Planning Council] (JMCSD 2001)	teachers, administrators, nonprofits	1. Group members willing to give up "turf" and not use time "protecting" resources or areas of responsibility. 2. Mutual interdependence—all members depend on one another to accomplish objectives and each team member participates and contributes. 3. Flexibility in roles and responsibilities—team members willing to shift and change their individuals roles and responsibilities depending on the nature of the task. 4. Group members have a common goal that all share and all members focus on and are committed to achieving. 5. Members understand group process skills—problem solving, consensus building, and conflict resolution. 6. Mutual trust and respect among group members. 7. Equality among group members, no member or members dominates or controls discussions or activities.
Principles of Intergroup Projects: A First Look [Association for the Study and Development of Community] (ASDC 1999)	foundations, nonprofits, government agencies, social scientists	1. Identify important common issue and work toward common goals to address the issue. 2. Bring together members as equals in terms of power, respect, and importance. 3. Provide opportunities for members to get to know one another as individuals. 4. Provide opportunities to identify similarities between groups. 5. Identify groups' assets and use and exchange them. 6. Identify and respect conflicts and transform them into improved capacity and relations. 7. Organize and carry out collective action. 8. Foster and sustain intergroup relations through frequent contact and cooperation. 9. Garner institutional support to promote intergroup relations. 10. Ensure that intergroup strategies operate at multiple levels—individual, relational, and institutional.

Three-Sector Initiative [Conference Board, Council on Foundations, Independent Sector, National Academy of Public Administration, National Alliance of Business, National Civic League, National Governor's Association] (Fosler 2002)	government, business, nonprofits	1. Leadership. 2. Citizenship to provide the base, reservoir, support, action arm, and accountability of leadership. 3. Knowledge and understanding about economic and social trends; about successful and unsuccessful experience elsewhere; and about the respective agendas, cultures, and operating practices of partners. 4. Communication and network management, including skills such as visioning, strategic planning, convening, facilitating, deliberating, attentive listening, coaching, consensus building, brokering, mediating, negotiating, contracting, monitoring, evaluating, assessing, reflecting, learning, and collaborative problem-solving. 5. Industry and service system structures, including well-designed markets, industries, social service systems, and policy arenas.
The Federal Government as Partner: Six Steps to Successful Collaboration [Treasury Board of Canada Secretariat] (Czerny 1995)	government, private sector, nongovernmental organizations	1. Shared or compatible objectives. 2. All parties contribute resources (e.g., money, information, equipment). 3. All parties share in the benefits of the collaboration. 4. All parties agree to a fair allocation of the risk-taking. 5. An explicit agreement, contract, or other instrument sets out the terms of the arrangement.

smoke from intentional and unintentional fires flow back and forth across the border, with a primarily northward trend in the Ambos Nogales area. The Santa Cruz River begins in southern Arizona, makes a 32-mile loop through Sonora, and returns to the United States east of Ambos Nogales, supplying drinking water from its groundwater aquifers to communities along its entire course and providing approximately half the supplies to the sister cities. An international trunk line constructed in the Nogales Wash carries wastewater and infiltrated groundwater from Ambos Nogales north and downhill to the International Wastewater Treatment Plant in Rio Rico, at which wastewater is treated and discharged to the Nogales Wash at its confluence with the Santa Cruz River. Sewage overflows from the leaky collection system in Nogales, Sonora, also flow directly into the Wash. In short, environmental problems of an interconnected, binational scope proliferate; they include poor air and water quality, deforestation, water scarcity, inadequately managed hazardous waste, and groundwater contamination.

Binational Initiatives in Arizona-Sonora

Several binational initiatives have evolved in this context, and maquiladoras have come to play a role in all of them. Mirroring patterns across the United States, in the post–World War II era border communities looked to private enterprise and economic development, generally in the form of industrialization, to improve the quality of life throughout the Arizona-Sonora region. Consequently, early initiatives focused on trade and programs to attract industry to the region, and these set the environment within which maquiladoras would later proliferate. In 1959, prior to the development of maquiladoras, the Arizona-Mexico West Coast Trade Commission and the Sonora-Arizona Committee for Social and Economic Promotion were formed to coordinate efforts to attract private enterprise and promote economic development (www.azmc.org/aboutus.asp?from=history). These organizations were established at a conference cosponsored by the University of Arizona and the University of Sonora in Hermosillo to expand cultural and trade relations between the two states. Governors Paul Fannin of Arizona and Álvaro Obregón of Sonora asked experts from each state to strengthen binational relations in agriculture, education, communications, economic studies, industry, livestock, public health, tourism, and trade. The organizations began by hosting five joint conferences, three in Sonora and two in Arizona. Binational collaboration was heralded at the time, and the two governors and their committees were invited to participate in the 1962 and 1964 World's Fairs.

Mexico's Border Industrialization Program began in 1965, and the first maquiladora opened its doors in Nogales in 1967. In 1972, under the direction of Arizona Governor Jack Williams, the Arizona-Mexico West Coast Trade Commission and the Sonora-Arizona Committee for Social and Economic Promotion evolved into the Arizona-Mexico Commission and the Comisión Sonora-Arizona. At that time, they included maquiladoras among their members. The commissions were intended to serve as the principal means of communication between the states. They continued to address trade and economic development issues. But, again following larger trends that by then acknowledged the limits of a narrow focus on economic development for improving quality of life, they began paying greater attention to factors such as health and education, and they established mechanisms to address specific concerns. By May 1984, for example, the commissions voted to approve the articles and laws establishing the Arizona-Mexico Border Health Foundation to assist in the diffusion of medical knowledge and to improve medical care to the less privileged citizens of both nations who reside along the border. In 1992, Arizona Governor Fife Symington and Sonora Governor Manlio Fabio Beltrones opened trade offices in the capitals of their sister states. Also that year, the Arizona-Mexico Commission recommended the creation of the National Law Center for Inter-American Free Trade and focused its committee work on positioning the regional economy to capitalize upon the increased international opportunities created by the upcoming North American Free Trade Agreement (NAFTA), then in negotiation.

Since their reorganization, the commissions have continued to expand to address issues, such as environmental pollution, that are of concern to the member states; thirteen committees and seven ad hoc committees now undertake a host of binational activities. Like the other committees, the Environment Committee meets twice a year at the commissions' biannual plenary sessions. The committee structure is typical: it is cochaired by directors of the state-level environmental agencies of Arizona and Sonora and by two private-sector representatives, one from each state; staffed by state agency personnel dedicated to border environmental matters; and composed of environmental professionals from all sectors in both states. Agendas for the plenary session committee meetings are developed by the staff and approved by the cochairs. Meetings are used to provide general information, supply updates regarding past recommendations, and develop recommendations to be adopted during the session. Recommendations for binational activities are presented at the closing plenary session, together with the recommendations from all committees, and endorsed by the governors of the two states. Commission plenaries have proven to be an effective means of establishing and authorizing binational activities based on regional and local input, without requiring bilateral, federal treaty negotiations between the two countries. Local and state officials have observed that the latter may be carried out by federal representatives with limited knowledge of the border area or the two-state region. Communication between the plenary sessions is largely driven by specific projects as well as joint participation in various other policy-setting forums, such as the Border Governors Conference and the Ten States Meeting, that also offer opportunities to develop binational policy for the two-state region and/or the border region as a whole.

Maquiladora involvement in the commissions has evolved along with the institutions. Initially companies focused on trade issues, and participation was dominated by the managers responsible for establishing and maintaining trade. By the late 1990s, maquiladora environmental and safety managers were taking an active role in the Environment Committee (see the section on maquiladora associations, below).

By the 1990s, rapid growth and associated problems along the border had attracted national attention in the United States. In 1993, the U.S. State Department established the Border Liaison Mechanism (BLM), a diplomatic instrument to achieve dialogue and coordination between sister cities on the U.S.-Mexico border. The BLM was designed with a flexible organizational structure to allow and facilitate binational, intergovernmental collaboration at local, state, and federal levels. Nine BLMs, chaired by U.S. and Mexican consuls, operate in "border pair" cities and

> have proven to be effective means of dealing with a variety of local issues ranging from accidental violation of sovereignty by law enforcement officials and charges of mistreatment of foreign nationals to coordination of port security and cooperation in public health matters such as tuberculosis. In conjunction with the 1998 New Border Vision, the United States and Mexico agreed that each BLM would establish three working subgroups: Economic and Social Development, Protection/Migration and Border Crossing Facilitation, and Border Public Safety (http://www.state.gov/www/background_notes/mexico_0899_bgn.html).

The Arizona-Sonora BLM is cochaired by the U.S. and Mexican consuls serving in Ambos Nogales and addresses issues of interest in the border communities of the two states. Meetings are held approximately three to four times yearly, and the consuls invite various participants, primarily from the law enforcement, diplomatic, and municipal sectors, based on their interest in and potential contributions to the various agenda topics. Communication between these meetings is largely driven by specific projects (for example, implementation of the laser visa system), developing events (such as the ever-mounting toll of deaths among those attempting to cross the border illegally into the United States), and the overall missions of the agencies involved. To the extent possible, issues raised are resolved at the local level; when this is not possible, policy matters are elevated to the appropriate authorities. Because of the travel distances involved, a geographic subgroup was recently established to address local issues arising in the Yuma–San Luis–San Luis Río Colorado area. Maquiladora representation on the BLM began in 2002 when participation in one project-oriented subcommittee was broadened to include nongovernmental institutions.

Maquiladora Associations' Contribution to Binational Environmental Initiatives

Maquiladoras have participated in binational initiatives as individual companies and through two associations. The National Council of the Maquiladora Industry (CNIME) is a civil organization (*asociación civil*) established in Mexico in 1988 to facilitate the manufacturing operations of foreign corporations in Mexico, serve as a bridge between the U.S. and Mexican legal and regulatory systems, and represent the interests of maquiladoras. Its thirteen committees address legal, labor, education, immigration, transportation, and environmental issues. In 2002, approximately 90 percent of the Nogales maquiladoras, and all of the largest plants, were members.

The Association of Environmental Protection Professionals (APSA) is a smaller organization formed in 1994 by a group of environmental engineers and industrial hygienists from various Nogales maquiladoras and other businesses as a forum through which environmental, health, and safety professionals in Nogales, Sonora, could discuss and address problems related to their professions (http://mx.geocities.com/apsa_ac/menu.html). The group's first president spearheaded the creation of the group when he moved from Mexico's Environment Ministry (SEMAR-

NAT) to a position in one of Nogales's maquiladoras. APSA's explicit purpose is to improve safety and environmental practices among the maquiladoras and within the larger community. APSA strives to create permanent, positive change in health, safety, and environmental law and practice at the local, state, and national levels. The group registered formally as a civil organization in April 2000, and its 2002 membership included thirty-five companies within the maquiladora sector and supporting industries, as well as independent professionals. Most of the APSA members represent large maquiladoras, but a primary function of the association has been to provide education, training, and mentorship to employees within smaller plants and Mexican businesses. The group provides its members with legal updates, free training courses, support in meeting legal requirements, a list of consultants and specialists, formal and professional representation in government assemblies, and a central archive of information related to these topics.

As part of its outreach, APSA sponsors educational activities and community service projects. In 1998 the association began sponsoring an annual conference for environmental, health, and safety professionals (Encuentro Estatal de Profesionales en Seguridad, Higiene, y Medio Ambiente). It also holds monthly meetings, which are hosted by its members at their own facilities and include educational presentations on topics of interest to its members. The association began in Nogales and has expanded statewide. Though APSA's members are primarily Mexican and its efforts have been aimed at Nogales businesses and neighborhoods, it has been an active participant in several recent binational initiatives for environmental improvement.

In 1997, recognizing that limited resources would render command and control approaches ineffective, the Arizona Department of Environmental Quality (ADEQ) developed the Arizona-Mexico International Green Organization (AMIGO) program, and APSA has been instrumental in its success. AMIGO was modeled after a program initiated in the early 1990s by the ADEQ to partner with industry in promoting the reduction of hazardous waste generation in the state. The Arizona Partnership for Pollution Prevention (P3) provided a means of networking among, and offering mutual assistance to, participants from various industry sectors. Pollution prevention refers to any operating, fabricating, housekeeping, or managing techniques that reduce pollutants. Pollution prevention activities include toxics use reduction, source reduction, recycling, waste minimization, reclamation, conservation, reuse, and material substitution. In this program, industry partners coordinated and planned meetings, scheduled speakers, arranged facility tours, addressed issues of interest, and shared waste-reduction accomplishments across business sectors. Because the P3 flourished as industry participants began to appreciate the economic incentives of pollution prevention, ADEQ staff anticipated that this nonregulatory and voluntary model to promote waste reduction in Arizona would have the same potential in the border region.

The majority of Nogales's maquiladoras have U.S. parent companies, but parent companies from countries such as Japan and Korea also established manufacturing facilities there. The 1983 La Paz agreement stipulates that any hazardous waste generated in the manufacturing process through the use of imported raw materials must be returned to the country of origin of the raw materials. Typically, for maquiladoras with U.S. parent companies, most, if not all, of the raw materials used in manufacturing originate in the United States. This creates a potentially large waste stream flowing into Arizona; and that, along with the lack of resources to ensure compliance with either Mexican or U.S. laws on their respective sides of the border, has generated concern in both countries (see other chapters in this volume). Consequently, many in the hazardous waste industry and regulatory agencies supported establishing a voluntary P3 initiative in the Arizona-Sonora border region to augment compliance efforts.

In 1997, the U.S. Environmental Protection Agency (EPA) solicited proposals for environmental projects that would support the efforts of the U.S.-Mexico Border XXI Environmental Program (Border XXI), a five-year framework established by both governments in 1996 to address environmental issues in the U.S.-Mexico border region. ADEQ submitted a proposal and was awarded a grant to establish the P3 program, named AMIGO, in the Arizona-Sonora region, with support from local, state, and federal officials in both countries.

The focus of AMIGO is to promote pollution prevention and improve waste management practices among industries in the Arizona-Sonora border region. Voluntary members share information on successful waste reduction activities and identify and resolve barriers to pollution prevention through meetings, workshops, and facility visits. Mexican officials in Sonora have supported the organization because it is based upon the concept of waste minimization and pollution prevention, and serves as a stepping-stone for developing the state's voluntary environmental audit program. Key support for the program also comes from Sonora State's environmental agency (Secretaría de Infraestructura Urbana y Ecología;

SIUE) and the state binational commissions. In its relatively short existence, the program has received support from industry and organizations such as APSA as well. Industries on both sides of the border that have hosted facility visits or conducted presentations at workshops include companies with recognizable names such as IBM, Raytheon, Intel, Weiser Lock, The Chamberlain Group, SUMEX/XEROX, and Motorola.

As part of AMIGO, an award program was established to recognize partners in the organization who have demonstrated leadership in implementing and supporting the goals of pollution prevention to reduce the amount and toxicity of hazardous wastes and the use of toxic substances in the Arizona-Sonora border region. The awards are divided into two categories: Process Improvements and Pollution Prevention Promotion. The program includes a call for entries and an application form with instructions in both English and Spanish. Applicants are evaluated on the criteria of Economic Benefits, Employee and Community Involvement, Environmental Benefit, Management Commitment, and Pollution Prevention Hierarchy. The awards are presented at the annual fall plenary session of the Arizona-Mexico and Sonora-Arizona commissions.

For each of the two categories, the ADEQ and SIUE, in coordination with the regional offices of the federal environmental agencies, select one award recipient. Each panelist individually scores each application, and then a consensus decision is formulated. The specific evaluation criteria used to select the recipients are identified in table 8.3. Promotion of the awards program begins during the summer months through mass mailings, presentations at meetings and conferences, and posting of information on the ADEQ Web page. Participation requires prior membership in AMIGO, so applicants are aware that a panel consisting of representatives from the four agencies will conduct the evaluations. The majority of applications come from maquiladoras, and the Mexican agencies provide notification to the other evaluation panelists if there are any compliance issues with the applicants. Additionally, for maquiladoras that have a twin plant in Arizona, an internal compliance status review of that facility is conducted.

According to data provided by the winners, in the last three years those companies alone saved nearly $1 million by implementing pollution prevention strategies. The success of these and other maquiladoras has helped to reach other companies, especially those without the resources to address environmental issues at their facilities, through mentoring and networking. The effort to promote these accomplishments has also lent support to environmental education efforts of APSA, local technical institutes, and state-level institutions of higher education.

Though not readily quantifiable, the acceptance and success of the AMIGO program in the Arizona-Sonora maquiladora sector can be attributed to a variety of factors that are fundamental to binational cooperation. These include the historical state-level collaboration generated by the Arizona-Mexico and Sonora-Arizona commissions and the support these institutions have imparted to the program; the low cost of implementing this type of voluntary partnership program; the longevity and stability of the ADEQ staff implementing the program, as well as key participants within APSA and the maquiladora sector, which is a vital component in establishing trust in a binational and bicultural setting; and the bicultural and bilingual skills of the involved staff.

UTILIZING THE FOUNDATION FOR ACTION: PURPOSE, PROCESS, AND PERFORMANCE

The remainder of this chapter will examine how the foundation laid by the various initiatives allowed a binational coalition of governmental, nongovernmental, industry, and academic institutions to come together with school groups and *colonia* (neighborhood) residents to promote revegetation in Nogales and establish a framework that would foster additional environmental and community development projects. Successful collaboration relied upon the established networks and required a clear *purpose*, careful attention to *process* so that participation did not depend on size or resources and so that responsibilities were delineated, and collective *performance* in specific actions that demonstrated commitment and achievement.

The BLM Economic and Social Development Subgroup: Addressing Air Quality

In 1999 the U.S. and Mexican consuls in Ambos Nogales recruited ADEQ and SIUE to assist them in establishing the Nogales Border Liaison Mechanism's Economic and Social Development Subgroup (BLM Subgroup) with the specific purpose of addressing the binational air quality problem in the region. The resulting binational, intergovernmental dialogue also was responsive to recommendations of the Arizona-Mexico Commission's Environment and Education committees.

Table 8.3. Evaluation Criteria for AMIGO Awards

Criterion	Definition
Economic benefits	Demonstrates financial savings or quality improvement to the product or other operations due to the implementation of pollution prevention.
Employee/community involvement	Employee or organizational involvement in pollution prevention activities in the community.
Environmental benefit	Illustrates environmental benefits through the reduction in volume or level of toxicity, the generation of hazardous wastes, or use of chemicals and related discharges or emissions.
Management commitment	Indicates management support relating to changes in policies, procedures, or operations to meet pollution prevention goals, and future planned actions to provide ongoing pollution prevention activities.
Pollution prevention hierarchy	Highlights the hierarchy of environmental management with highest priority placed on source reduction, followed by decreasing priority on reuse, recycling, and treatment, and with disposal as the option of last resort.

Since its inception, officials from ADEQ and SIUE, together with the two consuls, have cochaired this BLM Subgroup. The group benefits from the active participation of various departments of each of the local governments, other state and federal agencies focused on environment or health, and a variety of state and federal agencies with a role to play in reducing local particulate matter emissions. For example, because emissions generated by cars waiting to cross the border are a significant source of air pollution in Nogales, port-of-entry inspection agencies are members of this subgroup.

Air quality in Ambos Nogales is impaired by particulate matter (dust) contamination. This contamination has been estimated to have important health impacts for area residents, ranging from increased upper respiratory tract infections (for example, colds or flu), to more frequent and severe attacks among asthma sufferers and increased levels of premature death among elderly people who already suffer from an underlying heart or lung condition. Rates of health impacts attributable to particulate matter are similar in the two communities because they share a common airshed and their residents are thus exposed to similar levels of contamination. Air quality in Ambos Nogales regularly violates federal standards set for particulate matter in the United States and Mexico. For this reason, Nogales, Arizona, and other portions of Santa Cruz County—primarily Rio Rico—have been designated an EPA "non-attainment area" for particulate matter.

The first task of the BLM Subgroup was to develop a set of recommended actions to improve air quality in Ambos Nogales. BLM Subgroup members proposed and accepted a set of operational ground rules and a method for reaching consensus on all group decisions (see Saint and Lawson 1994). A "state of consensus" was achieved *when and only when* members could support a decision at least to the extent described in the following statement:

> I understand what most of you would like to do. It is not my first choice, but I feel you understand what my alternative would be. I have had sufficient opportunity to sway you to my point of view, but clearly have not done so. Therefore, I can live with <u>and support</u> what I consider to be an acceptable solution (Take Charge Consultants, Inc., at www.takechargeinc.com/).

Decisions were accepted by unanimous, formal consensus *when and only when* members had indicated, on a scale of 1 to 6, their level of support

Table 8.4. Steps in BLM Subgroup Consensus Process

1.	We will maintain mutual respect. This means we disagree with <u>ideas</u>, not with people. It also means we provide amnesty to any and all suggestions or ideas offered, no matter how odd they may seem to us.
2.	Disagreement will be viewed as an <u>opportunity</u> to identify many possible solutions, which enhances our decision-making process by offering a greater degree of choice.
3.	We will not <u>seek</u> conflict-reducing techniques, such as going along just to get along.
4.	A member's silence will be interpreted as showing his or her <u>agreement</u> with what is being discussed or proposed.
5.	Any move to block a decision <u>must</u> be accompanied by the reason(s) why the member feels the need to block the decision as well as a proposal for how to unblock the decision.
6.	All members <u>agree</u> not to withhold information that is vital to a decision-making process.
7.	All members are <u>obliged</u> not to compromise their own personal integrity.
8.	Members recognize that most decisions can always be recalled, revised, or revoked when presented with new information that makes such a change necessary or desirable.

for the decision under consideration and no one indicated they would block the decision or needed more information. Eight ground rules were adapted for local use to guide the group's deliberations and decision-making process (see table 8.4). Using this approach in a two-phase series of planning sessions, the BLM Subgroup developed a set of twelve recommended actions to improve air quality. In the first phase, a series of informational sessions focused primarily on five aspects of the air quality problem in Ambos Nogales: residential emissions (primarily from wood burning and garbage burning), soil erosion, unpaved traffic areas, traffic congestion, and vehicle emissions. These problems were identified in a binational air quality study conducted jointly by ADEQ and SEMARNAT (ADEQ 1999) and by local residents and environmental professionals.

The planning sessions concluded with a visioning session that ranked seventy-eight possible actions. Following review of financing sources and mechanisms, the BLM Subgroup sought final recommendations that would include long-term solutions but would focus on well-defined options likely to have greater impacts in the short and medium term. As directed according to the unanimous, formal consensus of the BLM Subgroup, ADEQ and SIUE worked together to revise the list of options and propose a refined set of recommendations for the group to discuss and modify. The revisions were based on a strategic review of the list of options as well as discussions with the municipal governments participating in the BLM Subgroup. After discussing the proposed revisions, the BLM Subgroup further refined the recommendations to distinguish "high" and "additional" priority items. Though high-priority items were to receive greatest emphasis, the group recognized that some items on the additional priority list, especially those that might be easier and quicker to implement, should also receive attention.

In support of the BLM Subgroup's first phase of activities, the University of Arizona evaluated the nature of deforestation and the potential for the success of revegetation efforts in reducing erosion in Ambos Nogales. The University's Bureau of Applied Research in Anthropology, in collaboration with the Department of Soil, Water and Environmental Sciences, led this assessment. The analysis included three primary components: (1) group meetings and individual interviews with organizations already involved in reforestation or revegetation efforts in Ambos Nogales to identify existing resources; (2) field studies combined with preliminary modeling efforts to identify the extent of erosion occurring in four different colonias of Nogales, Sonora, and the reductions that could be realized through revegetation; and (3) community interviews of residents in these four colonias and various neighborhoods in Nogales, Arizona, to determine resident attitudes toward plants and the environment, as well as the kinds of factors that might motivate residents to become more involved in revegetation and reforestation efforts.

The research group shared the results of the revegetation assessment with the BLM Subgroup during one of its informational sessions, reporting that revegetation had significant potential to reduce soil erosion on the sandy loam slopes characteristic of Ambos Nogales and that there existed potential support and organizational infrastructure for revegetation efforts. The assessment occurred after the Mexican government identified reforestation as a national priority; and a tree-planting program begun in 1998 by the maquiladora SUMEX was among those efforts identified during the assessment. The assessment findings sufficiently impressed the members of the BLM Subgroup that several immediate actions were identified and endorsed to promote revegetation. The Subgroup's final recommendations to improve air quality in Ambos Nogales included one directed at revegetation. The Ambos Nogales Revegetation Partnership emerged as one attempt to support revegetation efforts.

SUMEX and Maquiladora Reforestation Efforts

SUMEX has led reforestation programs in Nogales since 1998, when the company began giving away trees to its employees as part of its Earth Day celebration. At its Nogales facility, the company remanufactures printer cartridges and, in the process, recycles over 90 percent of all the production material used (personal communication with John Swanson, 2002). While SUMEX has adopted some of the standards of its parent company, XEROX, its managers have also established their own goal of being a leader in environmental stewardship. SUMEX was awarded an AMIGO award each year between 1998 and 2001.

SUMEX's reforestation project grew quickly, from distributing a thousand trees in its first year to over seventeen thousand by 2002, and it expanded to include all city residents. SUMEX worked with the Mexican and Sonoran governments to acquire trees from the government-run nurseries. Because of the national initiative to promote reforestation, residents were able obtain trees at no cost. SUMEX paid to transport the trees and developed a brochure about tree care to distribute with the trees to Nogales residents.

In addition to SUMEX, C.R. Bard, Chamberlain, Moen, Motorola, Tecate, Sunbelt, Megas, and Chermax had all participated in reforestation efforts in Nogales. However, SUMEX's efforts had been sustained over the longest period, and SUMEX managers began challenging other maquiladoras to become more involved in community environmental protection and improvement programs. They helped establish a revegetation committee within APSA to organize cleanup and revegetation campaigns. In addition, they worked with city officials to revise Sonora's 1990 ecology law (Ley 217) to better meet the needs of Nogales. The law requires that any trees that are removed during development must be replaced with three new trees. However, the lack of any requirement for maintenance has meant that few of the new trees survive. The revised law seeks to increase survival rates by requiring developers to transplant the vegetation cleared for new development and, when it is necessary to replace trees, to plant vegetation that is native to the Nogales region.

The Ambos Nogales Revegetation Partnership

One of the strongest messages of the revegetation assessment was that the people of Ambos Nogales believed there had been enough studies and wanted to see concrete steps taken to improve the environment and to foster a stronger sense of respect and care for their community. Platicamos Salud (Let's Talk Health), a department of the Mariposa Community Health Center in Nogales, Arizona, had received EPA funds to support local environmental improvement efforts, and several of the recipients were eager to continue and expand their work. As the assessment was coming to a close, the University of Arizona announced small grants aimed at fostering collaboration among institutions of higher education on both sides of the U.S.-Mexico border.[1] Three units within the University of Arizona, along with the Instituto Tecnológico de Nogales, submitted the grant, which included as partners the municipal ecology department,[2] a prepara-

---

[1] The grants were offered by the Consortium for North American Higher Education Collaboration, an initiative of the Ford Foundation and the William and Flora Hewlett Foundation through its Border Partners in Action (Border PACT) program.

[2] Partners include, in Mexico, the Departamento Ecología H. Ayuntamiento, the Centro de Estudios Tecnológicos Industrial y de Servicios 128, Escuela Ignacio W. Covarrubias, and SUMEX of the XEROX Corporation from Nogales, Sonora. The partners in the United States are the ADEQ, the Southeast Arizona Health and Education Center, the Arizona Department of Health Sciences Office of Border

tory school, a primary school, and SUMEX from Nogales, Sonora, and, from north of the border, the ADEQ, two health agencies, an organic farm and composting business, and a community health organization active in Nogales and Rio Rico, Arizona. A principal challenge for the partners lay in establishing mechanisms by which the institutions of higher education could obtain and distribute funds. In Mexico, for example, funds go first to Mexico City and then are sent to the local educational institution. The Instituto Tecnológico de Nogales had established a *patronato*, a foundation that works locally to raise funds for the institution, and this organization functioned as the award recipient.

The grant supported three pilot projects—a neighborhood park, a schoolyard habitat, and a nursery and composting facility. University students also produced guides to native vegetation of Ambos Nogales, water harvesting, and composting. The city's ecology department provided maps, background information for the guides, and permits for the projects. SUMEX provided barrels to serve as composting bins, information about how to obtain trees from the Mexican government's nurseries, and help dealing with border officials. Many of the neighborhood residents worked at maquiladoras, and they were able to obtain a grant from one of their employers to pay for fencing their park. ADEQ provided background information for and funded production of the guides. Terra-Cycle Technologies, the organic farm, provided gardening and composting workshops and compost for the planting efforts. Students and faculty from the high schools, technical college, and university worked with residents and provided ideas, information, and labor. New partners joined the effort as particular needs, such as workshops on desert ecology and water harvesting, were identified.

The revegetation partnership evolved to become a loose consortium of groups and individuals from the governmental, academic, business, and nonprofit sectors. Partners began holding monthly meetings to share information and identify areas requiring attention; in May 2003, participants adopted the name Asociación de Reforestación en Ambos Nogales, whose acronym, ARAN, means "they plow" in Spanish.

SUMEX managers initially became involved in the revegetation partnership as a way to build upon the success of their tree distribution program, help build local capacity for tree maintenance and care, and broaden local support for environmental protection. The maquiladora expanded its

---

Health, Terra-Cycle Technologies, and Platicamos Salud from Nogales and Rio Rico, Arizona.

participation in revegetation and environmental projects to include the donation of barrels to a local preparatory school for use as composting bins, the creation of a small grants program for environmental projects funded with monies received in exchange for recycling cardboard from the plant, and consultation with schools and neighborhood groups initiating revegetation projects. Interest within other maquiladoras led to a greater interaction between APSA and the revegetation partnership.

Weiser Lock

In response to interest expressed by several APSA members in revegetation efforts at their plant sites, two university students helped develop a pilot revegetation project at a maquiladora site. The students worked with APSA's revegetation committee to design and conduct an assessment of three maquiladoras and select the pilot site. At each maquiladora they assessed the land available for revegetation, the level of interest in and support for a revegetation project, and the willingness of managers to allow workers to participate in the project. The three maquiladoras included two large maquilas—Samson/Samsonite (a luggage manufacturer), which had operated in Nogales for thirty-two years; Weiser Lock (a lock and doorware manufacturer), which had relocated from Tucson in 1999; and Transformadora de México, a small recycling plant with fifty-seven employees, which opened in 1996. The students selected Weiser Lock because of the land, water, and human resources that would be made available to the project.

Weiser Lock is one of the newest maquiladoras in Nogales and is located in the New Industrial Park of Nogales, a 500-acre industrial zone.[3] Workers in the plant assemble doorknobs and other locking devices. In 2002, the plant employed over seven hundred workers, had over eight acres of land available for revegetation, and disposed of over ten thousand gallons of water a day that could be reused for vegetation. Both managers and workers expressed interest in revegetation, and senior managers agreed to allow employees to help with planting and maintenance during the workday. Weiser Lock employees gathered information about the wa-

---

[3] The Nogales community has criticized the creation of the New Industrial Park, which required the clearing away of native vegetation. Community members formerly referred to this area as "Nogal forest," after the native *nogal* (walnut tree) for which the city is named. Workers have expressed a personal interest in revegetating this area.

ter system, provided samples for water quality testing, and worked with the students to design a plan for their site. University students provided information about species and their availability, helped employees write a letter to the government nursery to request trees, and recruited a student in landscape architecture to help review the plan.

Planting at the site began in the summer of 2002. The workers received almost two hundred trees, including native manzanitas and sycamores from the government nursery located in Santa Ana, a small town two hours from Nogales. Though the workers had to balance their work responsibilities and their dedication to this project, moving between tree planting and their work stations inside the plant, the organizers maintained a commitment to the project.

Understanding Maquiladora Participation

Industry participation in community efforts is frequently viewed with skepticism, and the maquiladora participation in the revegetation partnership requires a closer look. Information for this analysis comes from the authors' participation in APSA meetings and revegetation efforts. In addition, Alba Jaramillo worked with the Weiser Lock project throughout 2002, participated in APSA's revegetation committee, and conducted interviews with maquiladora managers.

Nogales maquiladoras range in size from small companies operating out of trailers to large, well-financed operations tied to major multinational corporations. Many of the companies that are most active in the revegetation and other community projects are affiliated with large corporations. Their environmental managers are well versed in international codes and standards, are ISO 9000 certified, and are operating in a framework within which at least the rhetoric of corporate responsibility is widely shared. These individuals tend to be supported, if not actively encouraged, in their efforts. Still, the managers report that they have a significant degree of autonomy in determining the nature and extent of their environmental protection and community outreach activities. In some cases, they perceive their plants to be competing against others within the corporation for product lines and their headquarters' support. Though this sense of competition may spill over to community outreach, there is little evidence that successful public relations are sufficient for significantly increasing the status of the maquiladora within the corporate structure.

Furthermore, many of the maquiladora projects described above will generate little, if any, additional recognition in corporate headquarters. APSA's programs to mentor environmental managers in smaller maquiladoras and Mexican-owned businesses, SUMEX's participation in the revegetation partnership to increase the success of its tree planting and distribution efforts, and Weiser Lock's development of a revegetation project to utilize wastewater are examples. Comments of maquiladora managers and employees in planning meetings, project activities, and interviews reveal that the maquiladoras in Nogales have reached a point where they not only contribute to the formal infrastructure of commissions, committees, and boards, but they also, by providing relatively good jobs to local residents, help support, through their employees, the informal social infrastructure of the community.

The environmental problems of Nogales directly affect the managers' lives, and the managers link their participation in local projects to their ties to the community. For example, the leader of one of APSA's neighborhood revegetation projects is a resident of that neighborhood. At Weiser Lock, workers established the following goals for the project: provide shaded areas that the workers and their families could enjoy, make better use of the gray water (water processed through industrial use), create green areas within the maquiladora, and help beautify the plant site. Their project was the only one undertaken by the revegetation partnership on private land, and it was selected because the company agreed to make the space available to community residents.

When asked why they were involved in revegetation, most maquiladora managers expressed a common sentiment. Responses included "We have an obligation to our society"; "We want to respect the environment because natural resources are limited"; "There must be an interaction between maquiladoras and the community"; "We have a goal not just to offer jobs to the community but to promote the communal interest"; and "Our children live here." Others offered economic reasons such as, "It is good business to protect the environment; the company can profit from it."

Participation of maquiladora managers in environmental projects is also a reaction to the negative images about maquiladoras that are frequently shared in the news media and have become internalized by some workers. At an early meeting of the revegetation partnership, one individual stated that he wanted to participate in the group to do something good for the environment since his work at the maquiladora was per-

ceived as harming the environment. His employer had recently been recognized as a leader in environmental management, and his comment
demonstrated that the stereotyped images of maquiladoras affect workers
and managers regardless of the performance of individual plants. One
Weiser Lock manager suggested that the main goal of that project was to
"cambiar la visión"—to change the image of maquiladoras with respect to
the environment. In meetings and interviews, several people commented
that they are blamed for Nogales's environmental problems. At an APSA
meeting, one maquiladora manager brought a newspaper article that
charged a maquiladora for not properly disposing of its hazardous waste.
He told the group:

> It is our responsibility to answer publicity like this. The ma-
> jority of maquiladoras do a clean job, and the majority of
> maquiladoras spend a lot of money on training. As members
> of APSA, our responsibility is to produce a clean image of
> maquiladoras. We cannot stay quiet. Nobody is on the side of
> maquiladoras. As members of APSA we need to discuss the
> positive things that maquiladoras are doing.

His comment generated much discussion but no consensus about the
role APSA should play in policing or defending individual companies or
maquiladoras. The group members expressed the desire to see their organization continue to serve as a place where maquiladora managers could
come together to solve problems.

CONCLUSIONS

The maquiladora model has been criticized for its failure to require companies to contribute to the infrastructure of the community to which they
relocate. Local leaders have had little say over the nature and scope of
maquiladora development. Public officials and private citizens in Ambos
Nogales, including those who work in the maquiladoras, have been vocal
about the environmental problems that have resulted from rapid growth
and unplanned development. Irresponsible environmental practices at
individual maquiladoras have also generated outrage. At the same time,
in Nogales and other border communities, maquiladoras are now an inte-
gral part of the local economy; the jobs they provide support the civic
leaders and residents upon whose social capital communities are maintained.

In Nogales, a framework has been established within which maquiladora managers and workers can and do participate in local environmental improvement efforts, from physical enhancement of plant and neighborhood sites to legal reform. That framework was developed within a context where binational government-government and government-industry collaboration had been well established. These efforts are maintained by rules of participation that represent a compromise between an open-meeting model that allows anyone to come and participate and a closed-door approach to decision making. The framework provides forums within which participants can find common ground and develop trust. This framework also legitimizes less formal cross-border collaboration, such as the Ambos Nogales Revegetation Partnership (ARAN), within which maquiladora employees, city and state officials, educators, and residents gather in the same meeting rooms and neighborhood parks to plan and carry out projects.

This sociopolitical infrastructure is often overlooked, but it is as crucial to community development as is the physical infrastructure of roads and sewer systems, and it takes significant time and resources to establish. Like a system of roads or water pipes developed after homes and businesses have been built, the infrastructure that developed in Nogales to address environmental problems was not planned in advance, but emerged instead from the links and connections that already existed. At various points, such as the creation of APSA and the mobilization of the BLM Subgroup, a new design was laid out and deliberate connections were made. The persistence of the system will depend on both the integrity of the original design and the continued functionality of the links. Minor failures—such as the loss of an individual within a maquiladora or agency or the loss of a school or neighborhood group—can be overcome by redundancy. Critical linkages among the sectors, though, must be maintained. The integration of government, business, academic, and nonprofit interests and organizations is necessary to retain balance, resources, and credibility.

Sociopolitical links are facilitated by both individual and institutional histories. The movement of a Mexican environmental official to a job within a maquiladora was instrumental in the development of APSA and in the interaction among maquiladoras and between maquiladoras and the government; likewise, the movement of an EPA official to a position within the ADEQ was important for strengthening intergovernmental communication on the U.S. side. Though such linkages have the potential to restrict participation and limit the introduction of alternate ideas and paradigms, they are essential for establishing networks.

Several features of the collaborative efforts described here are notable. First, the binational partnerships have opened up new possibilities for learning and access to resources not otherwise available. The Arizona-Mexico and Sonora-Arizona commissions and their committees have given sanction and support to binational intergovernmental initiatives such as the AMIGO program, which, in turn, fostered the growth of APSA's environmental education and outreach efforts. In the revegetation partnership, initial small grants and seeds for native grasses and shrubs came from the United States, and trees and labor came mostly from Mexico. By the end of the first year, though, Sonoran residents had raised funds and acquired grants for their projects, nurseries were under development at several schools, and more students were being recruited from Arizona. At the end of 2002, several members of the partnership, including both managers and workers at several maquiladoras, were elected to Nogales's official Municipal Reforestation Committee, one of twelve established by the Mexican government within the state of Sonora. After those members engaged in considerable struggle to gain government approval, the University of Arizona was invited to become a member of the committee's higher education subgroup. This action demonstrated the depth of local commitment to cross-border collaboration.

The relative stability of both the institutions and key participants within the region has contributed to the success of these collaborations. Individuals have been crucial in bringing their institutions and organizations to the partnerships and holding them there. They have worked within their organizations to identify problems and motivate change, and they have shared their knowledge and experiences across groups.

Implications of Recent Trends

Long-term partnerships begin with shared goals, grow with trust, and are maintained by their members' considerable investments of time and energy. The collaborative efforts described in this chapter have benefited from continuity and the committed involvement of key participants. During 2002, the jobs and security of several people within maquiladoras, government agencies, and academia were threatened by the economic hard times felt throughout the region. Some people lost their jobs, and others were transferred to new positions where their opportunities for participation in collaborative efforts were limited. APSA, which has played an instrumental role in facilitating interaction among maquiladora managers and supporting community education and outreach efforts, was created during a period of growth and expansion. It remains to be seen how the recession and related layoffs will affect the organization and its role in the community.

Changes that are happening in the border region and within the maquiladora sector potentially threaten the social infrastructure. At the same time, they open opportunities to examine the resiliency of the collaborative partnerships that have developed. Continued expansion of maquiladoras to interior communities requires attention to whether and how multinational social infrastructure develops away from the border. The endeavors described here have depended on mutual recognition of common interests, frequent face-to-face interaction, and personal ties that existed prior to the formal efforts at collaboration and that were established through these efforts. Strong ties expanded into weaker ties that successfully linked many previously unassociated people with networks and organizations from which resources and support were drawn. Short distances facilitated the participation of many people, including busy government officials, residents, and students. Whether and among whom such infrastructure might develop elsewhere remains to be seen.

The authors are involved in several new initiatives that will allow further investigation. First, there are plans to replicate the revegetation partnership model in Ambos Nogales in a thermal-housing-construction training program aimed at investigating the potential for alternative approaches to housing construction that minimize the need for artificial heating and incorporate the principles of site design developed through the revegetation partnership. This partnership is anticipated to start with groups, including some local maquiladoras, that have participated in housing projects. Beginning during a period of economic distress, it would provide a basis for comparison. Though currently there are no links between the two initiatives, representatives from both groups have recognized the tremendous benefits that could result from working together. In addition, through a collaboration with the Universidad de las Américas in Puebla, Mexico, faculty and students from the border and interior regions have discussed the design and implementation of comparative studies of maquiladora and community development. They would investigate whether the leadership and ideas developed through groups such as APSA and the AMIGO program accompany the maquiladoras as they move, or whether the social infrastructure in those communities must be built from scratch.

The efforts described in this chapter illustrate that sociopolitical infrastructure for community development can and does develop within areas dominated by maquiladora industrialization. They nevertheless also illustrate that the process is lengthy and requires considerable inputs from people who have experience within government, industry, academia, and nonprofit organizations from both the host country and that of the parent corporation. It is important to consider the distance, both geographical and cultural, over which collaboration is possible and effective. The social and environmental impacts of maquiladoras, within the U.S.-Mexico border region and elsewhere, cannot be addressed without simultaneous action within larger national contexts, by both policymakers and the consumers of the goods produced at the maquiladoras. As maquiladoras move farther from the U.S. border, the challenge of getting and maintaining the attention of U.S. citizens and policymakers is likely to grow.

References

ADEQ (Arizona Department of Environmental Quality). 1999. "Ambos Nogales Binational Air Quality Study: Citizens' Summary." August.

Arreola, Daniel D., and James R. Curtis. 1993. *The Mexican Border Cities: Landscape Anatomy and Place Personality*. Tucson: University of Arizona Press.

ASDC (Association for the Study and Development of Community). 1999. "Principles for Intergroup Projects: A First Look." Report prepared for the Community Foundations/Intergroup Relations Program funded by the Ford and C.S. Mott Foundations. At www.capablecommunity.com.

Bendesky, León. 2002. "Crecimiento," *La Jornada Virtual*, May 27.

Czerny, Robert E. 1999. "The Federal Government as Partner: Six Steps to Successful Collaboration." Treasury Board of Canada Secretariat, November.

Davidson, Miriam. 2000. *Lives on the Line: Dispatches from the U.S.-Mexico Border*. Tucson: University of Arizona Press.

Fosler, R. Scott. 2002. "Working Better Together: How Government, Business, and Nonprofit Organizations Can Achieve Public Purposes through Cross-Sector Collaborations, Alliances, and Partnerships." Report prepared for the Conference Board, Council on Foundations, Independent Sector, National Academy of Public Administration, National Alliance of Business, National Civic League, and National Governors' Association.

Granovetter, Mark S. 1973. "The Strength of Weak Ties," *American Journal of Sociology* 78: 1360–80.

————. 1982. "The Strength of Weak Ties: A Network Theory Revisited." In *Social Structure and Network Analysis*, edited by Peter V. Marsden and Nan Lin. Beverly Hills, Calif.: Sage.

JMCSD (Jackson-Madison County School District). 2001. "Components of Successful Inclusion." Jackson-Madison County School District and Tennessee Developmental Disabilities Planning Council, www.acu.edu/academics/ education, last update July 2, 2001.

Kopinak, Kathryn. 1996. *Desert Capitalism: Maquiladoras in North America's Western Industrial Corridor*. Tucson: University of Arizona Press.

Saint, Steven, and James R. Lawson. 1994. *Rules for Reaching Consensus: A Modern Approach to Decision Making*. Amsterdam: Pfeiffer.

Smith, Geri. 2002. "The Decline of the Maquiladora," *Business Week*, April 29, p. 59.

Staudt, Kathleen, and Irasema Coronado. 2002. *Fronteras No Mas: Toward Social Justice on the U.S.-Mexico Border*. New York: Pargrave Macmillan.

Vélez-Ibáñez, Carlos. 1996. *Border Visions: Mexican Cultures of the Southwest United States*. Tucson: University of Arizona Press.

Zúñiga, Juan Antonio, and Roberto González Amador. 2002. "545 maquiladoras han salido de México desde junio de 2001," *La Jornada Virtual*, July 17.

9

Unions and Social Benefits in the Maquiladoras

CIRILA QUINTERO RAMÍREZ

This chapter analyzes the behavior of two types of unions in maquiladoras, one in Matamoros and the other in Ciudad Juárez. Particular effort is made to explain the unions' different levels of involvement in helping their workers gain economic rewards and meet their social needs, such as health, education, and housing. The chapter reveals a difference in the practices of the two unions. The agenda of the Matamoros union, identified here as a "traditional" union, integrates both economic demands and the kinds of social benefits referred to above. The "subordinate" union, in Ciudad Juárez, has minimized social benefits or linked them to the needs of production or the company's international dynamic.

The chapter reveals how traditional maquiladora unions are very similar in behavior to Mexico's older industrial unions, such as those of miners or oil workers, which incorporated a variety of social benefits into their collective bargaining contracts (CCTs), the principal documents to assure labor gains. The subordinated maquila union more closely resembles the traditional unions that failed to retain social benefits in their collective bargaining agreements or that linked these benefits to the needs of the company, especially in industries that depended on the international movement of capital,[1] as was the case with the maquiladoras established along Mexico's northern border in the mid-1960s. The chapter explains the

---

[1] A significant share of Mexican companies adopted this strategy as they attempted to integrate into the global market during Mexico's industrial restructuring. For more, see de la Garza 1993.

differences between these unions' behavior in terms of their development trajectory, the characteristics of their respective industries, and the labor context existing in their respective regions.

MEXICO AND WORKERS' BENEFITS

The maquiladoras presented a challenge to traditional Mexican unions; they represented a new kind of industry, more closely linked to the international market than to the domestic one that had predominated during Mexico's period of import-substitution industrialization (ISI). These new industries were displayed as showpieces for the new export-led development model the Mexican government adopted in the 1980s. The new industries demanded more from the workers in the production process—higher productivity and better product quality—in order to be competitive in international markets. The problem was that these demands were not paralleled by improvements in social benefits for the workers. On the contrary, social benefits began to disappear from collective bargaining agreements.

I use "social benefits" here as including all services and benefits that unions have obtained for their workers beyond the payment of wages.[2] These services are linked to the social reproduction of the labor force, defined as the social conditions a worker needs—housing, health care, education, and so on—to reproduce himself/herself and his/her family.[3] Social reproduction, then, implies two aspects: maintenance, first, of the worker and, second, of his/her replacement in the workplace by future generations (de Oliveira and Salles 2000). For both stages of social reproduction to occur, workers must have the means to satisfy their basic needs. However, reproduction of the labor force is not only biological; it is also ideological (de la Garza 1989: 123).

From a Marxist perspective, employers should be primarily responsible for providing the means for satisfying the reproduction needs of their workers and their workers' families. However, other actors, such as the

---

[2] The wage in maquiladoras is a front-burner issue, especially in terms of its level vis-à-vis wages in the United States. Cooney (2001) states that the Mexican wage is about 1/11th of the U.S. wage. The issue of wages' falling purchasing power is largely outside the scope of this chapter.

[3] This definition comes, in part, from Karl Marx, who states: "the value of the labor force is defined by the value of the indispensable articles of primary necessity for producing, developing, maintaining and perpetuating the labor force" (Marx 1974a: 56; author's translation).

state or labor unions, could also contribute to the satisfaction of these needs. Together, these actors participate in an *organized reproduction* of the social reproduction of workers, understood to include such aspects as education, food, leisure, transportation, public services, and training (de la Garza 1989: 122–23). The extent of each actor's involvement will depend on the specific social context.

The Mexican case offers a good example of the involvement of companies, the state, and labor unions, and the different ways in which these actors serve workers' social needs. According to Marx and others, wages (the price the capitalist pays for labor) should support not only the survival of the worker but also the procreation of new workers for the labor market (Marx 1974b: 162). Wages, according to Marx, are the price of the existence and reproduction of the worker and his family. Article 90 of Mexico's federal labor law (LFT), on the minimum wage, seems to acknowledge this:

> The minimum wage is the least amount that the worker should receive in cash for one day of work.[4] The minimum wage should be sufficient to satisfy the normal material, social, and cultural needs of a household head and to provide state-mandated education to his children (LFT 2001: 21).

Despite the official definition of minimum wage, there is a lively debate about the ability of the set minimum wage to cover workers' basic needs, especially in light of wages' lost purchasing power in recent decades and the gap between the rate of inflation and wage increases. According to Salas (2001: 6), Mexico's minimum wage—which is set each year by official unions, employers, and the federal government—lost almost half of its purchasing power between 1990 and 2000.

Wages' loss of purchasing power makes non-wage benefits even more important, and Mexico's labor law gives employers and the state important roles to play in the provision of social benefits. The law requires that companies not only pay wages but also fulfill workers' social needs. The state, for its part, develops complementary programs designed to satisfy social needs.

---

[4] The minimum wage is set by a tripartite National Minimum Wage Commission. Besides cash payments for each workday of labor, wages are integrated into a lump sum in the form of commissions or paid in any other mutually agreed manner (Bureau of International Labor Affairs 1996: 7).

In the area of education, federal labor law specifies that employers collaborate with labor and education authorities in literacy campaigns for workers and that they also provide educational support to workers' children. The law directs companies to establish scholarships for workers and/or their children and to cover the costs of their studies. The law also requires employers to provide worker training (LFT 2001: 31–32) and to improve workers' preparation. The state participates by providing all students with a free primary school education, a right established in the Constitution.

In support of workers' health, federal labor law obliges employers to offer a safe and clean work environment, "to prevent accidents and illness in the workplace" (LFT 2001: 32). The law emphasizes employers' obligation to take measures to avoid excessive contaminants in the workplace. Finally, the law asks employers to provide medicine and treatment in case of worker accidents or injuries; when industrial plants are located in areas with high incidence of disease, such as tropical zones, employers are required to provide preventative medicine to protect workers' health.

The state complements employer-provided health services through the Mexican Social Security Institute (IMSS), which is responsible for providing medical care and essential social services to those living at a subsistence level. The IMSS is also responsible for pensions (Ley del Seguro Social 2001: 523). IMSS services are for workers, their spouses, minor children, and live-in parents. Each company pays a set quota to the IMSS, according to the number of workers it employs. Each worker also pays a contribution.

With regard to housing, federal labor law specifies that "all industrial, agricultural, and mining companies must provide clean and comfortable housing for their workers." To this end, companies contribute the equivalent of 5 percent of their total worker payroll to the government's National Workers' Housing Fund (INFONAVIT) (LFT 2001: 36).[5] INFONAVIT uses these funds to provide workers with inexpensive credit with which to obtain clean and comfortable housing, as well as to build, repair, or improve their own homes.

Federal labor law also addresses sports and cultural activities, requiring employers to provide the necessary uniforms and equipment. The state itself has no special programs to support such endeavors.

The system of companies and government together providing social benefits for workers seems to have functioned adequately under the ISI

---

[5] Even if a company provides housing for its workers, it must still make its IN-FONAVIT contribution (LFT 2001: 30).

model. However, when Mexico adopted an economic model that made the country dependent on the international economy, it also changed the social system of protection for workers.[6]

> [Mexico's] development process lost its national character. It was transformed into a by-product of the global strategies of multinational companies. Development was no longer related to state or social priorities. Decisions were to be inserted into the strategies of corporations. The balance of power between national states and corporations began to favor the latter (Zapata 2001: 2).

The adoption of the free market model by most Latin American countries has meant that "some central questions, such as the price of the labor force, social protection, social security, health, and welfare of the workers, were determined according to the competitiveness of each economic structure" (Zapata 1993: 143).

In Mexico, two key changes occurred in social welfare programs: first, the government initiated a new pension system; second, it reformed workers' housing provisions. In the first case, the government created individual retirement accounts (IRAs), to which employers must deposit 2 percent of each employee's wage; employees may make additional voluntary contributions if they wish. Workers can access their pension funds at age 65 or receive a pension from the IMSS or private pension funds established by their employer (Bureau of International Labor Affairs 1996: 15).

The INFONAVIT contribution remains set at 5 percent of an employee's wage, but now the employee owns his/her account. Previously, the 5 percent housing contribution went directly into INFONAVIT coffers. Under the new system, INFONAVIT will no longer construct houses. Instead, its role will be to help finance housing construction and to provide mortgage guarantees (Bureau of International Labor Affairs 1996: 15).

The next section examines the participation of the third actor—unions—in the provision of benefits to support workers' social reproduction. My aim is to demonstrate that unions' level of participation in providing social benefits, both inside and outside the workplace, depends on their strength in the region. Whether or not they play a strong role is also closely related to the level of workers' identification with their unions.

---

[6] For an in-depth discussion of this transition in Mexico and elsewhere in Latin America, see Zapata 2001.

MEXICAN UNIONS AND THE STRUGGLE FOR SOCIAL BENEFITS

During Mexico's import-substitution phase, some industries, especially the parastatal companies controlled by the Mexican government (in the oil, mining, and electricity-generation sectors, among others), provided very good wages and social benefits to their workers, as evidenced in their collective bargaining contracts.[7] This situation was the outcome of trade-offs in which "official" unions ceded a great deal of control over labor to the government in exchange for benefits for the unions and their members, along with some political rewards, such as positions in government departments.

These generous benefits and wages were possible under the ISI welfare state given the state's participation in providing for social well-being. However, another powerful explanation involves labor struggles in the 1950s, especially in unions in parastatal industries, to extend their demands to new areas, such as the construction of housing, hospitals, and recreation centers for workers. These struggles were aimed at improving the lives of workers and their families inside and outside the plant. The unions' success at wielding economic power reinforced the support they received from the rank and file. Two features to note in these struggles are the unions' combativeness, especially in parastatal companies, and their willingness to support the provision of social services, not only through their collective bargaining agreements but also with the unions' own economic resources, which further consolidated the links between workers and unions.

However, Mexico's adoption of the neoliberal economic model weakened unions as industries were restructured to pursue competitiveness in the global marketplace. Privatization of parastatal companies and the introduction of "flexibilization" in the labor force and production processes undercut unions' past gains. The results were smaller wage increases and the loss of some social benefits, although unions continued to wield substantial power. Most affected by these changes were industries where unions were weak and hence more willing to bend to the political will of private capital, both national and international. Maquiladoras were among the industries most affected. De la Garza (1993) and others have discussed how these unions either began as a flexible labor force or lost labor rights and social benefits that they had enjoyed previously. In the following sec-

---

[7] De la Garza (1993: 106) states that most clauses in these unions' collective bargaining agreements were added in the 1930s and 1940s, and he notes that these unions also added clauses that mandate participation in the productive process.

tion, I examine how losing or holding onto social benefits depended on local labor history and the type of maquiladoras prevailing regionally.

UNIONS IN MEXICAN MAQUILADORAS

Contrary to popular perceptions, a substantial portion of workers in Mexican maquiladoras are unionized; in 2000 I found that almost 63 percent of maquiladora workers belonged to unions.[8] Most of their union locals were affiliated with official unions such as the Confederation of Mexican Workers (CTM), Revolutionary Confederation of Workers and Peasants (CROC), and Mexican Regional Labor Confederation (CROM).

Nonetheless, though they may belong to official unions, unions in the maquiladoras behave very differently. Elsewhere (Quintero Ramírez 1997) I have identified two types of unions in these industries: traditional and subordinate unions.[9] The "traditional" unions are concerned with achieving at least minimal improvements in their members' work conditions, while "subordinate" unions give priority to supporting their companies' pursuit of higher profits. I can add to this definition the fact that traditional unions are characterized by social unionism and concerned with social benefits, similar to the parastatal unions, while subordinate unions prioritize productivity and privileges to be obtained from the company over social benefits for their members.

Matamoros and Ciudad Juárez: Industrial and Union Characteristics

Matamoros, along with Tijuana and Ciudad Juárez, has one of the longest histories with maquiladoras in Mexico. The first maquiladora opened in this northeastern border city in 1964, and from this point forward we can identify three periods in the city's industrial evolution. During the first phase, in the 1960s and 1970s, industrial growth was uneven and irregular and took place outside of the industrial parks. In the second phase—the 1980s and 1990s—plants, especially those belonging to important transnational corporations (TNCs) like General Motors and AT&T, developed in industrial parks. And finally, the 1995–2001 period witnessed more moder-

---

[8] The figures by individual location are: Matamoros, 100 percent; Reynosa, 100 percent; Nuevo Laredo, 95 percent; Piedras Negras, 100 percent; Ciudad Acuña, 7 percent; Ciudad Juárez, 12 percent; Tijuana, 30 percent. The overall percentage would vary if different cities were included.

[9] For an extended discussion of these types of unions, see Quintero Ramírez 1997.

ate growth; this was especially true from October 2000 to December 2001, when the U.S. auto sector was in recession. In 2000, there were 119 maquiladoras in Matamoros, employing 66,023 workers, making Matamoros the fourth most important maquiladora city in Mexico (INEGI 2001: 64).

Labor relations have been very important in the growth of maquiladoras in Matamoros. Area unions are strong, and from the very beginning the maquilas have been 100 percent unionized.[10] The principal maquiladora union is the Union of Industrial Maquiladora Workers (SJOIIM), whose key demands, like those of other local unions, have been for wages and benefits above the minimum levels set under Mexican labor law.

The relocation of important auto industry transnationals like General Motors to Matamoros in the 1980s attracted sizable and stable investments in the city's international production sector. The outlook was very good for GM and its maquiladoras in Matamoros during the 1980s, and SJOIIM took advantage of the positive industrial environment to negotiate the best collective contract on the border.[11]

Labor's position weakened slightly during the 1990s as the TNCs pressed to hold down increases in wages and others benefits. Under pressure from the state government, SJOIIM acquiesced to some of management's requests. Among labor's concessions were the following: payment of the minimum wage to new personnel; temporary (three-to-six-month) contracts for some workers; and permission to merge maquiladoras and change company names as long as the "new" companies continued to respect the terms of existing collective contracts. The unions were, in fact, able to retain most of their gains, in large part because of the efficiency of the workers and the quality of their production, which had enabled their unions to obtain international certification in most of the maquiladoras.

Matamoros offers an example of union continuity and traditional union policy, with the fight for good wages and benefits forming the crux of its politics. Local union history and unity are the key factors explaining the ability to resist government and company pressures. The particular industrial characteristics of local maquiladoras also played a part.

---

[10] In the past, Matamoros had a strong labor movement in services and the cotton industry. A labor leader in the cotton industry unionized the first maquiladoras in the 1960s. Since then, all maquiladoras have been unionized.

[11] Most maquiladoras have the same collective bargaining agreement, although there may be some differences in wages or benefits depending on the particular company's economic situation. SJOIIM was able to negotiate a minimum wage and benefits package that exceeds the national level.

Ciudad Juárez, at the center of Mexico's northern border, is the largest employer of maquiladora workers in Mexico. In 2000, 308 plants employed a total of 249,509 workers (INEGI 2001). The first maquiladora in Ciudad Juárez was Nielsen de México, established in 1966 under the Border Industrialization Program (BIP). The evolution of the maquiladora sector in Ciudad Juárez has passed through four stages. From the 1960s to the mid-1970s, there was a proliferation of maquiladora plants. The second period—1976 to 1982—witnessed a sorting out and consolidation of maquiladora investments, when a substantial number of the maquiladoras established in Ciudad Juárez during the first stage closed or relocated.[12] Only the most stable investments remained. The third stage, from 1982 to the end of the 1990s, saw another growth spurt, especially in the number of employees in the automobile and electronics sectors. And finally, the fourth period, from 2000 to the present, has been characterized by recession and job losses.[13] The unevenness in the evolution of Ciudad Juárez's maquiladora sector exemplifies this sector's high dependence on the international economy.

Unlike Matamoros, Ciudad Juárez has no strong unions. Local unions have been weakened by company management and government, but also by internal factionalism, corrupt leadership, and infighting between the two principal official unions (CTM and CROC). These factors have ensured a low unionization rate; in 2000, only 12 percent of local workers were unionized.[14]

Unions in Ciudad Juárez have other important characteristics. First, they represent the transition from traditional unionism to subordinate unionism. Because they are weak, they have been forced to meet certain requirements set by management just to remain active; perhaps the most important such concession is acknowledging management's absolute freedom to introduce flexibility into the labor force. Second, the unions have subordinated labor's rights to company goals. And third, they have retained key union privileges, such as an exclusion clause for problematic

---

[12] Firm closure or relocation is something that all border towns have experienced, although Ciudad Juárez and Tijuana were particularly hard-hit. For more on this issue, see Carrillo 1985.

[13] For a detailed analysis of the stages of maquiladora development in Ciudad Juárez, see de la O Martínez 2001.

[14] For a detailed history of unions in Ciudad Juárez, see Quintero Ramírez 1996.

workers and payment by the company for the activities of union leaders, stipulations that benefit union leaders but not the rank and file.[15]

SOCIAL BENEFITS IN DELTRÓNICOS AND RCA COMPONENTES

This section analyzes the differences between two kinds of unions in maquiladoras, using as cases the most important maquiladora in each of two regions: Deltrónicos in Matamoros and RCA Componentes in Ciudad Juárez. I have examined their collective bargaining contracts to extract the clauses that refer to social benefits,[16] and I have interviewed union leaders in order to ascertain how they view the social benefits contained in their collective contracts and what these mean for the workers. I also analyze the influence of union strength and maquiladora type.

Plant Characteristics

Deltrónicos Operations (originally called Deltrónicos de Matamoros) belongs to Delphi Delco Electronic Systems, which is owned by Delphi Automotive Systems. The company was established in Matamoros in 1979 to manufacture car radios and electronics. According to company managers, in 2000 Deltrónicos manufactured 80 percent of the car radios that Delphi Delco Electronic Systems sold to clients throughout the world.

Until 1997, Deltrónicos was a direct investment of General Motors, which owned the Delco Electronics division of Hughes Electronics. In 1997 the company became part of Delphi Automotive Systems, a change that made it a leading producer of electronic systems for automobiles. All of the company's production was aimed toward export.

Deltrónicos obtained various certifications for production quality at the international level. In 1994 it received ISO 9000 certification, and in 1998 it obtained ISO 14000 environmental certification. The company's clients clearly recognize its high product quality. For example, the plant has received the NUMMI Partnership Award, the CAMI President's Award, and QS-9000 certification (Deltrónicos Operations 2000).

---

[15] For example, the collective bargaining agreement currently in effect at RCA Componentes contains five clauses referring to economic support for delegates' travel and conference expenses. One of these clauses notes further that "the company will give delegates a gift at the end of the year."

[16] I analyzed the collective contracts at Deltrónicos for 2000 through 2002, and those at RCA Componentes for 2001 through 2003.

For Deltrónicos, satisfying its international clients is the principal goal, and its motto is "to exceed client expectations." All of the company's output is exported to assembly plants, mostly in North America. Its clients include General Motors (60 percent of output); Toyota Motor Company in Japan and the United States; Phillips; Volkswagen in Germany and Mexico; and the truck lines of Peterbilt, Volvo, Freightliner, and John Deere.

Deltrónicos's success has meant an increase in the company's workforce. In March 2000, it employed 5,800 workers, mostly women (70 percent), in three shifts. The majority of workers do intensive, mostly unskilled work. They are organized in teams referred to as "operations," a structure that allows Deltrónicos to respond quickly to international market demand.

However, the most important factor in the company's success has been the union's support as the company changed its productive operations. Deltrónicos initially assembled electrical and plastic parts for car stereos; in the mid-1980s it introduced new procedures and technologies, especially in plastics molding and finishing for car stereos. During the 1990s, favored by Mexico's lower costs, the plant began manufacturing new products for NUMMI and other industries, especially compact disc players and DIN-8 radios. Finally, in the mid-1990s, the company stopped manufacturing older products, such as the "Cadillac E/K" and "Chevy 4," and began producing new ones, including audiotronics for the Chevrolet GMC truck. It also introduced logic boards for FM radios and a new Single-DIN high resolution radio.[17]

The union has collaborated closely with the company in implementing these product changes, and the company has guaranteed employment and committed to retain the benefits contained in the workers' collective contract. Negotiations have not been without tensions, however. The company urged the union not to press for more benefits and to accept smaller wage increases in order to keep Deltrónicos internationally competitive. The SJOIIM agreed to changes in work shifts, which affected a portion of union members, and also agreed to firing and hiring during periods of recession or growth, but it refused to allow benefits clauses to be dropped from the collective contract and petitioned that benefits be extended to all workers, both permanent and temporary[18] and including administrative employees.

---

[17] An in-depth discussion of production changes at Deltrónicos can be found in Quintero Ramírez 2000.

[18] Eighty-five percent of Deltrónicos workers are "permanent." Although temporary workers are the exception, their numbers have risen in recent years. According to

Despite the differences between the respective positions of the company and the union, both attained their objectives, at least partially. Deltrónicos remains internationally competitive, and its workers have a good labor contract.

The situation in Ciudad Juárez is quite different. RCA Componentes, S.A. was established in Ciudad Juárez in 1969,[19] with facilities in the Bermúdez Industrial Park. RCA Componentes has changed ownership at various times in its history. The plant was first owned by RCA Victor, was acquired by General Electric Inc. in 1985, and was sold to a French transnational, Thomson, in 1988.[20] The ownership changes, which are strongly linked to the movement of international capital, have deeply affected the labor force in terms of hiring and firing, especially during key periods. RCA Componentes enjoyed strong employment growth during the 1970s and 1980s. According to María Eugenia de la O Martínez (1994: 86), the plant employed almost 5,000 workers in 1987, mostly women. However, during the 1990s and at least until 2003, the plant reduced its labor force due to a contracting product market. Today RCA Componentes employs 3,500 workers. The principal problem at this maquiladora has been fluctuations in the number of plant workers because of production and market movements. In direct contrast to the employment security found in Deltrónicos, there is no permanent employment at RCA Componentes, and the company's workers experience a constant sense of job insecurity.

The company's chief activities—all done on production lines—are inserting microchips onto circuit boards, assembling television chassis, and soldering electronic components onto circuit boards. During the 1970s, the work was done manually; some activities, especially the insertion of microchips, were mechanized during the 1980s. If we follow the company's history as reconstructed by de la O Martínez (1994), we can deduce that the company's long residence in Ciudad Juárez has been based on the wide latitude it enjoys in hiring workers, as well as the interaction of different production systems inside the plant, including high technology, line assembly, and piecework.

---

the collective labor contract, all benefits and compensation at the plant are linked to worker seniority.

[19] For an analysis of historical data on RCA Componentes' industrial and labor characteristics up to 1988, see de la O Martínez 1994.

[20] Despite the changes in ownership, the plant's name has remained the same.

Union Characteristics in Deltrónicos and RCA Componentes

All Deltrónicos workers belong to the SJOIIM, the principal maquiladora union in Matamoros,[21] which was created in 1932[22] and is affiliated with the CTM. SJOIIM began as a union representing farmworkers in the region's cotton fields before becoming a maquiladora union in the mid-1960s. SJOIIM currently has 48,000 maquiladora worker members, 70 percent of whom are women (author interview with SJOIIM's general secretary, July 2002).

In Matamoros, there are no union sections or union companies. Instead, all local maquiladoras are integrated in a single large union. SJOIIM names a delegate for each plant, and this person deals with day-to-day problems regarding the labor force in the workplace and ensures that employers adhere to the collective contract. There are actually three delegates in the Deltrónicos plant, one for each shift. Delegates must inform the SJOIIM Executive Committee of any major problems; if they fail in this or other responsibilities, they are removed from their position, a situation that arose at Deltrónicos in the 1980s.[23]

The SJOIIM's primary success was negotiating the same collective labor contract with the first maquiladoras that had prevailed in the cotton industry, with only minor changes. This agreement remains the basis for the current contracts in the maquiladora sector. During the 1980s, the wages and benefits stipulated in the collective bargaining agreement increased substantially thanks to the growth of the GM maquiladoras, including Deltrónicos. During this decade, SJOIIM was able to add important clauses to its labor contract: a forty-hour workweek,[24] wages 100 to 130 percent above minimum wage; and linking all benefits to a worker's seniority. Moreover, the union used its funds to build and service various *colonias* (working-class neighborhoods) for the workers. The collective bargaining

---

[21] There are three other maquiladora unions in Matamoros besides the SJOIIM, but "Jornaleros" (the popular name for the SJOIIM) represents almost 85 percent of maquiladora workers in this region. All maquiladora unions, including SJOIIM, belong to the CTM, although they retain substantial freedom to negotiate their own labor agreements.

[22] SJOIIM celebrated its seventieth anniversary on July 15, 2002, which probably makes it the oldest union in the maquiladora sector.

[23] For more on this topic, see Quintero Ramírez 1997.

[24] The standard workweek under Mexican labor law is forty-eight hours.

agreements negotiated with the General Motors maquiladoras, especially Deltrónicos, became the prototypes for other companies in Matamoros.[25]

Compare this to the case of RCA Componentes, whose union was established at the same time as the company. In the beginning, the workers belonged to the National Union of RCA Victor, with headquarters in Mexico City. In the mid-1970s, the RCA Workers Union (SUTRCA) was established (with headquarters in Ciudad Juárez) and began representing RCA Componentes workers. Although this union is an affiliate of the CTM, this affiliation is a mere formality; in fact, SUTRCA has complete freedom in contract negotiations. Both cases presented here—Matamoros and Ciudad Juárez—give evidence that the CTM's supposed control over all Mexican unions is a myth. Indeed, the keys to understanding maquiladora unions are local power and local history.

SUTRCA has a poor history. The union has been weak in defending workers' rights, RCA Componentes employees lack job security, and the union has tended to submit to management's decisions. For example, in 1982, when 2,000 workers were fired, and again in 2001, when thousands more lost their jobs, the union did nothing to defend their workers, leading to numerous complaints from the rank and file. Workers have also denounced the close alliance between the company and the union, which led to an agreement to cut work shifts, putting employees out of work (de la O Martínez 1994: 125–26).

What is most worrisome is that SUTRCA has lost crucial ground in its collective labor contract. Among the benefits that have been sacrificed are measures to protect workers from work-related injuries and illness,[26] concessions that union leaders made in order to continue operating within the factory. Moreover, most of the worker benefits that have been retained are linked to the needs of production and new organizational forms of work, as are bonuses and other rewards to workers. The union has tried to recover the trust of the rank and file with small, mostly symbolic, company-supported social programs. However, interviews with the workers uncovered their deep discontent with the union (de la O Martínez 1994: 170–76).

Management did not hesitate to take advantage of the union's weakness. According to de la O Martínez, beginning in the 1980s RCA managers

---

[25] SJOIIM has basically the same collective contract in all the maquiladoras. Benefits such as holidays, Christmas bonuses, and so on are calculated according to each company's financial situation.

[26] The loss of these benefits can be seen by comparing the company's labor contracts from 1978 and 2000.

established a new policy for handling the labor force. The policy involved various motivational programs to address absenteeism and subtle strategies to control the workers and limit their discontent. The new labor policy mixed traditional forms of control, such as punishing and/or firing workers, with "humanized" approaches, such as meetings between workers and management, parties and sports events, productivity rewards, and so on. The program philosophy was to present the company as "one big family,"[27] in which all members (workers, supervisors, and managers) were important. Managers were encouraged to establish closer contact with the workers, and the workers generally accepted the new policies enthusiastically, especially the monetary rewards and the managers' "kind treatment."

The company's strategies for organizing and controlling the workforce were complemented by activities organized by the Maquiladora Industry Association (AIM), which also emphasized the importance of the workers' commitment to their companies. Below, I examine the social benefits that the two unions won for their respective rank and file,[28] including wage supports, recreational activities, and basic services such as health care, education, and housing to ensure the social reproduction of the worker and his or her family.

Wage Supports

Because of their proximity to the United States, Mexico's border communities have been hit particularly hard by the drop in wages' purchasing power and the devaluation of the peso, making wage supports increasingly important, especially in areas where most workers receive the minimum wage. Deltrónicos introduced wage supports—food supports and various kinds of incentives—to the collective bargaining agreement in the 1990s. The union leader at the time, Agapito González, objected to the inclusion of "food baskets" in the labor contract, asserting that workers should receive any added benefits in cash and decide for themselves how to prioritize their basic needs (Quintero Ramírez 1997). However, under govern-

---

[27] De la O Martínez (1994) reported that production lines were designated as "families," the aim being to reinforce the workers' connection with their production line. The best line (family) was rewarded with a prize.

[28] I use the labor contracts of Deltrónicos (2000–2002) and RCA Componentes (2001–2003) to compare these points. I complement the data analysis with interviews with labor leaders and with information from the companies.

ment pressure during the 1990s and facing enormous barriers to any wage hikes, SJOIIM accepted the introduction of some in-kind bonuses. These are seen as complements to workers' wages, while most social benefits and labor rights (such as severance pay for fired workers) remain linked to worker seniority and are enshrined in national labor law.

According to the collective bargaining agreement at Deltrónicos, the company will return to a worker in the form of food vouchers the amount that the worker has paid in dues for government health insurance (IMSS) and taxes (ISPT). Workers also receive a financial incentive for good attendance and punctuality equivalent to 5 percent of their weekly wage. Deltrónicos has stopped giving food bonuses.[29] However, a clause in the labor contract requires the company to increase wages under "emergency conditions," such as currency devaluations or an increase in the minimum wage. In the latter case, the objective is to retain the company's relative wage structure and prevent workers' wages from losing purchasing power. Thanks to the various kinds of wage supports that Deltrónicos provides, this company continues to offer some of the best wages in the maquiladora sector, especially to its senior workers, even though recent wage increases have been small.

In Ciudad Juárez, in contrast, wages are only slightly above the minimum, making bonuses and economic incentives very important in terms of meeting workers' basic needs. The collective bargaining agreement at RCA Componentes offers a good example. The company provides free transportation for all company personnel and two meals for workers during both the normal workday and overtime shifts. Also, the company gives all union workers coupons for a weekly food basket, worth about 113 pesos.[30] Employees working during company holidays (in July and December) receive two additional food basket coupons.

Moreover, to address the high turnover rate in Ciudad Juárez (almost 13 percent turnover monthly) and to ensure stable productivity levels, RCA Componentes also gives special bonuses for punctuality, attendance, and seniority. According to the terms of the collective contract, the company rewards a week of perfect punctuality with a bonus of 11 percent of that week's wage. The bonus for a week of perfect attendance is one week's

---

[29] As specified in the collective contract, the company has established a cafeteria where workers can eat meals they bring in. The cafeteria also sells inexpensive food items.

[30] The Mexican peso fluctuated in value between 9 and 10 cents (US$) between 1999 and 2002.

minimum wage. The seniority bonus is equivalent to 13 percent of the nominal wage. The company has also established a savings fund for the workers, to which the company contributes between 8 and 13 percent of a worker's nominal wage, depending on seniority. The worker makes an equal contribution.

Clearly, bonuses are very important in workers' incomes. For workers in RCA Componentes, as in most of the maquiladoras in Ciudad Juárez, bonuses can double and even triple workers' wages. One problem, however, is that these bonuses depend on company largesse.

Health and Social Security

In Matamoros, the SJOIIM's collective contract reflects key aspects of federal labor law regarding workers' health and safety in the workplace. Under the CCT, a company is obliged to register workers in the IMSS upon hiring. Also, the companies pay 60 percent of wages for the first three days of non-workplace-related medical incapacity, as specified by the IMSS. Most important, the SJOIIM has recovered funds that workers pay into the IMSS and in taxes. These are returned in the form of food coupons equivalent to the amount that each worker paid to IMSS and in ISPT. Matamoros maquiladoras also pay workers' costs for obtaining a health card, and they provide medical attention (on-site doctor's and nurse's care, plus first-aid supplies) to workers at the worksite. And the company provides eyeglasses to all workers who need them, up to twice over a two-year period (the IMSS prescribes the lenses).

Another important advance regards protection for pregnant women who are temporary workers. According to the CCT, temporary women workers who have been with the company for more than three months and have become pregnant during their contract period cannot be fired, and the company must pay all the benefits established under the law. Mexico's federal labor law specifies that women workers must be given maternity leave beginning six weeks before the projected delivery date and ending six weeks after the baby's birth. Women workers receive full pay and all labor benefits during this period. If a woman is unable to return to work at the end of her maternity leave, the leave can be extended for up to an additional sixty days at half wages (LFT 2001: 50).

In negotiating the most recent version of its collective labor agreement, the SJOIIM reiterated the importance of including the maternity clause, possibly because Deltrónicos has yet to fully implement this labor right for its women workers. Although Deltrónicos provides a space for workers to breastfeed their children,[31] the company has no child daycare, so its women workers must rely on the daycare services provided by the IMSS.

Finally, the Deltrónicos collective contract also contains a clause requiring workers to have a yearly medical examination to detect any condition that might require medical attention. It is important to note that this clause could function to the detriment of women workers, especially pregnant workers. Although these employees are protected under the contract, the company could, nevertheless, employ a variety of strategies, such as threatening to transfer the worker, to force a pregnant worker to quit.

In addition to the protections and services that SJOIIM obtains for its members through the collective labor contract, it also provides services outside the plants. SJOIIM has a well-equipped hospital staffed with general practitioners and specialists. Any SJOIIM member, including workers at Deltrónicos, can use the facility, paying only a small consultation fee. The union employs seven individuals whose responsibility is to ensure that SJOIIM's members[32] receive good treatment at the IMSS, in their consultations with doctors, their medical prescriptions, and so on (author interview with SJOIIM's general secretary, August 2002). Finally, in collaboration with the government, SJOIIM has created two daycare centers for the children of women workers.

The final social benefits to be discussed are pensions and retirement benefits. Retiring workers receive an IMSS pension, the amount of which is based on the money paid into the worker's account during his or her work life. Workers are also entitled to a pension if they are incapacitated by a workplace accident or workplace illness. However, some workers who are eligible to receive a pension prefer to continue working because the IMSS pension is quite small.

The SUTRCA case is quite different. Its labor contract contains few health-related protections. Like Deltrónicos, RCA Componentes also registers its workers in the IMSS. However, although the company has an on-

---

[31] According to federal labor law, the company allows women workers two 30-minute breaks for breastfeeding.

[32] SJOIIM members pay monthly union dues of 5 pesos. Workers can pay dues even when they are no longer working and continue to receive access to all the social services the union offers. This speaks to the union's independence from the companies. Traditionally, workers only pay dues while they are employed; when they are fired or quit, they lose their union rights. Also, most of the unions, especially subordinated ones, depend heavily on company payments, rather than on union dues, to support their services.

site doctor during the first and second shifts, there is no doctor on the third shift, and medical attention during these hours is provided by another worker whom the company has trained in first aid. The potential danger for anyone injured during the third shift is obvious.

Moreover, at RCA Componentes, in contrast to Deltrónicos, employees suffering from a work-related illness are allowed to continue working at the plant if the company can find them an appropriate position. For workers incapacitated by illness for a period from 8 to 208 days, the company pays only the difference between the IMSS disability payment for incapacitated workers and the worker's usual daily wage. Long periods of incapacity are uncommon. Much more common, according to the IMSS, are absences of about three days, and the company does not pay the worker anything during such a brief incapacity.

RCA Componentes has committed to cover the wage of one individual to support union employees (not all workers) who have problems with the IMSS. The company also offers life insurance (natural and accidental death coverage) to unionized workers. Coverage for prescription eyewear is available to only about 20 percent of the workforce (450 workers), with the union and company together deciding which workers will receive this benefit.

Like Deltrónicos, RCA Componentes offers workers regular medical examinations, performed by company doctors. But under a particularly worrisome clause in the labor contract, the company can also require a prospective employee to submit to a full medical examination as a prerequisite to employment, and it is very possible that this enables the company to refuse employment to pregnant women. No other health-related issues are addressed in the SUTRCA collective labor contract. Most egregious is the absence of protections for women workers, given that most workers at RCA Componentes are women. For example, there is no support for daycare.

However, SUTRCA complements the health benefits outlined in the collective labor agreement with a program called "La Feria de la Salud." This "health fair" brings together a variety of health professionals, including general practitioners, optometrists, dentists, and so on, from the IMSS and the private sector, who attend to RCA workers with minor health problems at a cost below that of private health services. The health fair is for the worker and his or her family members and aims to be preventative rather than treatment-oriented. The director of this program stated that they also offer IUDs and condoms, "especially on weekends" (author interview with the SUTRCA leader responsible for signing collective bargaining agreements from 2001 to 2003, August 2002). The health services that SUTRCA provides are fewer than those offered by the SJOIIM, and they are restricted to RCA Componentes workers, while SJOIIM health services are available to all members plus their families.

Education

This section reviews the kinds of educational supports offered to workers and their children. The Deltrónicos labor contract provides for the minimum in training and education that is required under Mexican labor law. To meet these minimum requirements, the company, together with the union, established a Joint Training Commission (Comisión Mixta de Capacitación y Adiestramiento); the company is required to design, present, and pay for all training courses. The SJOIIM's perspective on training is very traditional, leaving most decisions on training to the company. The union will soon open a training center and offer free classes in English, computers, and so on, rather than focusing on strengthening work skills.

As part of its support to education, Deltrónicos provides twenty-four scholarships (for high school or university work) to its workers and their children. Each scholarship is for 1,100 pesos, a rather paltry amount which makes this a largely symbolic gesture, especially given the size of its labor force (over 5,000 workers). Nevertheless, Deltrónicos is adhering to federal labor law, which requires companies to offer three scholarships for every thousand workers (LFT 2001: 31).

The support to education that SJOIIM provides to workers at Deltrónicos and other plants is more visible outside the plant. The union has built elementary schools in workers' neighborhoods and provided the furniture and materials necessary for their proper operation. Moreover, it has paid the teachers' salaries because the municipal government does not have the resources to do so. According to the head of the union, SJOIIM's objective is to ensure that the workers' children receive an education. Another service SJOIIM offers to workers and their children is the Union Library, which is housed in the union building and "is very well stocked ... and one of the best libraries in the state" (author interview with SJOIIM's general secretary, August 2002).

SUTRCA's case, as one might expect, differs in this area as well. Most training is offered inside the plant. Training is very important at RCA Componentes due to ongoing changes in production processes and technology. All workers, regardless of seniority, can participate in an advancement training program (Programa de Progresión) and receive an increase in wages as a result. This program encourages workers to attend the training courses the company gives to improve production or to introduce new technologies. Employees who do not attend are dropped from the advancement program and lose the chance to improve their working conditions. Under the CCT, workers can advance to higher work positions after passing a skills examination.

RCA Componentes also has a Joint Training Commission, as required under federal labor law. Like Deltrónicos, RCA Componentes is solely responsible for offering courses, and the union is responsible for ensuring that workers attend and abide by all skills evaluations the company considers necessary.

In the area of education, RCA Componentes is obliged to provide 750 scholarships of 500 pesos each to workers every three months. Every year, the company must give 3,000 scholarships to support the workers' education costs, especially book purchases. Also, under its collective labor agreement, RCA Componentes provides 359 scholarships of 200 pesos per month for the education of its workers' children. Overall, the number of scholarships that RCA Componentes offers is in good proportion to the size of its workforce.

To support the educational needs of its members, SUTRCA offers the Outstanding Student Program (Programa Aplicadísimo), whereby all workers' children with a grade-point average above 8.5 (on a 10-point scale) receive a backpack and all essential school supplies. According to the head of SUTRCA, the union also supports adult education programs inside the plant (author interview with the former head of SUTRCA, August 2002).

Housing

Under its collective labor agreement, Deltrónicos is obligated to deliver to the union a copy of its payroll and of the 5 percent payment the company makes to the local office of the Finance Ministry (Secretaría de Hacienda) as its contribution to the National Workers' Housing Fund (INFONAVIT). This enables SJOIIM to confirm that the wages reportedly paid are genuine. Also, the company must provide each worker with confirmation of the total amount paid to INFONAVIT so that the worker can present his or her claim for INFONAVIT funds.

SJOIIM has various programs to support worker housing. Most important, SJOIIM has purchased large plots, subdivided them into house lots measuring 25 by 20 meters, and sold these to workers at low cost.[33] These land extensions were the foundation for four working-class colonias. The union also introduced such basic services as electrification, water delivery, and sewerage in these colonias. According to the union's leader, "these lands allow workers to build an appropriate space to live with their families. They have more space and they don't have the problems with neighbors and neighbors' children over the use of space, as happens in INFONAVIT housing developments" (author interview with SJOIIM's general secretary, August 2002). Finally, SJOIIM subsidizes fire insurance, providing 5,000 pesos to owners of houses and 2,500 pesos to renters.

Under its collective agreement, RCA Componentes also agrees to observe federal labor law regarding INFONAVIT disbursements, although the agreement does not specify how this is to be done. The leader of the SUTRCA suggests that INFONAVIT has done a poor job of providing worker housing in Ciudad Juárez, and INFONAVIT houses are often built with inferior materials. A large percentage of workers must improvise housing, constructing with cardboard and scrap lumber, creating a very dangerous situation for working-class families in this region of extremely high summertime temperatures.

SUTRCA has established a Contingency Program (Programa para Contingencias) under which workers who have lost improvised homes to fire can obtain bricks and cement with which to rebuild (author interview with a former SUTRCA leader, August 2002). As is the case with other social benefits offered by SUTRCA, the Contingency Program is a superficial solution to the housing problem rather than the in-depth structural response that is required. SUTRCA would do well to reconsider their principal objectives, especially job security, wages, and benefits for their workers. Moreover, SUTRCA should develop a program of benefits outside the plant that is less dependent on the company; such an initiative would go far toward strengthening its image among the rank and file.

Sports and Recreation

This last section deals with an area that might be considered unimportant but is actually fundamental to workers' overall social development: recrea-

---

[33] According to the leader of SJOIIM, this money is used to purchase land for new worker colonias.

tion and use of leisure time. The collective contract at Deltrónicos requires the company to sponsor sports activities—to purchase all materials and equipment required to practice and play sports, and to support teams formed by the workers. The company and union are responsible for caring for workers injured while playing company-sponsored sports.

SJOIIM has complemented this support by building soccer and baseball fields, and the union helps organize soccer and baseball tournaments, which are often named for union leaders. In 2003, SJOIIM built a workers' gymnasium, complete with equipment and coaches for a variety of sports. Finally, as further support for workers' recreation, SJOIIM purchased two pieces of land where it installed playground equipment, walking paths, and picnic areas for workers' families.

The collective contract at RCA Componentes also includes support for sports. The company provides all necessary equipment, including uniforms and shoes, for workers participating in extramural sports. For participants in intramural sports, the company provides T-shirts only. RCA Componentes is also required to host a Christmas dinner and party for all of its workers. In Ciudad Juárez, unlike the situation in Matamoros, sports competitions and other recreational activities, including parties and picnics, are organized by company managers and the Ciudad Juárez Maquiladora Association (AMAC).

CONCLUSION: THE STRUGGLE FOR BENEFITS IN MAQUILADORAS AND THE RECONFIGURATION OF MEXICAN UNIONISM

This chapter has analyzed how, in this era of globalization, workers are securing the social benefits needed for the social reproduction of the labor force. Special attention was given to how the maquiladora sector, whose industries are closely tied to the international context, has modified the system of social benefits for workers that previously existed in Mexico. The Mexican government, through the country's federal labor law, has required employers to meet their workers' basic needs through wages that are at or above minimum levels and benefits packages for health care, education, and housing sufficient to guarantee the social reproduction of workers and their families.

Under past economic models in Mexico, employer-paid benefits were complemented by government programs to assist workers. However, the government's commitment to such social programs has declined since Mexico's adoption of the neoliberal economic model, which relegates social programs to the second tier in terms of importance.

The two maquiladora case studies examined here reveal how the benefits system is being reconfigured in Mexico and the roles that employers, workers, unions, and government are playing in this process. At the present time, the companies, which are now primarily responsible for the workers' social reproduction, are conceding the bare minimum of benefits specified under federal labor law. Moreover, the case of RCA Componentes in Ciudad Juárez demonstrates that the distribution of basic social benefits can be manipulated to support the company's need to remain internationally competitive. In each company, social benefits can be extended or reduced depending on the union's actions.

We found two types of unionism inside the maquiladoras. The more "traditional" union had achieved higher wages and slightly better social benefits, attributable both to the strength of the union and to the company's strong economic performance. This traditional union is able to complement the benefits obtained through its collective contract with important social programs provided outside the factory, reflecting both the union's focus on the workers' social well-being and its ability to build financial strength through the union dues it collects from the rank and file. Further, the combination of the workers' close contact with the union inside the plant—from hiring to firing—and their interaction in union programs outside the plant has built strong ties between the workers and their union and cemented their identity as different from their employers.

The "subordinated" union, by contrast, seems to have lost the essence of a labor organization. Even though it is officially recognized as a legal union, any concern with improving its members' wages and benefits has largely disappeared from its agenda. For this union, the company's objectives are paramount, particularly the firm's concern with remaining competitive in the global marketplace. This union is too weak to negotiate effectively with the company. It has ceded all control over the labor force, from hiring to firing, to the employer in exchange for the "privilege" of remaining active in the factory. The company is free to organize the workforce according to its production needs. Finally, although this union collects union dues, most of its funds come in the form of economic supports that the company provides for its activities. This economic dependence on RCA Componentes has prevented the union from developing social programs outside the factory. In combination, the union's failure to support workers inside the plant and its failure to provide social programs outside the plant have generated a dissociation between the workers and their union. Paradoxically, the union's deal with management—ceding control over the workforce in exchange for being allowed to continue representing the workers—aligned the workers' perspective more closely with that of the company. For example, workers see the majority of their benefits, and especially the food vouchers, as company generosity rather than as a product of union struggle.

Despite the fact that workers in Ciudad Juárez potentially have access to significant economic benefits, the analysis presented here clearly demonstrates that these payments—which are not enshrined in any collective bargaining agreement—are very precarious, and these workers still suffer a lack of protection in the workplace. Absent any real support from the company, the government, or their union, these workers seem to be assuming the cost of their own social reproduction.

References

Bureau of International Labor Affairs. 1996. *Foreign Labor Trends Report, Mexico, 1991–1992.* Washington, D.C.: U.S. Department of Labor.

Carrillo, Jorge. 1985. *Conflictos laborales en la industria maquiladora.* Tijuana: El Colegio de la Frontera Norte.

Cooney, Paul. 2001. "The Mexican Crisis and the Maquiladora Boom: Paradox of Development or the Logic of Neoliberalism?" *Latin American Perspectives* 118, vol. 28, no. 3 (May): 55–83.

De la Garza, Enrique. 1989. "Área de la reproducción social de la fuerza de trabajo." In *Un paradigma para el análisis de la clase obrera.* Mexico: Universidad Autónoma Metropolitana.

———. 1993. *Reestructuración productiva y respuesta sindical en México.* Mexico: Instituto de Investigaciones Económicas/División de Ciencias Sociales y Humanidades, Universidad Autónoma Metropolitana.

———. 1994. *Innovación tecnológica y clase obrera: estudio de caso de la industria maquiladora electrónica R.C.A Ciudad Juárez, Chihuahua. Mexico.* Universidad Autónoma Metropolitana–Iztapalapa/Miguel Ángel Porrúa.

———. 2001. "Ciudad Juárez: un polo de crecimiento maquiladora." In *Globalización, trabajo y maquilas: las nuevas y viejas fronteras en México.* Mexico: Plaza y Valdés/ CIESAS/Fundación Friedrich Ebert/ AFL-CIO.

Deltrónicos Operations. 2000. Typescript, March.

De Oliveira, Orlandina, and Vania Salles. 2000. "Reflexiones teóricas para el estudio de la reproducción de la fuerza de trabajo." In *Tratado latinoamericano de sociología del trabajo,* edited by Enrique de la Garza. Mexico: El Colegio de México/FLACSO/UAM/FCE.

INEGI (Instituto Nacional de Estadística, Geografía e Informática). 2001. *Industria maquiladora de exportación, estadísticas económicas.* Mexico City: INEGI, May.

Ley del Seguro Social. 2001. In *Colección Laboral*. Mexico: Ediciones Delma.

LFT (Ley Federal del Trabajo). 2001. In *Colección Laboral 2001*. Mexico: Ediciones Delma.

Marx, Carlos. 1974a. "Salario, precio y ganancia." In *Obras escogidas de Carlos Marx and Federico Engels*. Vol. 2. Moscow: Progreso.

———. 1974b. "Trabajo asalariado y capital." In *Obras escogidas de Carlos Marx and Federico Engels*. Vol. 1. Moscow: Progreso.

Quintero Ramírez, Cirila. 1996. "Sindicatos en Ciudad Juárez: historia y debilidad sindical," *Estudios Fronterizos*, June/July.

———. 1997. *Reestructuración sindical en la frontera norte: el caso de la industria maquiladora*. Tijuana: El Colegio de la Frontera Norte.

———. 2000. "Cambios productivos y condiciones laborales: la experiencia de Deltrónicos Operations-Delphi." Paper presented at the meeting of Asociación de Historia Económica del Norte de México, Baja California Sur, November.

Salas, Carlos. 2001. "Highlights of Current Labor Market Conditions in Mexico." RISEL (Red de Investigadores y Sindicalistas para Estudios Laborales), *Global Policy Network*, http://www.globalpolicynetwork.org.

Zapata, Francisco. 1993. *Autonomía y subordinación en el sindicalismo latinoamericano*. Mexico: Fideicomiso Historia de las Américas, Fondo de Cultura Económica/El Colegio de México.

———. 2001. "Free Market, Privatization and Latin American Unions." Paper presented at the ISA, Chicago, February.

10

So What Is to Be Done? Maquila Justice Movements, Transnational Solidarity, and Dynamics of Resistance

JOE BANDY

In the era of liberalized trade and investment in North America, manufacturing firms from around the world have been able to shed—or "externalize"—many costs of production onto the workers and natural environment of Mexico. In the midst of the social and environmental problems this has caused, workers have articulated critiques, and these critiques have led to action. Indeed, maquiladora workers have not been passive victims of labor exploitation. The history of export processing in Mexico, especially since the late 1980s, has been characterized by increasing worker militancy and the growth of transnational networks to support labor rights. In the wake of the North American Free Trade Agreement (NAFTA) and the impacts of maquila growth throughout the continent, maquila workers and their communities have formed coalitions with social movement organizations—including human rights organizations, women's groups, Mexican unions independent of the dominant political parties, U.S./Canadian unions, environmental justice groups, indigenous peoples' movements, and fair trade organizations.

With the emergence of popular movements against neoliberal development—from the Zapatista Army of National Liberation (EZLN) and its supporters in 1994 to the many protests against supranational institutions such as the World Trade Organization (WTO) and World Bank—there has been even greater interest among North American movements seeking more democratic and equitable development. Among hundreds of organizations that have participated in maquila labor struggles, several have become prominent in recent years, including the Coalition for Justice in the Maquiladoras (CJM), the Border Workers' Committee (CFO), the alliance between the United Electrical Workers (UE) and the Authentic Labor Front (FAT), and the AFL-CIO's American Center for International Labor Solidarity (ACILS).

Critiques of export processing in Mexico have varied considerably among these organizations, but the organizations have collaborated because of a common commitment to improving wages, working conditions, and the environmental health of workers. With increasing international attention and support, maquila workers have been able to organize more extensively by educating each other about their legal rights and their economic conditions, promoting regulatory oversight, changing corporate labor relations, and mobilizing for unionization. And with greater solidarity and organizational capacity, the scope of workers' movements also has grown, from critiques of local maquila management to that of neoliberal globalization, from goals of corporate managerial reforms to those of unionization and economic democracy. Indeed, the resistance to maquila labor and environmental conditions has been so great that, in an effort to secure continued production and profitability, maquila owners and government officials often have united to suppress workers' movements— through an alliance of personnel managers, Mexico's Labor Mediation and Arbitration Boards (JLCAs), company guards and police, and government-supported unions that obstruct independent unionization.

Endeavors of labor networks to empower maquila workers have had mixed results. Given the repression they face, their limited resources, and continuing internal conflicts, the very survival of cross-border labor networks for maquila justice has been a positive result. Beyond survival, however, some episodes of labor conflict have resulted in changes that workers have regarded as progressive. There have been corporate reforms to toxic dumping and abusive labor relations; workers have received precedent-setting legal verdicts and settlements in both national and international tribunals; labor rights education has informed countless citizens; and, as we will see, workers have had qualified successes in unionization and collective bargaining. In these efforts, coalition has functioned to magnify the strengths of individual organizations, and each success has fortified hopes for a transnational civil society that can shape a more democratic form of development. In many instances, however, workers' goals have not been achieved and the hopes of regulating transnational capital are dim. In these cases, corporations have fired and intimidated activists; Mexican government leaders and official unions have obstructed independent unionization and harassed workers; activists have had limited resources to devote to organizing; or workers' coalitions have conflicted over strategy, organizational development, or identity issues such as nationality, disrupting their unity and power. Indeed, at this moment in history, the forces of economic liberalization appear far stronger than those of democratic regulation, prompting social movements worldwide to ask, not unlike Lenin (1929), what is to be done?

To this question there may be as many answers as there are movements. Yet, among labor organizations, each episode of conflict with corporations and government has facilitated the development of common, coordinated strategies of resistance. To understand the most current phase of labor movement activism and the power dynamics between labor and capital in the maquilas, it will be helpful to discuss two of the most recent and prominent cases of labor mobilizations in the maquilas—that at the Han Young plant in Tijuana, Baja California, from 1997 to 1999, and that against the Kukdong/Mexmode maquila in Atlixco, Puebla, from 2000 to 2002. Clearly, there have been many precedent-setting labor struggles in Mexican maquilas since the late 1970s that could be discussed here— Solidev, Sony, ALCOA, GE, Maxiswitch, or Duro—yet Han Young and Kukdong are arguably the most instructive. Each movement was able to achieve new precedents of unionization: in one case, government recognition, and in the other, a labor contract. Further, each demonstrates slightly different paradigms of resistance to export processing, with distinct strategic opportunities, regional influences, and outcomes. Han Young represents at once one of the greatest successes and failures of maquila labor movements, while many regard that of Kukdong/Mexmode to be a new model for labor internationalism in North America. Thus a comparative analysis of these cases will provide insights into the industrial conflict in the maquila sector.

This discussion is grounded in ten extended (two-to-three-hour) interviews with the lead activists and workers participating in each conflict, conducted during 1997–1998 for the Han Young case and during 2001 for Kukdong. Additionally, government reports and movement documents— communiqués, monitoring reports, action alerts, protest faxes/letters, media packages, and so on—will be discussed. Lastly, this research was conducted as part of a much larger study of U.S.-Mexican labor coalitions involving over a hundred interviews with activists, maquila managers, and government officials, as well as over six years of selective participation in workers' movements, providing many other relevant insights.

DRIVING HYUNDAI TO THE BRINK: THE CASE OF HAN YOUNG

In early 1997, workers at the Han Young maquila in eastern Tijuana, a Korean subcontractor of Hyundai Precision, were concerned with several health, safety, and wage issues.[1] Han Young workers are almost all men, and the average age is around twenty-two. They produce chassis for Hyundai tractor-trailers, which requires lead welding. Due to a lack of safety devices, the lead welding frequently resulted in toxic exposure and eye injuries. Further, the large cranes used to transport chassis were failing, causing extremely heavy chassis to fall, which in turn resulted in severe injuries. Despite eleven inspections of Han Young by Mexico's Labor Ministry (Secretaría del Trabajo) and the documentation of "forty-one health and safety violations" (U.S. NAO 1998), including some that were near fatal, Mexican officials failed to act. Garett Brown of the Maquiladora Health and Safety Support Network (MHSSN) stated, "I fear that only multiple worker deaths in a catastrophic accident will jolt the Mexican Labor Department into action" (LaBotz 1998a). Additionally, according to the Support Committee for Maquiladora Workers (SCMW), management refused to pay profit-sharing bonuses required under Mexican law (Tong 1998).

Because in previous years many workers at Han Young had participated in a defense of their *colonia*'s land rights against government efforts to assist Hyundai's expansion, workers already had developed a critical perspective on maquila development and an understanding of how to mobilize. With strong community and transnational support, it did not take long for workers to organize a local of the FAT-affiliated union, the Metal Workers Union (STIMAHCS). STIMAHCS is one of the most active independent unions in Mexico, supporting industrial workers in both export-oriented and domestically oriented sectors. But when workers petitioned the state for collective bargaining rights, they found that the Unión de Trabajadores de Oficios Varios "José María Larroque," a local of the

---

[1] The discussions of the Han Young and Kukdong/Mexmode cases were drawn from a forthcoming book by the author, *Laboring against Neoliberalism in North America: Transnational Movement Coalitions between U.S. and Mexican Labor.*

Revolutionary Confederation of Workers and Peasants (CROC), already had them (U.S. NAO 1998).

In a corrupt but typical strategy, the CROC, an official union allied with the Institutional Revolutionary Party (PRI), signed this contract to obstruct the workers' organizing initiatives. The contract did not have worker consent and it did not challenge any health, safety, or wage policies. Labor lawyer Jesús Campos Linas claims there are thousands of such "ghost" or "protection" contracts in Mexico: "the government basically uses these labor federations to get votes during elections.... Companies make hefty regular payments to union leaders under these contracts, and in return get labor peace" (Bacon 1999). To replace the CROC with their own union, 70 percent of the Han Young workforce signed up as STIMAHCS members and forced a union election. They also held a work stoppage in June to prompt Hyundai to recognize and bargain with their union (under Mexican law, Hyundai is the sole contractor and thus responsible for Han Young's actions) (Faulkner 1998; Comelo 1997).

To initiate a runoff, STIMAHCS applied for *titularidad*, or entitlement to sole bargaining rights with the local JLCA. Composed of three representatives—one from the corporate sector, one from government (in this case the National Action Party, or PAN), and one from the official union movement—the JLCA is typically an unwavering opponent of independent unions. To thwart independent unionization and any potential escalation in labor costs for foreign investors, the JLCA urged Han Young to hire Luis Manuel Escobedo, a union-busting consultant (Faulkner 1998), as its new human resources manager (Tong 1998). Despite the fact that Han Young had already begun discussions with STIMAHCS to resolve the conflict, the company relented, negotiations were halted, and activists were fired. Escobedo then began "psychological warfare" against workers by enlisting CROC supporters to spread rumors depicting activists as self-serving, corrupt, and under the influence of foreign agitators (Tong 1998). Workers even reported that one activist was physically attacked by the CROC (U.S. NAO 1998).

The PAN governor of Baja California, Héctor Terán Terán, then ordered the JLCA to defer the election for a month due to an "incorrect docket number" on the petition (Tong 1998). Because this granted anti-union organizers more time to demobilize workers, workers protested at JLCA headquarters. JLCA President Antonio Ortiz surprisingly yielded to pressure by setting an October 6, 1997, date for the election, an action that most observers believe led to Ortiz's forced resignation (Faulkner 1998). But counter-movement tactics were far from over. On election day, many activists from the United States and Mexico were present as observers to hold the JLCA and CROC accountable; they included members of the SCMW, CJM, AFL-CIO, and the International Labor Rights Fund (ILRF). Also present were thirty-five CROC supporters, all of whom were hired that morning by Han Young (U.S. NAO 1998). These "ghost" workers demanded to vote, shoved STIMAHCS supporters, and insisted that foreigners cease interfering in national affairs. Despite protests, the JLCA allowed them to vote, even though they had to be coached by management at the voting booths. A total of 5,129 workers voted, yet because the CROC miscalculated the number of votes needed, STIMAHCS prevailed, winning 55 percent to 34 percent (U.S. NAO 1998).

In response, Governor Terán Terán claimed that "foreign political interests" had engineered the victory and that it did not represent the interests of Han Young workers. He placed a three-day gag order on regional press coverage, and the SCMW was barred from future entry to Mexico (Faulkner 1998). On November 10, the JLCA nullified the election, "on the grounds that STIMAHCS had failed to adequately substantiate that it had the support of the majority of the workers at the plant and that it lacked the proper registration" (U.S. NAO 1998). STIMAHCS, SCMW, ILRF, and the National Association of Democratic Attorneys (ANAD) filed a complaint with the U.S. National Administrative Office (NAO) that oversees violations of NAFTA's labor side accord. Like many other NAO complaints, it stated that workers were denied legal rights to free association, ultimately leading the NAO to recommend ministerial-level consultations between U.S. and Mexican labor ministers (U.S. Department of Labor 2002). The SCMW and UE organized letter campaigns to Hyundai President and CEO Ted Chung, Governor Terán Terán, and Mexican President Ernesto Zedillo. And they organized protests at Hyundai dealerships in twenty-five U.S. cities. Even Representative David Bonior (D-Michigan), who met Han Young workers in the midst of the NAFTA fast track debates, saw Han Young as a "test case" of NAFTA's labor side accord (Tong 1998):

> Han Young management, the Tijuana labor board, and the Mexican government are engaged in a systematic effort to deny Han Young workers their right to an independent union through harassment, intimidation and fraud.... In the last few days, Han Young management and government officials appear to have broken Mexican law and engaged in blatant voter fraud to crush the independent union.... These actions

could have long-term implications for U.S. trade policy. The United States has a moral obligation to exercise leadership to ensure that our trading partners respect basic democratic rights (SCMW 1998).

Despite such pressure, Han Young began mass firings of STIMAHCS supporters, replacing them with workers from Veracruz (U.S. NAO 1998). The government sent two hundred police officers into nearby workers' communities, arresting STIMAHCS supporters and intimidating others. This only strengthened the workers' resolve, and three recently fired employees—Fernando Flores, Miguel Meza, and Miguel Sánchez—began a hunger strike that would last three weeks (Comelo 1997).

Representative Bonior appealed to President Clinton, who conferred with Labor Secretary Alexis Herman and Mexican President Zedillo. The latter then pressured Mexican officials to resolve the conflict (Tong 1998). According to the U.S. National Administrative Office,

> Following considerable publicity on the case, the Mexican Federal Government intervened and mediated an agreement among the parties. The agreement called for a new representation election, to be conducted under the supervision of state and Federal authorities. The parties agreed to abide by the outcome of this election, suspend all legal action they had undertaken, and desist from further conflict within Han Young (U.S. NAO 1998).

At the urging of President Zedillo and the NAO, Mexico's labor minister facilitated the scheduling of a second union election, to be held at Han Young on December 16, 1997. The independent union prevailed again, this time over both the Confederation of Mexican Workers (CTM) and the CROC. After all the hardships and opposition, on January 12, 1998, the JLCA granted recognition to the "October 6" Union of Industrial and Commercial Workers (Sindicato de Trabajadores de la Industria y del Comercio "6 de Octubre"), mandated that fired workers were to be reinstated, and asserted that there should be no further CTM or CROC interference (U.S. NAO 1998). Historically, there have been maquila unions affiliated with official unions, such as the CTM unions in Tamaulipas, and at times these have functioned to benefit workers. There also was one historic union, the Sindicato Independiente Solidev at the Solidev Mexicana maquila in Tijuana, that was locally organized, officially recognized, and which even won a contract between 1979 and 1982. At a time when the CROC/CROM had not yet consolidated their dominance in Tijuana, the Solidev union also had relatively friendly relations with the CROC, even affiliating with them before the Solidev factory closed in 1983, breaking the union (Iglesias Prieto 1997: 81–97; Carrillo and Kopinak 1999: 119). Despite this precedent, "October 6" became the first officially recognized and fully independent union in the maquila sector (U.S. NAO 1998). Yet, even with this victory, problems persisted.

Under Mexican law, negotiations with a union cannot begin until one year after the signing of the previous contract, and since this had been signed in May 1997 by the CROC, "October 6" negotiations were deferred until May 1998, allowing for a new wave of anti-union tactics. In 1998, Han Young hired more pro-CROC workers from Veracruz, setting the stage for yet another union election. The company also pressured union supporters to resign by offering bribes of $1,200 (*Labor Notes* 1998: 9). Further, while "October 6" representatives were barred from the maquila, a CROC operative continued to work as human resources manager. Management eliminated worker bonuses and set higher production quotas, causing speedups that increased the risk of accident. Workers again engaged in several work stoppages, including a full shutdown of the plant on January 23, 1998. On May 22, workers struck to pressure the company to negotiate, reiterating demands for safety precautions and a raise from fifty or sixty pesos to one hundred pesos per day (SCMW 1998). In response, Pedro Martínez, director of the state Mexican Employers Council (COPARMEX), and José Calleros Rivera, head of the Mexican Maquiladora Association (AMM), warned that the strike was a threat to all investment along the border (Bacon 1999). On June 2, the Baja California state subsecretary, Ricardo González Cruz, declared the strike "nonexistent" since strike banners were posted a few minutes after the 8:00 a.m. deadline (Bacon 1999). Police destroyed strike banners, physically attacked workers, and demanded that they return to work (SCMW 1998). When workers refused, arrest warrants were issued for an "October 6" organizer, and hundreds of special forces and public security police escorted replacement workers into the plant.

By this point, there were many voices calling for justice. Representative Bonior called for monitoring and enforcement of NAFTA's side accord. Mexican Senator Rosa Albina Garabito declared that the "violation of the rule of law by actions of the authorities themselves betrays an inadmissible contempt which we cannot tolerate" (Bacon 1999). AFL-CIO Secretary-Treasurer Art Pulaski personally told President Zedillo that "union members and working families are watching events there [at Han Young] closely because in the expansion of the global economy, workers and their rights must be protected by every nation" (Bacon 1999). Company officials and their government allies ignored these appeals. As the struggle wore on, many workers feared losing the conflict and became increasingly weary of the hardships suffered: limited work and family income, police harassment and arrest, and the relentless rigors of organizing. The limited resources and size of border labor movements relative to extensive government and corporate power only served to heighten frustrations (La Botz 1998b). As tensions grew, conflicts arose within the movement. First, "October 6" organizers became critical of STIMAHCS/FAT leaders, who at times seemed unresponsive to worker demands and who were willing to meet with company representatives without full worker participation. This sentiment included long-standing suspicions of corrupt unionism, and it led to the disaffiliation of "October 6" from STIMAHCS, leaving workers with even fewer resources and allies. Second, workers grew frustrated with unions in both countries and with regional labor support organizations along the border, since they sometimes appeared to use the Han Young struggle to further their own interests. They also advocated militant strategies that only magnified local worker hardships and risked jobs, if not lives. As tensions mounted and defeat loomed, activists accused one another of misguided strategies and self-interested goals.

These disagreements never found resolution, since in the summer of 1999, rather than face continued public relations problems, political pressure, and labor resistance, Han Young closed the factory. What foreign investors, government officials, and workers feared ultimately came to pass: capital flight. Along the border many maquila owners have threatened to relocate in the face of labor activism, and in this case Hyundai and Han Young were able to carry out the threat. With the closure of Han Young, the "October 6" union was closed as well. Despite the effective and militant organization of workers—and the successful efforts of a transnational network to pressure both government and corporate representatives to recognize the union—the official unions, company management, and government leaders were intractable in their counter-resistance. With every worker success, the CROC leadership and key officials in the Mexican state became entrenched in their efforts to break the movement and avoid a precedent for unionization. As they did so, workers fought among themselves. In the words of Benedicto Martínez of the FAT, "They could have been the union alternative in Baja California.... [But instead] it was a resounding failure.... For us it was a bitter experience, because we had the victory in hand. We could have consolidated this first union, because we already had all the potential to make it work ... but it was lost" (author interview, Mexico City, November 2001).

MAKING NIKE SWEAT FOR A CHANGE: THE CASE OF KUKDONG

On January 9, 2001, eight hundred of the nine hundred workers assembling apparel at Kukdong Internacional México began a sit-down strike and an occupation of the factory (Alexander 2001). Kukdong is a South Korean–owned, 25-million-dollar plant (Thompson 2001) in Atlixco, Puebla, southeast of Mexico City, an area central to Mexico's textile industry. Kukdong, in Mexico, Indonesia, and Brazil, produces principally Nike-brand sweatshirts (but also Reebok, Pierre Cardin, and others) for universities such as Duke, Michigan, and California (Boje, Rosile, and Alcántara Carrillo 2001). In 2001, women represented 85 percent of the workforce (Boje, Rosile, and Alcántara Carrillo 2001), averaging twenty years in age (Verité 2001a); most were single mothers (CLR 2001a).

The striking workers cited familiar grievances. Workers experienced many incidents of forced overtime, especially for workers under age sixteen, who under Mexican law can work no more than six hours a day but who frequently were working up to ten. Employees also suffered verbal and physical abuse at the hands of managers speeding up production. This includes management screaming racial epithets and obscenities (WRC 2001: 3) as well as a "range of physical assaults such as blows by hammer and screwdriver, to slaps on the front and back of workers' heads." Management also fed workers rotten meat and worm-ridden rice for lunch (author interview with Blanca Velásquez Díaz, Mexico City, November 2001). The substandard food caused rashes, fevers, and stomach disorders (WRC 2001: 4). Further, the company failed to grant workers legally mandated benefits such as Christmas bonuses (Boje, Rosile, and Alcántara Carrillo 2001) and maternity leave (WRC 2001: 3). Workers also complained of low wages; in 2000 the average daily wage was 43 pesos (<US$5), well below the Mexican median of 66 pesos (Boje, Rosile and Alcántara Carrillo 2001). According to a report by the Worker Rights Consortium (WRC), "wages are grossly insufficient to meet the barest needs of a family of three.... A worker with one dependent would fall below the commonly recognized line of 'extreme poverty'" (WRC 2001: 4). In a National Public Radio interview, one worker, Josefina Hernández Ponce,

claimed Kukdong paid only thirty-five dollars a week, "not quite enough to buy a pair of the pants" she sews ten hours a day. In fact, Hernández feared that workers' living conditions in central Mexico would become like those of the northern border, "crowded unsanitary factory slums" (Hadden, in Boje, Rosile and Alcántara Carrillo 2001).

In December 2000, five workers refused to eat their rotten lunches and began organizing. By January they were fired for insubordination. With support from their families, the Worker Support Committee (CAT), and the confederation of independent unions (the National Workers Union, or UNT), workers decided they wanted to unionize (Thompson 2001). According to Gabriela Cortés of the CAT, "Through experience we know that a union is elementary for workers to get what they deserve" (author interview, Mexico City, November 2001). Kukdong managers forced the retirement of twenty-five additional workers (Axthelm and Pitkin 2001) by threatening to refuse workers their severance pay (author interview with Blanca Velásquez Díaz, November 2001). More significantly, as at Han Young, management told workers that the company had already signed a contract with the CROC in 1999 (Alcalde Justiniani 2001; CLR 2001b). Workers were furious. In the words of Gabriela Cortés, the workers routinely asked:

> Why do they [the CROC] represent us as a union when not one of them has worked, when they have never sat down at a machine ... when not one has worked ten-hour days? Why does a person such as this represent us? Why is it a person who doesn't know that we go home hungry to our villages, and at times we must choose to use our meager wages for clothes or for food, to send our children to school or to buy them shoes, but never both? Why is a person such as this going to be our union director? Why not us? Why these guys, who don't know of labor rights?... How are they going to defend us? (author interview, November 2001).

Workers rejected the CROC and formed their own organization, tentatively named the Kukdong Workers Coalition (CTK). The company refused to recognize the workers' independent union and hired additional armed guards to man the factory gates. On January 11, 2001, CROC "enforcers" and two hundred riot police confronted three hundred picketing workers, announcing that the governor of Puebla had ordered their removal from the area. Although the strikers put up no resistance, the police beat fifteen workers severely enough to require visits to the hospital. Two needed extended hospitalization (author interview with Blanca Velásquez Díaz, November 2001; CLR 2001c), and two women suffered miscarriages (Boje, Rosile, and Alcántara Carrillo 2001). According to the WRC and the ILRF, these actions violated Nike's code of conduct, Mexican federal labor law (Articles 357, 358, 373, 389, and 391), and the principles of the International Labour Organization (ILO) 1998 Declaration of Fundamental Principles and Rights at Work (Conventions 87, 98, and 154), each of which claims that workers' rights to association shall be honored (WRC 2001; CLR 2001d). With little recourse, the workers went on strike.

The CTK and CAT began a two-pronged strategy, one focused on grassroots mobilization, the other on international solidarity. Locally, they educated workers to resist Kukdong management, the CROC, and their government supporters. In response to Kukdong efforts to bribe strikers to return to work, Cortés said, "We made a point again of visiting the villages of workers and explaining to them that, if they accepted the bribes, they were not going to win ... a big victory, and that what they had won so far was nothing compared to what they could win" (author interview, 2001).

Internationally, they wrote letters to publicize their cause and request support. Hernández Ponce wrote:

> We write you to ask for your support and solidarity with the work stoppage we have begun. We don't want to hurt the company, we just want to remove the union, since we were forced to join it and threatened with being fired if we did not. The union gained power, but this power was not to help the workers but to serve the union's and the company's interests. Therefore we were forced to stop work to show our disagreement and to be heard (CLR 2001e).

Additionally, Kukdong workers gained the attention of the United Students Against Sweatshops (USAS), the UE, the FAT, the Maquiladora Solidarity Network, and the AFL-CIO, which had established a labor support office in Mexico City. Workers also submitted a formal complaint to the Worker Rights Consortium on January 18, 2001, which resulted in investigations and well-publicized monitoring (WRC 2001: 1). They even received moral support from the Korean House for International Solidarity. The United Students Against Sweatshops immediately contacted its campus-based organizations in the universities for which Kukdong was a producer, most notably Indiana University's NoSweat! Similarly, the UE contacted its thirty-five thousand members. Each urged its constituents to send letters and faxes of protest to Kukdong and Nike. NoSweat!'s message was:

> Do not "cut and run." Nike cannot escape from these problems by moving production to another location and leaving these workers behind. As an entire company, you made a commitment to protect your workers' rights and you must follow through on that commitment.... The Kukdong Workers Coalition is the legitimate representative of the workers and must be recognized as such. We demand that you officially recognize this organization and allow all workers to return to work, including those previously fired for union activity (in Alexander 2001).

Meanwhile the UE's president, John H. Hovis, Jr., stated in his letter to Nike,

> I am writing to you on behalf of the 35,000 members of the ... UE.... The UE is well aware of the practice by companies which operate in Mexico of imposing ghost unions and protection contracts to deprive workers of their rights. We also know from experience that companies and official unions often use violence and other illegal pressure, frequently with the complicity of the Mexican labor authorities. Nike has received much negative media attention regarding your labor practices in Asia and this situation—much closer to home—promises to become a new focus of attention if it is not rapidly resolved. We encourage you to take immediate action to ensure that your code of conduct is honored by Kukdong and that the workers' rights of association are fully respected (in Alexander 2001).

Receiving little response from Kukdong or Nike, the workers organized to oust the CROC. They adopted statutes, elected leadership, and met all legal requirements to force an election, naming their organization the Kukdong Workers Independent Labor Syndicate (SITEKIM). According to NikeWatch, the combination of local worker movements inside the factory and consumer pressure from without made Kukdong potentially the most hopeful effort for gaining collective bargaining rights in a Nike supplier (Connor, in Boje, Rosile, and Alcántara Carrillo 2001). In early March 2001, an independent monitor hired by Nike (Verité 2001b) released findings that Mexican law and Nike's own code of conduct had indeed been violated: "18 of 29 workers interviewed reported that the factory does not permit workers to form and join unions of their choice.... Most workers at the factory either do not want the CROC as their union or want no union. Only a small number of workers reported that they were satisfied with the CROC" (Verité 2001b). The pressure was increasing.

In an unprecedented response, Nike outlined a plan of actions to be taken by Kukdong and gave a timeline for compliance. Nike agreed to the following: eliminate forced resignations, bring safety conditions up to standard, and, most importantly, support workers' rights to independent union representation. As a result, four hundred of the eight hundred striking workers returned to work, including those fired for activism. Despite this, Kukdong remained hostile to independent union organizing, and many workers chose not to return for fear of abuse. Further, the CROC retained access to the factory floor and the public-address system, and one CROC official even drove near the homes of SITEKIM leaders in the interest of, in his words, "guarding the chicks so that they would not step outside the fence" (CLR 2001f). In addition, SITEKIM still did not have recognition, and Nike failed to offer a secret ballot election between SITEKIM and the CROC, leaving workers open to intimidation (CLR 2001f). And not unlike Han Young, Nike began to warn the USAS in April 2001 that the company might have to pull out of Mexico because "Kukdong is doing so poorly financially" (Boje, Rosile, and Alcántara Carrillo 2001). In the summer of 2001, activists were targets of continuing intimidation, bribes, and beatings at the hands of managers and the CROC, coordinated by Kukdong's Alberto Cedano and the CROC's José Luis Ruiz.

Nevertheless, SITEKIM applied for union registration in May 2001. Puebla's JLCA delayed its decision throughout the summer, prompting many workers to look for jobs elsewhere (USAS 2001a). However, the Campaign for Labor Rights (CLR) organized delegations that brought letters to forty of the forty-five Mexican consulates in the United States. Meanwhile, monitoring continued by the WRC, the ILRF, and independent researchers such as economist Huberto Juárez Núñez (CLR 2001g). USAS organized student delegations to visit with workers, provided organizational support, and publicized the issue on college campuses. The Mexico City office of the ILO organized "freedom of association trainings" with Kukdong management, although CROC operatives were present. In short, despite having no clear victory in sight, international pressure continued. Marcel Muñoz, a twenty-two-year-old line supervisor and a leader of

SITEKIM, claimed to the *New York Times*, "Eyes around the world have been focused on us" (Thompson 2001).

By September 17, 2001, all parties relented and Kukdong changed its name to Mexmode to facilitate a dissociation from the CROC and recognition of the independent union, now renamed the Mexmode Workers Independent Labor Syndicate (SITEMEX) (USAS 2001a). On September 21, SITEMEX signed a collective bargaining agreement that ousted the CROC, reinstated fired workers, created a formal grievance process, granted legally required bonuses, addressed complaints of harassment, and improved the cafeteria food (Thompson 2001). Of the 450 workers employed at Mexmode at that time, 399 signed the application for the independent union (Boje, Rosile, and Alcántara Carrillo 2001), and as of November 20, 2001, 95 percent of Mexmode's workers were affiliated with SITEMEX (USAS 2001a). On April 1, 2002, without the threat of a strike, SITEMEX negotiated a new contract with Mexmode that granted workers a 10 percent increase in wages, a 5 percent increase in benefits, and attendance bonuses—in sum, enough to give a single person a living wage and some surplus for her family. Workers also have labored to improve health/safety equipment, social security enrollments, and clinic services (USAS 2001a). Workers were pleased with the new union democracy and its mechanisms of representation and accountability (CAT 2002). After a few months, SITEMEX's Marcel Muñoz told National Public Radio, "We've won lots of good things. In the first place, we got our jobs back.... Second, last year we barely got two raises; now, in less than six months we've had two raises and we're expecting a third. Now we have a new cafeteria with more options" (USAS 2001b).

Clearly Nike's public image was bruised. Nike, the world's largest athletic shoe and clothing manufacturer, has been a lightening rod for sweatshop campaigns in recent years, especially related to the company's subcontracting relations in Asia. In the words of Ginger Thompson of the *New York Times*, high-profile campaigns have "threatened the image of the Nike swoosh" (2001). During SITEMEX negotiations, Nike spokesman Vada Manager said the company takes seriously its power to ensure that its suppliers comply with fair labor practices and that fifty Nike employees were assigned to monitor subcontractor compliance. Nike's Vice President of Compliance Dusty Kidd and Director of College Sports Marketing Kit Morris announced that the company vowed to renew orders from Mexmode after SITEMEX's recognition as well as attend public forums at several universities on the company's code of conduct. Indeed, after the struggle at Kukdong/Mexmode and the public relations problems Nike suffered, the company's language began to reflect that of the activists:

> We believe collaboration can yield positive, successful results for workers in delicate situations like Kukdong/Mexmode. Companies like Nike (and Reebok who contributed to the costs of the Verité report) can make an immediate impact in reaching resolution because we have the ability to place or terminate orders which can affect the factory's ability to be profitable and attract other buyers. We are always concerned that workers can be unduly affected if we choose not to continue production at a factory, thus we do not take our responsibility lightly (USAS 2001b).

However, it is worth noting that, although Nike was aware of labor violations via a Price Waterhouse Cooper report as early as March 2000 (Boje, Rosile, and Alcántara Carrillo 2001), the company failed to pressure Kukdong to recognize the independent union until the labor network increased public pressure. Only then did the company force the hand of its subcontractor and use its power as the workers and their allies had hoped it would, setting a precedent for higher labor standards in export processing. Gabriela Cortés, of the CAT, summarized the company's decision as follows:

> What occurred here at Kukdong was based on pressuring the company. Pressuring the company allowed it to see that its profits would diminish, that its expected production would diminish. It was obliged to see the reality that it is the workers who are producing; therefore they must treat the workers well. Because if it is not all right with the workers, the company will not have the helping hands of the workers. It will not get [the workers' help] with the Junta Local [JLCA], and it will not get it with the CROC. So what the NGO [nongovernmental organization] support did—in this case, the USAS—was to pressure the brands.... The only exit was for the company to accept the independent union and to reject the CROC (author interview, November 2001).

According to Huberto Juárez Núñez, "This fight showed that globalization has another face.... Companies are going to be required to do more than abide by weak regional laws. Their codes of conduct must set global standards that treat workers as world citizens and guarantee them certain levels of dignity and respect" (in Thompson 2001). For workers and anti-sweatshop opponents throughout North America, this was precedent-setting; no maquila union before has achieved both official recognition and a labor contract. Yet it should be noted that, as of this writing, international monitoring efforts and foreign pressure have waned, and Mexmode has renewed threats of speedups, downsizing, capital flight, and contract rene-gotiations.

COMMON STRATEGIES OF MOBILIZATION AND SOCIAL CHANGE

There are many striking similarities and differences between these two cases. Among the similarities are the political-economic context of the two factories, the repertoire of strategies deployed by workers' movements, and the actions taken by state/corporate officials in their endeavors to thwart labor democracy in the maquilas. First, at a structural level of analysis, Han Young and Kukdong were each subcontractors principally for one company—Hyundai for Han Young and Nike for Kukdong—and these two major companies possess prominent public images. This was not lost on activists within labor support organizations, who regarded Han Young and Kukdong as opportunities to focus extensive public support on labor justice in export-processing zones.

Second, one could argue that both Hyundai and Nike did not have complete freedom in relocating production, giving workers greater lever-age. Despite the fact that Han Young/Hyundai ultimately closed its Ti-juana facility and despite the fact that labor-intensive production in the apparel industry may be more easily relocated, activists such as Jeff Her-manson (AFL-CIO), Antonio Villalba (FAT), and Martha Ojeda (CJM) are confident that companies do not wish to leave Mexico. This is because Mexico's maquilas, especially the 2,603 maquilas in Mexico's northern border states (INEGI 2001. 2–3), have what Storper and Walker have termed "locational advantages," such as proximity to U.S. consumer mar-kets, U.S. ports and supply chains, U.S. management and investors, as well as the streamlined, low-cost advantages of investing in a NAFTA nation (Storper and Walker 1989: 70–76; Gertler 1997: 58). Further, both Hyundai and Nike had large contracts with their maquilas; thus it was not easy for them to switch their production lines to other factories. This was especially true for Hyundai, which had the added difficulty of relocating the large, expensive production processes necessary for manufacturing truck chassis.

These structural political-economic similarities made both Han Young and Kukdong vulnerable to labor strategies such as work stoppages and international public pressure campaigns.

A third similarity is that both maquilas had South Korean ownership. Although this trait may not have made the maquilas especially vulnerable to labor mobilizations, activists argue that the labor relations of the typical South Korean plant are more authoritarian and abusive, leading to labor unrest. Even though approximately 90 percent of maquiladora investments have been based in the United States (United States–Mexico Border Progress Foundation 1996; SCMW 1996: 1), South Korean firms are a large proportion of the most recent foreign direct investment in Mexico, especially in Tijuana. There, stories abound of South Korean labor relations. At the Dae Wan maquila, in order to speed up production, management removed laser-sighted safety devices from machines designed to bend sheet metal. Because these devices had been developed to protect workers from thousands of pounds of hydraulic pressure, management put workers at risk of mutilating injuries. The results were horrific, with workers losing fingers, hands, and even arms, crippling not only bodies but the livelihoods of entire families (Cota 1996, and author interview with Jaime Cota, Tijuana, March 1997). A manager at another South Korean maquila, upon hearing two women workers laughing during a lunch break, approached and hit the workers; he was subsequently detained by police when the workers complained. Workers at Kukdong and organizers with CAT also cited Korean managers' verbal abuse, which entailed racist and sexist epithets and, most notably, use of the word "garbage" to refer to women workers at the plant (author interview with Blanca Velásquez Díaz, November 2001). While abuse is not exclusive to South Korean firms, workers claim that South Korean managers have been far more abusive than their U.S. or European counterparts, and far more reactionary in their retaliation against workers' efforts at organizing. This managerial culture has provoked many grievances from workers, prompting labor networks to pressure management and their contractors. Together, these three similarities offer what Tarrow (1994) terms a "political opportunity structure" for labor mobilization.

Other similarities between Han Young and Kukdong pertain to the character of the labor mobilizations themselves, particularly the trajectory of resistance and conflict. Workers/activists assessed the possibilities for change and built consensus around the goals of collective bargaining with a democratic union. Network supporters lent their expertise to multiple strategies of pressure. Workers educated and mobilized fellow workers for petitions, protests, and strikes. Human rights and union activists provided legal and economic advice, and they assisted in the pursuit of government registration and union runoffs. Public education and corporate pressure tactics familiar to human rights organizations were also common. Activists and concerned citizens throughout North America, but principally workers and students, participated in tours and conferences with workers in their communities. They returned home with documentation and personalized stories to help mobilize their members. Further, in both cases there were efforts to educate consumers and have them urge adherence to labor standards, whether it was via protests at Hyundai dealerships in California or USAS and WRC teach-ins on college campuses. And, of course, workers at both plants used the strike to demonstrate their importance to maquila profitability and as a powerful pressure tactic to force labor rights compliance.

However, counter-movements also mobilized in both cases, and with the opposition of labor boards, official unions, police, and corporate management, each of these strategies of resistance assumed greater urgency. When activist workers were fired, denied certification, or arrested and beaten, many workers undoubtedly felt trepidation. Yet workers in both cases recognized that their national constitution, federal labor law, and human rights were violated, and all for the sake of the profit of foreign investors. With support from an international community of citizens articulating a discourse of universal human rights, corporate-state alliances seemed illegitimate and resistance grew. Labor networks began more intensive monitoring and publication of human rights violations while at the same time instigating legal strategies to have international institutions condemn illegalities. In the case of Han Young, the NAO condemned violations and helped influence the Mexican government to recognize the "October 6" union. At Kukdong, NAO petitions were regarded as unnecessary until the full impact of investigations by the WRC, Verité, and Nike were felt, and these were sufficient to yield contract negotiations. Yet even after initial successes, both workers' movements had to remain vigilant if they were to gain collective bargaining. Each success only provoked greater harassment, bribes, and violence, which in turn incited more intensive efforts on the part of workers to strike, protest, and mobilize foreign support. Indeed, both cases reveal that an intensification of conflict between workers and government is likely to build until corporations step in to end the matter.

Both cases give cause for pessimism. Han Young ultimately closed, and Kukdong workers still must remain diligent in overseeing the implementation of labor contracts. Neither case sparked sweeping reforms in the maquila sector or a mass movement for fair trade and labor democracy in North America. Despite some successes, independent unions have received recognition at only 2 of the 3,590 maquilas in Mexico (INEGI 2001: 2–3), and Jaime Cota estimates that only 2 percent of maquila workers have been organized in any way (author interview, March 1997). Further, the Mexican state has been inflexibly opposed to labor militancy, and neither the National Action Party nor the Institutional Revolutionary Party is tolerant of the threat that such militancy poses to a sector vested with so many hopes of national development. This inflexibility has intensified as foreign investment is threatened by international political and economic factors, whether competition from countries throughout the Pacific Rim, such as China, or geopolitical and economic uncertainty in a time of war and terrorism.

Nonetheless, in both Han Young and Kukdong we can see how, at least for workers in individual maquilas, reforms are possible. Both cases reveal that the right combination of organizations, strategies, and structural opportunities can grant workers sufficient power to unionize and achieve concessions from transnational companies. The politicization of workers' communities and the development of grassroots organizations are possible through dedicated worker activism and transnational support. These organizations, in turn, revealed an ability to pressure for change by combining diverse strategies in a flexible division of labor among labor networks. More practically, these succeeded in ousting ghost unions, gaining state recognition, and exerting political pressure to have Mexican authorities and transnational capital adhere to labor rights. They strengthened existing organizations and inspired new ones to help monitor and resist abusive labor conditions throughout Mexico, expanding the base of experience necessary for greater successes in the future. Just as important, these strategies succeeded in educating North American workers and citizens about the social costs of free trade and export processing, politicizing entire communities. According to Blanca Velásquez Díaz of the CAT, many came to understand that maquila clothes are "based on oppressions, based on suffering, based on sleeplessness, based on starvation wages" (author interview, November 2001).

They also succeeded in doing something that is often underestimated in social movement analysis. They built a culture of hope among workers of

North America, a hope in cross-border solidarity and an emergent transnational civil society to promote a radically democratic form of development. As is obvious, workers from both struggles had a great sense of common purpose and a mutual commitment to each other's well-being. Local and international solidarity was strong, and each reinforced the other throughout the struggle. Locally, workers' meetings were both church and festival, places of reverence for one another and celebrations of what might be accomplished. They were also places of consolation and support, giving workers the resolve to continue against great odds and abuse. Blanca Velásquez Díaz, an activist in the Kukdong struggle, claimed:

> I have always said that one of the things that helped most ... was the resistance of the workers, and, over all, their unity.... With this resistance, we planted our feet on the ground.... Shoulder to shoulder, hand in hand, we never left them. We were always so strong. In problems, in threats, we were always united. I believe that this was the best strategy, the unity of the workers with one another (author interview, November 2001).

This local solidarity inspired national and foreign organizations to dedicate strategic resources to local activists and to build extensive cross-border coalitions. Coalition support, in turn, emboldened local activists with a sense that their resistance had global significance, and it gave them new capacities and dedication to seek out broader international coalitions. Workers in the "October 6" union cited the encouragement they received from the SCMW, CJM, and ILRF. Gabriela Cortés reported that, "Suddenly there were letters of solidarity from other countries.... It motivated us because they were making things better for workers elsewhere.... [W]hen the boys from USAS came to Atlixco, we realized that there are other organizations that are interested in our well-being" (author interview, November 2001). U.S. workers and activists also learned to appreciate the full humanity of maquila workers, not just their victimization. Blanca Velásquez observed this firsthand:

> I went to Chicago to a conference that the USAS hosted. There, one of the girls that had come to Atlixco ... said something funny.... They had an image of Mexican workers. They believed that they were going to arrive to find tired workers, workers without aspirations, making nothing in a poor

town.... But when she visited, she opened her eyes and realized to whom they were sending support. When she met the workers, we played soccer. They realized that we're really human beings above all. She said, "The maquiladora is like a university where the youth go. But what do they gain there? They may finish work, but the work finishes them also" (author interview, November 2001).

Jeff Hermanson of the AFL-CIO put it this way:

Until the Kukdong struggle, there's been a real failure for that movement in the United States and Canada to link up with effective worker organizing.... In Kukdong ... the students who ... came down here to actually involve themselves in the campaign on the ground—as observers, as people who were there to document what was going on and to take the message back—actually saw the Mexican workers not as victims but as brave fighters capable of organizing themselves. That is a tremendous thing. It really builds the enthusiasm in the movement in the United States, that we're working with people that, you know what?, are the same age as we are, they're women, young women who are our age, who are leading a fight against the whole mechanism of government, politics, corrupt unions, employers ... and they can win....

And [there is] the same perception on the part of the Mexicans that, yes, these people are helping us and without them we probably couldn't win, but we are the ones that are in the lead, that our campaign is driving the support. I think this is a social-psychological change that is of great significance on both sides of the border.... And for that, the Kukdong and the Nike struggle in Puebla was a very, very important one in which students learned a great deal about organizing, about Mexican workers; and Mexican workers learned a great deal about possibilities for alliances with American civil society.... That can be a tremendous area of work that has to be developed (author interview, Mexico City, November 2001).

With the victory at Mexmode, U.S. activists have felt even more inspired. As Scott Nova of the WRC put it, "The burning question on U.S. campuses has been whether colleges and universities can really make a difference in the conditions in overseas factories. Now we know the answer is yes" (in Thompson 2001). And in Mexico, too, workers have felt encouraged to continue their activism and begin new struggles for labor rights (Juárez Núñez 2001). Also, these successes have even inspired workers beyond North America, as when the SITEMEX contract moved a semi-independent union at a shoe factory in China to win new rights for its workers (Thompson 2001).

DIVERGING EXPERIENCES IN MAQUILA REFORM

However, the Han Young and Kukdong movements differ significantly in their grievances, in their organization, in their strategies, and certainly in their results. From those who have participated in these struggles to those who have observed them from afar, the differences between these cases have been lessons in the problems and possibilities of labor conflict in the maquila sector.

First, although both groups of workers had similar grievances around wages and speedups, the catalyzing frustrations were different. At Han Young, workers complained of health and safety problems, while at Kukdong the primary frustration was with verbal abuse and physical discipline of line workers. These differences may be attributed to the fact that the firms represented different sectors of maquiladora production. Han Young was an auto industry maquila with a technologically intensive work process involving heavy machinery, in which lowering the costs of production involved management urging workers to use equipment in fast and often unsafe ways. Kukdong, by contrast, is an apparel manufacturer with a labor-intensive process, in which lowering costs and improving productivity were sought via draconian methods of worker discipline.

Further, much of the difference in worker grievances is attributable to the fact that Han Young had a predominantly male workforce, while Kukdong employs almost all women. Women may be subject to physical forms of intimidation and discipline in the workplace that men are not. For female workforces, common practices of sexual harassment, physical abuse, and even sexual assault at the hands of managers function as a form of labor discipline, if not terror. Women workers have been subject to well-publicized incidents of sexual harassment such as offers of money for sex, threats of sexual assault, and the use of sexual favors to determine promotions. In one egregious case, the CEO urged workers at a company picnic to perform in a bikini contest or lose their jobs (CJM 1998; author interview with Mary Tong, Tijuana, July 1996). One woman worker subjected to this demand said that "he [the CEO] treated us like objects.... We are not his property." After workers sued this CEO for sexual harassment in Mexican courts, the plant closed and Mexican officials refused to hear the case. Subsequently, the plant closing was the subject of another suit, this time in U.S. courts, which eventually leveraged a settlement for former workers that these workers described as "satisfactory" (Tong 1998).

Activists have argued that this status quo sexual harassment is an effect of sexist and misogynist tendencies of both Mexican and foreign managerial cultures converging in a deregulated, permissive context. These abuses occur in addition to the more routine aggravations and punishment that men experience, though far less frequently; these include verbal insults, slaps, kicks, denial of bathroom breaks, and, in one plant, detainment in a "punishment room" (author interview with Mary Tong, Tijuana, September 1997). Women workers at some plants also have been subject to violations of reproductive freedoms, by having to take pregnancy tests as a condition of being hired or by being fired for becoming pregnant, all because managers wish to avoid the costs of legally required maternity leave and health care (Human Rights Watch 1996: 19–26; U.S. Department of Labor 2002).

Although male workers, such as those of Han Young, may also be subject to physical discipline, abuse, and unbearable humiliation, clearly many forms of punishment and worker discipline are reserved strictly for women. And the consequences are great. A gendered labor discipline serves to polarize a gendered division of labor between high-skilled male employment and "lower-skilled" women's work, diminishing wages and labor conditions for women, but also placing downward pressure on the work and wages of men. Mary Tong, of the SCMW, confirms this: "the problem is that sex harassment is an effect of how the entire industry fails to respect its workers, that sex harassment is merely one instance of this, and that all sex harassment policies do is mask the root of the problem— exploitation" (author interview, July 1996). Structurally, gendered differences between workers function to allow many maquilas to further externalize or socialize the costs of production onto workers. That is, insofar as women's work is socially devalued and there exist gender-segregated labor markets, maquilas may take advantage by employing a feminized strata of low-wage, labor-intensive workers. As maquilas compete to lower wages and displace the costs of production onto workers, pressure builds for the lowering of wages and the de-skilling of workforces throughout export sectors, female and male. In reference to our cases, because of a distinctly gendered form of abuse on the factory floor as well as racialized verbal epithets, Kukdong workers shared more than the class-based or communal identity that galvanized workers at Han Young, enhancing their sense of solidarity and opposition. This gendered solidarity was strengthened by workers' common belief that, in a Catholic society, women possess a dignity and value that is god-given and worthy of recognition by employers and policymakers (Chaney 1979: 142-55).

A second social difference between these cases is that of regional labor politics. The Han Young struggle occurred in Tijuana, an area of maquila development that, as Cirila Quintero Ramírez has argued, is a primary national site of "subordinated unionism":

> a unionism that is unknown to workers, dominated by a marginal labor power, the CROM [allied to the CROC], openly pro-business.... It defends an anti-worker politics in work conditions and labor benefits, and it permits in its collective contracts the introduction of pro-business clauses. In synthesis, it is a unionism that has subordinated and conditioned its labor struggle to the needs of the maquiladoras (1990: 115).

Consequently, in the shadow of this government-supported pro-business unionism, workers in Tijuana have had few precedents for independent unionism and have faced a well-organized, entrenched opposition. The struggle for unionization was plagued with uncertainty and doubt, especially given the intensive opposition of the Tijuana JLCA, the CROC, and Han Young, which had no tolerance for labor militancy. By contrast, Kukdong workers live and work in Puebla, a state in which subordinated unionism has yet to achieve complete dominance over "traditional unionism"—a unionism with ties to state development policies but one that retains significant autonomy and populist sensibilities with which to struggle for improved conditions, compensation, or rights. To be sure, the opposition in Puebla was strong but not as entrenched as that in Tijuana. Unlike the government-CROC alliance in Tijuana, which did not relent even under NAO and presidential pressure, the alliance in Puebla was persuaded to step aside. Further, unlike Han Young workers, the community surrounding Kukdong had prior experience with unionization struggles; many previously had been active in the Siemens/Volkswagen movement. Although this movement failed to win a contract for workers, it provided Kukdong employees with the politicization, the organizations, the strategies, and the support networks to be effective in pressuring for their demands.

Other differences between Han Young and Kukdong were strategic. The first is that labor activists at Han Young focused more attention on pressuring state institutions to grant registration to the independent union, while at Kukdong more emphasis was placed on corporate pressure tactics. This is always a matter of debate in maquila activism, with different movements bringing different strategic repertoires and organizational cultures to transnational networks. Yet most activists recognize that multiple coordinated tactics are best, especially because the weakness of labor relative to transnational capital makes it imperative to use any leverage available. Quoting a Brazilian maxim, Peter Evans summarized this attitude: "If you don't have a dog, hunt with a cat" (2002). Using all of the "cats" at their disposal, Kukdong labor networks took advantage of prior unionization experiences among Puebla communities, but also a well-organized U.S. student/consumer/labor opposition to Nike.

By contrast, neither Han Young nor Hyundai had been lightening rods for such movements in the United States or South Korea; and even if they had, coalitions between South Korean and Mexican workers would have been far more difficult to organize. Hence Han Young activists had fewer opportunities to pursue extensive direct action campaigns against Hyundai, leaving them with government-based appeals and maquila-level actions of strikes and protests. When asked to discuss these two cases, Jeff Hermanson stated that the anti-corporate alliance made the difference:

> I think too many of them [activists in the Han Young and Duro struggles] are focused on political and legal aspects, and not enough on on-the-ground organizing campaigns. And so you end up with no real worker organization, or a group of five workers who clearly have been treated unfairly, but they're not capable of bringing the struggle into the plant and really putting pressure on the employer. [Without this, nongovernmental organizations] end up pressuring the governor, they end up pressuring the general public and denouncing all the abuses, and that's all fine. But it doesn't change things.... In my opinion, the employers are the key, where in the Mexican tradition and consciousness it's the government. They immediately move their struggle from the factory gate to the zócalo [public plaza] or in front of the municipal palace.... How are we going to fix it? How are we going to prevent that? Well, in Kukdong the focus was all on

the employer, it was all on Kukdong and Nike.... And once they convinced the employer ... that he had to deal with the independent union, the employer went to the governor and said, "hey, you've got to let me out of this sweetheart contract with a crook so I can sign a deal with these workers, because otherwise they're not leaving me alone." And the governor said o.k. And the CROC was gone. I mean ... obviously pressure was put on the government ... but that wasn't the primary emphasis (author interview, November 2001).

Beyond corporate-versus-government strategies, Hermanson points to yet another very important difference between these two cases—namely, the nurturance of grassroots solidarity throughout the entirety of the conflict. To be sure, both struggles began with great participation and commitment, and each had international networks of labor and human rights organizations lending much-needed resources. However, as the conflicts dragged on, Han Young workers experienced significant internal disunity while international support, although consistent, remained largely advisory. The regional culture of labor repression in Tijuana, the relative lack of experience in protracted union struggles, and the limited leverage that Han Young workers had over their corporate opponents made it easy for counter-movements to resist unionization. Workers' hopes began to wane, doubt turned inward, and animosity was directed toward fellow activists, creating suspicion that led to accusations and fissures. Despite differences among Kukdong workers, they retained their solidarity and were buoyed by well-organized exchanges between U.S. and Mexican activists. The greater opportunities for success also allowed Kukdong workers to retain hope and optimism rather than experience fear and uncertainty, and this strengthened mutual trust and commitment. Thus the solidarity of the Kukdong network—both locally and internationally was arguably stronger than that of the Han Young coalition, and it faced fewer challenges in a shorter, better-organized struggle.

CONCLUSIONS

It is clear that these episodes of conflict do not give us a complete perspective on the problems of the maquilas nor any blueprint for resolving them. However, Han Young and Kukdong have been watershed events in the recent history of maquila workers, and they do suggest certain guideposts for activists and scholars of maquila reform movements. Most practically, the successful pursuit of reform at individual maquilas is more likely when the following ten conditions exist:

- Maquilas and/or parent corporations commit obvious and egregious labor injustices.

- Maquilas and/or parent corporations are well known, vulnerable to public relations pressure, already subject to popular protest, and unwilling to relocate.

- Regional or national labor culture is not dominated by repressive anti-labor forces.

- Workers have allies in government—locally, nationally, internationally—to aid in pressuring government to abide by codified labor rights.

- Workers have previous experience in social movement organizations, especially labor.

- Workers possess strong local solidarity, a common sense of purpose, and mutual trust forged by a shared identity of resistance—whether regional, gender, class, or something other.

- Workers have well-organized support from a diversity of movements (labor, women's, consumer, and human rights, among others) locally, nationally, and internationally.

- Workers have strong relations with allies in nations that are home to maquila investors.

- Supporters form a flexible and democratic network that can share resources effectively and respond to new challenges by coordinating a diverse set of strategies.

- Worker and network solidarity is lasting and able to withstand the demobilizing effects of counter-movements.

Given this list of facilitating conditions, today's social context does not lend optimism. The majority of maquilas that commit labor rights violations do so in ways that are not egregious or obvious but status quo. Many maquilas are not well known, or their relationship to contractors is indirect, obscure, or impermanent. Even if transnationals have a public image, they may have no organized opposition at home or abroad, or they are willing to relocate contracts if labor militancy surfaces, especially during times of economic uncertainty. Maquila workers' communities are often migratory and poorly organized, and few have well-established community organizations or local labor networks. It is also no coincidence that the fastest-growing area of maquila investment in Mexico is Baja California, a state dominated by pro-business union-government alliances, a region that wishes to remain competitive vis-à-vis other regions of the Pacific Rim. At national and international political levels, workers have some allies within government, but often they are marginal in what has become a political-economic hegemony of neoliberal development in North America.

Indeed, few conventional avenues of political change—lobbying, legislation, party organizations—have been open to those who question the wisdom of export processing and liberalization. Democratic labor organizations in Mexico must confront a seventy-year history of official unionism, not to mention repression, corrupt patronage networks, and a two-party hegemony when they seek to work within the state. Meanwhile, in the United States, despite significant resources dedicated to lobbying, political contributions, and grassroots mobilization, the labor movement remains a political pressure group, standing outside a political system that is abandoning the welfare state and any Keynesian compromise between labor and capital. Thus workers face what Seidman terms a "deflated citizenship" (2001) in which civil society is forced to struggle alone, with minimal support from the state and private capital. This can reduce labor movements to reactive and compromised strategies—urging government and capital to adhere to existing law, cooperating with corporations, instigating only plant-by-plant campaigns. These restrict proactive strategies that demand democratization and economic redistribution via party politics, policy initiatives, electoral campaigns, or sector-wide organizing against export processing through union/consumer confederations. Indeed, if movements against neoliberal development are to be successful, it is necessary for them to engage in more extensive political endeavors to transform state institutions and thus establish new state-society regulatory regimes.

In civil society itself, Mexican independent unions such as the FAT have been of great aid to many maquila workers, but they have a small pool of resources dedicated only to those movements with the greatest potential for success. Meanwhile, the UNT federation of independent unions has lent merely advisory assistance in maquila struggles as it negotiates new accommodations with the rising National Action Party. U.S. unions in Mexico are limited by law to function only as informal advisers, but even in this role they struggle to overcome nationalist ideologies of trade protectionism and a paternalism toward Mexican labor. Indeed, tensions exist between U.S. and Mexican activists over strategic planning, resources, organizational form, political ideology, and cultural identity; and each threatens to loosen the bonds of international solidarity. These tensions can be exacerbated by reactionary nationalisms that typically resurface in moments of international political conflict and economic crisis. And tensions can grow when unions or consumer movements encourage pressure tactics that unintentionally put workers at risk of further abuse or job loss. Moreover, even when foreign union or consumer pressure prompts reform, abusive labor relations often return when monitoring wanes.

Further, many community-based activists, especially women, openly question whether the trade unionism common to Mexico and the United States might transform maquila justice movements into merely a new form of business unionism—bureaucratic, hierarchical, corrupt, or patriarchal—rather than a social movement unionism that addresses broad aims of equitable and sustainable development. This would continue to compromise the interests of workers and fail to build a diverse labor movement that can effectively address the needs for policy change and sector-wide industrial organizing against export processing. Without these levers of empowerment, workers may continue to find themselves trapped in shopfloor struggles where they must compromise with management around minimal gains or risk capital flight. And without immediate signs of effectiveness and progress, it can be difficult for international labor coalitions to maintain the participation and resources necessary to engage in broad coordinated campaigns. More abstractly, some observers (see, for example, Poster 2002) have questioned whether the rights-based discourse of "anti-globalization" movements really takes us that far from the ideologies of Western liberalism, causing movements to reproduce, in subtle and not so subtle ways, the power inequities of an imperial and capitalist world system.

In the face of these challenges, it appears that the answer to our initial question—"What is to be done?"—may be "not much." However, while we have some reason to adopt what Gramsci termed a "pessimism of the intellect," we also have reason for his "optimism of the will" (1971: 175). The endeavors of a transnational civil society to prompt regulation of transnational capital, especially in North America, are in their infancy. European and U.S. movements for labor justice achieved changes in law and economic policy only after many decades of struggle, as did U.S. racial justice and civil rights organizations. The revolutionary Mexican state came into existence only after a nearly forty-year period of bloody conflict and shifting allegiances, and many argue it has yet to be completed. Even NAFTA's policies of trade and investment developed after almost forty years of Bretton Woods experimentation (by the World Bank, IMF, and GATT) and regional negotiations. Thus it would be shortsighted and of the most romantic utopianism to believe that North American labor networks should achieve systematic reform in the maquila sector within ten or even twenty years. In fact, despite the achievements of maquila unionism, activists often express the greatest satisfaction with the mere survival of transnational labor coalitions and the continuing efforts of labor education. Given the challenges of repression, limited resources, and the difficulties of cross-border coordination, the survival and growth of labor networks is, in itself, an indication that an ongoing and expanding campaign for labor democracy is possible in the region. And as movements worldwide experiment with opposition against liberalization and the advocacy of alternatives, there is potential for increasing leverage against transnational capital and governments in North America.

Further, despite the problems that movements encounter during times of political conflict and economic failure, recurring financial crises throughout the world—East Asia, Mexico, Russia, Argentina, Brazil—have prompted critiques of neoliberalism even within the halls of power. In fact, Evans (2000: 240) speculates that neoliberal policy and its crises may prompt the development of transnational regulatory principles and institutions, ones that may be leveraged by workers for the creation of a more socially just international economy. As the social costs of financial and trade liberalization become familiar topics of debate, there will be opportunities for globalization's discontents to pressure for change. And as transnational civil societies emerge to challenge the hegemony of neoliberalism, a broader public dialogue is beginning about what the future for working people can be, and how to get there. It is uncertain where this dialogue may take us, but if it can offer social critiques of the costs of liberalization and promote the possibility of a radically democratic global economy, it is a dialogue worth joining.

References

Alcalde Justiniani, Arturo. 2001. "Documents of the Mexican Labor Movement in Translation: Opinion Presented by Arturo Alcalde Justianiani Regarding the Case of 'Kukdong International' [January 30th]," *Mexican Labor News and Analysis* 6, no. 2 (February).

Alexander, Robin. 2001. "Strike at NIKE Plant in Mexico: TAKE ACTION NOW." United Electrical Employees listserv. January 12.

Axthelm, Joan, and Daisy Pitkin. 2001. "Workers Meet to Form Independent Union; Campaign Succeeds in Pressuring Nike to Take a Stand!" Report on Kukdong, U.S. Labor Education and Action Project (USLEAP). www.usleap.org/Kukdongmain.html, March 22.

Bacon, David. 1999. "Free Trade Endangers Rule of Law on Border," *Labor Alerts/Labor News*. Campaign for Labor Rights listserv, July 24.

Boje, David M., Grace Ann Rosile, and J. Dámaso Miguel Alcántara Carrillo. 2001. "The Kukdong Story: When the Fox Guards the Hen House." Las Cruces: New Mexico State University, October 20.

Calvo, D. 1997. "Tijuana Workers Win Labor Battle." Associated Press, December 17.

Carrillo, Jorge, and Kathryn Kopinak. 1999. "Condiciones de trabajo y relaciones laborales en la maquila." In *Cambios en las relaciones laborales: enfoque sectorial y regional*, edited by E. de la Garza and J. Alfonso Bouzas. Mexico: AFL-CIO/FAT/Universidad Autónoma de Mexico.

CAT (Centro de Apoyo al Trabajador). 2002. "Mexmode Workers Win a Raise." E-mail report to supporters. catpuebla@yahoo.com.mx, April 4.

Chaney, Elsa M. 1979. *Supermadre: Women in Politics in Latin America*. Austin: University of Texas Press.

CJM (Coalition for Justice in the Maquiladoras). 1998. *Correspondence*. San Antonio, Tex., October–November, p. 1.

CLR (Campaign for Labor Rights). 2001a. *Labor Alerts/Labor News*. CLR listserv. clr@igc.apc.org. www.summersault.com/~agj/clr, January 12.

———. 2001b. *Labor Alerts/Labor News*. "Kukdong Workers Establish an Independent Union." CLR listserve. clr@igc.apc.org. www.summersault.com/~agj/clr, March 22.

———. 2001c. *Labor Alerts/Labor News*. "Background: The Kukdong Story: A Strike, A Police Attack, An Agreement, and Mass Firings." CLR listserv. clr@igc.apc.org. www.summersault.com/~agj/clr, March 22.

———. 2001d. *Labor Alerts/Labor News*. "Nike Pressured to Take a Stand." CLR listserv. clr@igc.apc.org. www.summersault.com/~agj/clr, March 22.

———. 2001e. *Labor Alerts/Labor News*. "Letter from a Kukdong Worker." CLR listserv. clr@igc.apc.org. www.summersault.com/~agj/clr, January 12.

———. 2001f. *Labor Alerts/Labor News*. "Hostility Still Reigns, Where's Nike?" CLR listserv. clr@igc.apc.org. www.summersault.com/~agj/clr, March 22.

———. 2001g. *Labor Alerts*. "Breakthrough in Mexico: Kukdong Workers Win Independent Union." CLR listserve. clr@igc.apc.org. www.summersault. com/~ag j/clr, September 26.

Comelo, Anibel. 1997. "Background of Hyundai Struggle." E-mail report, December 16.

Cota, Jaime. 1996. CITTAC presentation at CJM semi-annual meeting, Tijuana, October.

Evans, Peter. 2000. "Fighting Marginalization with Transnational Networks: Counter-Hegemonic Globalization," *Contemporary Sociology* 29, no. 1: 230–41.

———. 2002. "Discussant Response." Labor and Labor Movements panel, meetings of the American Sociological Association, Chicago, August 18.

Faulkner, Tina. 1998. "Management Dragging Its Feet as Safety Problems Go Unaddressed," *BorderLines Updater*, February 17.

Gertler, Meric S. 1997. "Between the Global and the Local: The Spatial Limits to Productive Capital." In *Spaces of Globalization: Reasserting the Power of the Local*, edited by K. Cox. New York: Guilford.

Gramsci, Antonio. 1971. *Selections from the Prison Notebooks*. New York: International Publishers.

Human Rights Watch, Women's Rights Project. 1996. *Mexico. No Guarantees: Sex Discrimination in Mexico's Maquiladora Sector*. New York: Human Rights Watch.

Iglesias Prieto, Norma. 1997. *Beautiful Flowers of the Maquiladora*. Austin: University of Texas Press.

INEGI (Instituto Nacional de Estadística, Geografía e Informática). 2001. *Industria maquiladora de exportación*. Aguascalientes: INEGI, April.

Juárez Núñez, Huberto. 2001. "The VW Strike of 2000: Worker Resistance in a Setting of New Industrial Integration." Translated by Steve Babson. Puebla, Mex.: Center for Graduate Studies and Research, Universidad Autónoma de Puebla, November 1.

Labor Notes. 1998. "No End to Han Young's Union Busting," vol. 231, no. 9 (June).

LaBotz, Dan. 1998a. "Mexico's Labor Year in Review," *Mexican Labor News and Analysis* 3, no. 1 (January 1)

———. 1998b. "First Workers' Health and Safety Complaint to be Heard under NAFTA Labor Side Agreement," *Mexican Labor News and Analysis* 3, no. 4 (February 16).

Lenin, Vladimir Ilich. 1929. *What Is to Be Done? Burning Questions of Our Movement*. New York: International Publishers.

Poster, Mark. 2002. "Citizenship, Digital Media, and Globalization." Presented at the meetings of the American Sociological Association, Chicago, August 16.

Quintero Ramírez, Cirila. 1990. *La sindicalización en las maquiladoras tijuanenses, 1970–1988*. Mexico City: Consejo Nacional para la Cultura y las Artes.

SCMW (Support Committee for Maquiladora Workers). 1996. "Fact Sheet." San Diego: SCMW.

————. 1998. "Alert: Han Young Strike Is Forcibly Set Aside despite Fed Court Order." San Diego: SCMW.

Seidman, Gay W. 2001. "Deflated Citizenship: Labor Rights in a Global Era." Presented at the meetings of the American Sociological Association, Chicago, August 18.

Storper, Michael, and Richard Walker. 1989. *The Capitalist Imperative*. Cambridge: Blackwell.

Tarrow, Sidney. 1994. *Power in Movement: Social Movements, Collective Action and Politics*. Cambridge: Cambridge University Press.

Thompson, Ginger. 2001. "Mexican Labor Protest Gets Results," *New York Times*, September 8.

Tong, Mary. 1998. "Two Cases of Cross-Border Organizing." Los Angeles: Social and Political Responses to Globalization in Latin America Project (LAREGLO) and Latin American Studies Program, California State University, Los Angeles, April 15.

United States–Mexico Border Progress Foundation. 1996. www.borderprog.org.mx/fbp.html.

USAS (United Students Against Sweatshops). 2001a. "La Lucha Sigue: Part II." Website report.

————. 2001b. "Kukdong/Mexmode Update from Nike, 11/30 (fwd)." USAS listserv, November 30, 5:57p.m. EST, from Nancy Steffan. usas@yahoogroups.com.

U.S. Department of Labor. 2002. "NAO: Status of Submissions" website. www2.dol.gov/dol/ilab/public/programs/nao/status.htm, April 20.

U.S. NOA (United States National Administrative Office). 1998. "Public Report of Review of NAO Submission No. 9702." U.S. Department of Labor. www.dol.gov/dol/ilab/public/media/reports/nao/pubrep9702.htm, April 28.

Verité. 2001a. "Comprehensive Factory Evaluation Report on Kukdong International Mexico, S.A. de C.V. Atlixco, Puebla, Mexico (Audit Date February 5–7, 2001)." www.verite.org.

————. 2001b. "Mexican Nike Workers Beaten for Supporting Independent Union." Update no. 3 (April 11).

WRC (Worker Rights Consortium). 2001. "WRC Investigation re Complaint against Kukdong (Mexico): Preliminary Findings and Recommendations." Washington, D.C: WRC, January 24.

11

Development Diverted: Socioeconomic Characteristics and Impacts of Mature Maquilization

JAMES M. CYPHER

THE MAQUILIZATION MODEL

Steadily from the early 1980s onward, the Mexican socioeconomic structure changed dramatically as the policies of neoliberalism have become hegemonic, both ideologically and in practice. The neoliberal approach emphasizes above all that low income nations such as Mexico must turn away from state-led economic policies and focus with singular intensity on building an economic structure open to both imports and foreign direct investment (FDI) by transnational corporations (TNCs). In the early 1980s the U.S. government under Ronald Reagan and the British government under Margaret Thatcher urged neoliberal policies on the International Monetary Fund (IMF) and the World Bank. Neoliberals, uniting under the banner of the "Washington Consensus," argued that nations such as Mexico should restructure their economies to specialize in exports. According to their understanding of comparative advantage, Mexico would be most efficient if it ceased attempts to build a balanced industrial economy that relied upon growth driven by internal demand. Instead, Mexico would grow faster, with greater stability and benefits for its populace, if the nation specialized in what it did best and imported products that it had no natural advantage in producing. As the emphasis on exports mounted through the 1980s and 1990s, Mexico's competitive advantage in cheap, unorganized, low-skill labor became ever more important—and this has meant that the maquiladora sector has attained a greater and greater role within the socioeconomic structure of Mexican society.

As earlier chapters in this volume have shown, the results of what is probably the world's most significant experiment with neoliberal economics have not been promising. From 1940 to 1980 Mexico's real gross domestic product (GDP) grew at an average annual rate of approximately 6 percent. In the 1980s, growth was virtually nonexistent as Mexico slogged through the "lost decade." The 1990s, though, promised to be different. Driven by strong neoliberals such as Presidents Carlos Salinas and Ernesto Zedillo, Mexico consolidated its commitment to neoliberal policies, with the signing of the North American Free Trade Agreement (NAFTA) in 1993 being the best example. While it was argued that the failures of the 1980s were due to "transition costs," it is difficult to maintain that the poor performance of the 1990s was due to the short-run effects of adoption of the new model. From 1990 through 2002, real GDP increased at only a 3.2 percent annual rate—half the annual level attained in the era of import-substitution industrialization (ISI) (Banamex 2002a: 428). Adjusting for a population growth rate of 1.6 percent, real per capita income has risen only 1.8 percent per year (World Bank 2002: 233). However, if the entire neoliberal period is compared—1982 to 2002—the annual real growth of GDP falls to 2.3 percent, with annual per capita income growth averaging a mere 0.7 percent (IDB 1985: 389, 1996: 359; UNDP 2001: 155). In light of the 6.6 percent average annual growth achieved in the 1970s, which included a strong annual increase in per capita GDP of 3.6 percent, Mexico's neoliberal era as measured by an objective standard would appear to be a colossal failure (IDB 1996: 359).

Under this new regime, exports as a share of GDP have risen from their average level of 12 percent of GDP in the 1980–1993 period to 29 percent in 2000 (Banamex 2002b: 35). This process has been led by the maquila firms, whose numbers soared from 588 in 1982, when the neoliberal shift began, to 3,700 plants in 2000 at the peak of the maquila boom, and dropping to 3,200 plants in early 2002 (Buitelaar and Padilla Pérez 2000: 1631; Rodríguez Gómez 2002a: 11). Employment in the plants rose in the same period from 123,000 to 1,076,000, with this employment reaching a high of 1,339,000 in October 2000 (Buitelaar and Padilla Pérez 2000: 1631; Secretaría del Trabajo 2002). As the economy became increasingly reliant on exports, the maquilas played an increasingly important, and then dominant, role.

Maquila exports as a share of all exports rose from 34 percent in 1990 to 48.6 percent in 2001 (Gruben 2001: 13; INEGI 2002a).

With almost all (93 percent) of the value of all exports coming from manufacturing, it is important to note that a considerable and growing portion of the non-maquila manufacturing exports were actually competitive in international production due to their links to the maquila industry. Under complex but changing rules, maquilas have been free to sell a portion of their output into the domestic market since 1983, with 2001 marking the date for full allowance to sell any portion of maquila output into the domestic economy (Buitelaar and Padilla Pérez 2000: 1630). What this means is that the role of the maquilas is even greater than the data and trends cited above would suggest. One important example will convey this interconnection: In 2001, 42 percent of the non-maquila manufacturing exports were in the auto industry (Durán 2002a: 29). One of the two main pillars of maquila manufacturing is the autoparts industry, which was largely free to sell autoparts to the automobile sector. Thus a considerable portion of the value of cars and trucks shipped from Mexico arose in the maquila sector but was accounted for in the trade data as non-maquila exports.

The issue of the interconnectedness of the maquila/non-maquila sectors is much deeper than the above example of the auto/autoparts interrelationships. Enrique Dussel Peters estimates that when other temporary import/export programs, such as the PITEX and ALTEX programs, are considered, the maquila and the *maquila-like* sectors constituted 78 percent of all of Mexico's exports in the 1993–2001 period (Dussel Peters 2002: 8).

Another way of looking at the growing importance of maquiladora industries is to view their rising share of total manufacturing employment. In 1994 the ratio of maquila to non-maquila manufacturing employment was 41.8 percent, while in 2000, at the peak of the maquila boom, the ratio stood at 87 percent (Secretaría del Trabajo 2002). As the economy and society have steadily shifted toward greater and greater emphasis on the maquilas, this program, long viewed as peripheral to Mexico, has moved to the very center of Mexico's economic system. This trend has been insufficiently noted and understood. To revise dominant perspectives on the Mexican socioeconomic structure, it would be more accurate and realistic to adopt the term "the maquilization model" to describe the path Mexico has taken, rather than the less specific "export-led economy." Another striking statistical relationship conveying the newly emerging nature of the Mexican socioeconomic structure is the fact that between 1993 and 1998 more than 50 percent of all new jobs created in Mexico arose in the maquila sector (Salas 2002: 2). The trend has continued, with Mexico's Coordinator of International Trade Fernando de Mateo noting in 2002, "in the last several years exports have created more than 60 percent of Mexico's new jobs" (Becerril 2002a: 14).

Yet shifting more of Mexico's formal system to maquila production has not been associated with anything more meaningful to the mass of Mexicans than growing immiseration. Average wages fell precipitously from 1982 onward. In 2000, average wages were 76 percent below their 1981 level, while between 1994 and 2000, average wages fell 21 percent even as Mexican and U.S. officials praised Mexico for its strong recovery in the 1996–2000 period (Bacon 2001; Salas 2002: 2). And, in this context, the level of poverty remained startlingly high, reflecting the fact that the maquilization model could not create an adequate number of jobs for the populace. According to CEPAL/ECLAC, the level of poverty in Mexico in 1981–82, before the adoption of the neoliberal approach, was 36.5 percent of the population. This ratio rose to 47.8 percent in 1989 and again during the crisis of 1994–1996, and was estimated to be 42.8 percent in 2002 (Boltvinik 2002: 4–7). Since President Vicente Fox's election in 2000, the number of Mexicans falling into poverty has been 3 million, according to Mexico's top poverty researcher, Julio Boltvinik (2002: 6). In brief, rising exports, driven directly and indirectly by the maquila industry, have been accompanied by a long-term trend of falling wages and a rising index of poverty. Harlow, Denman, and Cedillo's chapter in this volume discusses the negative health impacts of poverty on maquiladora workers and their families.

The results of this great transformation have been portrayed with striking difference by the proponents and critics of the new export-led model of socioeconomic organization. In effect, the proponents of the model have sought to hegemonize even the very terms of the discussion as to what constitutes reasonable or acceptable criteria for the evaluation of the export-led model. This chapter reviews the criteria and arguments for the view that the maquila sector *has* been a viable development strategy. It then turns to the evidence demonstrating that the maquilization model has been a diversion of Mexico's developmental effort, while it has served as a lucrative project for transnational capital and for a few large "groups" (*grupos*) of national economic power. Particular focus is placed on the failure to build viable linkages between the mostly foreign-owned maquila firms and domestic producers. Following this, the chapter focuses on a critical assessment of the slump of 2000–2002 and the implications for the maquilization model that have emerged from that period. Some observers of the maquila sector have stated that there is now a profound transformation taking place in this sector, with "third-generation" producers emerging to spread the benefits of learning, technological transfers, and spin-offs throughout much of the Mexican economy. This approach is critically reviewed in the subsequent section of this chapter. The final section highlights the massive social costs endemic to the maquilization model, costs that are rarely juxtaposed to the meager and selective benefits that the mass of the Mexican populace receives from the maquilization model.

A Case of Success?

In support of their argument, the proponents of the model cite:

- the rapid growth of exports, particularly in the course of the 1990s, led by the maquiladora industry;

- burgeoning trade with the United States (reaching the point where Mexico has surpassed Japan as a U.S. trading partner);

- the ability to finance a trade current account deficit (exports < imports) through high levels of foreign direct investment (signifying "confidence" in the neoliberal model);

- high levels of overall economic growth—when growth *is* high—and the ability to withstand downdrafts in the economy (1994–1996; 2001–2002) when growth is low; and

- low(er) inflation levels since the late 1980s, attributed to "solid" monetary policy and to a public-sector budget that is usually close to being in balance.

Proponents of the model are fond of the praise they receive from multilateral institutions such as the World Bank and the IMF, along with the U.S. Federal Reserve Chair, for their ability to operate "sound" macroeconomic policy.[1] Much of the strength of the model, according to proponents,

---

[1] A particularly strong example of this effect appeared as the lead front-page article in *El Financiero* in 2002. The general director of the Bank of International Settlements (BIS) eulogized Mexico for its fifteen years of "reforms" and faithful monetary policy as well as its "fiscal prudence" (Salgado 2002). Yet on the same page a smaller article pointed out that the level of poverty had grown rapidly in the 2000–2002 period—four million more Mexicans had fallen below the poverty line. And

is attributable to the steady "opening" of the Mexican economy via the gradual elimination of restraints on foreign direct investment in terms of ownership of Mexico's assets, including assets that had once been conceived part of the *"patrimonio nacional"* (national heritage) in the form of a vast array of "parastatals," or state-owned firms. Although the early legislation surrounding the beginnings and entrenchment of the maquila industry was clearly seminal, Mexico's entry into the General Agreement on Tariffs and Trade (GATT, now the World Trade Organization or WTO) in the 1980s and the signing of the NAFTA accord in late 1993 were clearly benchmarks in the rapid adoption by the nation of the export-led maquilization model.

Many of the criteria the neoliberal advocates used to attempt to burnish the image of the wrenching changes undertaken over the last twenty years are strictly financial, such as boasting of:

- the size of Mexico's hard currency reserves (viewed as a buffer against a speculative attack on the peso);

- the exchange-rate stability of the peso (in light of the collapse of the Argentine and Brazilian currencies);

- the relatively smaller size of the foreign debt in relation to GDP (compared to historical data); and

- the "single-digit" inflation rate of the late 1990s, which has become an official refrain.

Much of the art of hegemonizing the discourse pertaining to the socioeconomic state of affairs consists of either ignoring uncomfortable facts or placing a uniquely audacious "spin" on matters that pertain to the profound economic and social costs relating to the rise of the neoliberal model. While silence and evasion are essential tools deployed in the battle to uphold the neoliberal model, so, too, is the persistent barrage of "spin" arguments intended to more tightly anchor Mexico to the export-led model. Currently, although the proponents of neoliberalism within the Fox administration are forced to acknowledge the weak economic performance— avoiding the analytical term of recession—experienced in 2001–2002, the cause(s) of the slowdown are never viewed as directly attributable to the

---

due to budgetary cuts, the public sector support for anti-poverty programs would be cut by 1.5 percent in 2003.

neoliberal/maquilization model. Rather, low productivity and lack of "competitiveness" are viewed as correctable when and if Mexico has a new national labor law (Ley Federal de Trabajo) which will permit much greater "flexibilization" of the labor force. Meanwhile, the modest size of the public sector and its weak financial base will be enhanced by a curious "tax reform"—one that will impose more regressive taxes. Greater efficiency, it is argued, will arise through the piecemeal privatization of the state-owned electrical utility companies and the petroleum company, PE-MEX. These three initiatives constitute the core of the "structural reform" that President Fox, the World Bank, and the IMF are currently seeking to impose on Mexican society. Through an act of alchemy yet to be revealed by proponents, it is argued that, with such a new and deeper embrace of the "free market" tenets of neoliberalism, Mexico will overcome its current stagnation. In short, brief bursts of economic growth—such as the 1997–2000 period—are glowingly portrayed as the logical/inevitable outcome of the neoliberal/maquilization model, while periods of crisis or stagnation (1994–1996, 2001–2002) are viewed as moments/opportunities to *deepen* Mexico's commitment to the model.

Another example of applying some particularly bold spin to maquiladora industries is the claim that they are leading Mexico into a serious process of restructuring through capital deepening, skill enhancement, and the development of human capital. As this claim is presented, the eventual impact of the evolution of the maquiladora industry will be to spin off new firms, entrepreneurs, and technological transfers as engineers and technicians leave the maquilas to form their own startup firms. According to the sequencing claim, it is currently possible to witness the blooming of the "third-generation" maquilas—high-tech, versatile, "Toyotist"-style firms using just-in-time/quality-circle advanced management forms and that are engaged in manufacture and design of highly complex, technologically demanding production processes. The "third-generation" firms will gradually be supported by quality-conscious, technologically competent, Mexican-owned supplier firms that will create clusters and dense webs of supplier/producer linkages in industrial production. As the evolutionary process is portrayed, these third-generation firms are steadily supplanting the "second-generation" firms, firms that involved capital deepening, manufacturing, and more complex production skills embodied in the workforce. And in the receding past are to be found the low-wage, assembly-process "first-generation" maquilas, with some firms remaining in this mode (Villavicencio and Lara 2002; Carrillo 2001).

While unquestionably there has been *some* evolution in the production processes of the maquiladoras, the "third-generation" argument has not been presented in a quantitative fashion. The question is, have the noted shifts resulted in a change of *form* or a change of *substance*? CEPAL researchers have been unable to document substantive change, noting that, although the maquila form of production clearly is the dominant form taken through the process of internationalization driven by transnational capital in Mexico, maquilas as a whole overwhelmingly remain first-generation assembly operations (Mortimore and Peres 2001: 55; Buitelaar and Padilla Pérez 2000). It is possible to find some examples of third-generation production processes, but they are part of a larger transnational corporate whole, wherein simple first-generation assembly remains the underlying purpose and focus (Buitelaar and Padilla Pérez 2000: 1633–35).

A Case of Failure?

Critics of the maquilization model have much to point to (discussed below), but they have difficulty gaining traction as the "spin" specialists attempt to rapidly shift the focus of the analysis toward whatever positive context can be found. During periods of expansion, as the triumphalist discourse mounts, the critics are marginalized. In times of crisis, the critics are able to gain conceptual space; their arguments receive a hearing and increasing credibility in the press and, to some degree, at the level of policy debate. The cyclical nature of the discussion should yield to closure. Either the maquilization model unquestionably achieves institutional and ideological hegemony, or Mexican development policy turns toward another attempt to build an accumulation model, perhaps adopting a neostructuralist approach (Sunkel 1990).[2] Such a turn may seem remote in the cur-

---

[2] Neostructuralism remains a largely undefined project. The key concept would be to replace the attempt to develop from "without"—via exports, free trade agreements, the unconditional acceptance of foreign capital—with macroeconomic policies that would emphasize a strategy of "development from within." Such an approach, categorically, would *not* be driven by nostalgia for the ISI era, but *would build on its many positive elements*. It would draw inspiration from the works of Raúl Prebisch and other leading strategists from the CEPALista school of thought in Latin America. As structuralists, they emphasized the weakness of any strategy that cast the fate of Latin American nations to the capricious nature of global markets that tended to drive down prices for raw materials exported by Latin America while pushing up prices of imported manufactured goods. Today it is the price of cheap-labor products, foremost the labor-intensive maquila products, that face long-term pressures of overproduction, global market satiation, and a declining

rent context, yet the questions remain. How far can the excluded popular classes of Mexico travel on the neoliberal road? Are the abrupt policy turns away from the neoliberal model to be noted in 2001/2002 in Argentina and Brazil harbingers of a new era for Mexico? A quick and solid economic recovery for Mexico would serve to dampen the credibility of the critics, but such a recovery appears unlikely. Nonetheless, Mexico has achieved a "special relationship" with the IMF and the World Bank, as well as with the U.S. government. All three have proven willing to grant Mexico extraordinary credits in earlier periods of economic stress. Thus, while expounding upon the virtues of free market forces, the neoliberals have the liberating option of tapping into the broad rivers of credit needed to cushion a downward spiral in the economy.

The critics present their case in terms of the economic and social costs of the maquilization model—precisely the terms that the proponents deny have legitimacy. One common approach is to point out that Mexico needs to create approximately 1.2 million new (formal) jobs every year if Mexican youth leaving the educational system for the labor market hope to avoid the twin pits of the neoliberal model: the informal economy and migration to the United States. Even during the 1997–2000 period, employment growth was not sufficient to meet the demands of the growing labor force. Since 2000, growth of the formal employment sector has been nearly nonexistent. In this context, the 200,000 to 300,000 jobs lost in the maquila sector are certainly notable, for it was precisely in this sector that the highest rate of growth of job creation was to be found in the course of the 1990s. Throughout this period proponents of the neoliberal/maquilization model were not hesitant to flaunt the growth of maquila employment, insisting that much of this new employment was to be found in "third-generation" skill-intensive careers that promised profound spin-off effects in terms of deep linkages to the broader economy. Rather than a "maquila enclave," the post-NAFTA surge in the maquila sector indicated that spread effects

share of global value-added, as will be discussed below in the case of Mexico. Neostructuralism would refocus the state's role, ending the demonization of the state that has been a focal point of the neoliberal strategy. Development from within would also address the growing maldistribution of income and entrenched poverty in order to drive the accumulation through a *wage-led process*. Brakes would have to be put on the "freedom" of speculators, transnational corporations, and the national elite to engage in "capital" strikes and the flight of capital from nations bent on achieving positive social change. It remains to be seen whether the election of "Lula" in Brazil in 2002 marks the beginning of a serious shift toward neostructuralist strategies.

would be profound as a process of "deep" or "thick" globalization unfolded.

Yet research on the linkage effects of the maquilas clearly points to a process of "thin" globalization wherein the affiliates of foreign transnationals and the Mexican-owned maquilas operated at the lowest end of buyer-driven (and sometimes producer-driven) commodity chains, largely free of any linkage effects (Kopinak 2003; UNCTAD 2001, 2002).[3] Indeed, Kopinak found that in Tijuana a collaborative relationship between U.S.-owned maquila firms and Mexican managers served to ensure that technological diffusion would not be the central focus of these managers. Through organizations such as the Association of Industrial Executives and the Technological Institute of Tijuana, Mexican technicians/managers sought primarily to enhance FDI within the Tijuana area. They have served, in the first instance, as perpetuators of Tijuana's "competitive advantage" in cheap labor. Only secondarily, and occasionally, have they served as catalysts for technological transfer and deepening of linkages, building toward high-tech production processes. In any case, Mexican engineers and managers have sought self-aggrandizement, seeking to both attract foreign capital and assume high-level positions within the manage-

---

[3] Buyer-driven chains are defined as commodity chains that are dominated by the demands and specifications of the buyers, a common arrangement in the apparel industry, the largest maquila sector. Under such conditions, the relationship between the contractor and the maquiladora is weak. Arms-length relationships dominate, and technology transfers are minimal. Buyers have no firm commitment to the supplier maquiladora. Under producer-driven chains, the contracting firms have tighter relations with the contractor. The level of technological mastery is higher; technology sharing and technology transfers occur to some degree. The labor force and management cadre undergo periodic upgrading to meet the complex demands of the contractor, often under capital-intensive forms of production. Producer-driven chains are thought to create some linkages. In the case of Mexico, some producer-driven chains are to be found in the electronics and autoparts industries. Gary Gereffi has sought to argue that Mexican maquilas are evolving toward producer-driven commodity chains (Gereffi 1996, 2002). Nonetheless, by 1998 the apparel industry alone generated approximately as much new employment per year as did the electronics and autoparts industries, according to Buitelaar and Padilla Pérez. In 1988, 7 percent of employment growth in the maquila sector was related to apparel; in 1998 it was 21 percent (Buitelaar and Padilla Pérez 2000: 1632). Susan Fleck, citing data from Mexico's National Institute for Statistics, Geography, and Informatics (INEGI), finds the apparel industry employing 141,000 in 1998, considerably fewer workers than electronics (201,000) and autoparts/transportation (153,000) (Fleck 2001: 146). Still, the growth trend in apparel has been dramatic, and it definitely points to a rising trend in processes associated with thin globalization.

rial structure of the transplanted foreign firms (Kopinak 2003: 15). As such, although these engineers may function well in the context of high-tech production and may inadvertently pull some high-tech production into Mexico, such processes do not indicate that Mexico will be experiencing a new wave of more technologically deep linkages and spin-off benefits.

LINKAGES AND VALUE ADDED: THIN GLOBALIZATION

The United Nations Conference on Trade and Development (UNCTAD) has devoted considerable attention to industrial linkages as a primary means of achieving deep/dense processes of globalized/internationalized production based in technology sharing, stimulating technological diffusion. Such processes have been achieved, most notably in East Asia, through the conscious effort of developmental states, but not in Mexico.[4] One indirect measure used to calibrate the "density" of a nation's integration into global production is to analyze the global share of manufacturing exports produced by a nation in relation to the global share of value added in manufacturing. By this measure it can be determined if a nation is actually developing a more complex system of production which then raises wages and local content. That is, value added is defined as the difference between the value of total output and the value of all inputs. If a nation's share of world exports rises but its share of value added falls, it is presumed that the nation has become more of an entrepôt—shipping more in and out but not really experiencing the dynamic developmental effects of rising local content. This is exactly the state of affairs that describes the Mexican experience, driven by the maquilization process:

> It is particularly notable that between 1980 and 1997 Mexico's share in world manufactured exports rose tenfold, while its share in world manufacturing value added fell by more than one third and its share in world income [fell] by about 13 percent. By contrast, the Republic of Korea, Singapore and Taiwan ... recorded the highest gains in terms of their share in world manufacturing income, without concomitant in-

[4] For a discussion of developmental states, see Meredith Woo-Cumings's *The Developmental State*, particularly the essays by Chalmers Johnson and Ha-Joon Chang (Woo-Cumings 2001). For an exhaustive examination of the empirical record of attempts to build upon a state-led process of development, see Alice Amsden's important book, *The Rise of "the Rest"* (Amsden 2001).

creases in their share in world manufactured exports (UNC-TAD 2002: 80–81).[5]

Thus, while the developmental states of Asia were able to increase their share of world manufacturing income through strategies and policies that emphasized the internal market as much as the external market, Mexico's singular focus on maquila-led exports did not yield spillover effects to the nation in terms of wage increases and the use of nationally produced materials and inputs. Mexico, embedded in globally integrated production systems, did not necessarily receive all of the domestically produced value added. Transnational corporations operating in Mexico—the maquilas—had a strong and probably growing claim to value added since they generate their locally derived profits from this sum of value added. Although data do not seem to be readily available to categorically demonstrate this proposition, it is to be inferred from the work of Michael Mortimore and Wilson Peres. They find that, in terms of the sales of the five hundred largest firms in Latin America, those of the national firms fell from 39 percent of the total in 1990–1992 to 37 percent in 1998–1999. Meanwhile, the sales of transnational firms increased from 27 percent of the total in 1990–1992 to 44 percent in 1998–1999 (the remainder being sales of parastatal firms). For the one hundred top firms, the shift was also dramatic: TNCs raised their share from 53 percent of total sales to 62 percent, while national firms experienced serious displacement as their sales share dropped from 43 percent to 37 percent (Mortimore and Peres 2001: 47).

While these data are for all of Latin America, there is reason to believe that in Mexico's case the displacement effect for national capital was even stronger than that experienced in general in Latin America. Mexico, with its relatively strong export position, accounted for 54 percent of the value of the sales of the twenty largest export firms operating in Latin America in 1999, while ten of the top twenty are Mexico-based firms, including Pemex

---

[5] Buitelaar and Padilla Pérez elaborate on this point: "The national component of value-added shows a declining trend. Over a third (36.3%) of value added was of Mexican origin in 1974. This figure declined steadily until reaching 18.6% in 1996.... This decline is due to the relative and absolute drop in the wage bill, which went from 22.4% of value added in 1974 to 10.6% in 1998. Not only the drop in real wages but also the increasing capital intensity of *maquila* production accounts for this trend.

"The above data explain why the total value added in *maquila* in 1998 was only about 12.7% of value added in [other Mexican] manufacturing industries" (Buitelaar and Padilla Pérez 2000: 1636).

(Mortimore and Peres 2001: 49). And it was precisely in the sectors where exports were the greatest that we find the highest level of displacement toward foreign-owned firms. The two hundred largest exporting firms, accounting for 47 percent of all the value of exports in Latin America, were analyzed in terms of their ownership. Transnational firms increased their share of export sales of the top two hundred from 29 percent in 1990–1992 to 43 percent in 1998–1999 (see table 11.1).

Table 11.1. Transnational Firms in Latin America

	1990/92	1998/99
TNCs' exports as percent of exports of top 200 exporters	29%	43%
Share of sales of the top 500 firms		
National firms	39	37
TNCs	27	44
Parastatals	24	19
Share of sales of the top 100 firms		
National firms	43	37
TNCs	53	62
Parastatals	4	1

Source: Mortimore and Peres 2001: 47.

From the above data showing increasing significance for TNCs, it is safe to infer that a *growing share* of Mexico's manufacturing value added was absorbed as profits received by TNCs—particularly maquila firms—operating in Mexico. Thus, even as Mexico's share of world manufacturing exports rose spectacularly—from 0.2 percent of world exports to 2.2 percent between 1980 and 1997—the share of world manufacturing value added *fell* from 1.9 percent to only 1.2 percent (UNCTAD 2002: 81). And, it can be safely inferred, the portion of the 1.2 percent of world value added that remained in Mexico to support national development also *fell*.

These relationships and inferences are relatively straightforward. Yet it is impossible to find any mention of the above trends in daily triumphalist neoliberal discourse as portrayed by government and business leaders in Mexico's business press, such as "Mexico is the seventh largest exporter in the world in 2002"; "it accounts for 72 percent of all of Latin America's manufacturing exports"; "it has a trade surplus of $37 billion with the

United States"; "60 percent of all new jobs in recent years have been created by exports"; and so on (Becerril 2002a: 15).

Why Mexico seems to show quantitative improvements in the export sector and qualitative deterioration in simple measures such as world share of value added can be readily discerned. Unlike many East and Southeast Asian nations, Mexico has done little to effectively build backward linkages from the transnational firms (particularly the maquilas) into the Mexican economy. Although some small steps have recently been taken to focus on methods of enhancing linkages and technological sharing—particularly in Tijuana—Mexico's insipient efforts are dwarfed by those of Singapore, Malaysia, and Thailand, where real benefits have been achieved (UNCTAD 2001: 200–203, 187–88, 176–77, 149, 146–47). UNCTAD's *World Investment Report 2001* was devoted to the issue of "promoting linkages" between TNCs and domestic producers. Nations that have strong linkages also have strongly rising value-added shares of world production, matching the trend direction of their world exports shares. Mexico is unique in relation to Korea, Taiwan, Singapore, Malaysia, and Thailand, all of which produced strong increases in their share of global manufacturing exports *and* in their share of world value added. Of this group of strong exporters, only Mexico found its share of world value added declining, and the decline was a striking 37 percent (UNCTAD 2002: 81). Comparing Mexico and Malaysia, UNCTAD found:

> In both [countries] ... manufactured imports and exports exceed value added by a large margin.... In both countries exports have high direct import contents due to their close involvement in international production networks. For example, one recent study estimated that in Mexico imports for further processing constitute as much as one half to two thirds of the total sales of affiliates of United States TNCs in industries such as computers and office equipment, and transport equipment. In Mexico, growth in manufacturing value added has been negligible compared to the surge in its manufactured imports and exports. Malaysia, however, has had a very strong growth in manufacturing value added in the past two decades, in part due to the establishment of local suppliers' networks based on foreign ownership (UNCTAD 2002: 77–78).

More generally, UNCTAD found that establishing linkages to local supplier networks arose only when nations had "strong political commitment" at the national level to a policy fostering local linkages. They also noted that there must be "effective public-private partnerships" (UNCTAD 2001: 191). Yet since the early 1980s, under President Miguel de la Madrid, Mexico moved steadily to adopt the neoliberal ultra-free-market stance that eschews public-private partnerships, arguing that the state—by its very nature—was unproductive and parasitic in terms of absorption of resources (Cypher 1990). More generally, UNCTAD developed this point through reference to successful national development strategies, strategies that top policymakers in Mexico have failed to adopt or even consider. Mexico's model has remained rooted in a low-skilled, labor-intensive assembly paradigm based in an indiscriminate opening to FDI. The consequences are clearly demonstrated in contrast to the linkage-building approach of several Asian nations:

> A strategy of development based on participation in labour-intensive processes in global production networks is substantially different for the successful post-war experiences of industrialization in East Asia, where the location of countries in the international division of labor resulted from well-targeted trade and industrial policies. Such policies were particularly important in the first-tier [newly industrializing economies], notably ... Korea and Taiwan ... as they moved out of labour-intensive manufactures and into more technologically sophisticated and capital-intensive activities. As part of a strategic approach to FDI inflows, their policy makers sought to maximize the benefits in foreign exchange and technology that they could extract from TNCs, and to ensure that these complemented—rather than substituted—efforts to strengthen domestic capacity (UNCTAD 2002: 76–77).

As numerous case studies show, at both the national and sectoral levels, success depends on many factors but often centers on the role of an *embedded* state that has nothing in common with the neoliberal state model that has existed in Mexico for the past two decades (Cypher 2003). How can the state foster linkages? UNCTAD's case studies point to several factors:

- *Information provisioning.* Here the government functions as a provider of information on the possibilities of creating linkages, maintaining a comprehensive updated data bank.

- *Matchmaking.* In this area it is incumbent upon the state to operate through many avenues to bring domestic producers and TNCs together, taking potential domestic producers to plants, facilitating negotiations between local producers and TNCs, and sponsoring a variety of activities such as conferences and trade fairs designed to build linkages. Matchmaking involves encouraging domestic suppliers to increase their ability to meet global quality standards.

- *Technology upgrading.* States should adopt strategies that will enhance technological cooperation between local producers and TNCs. States can use their power to impose performance requirements—reciprocity—as a concomitant to tax reductions/holidays and/or to the provisioning of infrastructure to TNCs. At the same time, governments should influence potential local suppliers to reach global quality standards such as ISO 9000 quality levels. States can set up technology transfer programs as joint ventures or strategic alliances with the affiliates of TNCs. Here, an agency of the government would locate potential suppliers and then TNCs would share technologies and skills. The state would provide the organizational structure for such an interface and financing for the local suppliers. States involved in such programs would establish incentives, such as tax allowances, for domestic suppliers who increase their outlays for cooperative research and development with TNCs and/or other firms and/or research institutes, national laboratories, and universities. *But such tax allowances, or incentives, or _any other tax allowances_ must be based upon _reciprocity and compliance_* in terms of the performance of firms (Amsden 2001). The state must have sufficient autonomy from both TNCs and national firms to impose meaningful sanctions for noncompliance.

- *Training.* Supplier associations, assisted with public funds, can encourage the exchange of skills between large suppliers and TNC buyers. Benefits provided to TNCs can be conditioned on requirements that a portion of the foreign affiliate's budget be devoted to seminars and other programs that will facilitate learning and skills upgrading among the employees of domestic suppliers.

- *Financial relationships.* Government must build institutions to protect local suppliers from the leverage that TNCs can exert over the price of locally supplied products. To do so may involve the willingness to provide subsidized legal assistance to local suppliers. In nations with shallow financial systems, the state can impose requirements that lead to some financial credits extended by the TNCs to their domestic supplier firms. TNCs often use their leverage over local suppliers to delay payment, but governments can legislate and enforce requirements for prompt and fair payment. Tax credits or other incentives can be used to encourage TNCs to provide long-term credits to their local suppliers while states can operate development banks to target credit to local supplier firms (UNCTAD 2001: chap. 5).

As UNCTAD demonstrates, many low-income nations have successfully employed numerous elements of the linkage promotion strategies outlined above—but not Mexico, except to the degree that some very incipient and untested programs have been introduced in Tijuana in recent years. Other programs designed to address aspects of the linkage issue, some dating from 1987, have shown minimal impact (UNCTAD 2001: 200–202). Although a descriptive list of Mexico's efforts to stimulate supplier linkages suggests that the Mexican state has addressed many of the most important issues, nowhere is Mexico featured when UNCTAD turns to illustrative cases demonstrating the range of successful accomplishments many nations have realized in deepening linkages between TNCs and local suppliers. Based on the broad research that UNCTAD has undertaken on the issue of industrial linkage effects, they determine that linkage programs can be successful *if:* (1) states show strong political commitment to their linkage programs; (2) states pursue programs that are coherent, with strong delineation of priorities; and (3) states are "embedded" in public-private relationships that are led by professionals who operate under conditions of mutual trust.

While the ingredients that are needed to propel a linkage development program seem sufficiently clear, and while successful examples are readily found, success has eluded Mexico. Mexico's status as the IMF/World Bank's number one subaltern and the staunch neoliberal posture of all Mexican governments since 1988, are sufficient to explain the failure of any serious linkage program in Mexico. For, as the necessary conditions listed above demonstrate, the deep commitment and participation of the state in the linkage programs constitutes the antithesis of the neoliberal conception of the role of the state: minimal and passive, never entrepreneurial or willing to challenge the failures of market arrangements. While commentators continue to feign surprise or dismay, it should by now be an accepted standard that—aside from direct labor—Mexico's domestic inputs are trivial. Domestic inputs constituted roughly 2 percent of the value of maquiladora output in 1980, and they stood at a mere 2.9 percent in 2002 (Cooney 2001: 75; Rodríguez Gómez 2002b: 29). In contrast, Taiwan pushed local content from 5 percent to 27 percent between 1967 and 1978; Korea raised local content from 13 percent to 32 percent between 1972 and 1977; and Singapore achieved a local content level of 40 percent in the same period (Wilson 1992: 23).[6]

THE SLUMP OF 2000–2002

Amid the growing triumphalist chorus of the late 1990s it was difficult, but certainly not impossible, to locate critiques of the maquilization model (Cypher 2001a). The crisis in the maquila sector beginning in October 2000 has persisted. As a result, Mexico's economy stagnated in 2001 with a 1 percent growth rate, and it dropped 1.6 percent in 2002. Leading the decline was the maquila sector, where 473 plants closed (13 percent of all plants) and 287,000 jobs were lost between October 2000 and March 2002.[7] Between August 2000 and August 2002, total hours worked in the maquila sector fell 19 percent as some workers were left unemployed and remaining workers encountered shorter shifts and reduced overtime (Becerril 2002b: 14). The cause, of course, was the recession in the United States, which seemed to take Mexican policymakers by surprise. President Fox, after all, had campaigned on the idea that he could promote 7 percent growth for six years. Mexico, in this interpretation, had been restructured. The strong growth of the late 1990s "proved" the desirability of the maquila-led export platform economy.

---

[6] Alice Amsden's work is the most detailed and systematic available on the subject of national strategies to enhance linkages (Amsden 2001).

[7] The decline in total maquila plants is a net number. Two recent announcements reflect the "race to the bottom" from which Mexico both benefits and loses. One of the major "third-generation" plants, which, according to advocates, were to reflect a new and higher stage of maquila production, abandoned Mexico, leaving 900 workers unemployed at the Phillips Electronics plant in Ciudad Juárez, where workers had been building PC monitors until November 2002. The jobs have gone to China, where labor costs are less than half those in Mexico. Yet, at the other end of the spectrum, Mexico will benefit and U.S. workers will lose when Maytag Corporation relocates its refrigerator plant from Illinois to Reynosa, Tamaulipas, which may "replace" all the jobs lost at Phillips (Reuters 2002: 47; Malkin 2002). As this churning occurs, the precariousness of the maquila sector comes to the foreground. Any benefits that workers might extract over time are conditioned on the flight of FDI to even cheaper labor areas. There seems to be a possible trend appearing in these movements, whereby Mexico gains simple assembly plants and loses so-called third-generation plants. The Japanese shuttered nine plants in Tijuana in 2001–2002, including ones run by Casio, Canon, and Epson, turning out over 7,000 maquila workers.

What had gone wrong? For the neoliberals in the Fox administration, the slump revealed nothing wrong in the fundamental model. Rather, to make the model work still better, the state would have to impose even deeper structural changes leading to a higher level of market autonomy. A new fiscal regime, lowering tax burdens on "savers" and "investors," along with a new labor law imposing a more "flexible" labor regime, would serve to raise the efficiency of the Mexican production sector. Taking these "structural" steps toward deepening the neoliberal model would, advocates maintained, allow Mexico to re-attain solid economic growth in 2003.

Yet the slump of 2000–2002 should have revealed one of the more serious consequences of maquilization: Maquilization has led to the deindustrialization of Mexico's domestic economy as imports have surged and many firms have been bought and mergered into TNCs. At the same time, since the maquila system is primarily built on substandard wages and working conditions that do not allow for the reproduction of the labor force (see Quintero Ramírez, this volume), maquila workers are able to purchase relatively few locally manufactured goods. The shift from a manufacturing sector dominated by more highly paid industrial workers in the national manufacturing sector to a manufacturing sector that is increasingly defined by the labor of the maquiladora workers means that internal effective demand (or total purchasing power) received by workers for a rising mass of manufacturing output actually declines *in relation to what it would have been had manufacturing employment grown sufficiently fast to maintain the 1994 ratio of maquila to non-maquila workers.* Alternatively, as the share of the manufacturing labor force shifted rapidly from 42 percent maquila workers in 1994 to 87 percent maquila workers in 2000 (as indicated in table 11.2), the overall purchasing power of manufacturing workers barely changed, for reasons discussed below in greater detail. Manufacturing employment (maquila plus non-maquila) went up 40 percent from 1994 to 2000, with virtually all the growth coming from the booming maquila sector (compare columns 1 and 2 in table 11.2). By 2000, the ratio of maquila workers to non-maquila workers in the manufacturing sector had reached 87 percent (column 3), up from just 41.8 percent only six years earlier.

But maquila workers were paid considerably less than non-maquila workers. Table 11.3 presents a comparison of the average daily pay for both non-maquila manufacturing workers and maquila workers. This comparison is made in "current pesos" and in "real wage 1994 pesos." The second comparison accounts for wages in terms of constant purchasing power, using 1994 as the base year. The comparison ratio of these workers' wages was nearly 2:1 in 1994 (46.5/26.2, or 1.78), falling to 1.52 (41/27) in 2002. This meant that, through the period, a declining wage "premium"— falling from 78 percent to 52 percent—was received by non-maquila manufacturing-sector production workers (*obreros*) in relation to maquila workers (*obreros*). Note that table 11.3 also demonstrates that non-maquila manufacturing workers had recovered only 88 percent of the wage decline they suffered from 1994 to 2002; real wages *fell* from 46.5 to 41 pesos per day, even as the real GDP rose by 26.5 percent in the same period. Meanwhile, maquila workers were paid roughly 3 percent more; in inflation-adjusted terms, their wages rose a miniscule amount above the 1994 level in 2002, but they were 4 percent *below* the 1994 level in 2001, suggesting that the recovery of wage levels might be only temporary.

Table 11.2. Numbers and Compensation Shares of Mexico's Manufacturing Workers and Maquila Workers, 1994–2002

	(1)	(2)	(3)	(4)
			[*in percentage terms*]	
Year	Manufacturing Workers	Maquila Workers	(2) (1)	Total Compensation, Maquila Workers/ Manufacturing Workers
1994	1,394,000	583,000	41.8%	20.5%
1995	1,273,000	648,000	50.9	24.6
1996	1,314,000	754,000	57.4	31.1
1997	1,388,000	904,000	65.4	38.0
1998	1,444,000	1,014,000	70.2	40.5
1999	1,457,000	1,143,000	78.2	46.2
2000	1,478,000	1,285,000	87.0	51.4
2001	1,413,000	1,202,000	85.0	56.5
2002a	1,350,000	1,076,000	79.7	51.7

Sources: Columns 1 and 2, Secretaría del Trabajo, at www.stps.gob.mx. Column 4, "Compensation," includes all payments as "*remuneraciones*" to both workers (*obreros*) and technicians and professionals (*empleados*), including in both categories payments for vacations, bonuses, incentives, *aguinaldos* (end-of-year bonuses), *comisiones*, all social benefits paid by employers, social security program payments made by employer and profit sharing, etc. INEGI, http://dgcnesyp.inegi.gob.mx/BDINE/.

a Through August 2002.

Table 11.3. Production Workers' Average Daily Wage Income in Mexico, 1994–2002

Year	Non-maquila Manufacturing Wage (current pesos)	Non-maquila Manufacturing Wage (real wage 1994 pesos)	Maquila Wage (current pesos)	Maquila Wage (real wage 1994 pesos)
1994	46.5	46.5	26.2	26.2
1995	52.7	36.4	31.9	22.7
1996	65.0	32.4	39.4	20.2
1997	80.1	33.2	50.3	21.6
1998	96.2	34.9	59.6	22.2
1999	115.8	36.2	69.7	22.3
2000	135.1	38.8	79.3	23.2
2001	152.0	41.2	91.2	25.2
2002[a]	155.0	41.0	99.7	27.0

Sources: Secretaría del Trabajo y Previsíon Social, "Salarios medios en la industria manufacturera" and "Salarios medios pagados a los obreros en las maquiladoras," www.stps.gob.mx/01-oficina/05-cgpeet.

Note: Conversion to real 1994 pesos computed from the consumer price index, Banamex, *Review of the Economic Situation in Mexico*, May 2002, p. 212.

[a] Through September 2002.

Returning to data presented in table 11.2, column 4 (total compensation of maquila workers/manufacturing workers) measures the approximate level of "effective demand" generated by the maquila sector in relation to the manufacturing sector from all workers' incomes combined for each sector. Maquila total compensation rose from 20.5 percent of manufacturing compensation in 1994 to 51.7 percent in 2002. This occurred for two reasons. First, the number of maquila workers increased by 84.6 percent while the number of manufacturing workers declined by 3.2 percent (table 11.2, columns 2 and 1, respectively). Second, real wages of manufacturing production workers (adjusting for inflation in terms of 1994 constant peso purchasing power) declined while maquila wages rose (slightly), as mentioned. The *positive* contribution of wageworkers in terms of sustaining the internal (domestic) market via workers' consumer purchases has thus been increasingly dependent upon the spending of maquila workers, since they account for 90 percent of the net growth of jobs for the two sectors. As the Mexican economy progressively shifts to the maquilization model, the macroeconomy is undercut through the effects of a widening vicious circle of forces endemic to the maquilization model. This model mandates that Mexico's competitive advantage be reduced to low-wage, pliant workers. In doing so, and in raising the relative weight of the maquila sector in relation to all manufacturing, the positive impulse to the internal market through the creation of derived employment from a given net addition to the manufacturing workforce is steadily diminished. This is so because employment in the manufacturing sector (with a wage premium of more than 50 percent in relation to maquila workers) has declined, and virtually all net new jobs have been created by workers whose lower wage levels mean that each new job supports more than 50 percent fewer opportunities for derived employment as workers spend their earnings. To be considered here, in terms of the reduced spending stimulus felt in the Mexican economy as this great shift has occurred, is the fact that the maquiladoras continue to be located, overwhelmingly, on the northern border. Thus it is inevitable that a certain, probably sizable, amount of the positive spending effect of workers' wages actually bleeds into the U.S. economy as the geographical proximity of U.S. retailers proves attractive in terms of consumer purchases.

Alternatively, as the entire manufacturing sector is increasingly represented by the maquila sector—49 percent of all manufacturing workers were maquila workers in 2002—and as the maquila wage represents only two-thirds of the manufacturing wage, the Mexican economy's prospects for internally driven growth based in mass purchasing power steadily declines. As this occurs, policymakers seek to *deepen* the maquilization model, viewing the growth of the export market as the only means of utilizing Mexico's industrial capacity. The maquilization model, based in low wages and "flexible" production schemes, is steadily spreading its own set of capital-labor social relationships (protection contracts, denial of the right to independent collective bargaining, and so on) to the non-maquila manufacturing sector. In so doing, the collateral impacts of the new model unleash further vicious circle effects: From 1994 to 2002, non-maquila manufacturing workers' productivity increased by 39.2 percent, even as wages fell by 12 percent (INEGI 2002b). *Had* the compensation for these workers matched the rate of increase in productivity, thereby allowing for a fundamentally fair-share distribution of the gains from economic growth, the total compensation of all non-maquila industrial workers would have been 39 percent higher. *Had* the shrinking number of non-maquila manufacturing workers been fairly compensated in terms of productivity sharing, the maquila workers' share of total compensation vis-à-vis non-maquila manufacturing workers (table 11.2, column 4) would have been 36.6 percent. Instead, it was 51.7 percent, representing approximately US$552 million that non-maquila manufacturing workers did *not* receive as the maquilization model spread steadily into the manufacturing sector. Thus the increasing relative weight of the maquila sector is simultaneously an indicator of the immiseration of both the maquila workers—who languish at a sub-subsistence wage—and the manufacturing-sector workers.

The implications for Mexico's economy of the shift toward higher and higher levels of manufacturing workers in the maquila sector go beyond the steadily weakening linkages between job creation and effective demand: For reasons that have yet to be clarified, maquila workers appear to create considerably lower "multiplier" effects within the economy than do non-maquila manufacturing workers. (Multiplier effects capture the downstream jobs and spending created by additional employment at the maquilas. Therefore, the multiplier effect measures the number of additional jobs and/or spending supported by a maquila worker or a given number of additional pesos of purchasing power pumped into the economy due to maquila employment growth.)

In a 1992 study, R. Guajardo estimated that the multiplier effect from maquila employment was dramatically lower than that from domestic manufacturing (Buitelaar and Padilla Pérez 2002: 1631, 1636). Guajardo divided the multiplier effect into two components: (1) the jobs created by the spending of the workers (consumption spending), and (2) the jobs created in supplier industries by the hiring of the new workers. Given that maquila workers create relatively few jobs in the second category because most inputs are imported rather than locally supplied, Guajardo found a multiplier effect of only 1.58 for maquila apparel workers versus 2.52 for non-maquila apparel manufacturing that relied upon a high level of local inputs. In other words, each new maquila job that was created led to 0.58 of another new job being supported, while the equivalent increase in per-job spending in the non-maquila manufacturing sector supported 1.52 new jobs. To the degree that this is accurate, then, while manufacturing employment went up 33 percent between 1994 and 2000, the job multiplier effect of this increase in employment was weak because 90 percent of the new manufacturing jobs were in the maquila sector (constituting more than *50 percent of all jobs created in the Mexican economy from 1994 to 2000*). That is, the 19,000 new non-maquila jobs helped create 47,880 jobs through the multiplier effect (table 11.2, column 1, job growth X 2.52 = 47,880 jobs), while the 702,000 jobs created in maquila manufacturing induced 1,112,320 jobs (table 11.2, column 2, job growth X 1.58 = 1,112,320 jobs). *Had* the proportions been reversed, the manufacturing sector—with 90 percent of the job growth coming in non-maquila manufacturing—would have created 1,769,040 jobs. In the maquila sector, only 30,020 jobs would have been created. The net jobs lost comparing this hypothetical situation to what actually occurred (1,769,040 jobs potentially created versus 1,112,320 jobs actually created) leaves a shortfall of 55 percent in terms of possible jobs created. And *had* Mexico's growth been directed away from the maquilization model and toward the domestic market and domestic manufacturing, the total wages earned by these workers would have been much higher. The premium that manufacturing wages held in 1994 over maquila wages—78 percent—would likely have remained (46.5 pesos per day versus 26.2 pesos per day). Thus the *economic cost* of the model can be calculated/estimated in terms of the opportunity cost (the viable alternatives not taken) of the maquilization model. Another, interrelated way of looking at this issue is to view the rapid expansion of the "informal" labor sector and the persistent export of Mexican workers as emigrants to the United States as manifestations of the economic cost of the maquilization model.

The slump of 2000–2002 revealed the level of external dependence of the maquilization model, since the recession was totally a product of the slowdown in growth in the United States. That is, William Gruben found that a 1 percent increase (decline) in U.S. industrial production led to a 1.3 percent increase (decline) in maquila employment (Gruben 2001: 18). This asymmetrical relationship means that any downturn in the United States will induce a downturn in the maquila sector approximately 30 percent larger than the proportional impact felt in the United States. As the maquilization model has expanded to become paradigmatic, the consequences of this asymmetrical relationship on the downside have become profound. Yet, while the slump has generated some soul-searching on the part of Mexico's policymaking elite and those who represent the top business groups (Business Coordinating Council [CCE], Coparmex, and others), the general response has been to search for strategies that will further tie Mexico's socioeconomic structure to the maquilization model (Ramírez 2002: 54).

COMPETITIVENESS

Even though Mexican officials are fond of claiming that Mexico is the seventh-largest exporter in the world, a plethora of data demonstrates that Mexico is not a competitive trader. The World Economic Forum has ranked many nations, including Mexico, in accordance with their "competitive-ness" in several areas. For 2001, Mexico received an overall ranking of 51, down from 34 in 1999 in overall "competitiveness" compared to seventy-four other nations (Rodríguez Gómez 2002c: 12). These measures and Mex-ico's 2001 ranking in comparison with all nations ranked (when stated/available) were: infrastructure, 45 of 49 nations ranked; education, 55 of 75; business "climate," 36 of 49; technology, 47; macroeconomic pol-icy, 21; and microeconomic competitiveness, 55 (Guadarrama 2002: 18; Zúñiga 2002: 1). In infrastructure—vital for the maquila industry—the highway system is largely inadequate, with only 6 percent of highway miles in the country included in the national highway system, and with only 61 percent of this highway system classified as completely modern. Only 32 percent of the entire road system is paved, and 66 percent of the total consists of rural roads (Rodríguez Gómez 2002d: 12). The education system is another yawning chasm of backwardness: 50 percent of youth between the ages of fifteen and nineteen do not attend school, while 44 percent of the fifteen-year-old students were classified as "functional illit-erates" in an OECD study that put Mexico in last place in education in relation to the other members of the OECD (Ramírez de Aguilar 2002: 56).

No measure of Mexico's lack of competitiveness could be more impor-tant than that of technology. Here Mexico's deficiencies have been well chronicled. Compared to the OECD average of 2.2 percent of GDP devoted to research and development, Mexico devoted 0.4 percent of GDP to R&D in 2001, with the private sector funding only 17 percent of the total, while most of the outlay was for science scholarships (Macías 2002: 50; Cypher 2001b: 18–19). While it is commonplace to encounter claims that Mexico's export sector is threatened by "high" wages, it is clearly the case that Mex-ico's competitive weaknesses arise in numerous areas, most beyond the narrow sphere of neoliberal economic analysis. Of particular importance is the inability of Mexican firms to meet global quality standards. Only three thousand manufacturing firms—0.36 percent of all manufacturing firms—have earned the ISO 9000 standard for quality awarded by the Interna-tional Organization for Standardization (Gutiérrez 2002a: 20). In England, or in any other OECD nation, ISO-level production is virtually ubiquitous.

Mexico's comparative/competitive advantage is composed of a dismal and socially unsustainable wage level where, particularly in the maquila sector, wages and working conditions are controlled through the collabora-tion of company unions and corporations operating with aid of the "pro-tection" contract, as Cirila Quintero has shown in her chapter in this vol-

ume. These contracts cover roughly two-thirds of the "represented" laborers, with the portion being considerably higher in the maquila industry
(Fonte Zenteno et al. 1999: 548). But beyond the central issue of the control
of labor, Mexico's other comparative advantages are: (1) proximity to the
United States, and (2) the decision by the U.S. auto industry in the early
1980s to build a Canada-U.S.-Mexico auto corridor. The auto industry continues with expansionary steps, seconded by the Mexican government in a
decidedly non-neoliberal way, to build production capacity. Mexico's auto
industry is currently the ninth largest worldwide, with auto exports (ex-
cluding direct export shipments by the autoparts maquilas) accounting for
42 percent of the value of non-maquila manufacturing exports (Durán
2002a: 29).

Realizing that the Mexican economy is rapidly losing ground in terms
of competitiveness, in October 2002 the Fox administration revealed a plan,
the Auto Industry Competitiveness Program, designed to provide government assistance to supplier firms, particularly maquilas, to improve
their technology levels, quality standards, and plant size (Durán 2002a: 29).
The government will go to great lengths with this program (designed to
bring US$20 billion of new FDI to the Mexican auto sector in the next seven
years), perhaps raising output from 1.8 million to 4 million vehicles, dou-
bling the employment in this sector, and necessitating the creation of five
hundred to seven hundred new supplier firms, most of them, it would
seem, being maquilas (Durán 2002b: 35). Since the dynamic here is really
initiated by Detroit and not Mexico City, the auto sector is known for its
global competitiveness.

Beyond the auto sector, where some considerable part of the grandiose
expectations will likely be met, the government in late 2002 unveiled a
"strategic plan to stimulate the maquiladora sector" (González Pérez 2002:
10). This plan essentially offers a series of tax exemptions, a broadening in
categories of imports exempt from tariffs, faster service with customs pa-
perwork regarding imports/exports, and greater police security guarding
the transport and storage of goods and materials. Mexico's Economic Ministry (SE) announced two new sector programs to help expand high-tech
production of electronics (such as digital television) and computer software in the maquila sector. At the same time, recognizing the issue of production quality, the National Council of the Maquiladora Industry
(CNIME) and the government have set up a maquila quality standard to be
awarded to only three hundred firms that meet certain quality norms and
import more than US$200 million (Silva 2002: 17). They will receive fa-

vored treatment on their shipments across the border. Tying these various initiatives together is the concept of developing and strengthening supply chains through a variety of government and public-sector/private-sector projects. At the same time, the neoliberal advisers to President Fox increased public-sector credit allocations to exporting firms through Bancomext (the government export bank) by 64 percent in 2002 (Gutiérrez 2002b: 18).

The above measures, long overdue and very basic compared to programs adopted by strong exporters throughout much of Asia, will likely receive little funding or support. Mexico's overall tax level—9.8 percent of GDP is miniscule compared to many nations. (Chile, thought to be an example of neoliberal probity, has a tax level of 19 percent of GDP.) The question, given the small tax base, is how large are the funds the government can actually devote to the maquila sector?

Two recent critiques of the maquila program are significant in addressing this question. For the first time, an official of the Treasury has revealed the fact that the maquila sector pays nearly no taxes—the total tax take (net of direct subsidies such as tax credits) from the maquilas was only an estimated US$300 million in 1999, less than one-half of one percent of all tax revenues and clearly trivial in terms of the magnitude of the entire sector (Vázquez Tercero 2002: 67). How, then, can the government hold out tax cuts as awards for desired behavior when maquilas pay virtually nothing for all the services (indirect subsidies) provided them by the public sector? As noted at the outset of this chapter, Enrique Dussel Peters maintains that *all* the temporary import-to-export programs—for example, the maquila program and the ALTEX and PITEX programs—have accounted for roughly 80 percent of Mexico's total exports since the late 1990s. Producers under all these programs are exempt from import tariffs and the value-added IVA tax; they are able to sidestep the income tax (ISR), and they obtain the above benefits because they are classified as "temporary importers." These firms constitute the core of the maquilization model.

The underlying purpose of all the new programs and initiatives outlined in the previous three paragraphs is to build the supplier base, accelerate and deepen the process of creating linkages, and thereby create a basis for more TNCs to locate and stay in Mexico, while raising domestic content and increasing the multiplier effects of the maquilization model in terms of employment, skill enhancement, and income. Dussel Peters notes, however, that to create such linkages, locally owned firms would have to develop while facing import tariffs that can reach 20 percent, an IVA tax of

15 percent, and an ISR tax that can reach 35 percent. How, then, do the government and the elite private-sector business organizations seek to facilitate the linkages between one group of firms that pays essentially nothing in taxes as they take advantage of the maquilization model and another group of locally owned firms that can pay effective tax rates above 50 percent of their cost of production (Dussel Peters 2002: 12)?

The answer, of course, is that they cannot. Nor can the government, with its slim tax base, target tax cuts to the potential domestic supplier firms. Given the established structure of the maquilization model, it is seemingly impossible for the state to carry through on its new-found goals of attainment of a much higher level of integration between the maquilization model TNCs (plus some national producers) and the potential domestic suppliers. Dussel Peters refers to the "farce" of thirty-seven years of policies and programs of integration. In this light, it is difficult to anticipate that the temporary conversion of President Fox's neoliberal advisers will either last or bring lasting results.

LEARNING, INNOVATION, AND HIGH-TECH PRODUCTION IN THE MAQUILIZATION MODEL?

Earlier works (Carrillo 2001; Villavicencio and Lara 2002) have been cited as examples of a school of thought arguing that the maquilization model is carrying with it deep unintended consequences that are fundamentally transforming the production base of the economy, spreading learning, innovations, and the increasing ability to engage in a high-tech, high-value-added production process. "Third-generation" maquilas are leading this process, it is claimed. It is argued that as more maquilas are producing products demanding high skill levels and an intensive level of technology (the third-generation firms), there is more learning by the workforce, including the workforce of suppliers. This "learning"—adoption of more complex work processes, organizational methods, higher levels of knowledge regarding the use and application of more complex machinery and equipment, new skills acquired in repairing and maintaining more advanced equipment, and so on—creates "spillover effects" within the plant, within the firm, and within the region as the learning is "spun off" due to labor turnover and the assimilation of work processes by competitor firms and many other, even nonrelated, producers in the region. More technicians are needed to operate the more complex production processes, while older technicians retrain, sometimes at universities or other educational and training institutions. In short, "upgrading" of the labor force—low skilled, intermediate-skilled, and highly skilled—takes place. New FDI embodies new labor and organizational processes; and once these are adopted in a region, certain positive externalities will occur.

Missing from the works of Carrillo and others known for their advocacy of these assumed positive dynamic effects of the maquilization model is any quantitative analysis of the magnitude of such trends. There is, in fact, some evidence of the emergence of rather isolated examples of higher-skilled production processes. The real issue is the *magnitude* of these processes. The avoidance of any quantification of the "third-generation" trend is a telling criticism of the concept that cannot be deflected through long and repetitious accounts of certain specific firms or programs that have moved some of their production processes beyond the narrow confines of assembly operations.

The issues relating to learning were well analyzed in UNCTAD's *World Investment Report 1999* in a chapter entitled "Generating Employment and Strengthening the Skill Base" (UNCTAD 1999: 257–87). The proponents of the skill upgrading/learning hypothesis intend to argue that the maquilization model is a *viable* and sustainable model because it is bringing economic development to many parts of the country. Yet, as UNCTAD stressed, the possibilities of achieving "learning" are restricted to nations that make a serious, strategic effort to restructure their export industries:

> Good policies are crucial, as governments pursue the twin goals of generating employment and enhancing its quality. Policies affecting employment are not made in isolation, but are closely linked to institutions that evolve over time. The latter comprise the labor market framework, including, among others, industrial relations and collective bargaining mechanisms; the framework for business, including commercial laws and competition policy, and business sector organizations such as chambers of commerce; and the system of education and training institutions that provides generic and specialized skill development (UNCTAD 1999: 277).

But those who find a pattern of evolution leading to the climbing of skill ladders through the ascendance to the "third-generation" maquilas are essentially hyperglobalists. They see a beneficial process unfolding through autonomous market forces, perhaps even production/product life cycles where more and more advanced production takes place in maquila and maquila-related firms. Their work rarely turns to the need for "good policies" as defined above. Yet the maquila sector, with some exceptions, is known for the *absence* of "good policies," including the absence of meaningful industrial relations and collective bargaining, along with an exceedingly weak system of education. It would be surprising, then, to find evidence of widespread and meaningful "learning" and a deep and sweeping enhancement of the skill base. There is little evidence that such a change has occurred, as Alfredo Hualde has shown in a careful case study of the Tijuana region, presented in this volume.

Table 11.4. Composition of Exports and Global Share of Exports for Mexico and All Developing Nations (percentages)

	1980	1985	1990	1998	
Export Category	DN[a]	M[b]	M	M	DN
Natural resources	51%	54%	33%	16%	19%
Resource-based manufacturing	22	13	12	9	23
Low-skill/technology-intensive manufacturing	6	7	14	20	7
Medium-skill/technology-intensive manufacturing	8	15	26	33	17
High-tech manufacturing	12	8	8	9	31

Sources: Data from Mortimore and Peres 2001: 44; UNCTAD 2002: 65. Figures have been rounded, and a category of nonclassified production has been excluded. Therefore the total is < 100.
[a] DN = all developing nations.
[b] M = Mexico.

The perception that such a process is occurring in the maquila sector is relatively widespread in Mexico, and that perception is partially driven by data suggesting that the quality and nature of Mexico's exports have changed drastically. Table 11.4 outlines the changing structure of Mexico's exports in terms of broadly used categories. In the years analyzed, a rapid double movement from raw material exports to manufactures, and within manufactures toward medium-skill/medium-technology manufactured products, has occurred. Note that the high-technology/high-skill production levels merely keep pace with Mexico's export boom, whereas for developing nations as a whole between 1980 and 1998 the share of exports in this category rose from 12 to 31 percent (UNCTAD 2002: 68). Rather than being a leader in this shift toward higher-skill-intensive production processes, Mexico lags far behind the global trend. Note that the data suggest a growing proportional reliance on low-skill operations, reflecting labor trends observed by Fleck (2001). The jump is impressive: nearly a 200 percent proportional increase (from 7 percent of Mexico's exports to 20 percent in only thirteen years). Medium-skilled output, reflecting the growth in autoparts and machinery, rises proportionately by over 100 percent, from 15 percent to 33 percent of Mexico's exports. This seems to corroborate the enhanced learning scenario suggested by many observers of the maquila sector. Note, however, that there is relative stagnation in high-technology manufacturing activities, a result strongly in contrast to the assertions of those who argue that "learning" is occurring due to the growth of maquila production. On the face of it, the data suggest a stronger shift toward medium-skill processes (an increase of 17 percentage points) over the shift to low-skill production (a 13-point increase).

Care must be taken, however, in analyzing these trends. It cannot be assumed that, because the product is classified as either "intermediate" or "high" technology, the production process has undergone a necessary upgrade. Dussel Peters, in fact, maintains that this perception, or leap in logic, is flawed; Mexico is not experiencing "learning" through some autonomous evolutionary process in the maquila sector:

> One possible conclusion is that because we can locate high-technology products—that is, those products wherein Mexico has been integrated into certain segments of value-added [global] production chains in electronics, autoparts, or autos, among others—this also implies that in Mexico [production] processes involve high levels of innovation and/or technological applications. But the preceding is incorrect from the perspective of analyzing production processes. By definition, with certain exceptions which should be analyzed in the future, the use of temporary imports for the purpose of export implies relatively simple and primitive production processes. To achieve a higher level of "local content" or to achieve a greater level of national integration [with the production processes of the TNCs] requires the payment of higher tariffs, or income taxes, or value-added taxes [by domestic producers in relation to TNCs] (Dussel Peters 2002: 13–14).

Earlier in this volume, Hualde reported that the number of technicians and administrative personnel in Tijuana—a proxy for the "upgrading" of the maquila labor force—went up only from 18 percent in 1994 to 21 percent in 2002. Taken all together, Hualde finds that the entire maquila labor force has a *lower* level of professionals and technicians than does the general labor force in Tijuana. This hardly suggests "upgrading," but it is consistent with Dussel Peters's hypothesis that Mexico has continued with essentially low- and some intermediate-skill-level production processes even as the proportion of products produced under the heading of "technology-intensive" production has risen dramatically.

The critical observations of analysts such as Hualde and Dussel Peters have been seconded from an unexpected quarter. Canacintra, a Mexican business organization that brings together Mexican-owned manufacturing firms, has essentially adopted a critical stance regarding the purported automatic upgrading process Mexico has experienced as exports have exploded. The head of Canacintra has advanced a sweeping condemnation of the neoliberal, export-at-all-cost model, charging that there must be a massive reorientation of the model to focus on the internal market as a means of creating employment and production opportunities for medium and small firms as well as low-skilled workers (Bercerril 2002b: 12). The leader of the Business Coordinating Council, Mexico's peak business organization, has directly responded to Canacintra's charges by claiming that Canacintra's views are totally without merit and that the existing free market model is "adequate." *If spread effects, learning effects, skill upgrading effects, and innovation effects* were widespread or even a strong tendency in Mexico, it is impossible to imagine that Canacintra would not notice the impact on its 37,000 member firms throughout the country. If the maquila sector were creating linkage effects of any magnitude, it would be precisely Canacintra member firms that would be the most affected. Rather than using their organization to launch withering attacks on the neoliberal model, Canacintra would, it seems, be the strongest proponent within the business sector of the maquilization model.

The split between Canacintra and the peak business organization, the CCE, became so shrill in October 2002 that the CCE suspended Canacintra's membership rights within the CCE, of which it forms a minor part. Thus, while the CCE can claim to represent Mexico's largest capitalists and perhaps intermediate-sized merchants, it is clearly no longer representing or advocating programs that are perceived to be in the interest of Mexican-owned manufacturing firms. This unprecedented open rupture within business interests demonstrates the tensions that have been created as the transnationalized corporate elite of Mexico, combining with those interests that derive their sustenance from trade and finance, have sought to come to terms with the maquilization model.

THE ISSUE OF SOCIAL COSTS: SOME CONCLUDING COMMENTS

The maquilization model has been presented as one that carries *positive externalities*, particularly relating to learning effects, as discussed above. While evidence of such positive externalities is difficult to locate, an immense body of documentation has demonstrated that the maquilization model carries with it a crushing mass of *negative externalities*. Social cost has been defined in the authoritative dictionary of economic ideas, *The New Palgrave*, as the sum of the private costs plus the external costs of an activity undertaken by a society (Graaff 1998: 393). As mentioned earlier in this chapter, the private costs can be construed as the opportunity cost—what is *given up* to pursue a particular activity. In the case of the maquilization model, Canacintra has taken the position that Mexico has given up a viable national economic strategy based in the internal market for one with deleterious consequences for the majority of Mexicans, but which works well for Mexican and foreign finance and trade capital as well as (above all) for the TNCs. *Adding* to this opportunity cost the range of negative externalities associated with the maquilization model will yield an estimate of the social costs of the great neoliberal experiment.

Previous chapters in this book have begun to move toward the broad goal of detailing the negative externalities. Much more research is needed to fully understand them. By way of conclusion, I delineate the general categories into which negative externalities might best be grouped.

- *Health.* To the degree that new organizational techniques have been employed in the export firms, "Toyotism" or "lean production" methods have become more widespread in Mexico, Labor economist David Fairris finds, in a study of such practices in the United States, that lean production is strongly associated with a rise in workplace safety and health problems, problems that are to some degree mitigated when good collective bargaining institutions prevail (Fairris 1999). One can only deduce that in the absence of solid labor representation and fair collective bargaining practices—a situation throughout the maquila/export sector—the negative external consequences of lean production on the workforce of Mexico will be even greater than those found elsewhere (Bacon 2001). Other dark pathologies can be noted, such as the fact that reported drug use in the border regions most closely tied to the maquilization model is much higher than elsewhere in Mexico (it is 50 percent higher than the national average in Ciudad Juárez and 152 percent higher in Tijuana, the two areas most affected by maquila production) (Ramírez 2002: 47). However, as Harlow, Denman, and Cedillo show in their chapter in this volume, the miniscule amount of research that has been carried out on the health impacts of maquilization does not even allow for the estimation of baseline measures. More research is especially needed in this area, and Harlow, Denman, and Cedillo suggest that it might be focused on following up findings that mothers working in maquilas tend to give birth prematurely and to babies with low birth weights more often than those employed elsewhere or working in the home. These authors also point to the need for more focus on the joint impact of exposure to hazards in both the workplace and the community, especially for women. Moreover, there needs to be better official surveillance of the health impact of maquiladora work, such as keeping records on the frequency of carpel tunnel syndrome among workers.

- *Environment*. George Kourous (1998) has chronicled the vast body of research pointing to the negative externalities relating to the use of chemicals and other substances in the maquila sector in Mexico. The negative externalities associated with the lax regulation of hazardous wastes from the production process have been the focus of considerable research (Kopinak 2002). The chapter by Varady and Morehouse in this volume adds a much-needed analysis about how insufficient and poor-quality water in many maquila cities has been exacerbated by industrial growth. Blackman's chapter assessing the negative impact of maquiladoras and other polluters on air quality provides a model for future investigation.

- *Infrastructure*. A negative externality inextricably linked to the private cost of the maquilization model is the inadequate social and economic infrastructure associated with the border region and with export industries in general. The lack of adequate schools, medical facilities, parks and recreation sites, and sewage and waste disposal, as well as water treatment facilities and publicly supported housing, is all a direct but external result of the maquilization model that imposes virtually no effective taxes on the export firms. Austin, Mendoza, Kimpel Guzmán, and Jaramillo demonstrated, in their chapter in this volume, how globalization "from below" has worked in one maquiladora city to begin the kind of revegetation that is so badly needed in many communities in northwest Mexico.

- *Constructing and maintaining a labor force.* High labor turnover is a well-documented externality of the maquilization model as firms have been allowed an extreme degree of latitude in terms of retaining and maintaining their labor force. In his chapter in this volume, Hualde detailed its negative effects in the Tijuana region. In times of economic downturn, turnover is no longer a problem to firms, but unemployment becomes a heavy burden on the general population and communities that house maquila industries. There has been no research on what maquiladora workers do when fired and how they support themselves and their families.

- *Labor rights.* Weak judicial institutions, systematically biased against the rights of workers and against the social interests of the citizens in the maquila regions, is yet another negative externality of the model, since this judicial laxness is actually part of a broader arrangement whereby the export firms receive the "infrastructure" they seek when they site "low-road" production operations in Mexico. Quintero's chapter in this volume showed how the Tamaulipas region's unions have resisted the problems associated with a weak judicial system. Joe Bandy's chapter addressed the complex situation of cross-border support for independent unions in the industry.

- Finally, *poverty*, at astonishing levels for a nation such as Mexico, which portrays itself as a success (and is cited by IMF and World Bank officials as a success), must to some degree be the by-product of production processes and systems that routinely discharge older workers and those who have suffered impairments arising from the production process. María Eugenia Trejos's chapter in this volume discusses the inability of maquiladora growth to spur development in Central American countries and its contribution to poverty there.

The above list is far from exhaustive in terms of the negative externalities that the maquilization model imposes on Mexico, and not every dysfunctional occurrence can or should be linked to the existence of export processing. But this list is sufficient to demonstrate that in addition to the very high opportunity or economic costs of the model, when the externalities are factored in, Mexico has for more than thirty-seven years tied itself closer and closer to an economically, socially, and environmentally unsustainable project. There are some signs that, in official circles, the lack of spin-offs, linkages, learning, spread effects, and upgrading processes arising from the maquilization model will receive some attention, particularly the need to provide some semblance of a minimally adequate infrastructure in some regions (Cadena 2002: 11). Such steps, however, appear intended to tighten the grip of the maquilization model. No noticeable effort, however, has been made to address the plethora of negative externalities associated with the model. Indeed, the social costs of this project are so high that there can be only one desirable course for Mexico as a nation and as a people. The maquilization model deserves, by any accounting, to be interred.

The 2001–2002 slump, centered on the export sector, may help create a broad coalition focused on a realignment of Mexico's paradigm of accumulation and growth. Mexico has polarized economically and socially, and it is undergoing a profound process of disintegration among various strata of the industrial sector. These tensions have created, and will create, new political alignments in Mexico that will at least cast the discussion and dispute over macroeconomic policy in a new form—to some degree highlighting the magnificent failures of the maquilization model. But there are many elements to consider in the context of this dispute, including the interests that U.S. capital, particularly in the auto sector, have in strengthening the status quo. The largest industrial "groups" have found an accommodation with the maquilization model, and they are now caught in a "path-dependent" process seeking to deepen neoliberalism.[8] If the United States should reenter a period of extremely vigorous economic growth—pulling along Mexico's exporters—the current climate of doubt and tension and *opportunity for a viable critique* would likely come to an end. But the

---

[8] Path dependence refers to the fact that current processes and practices are rarely the result of unconstrained options. Furthermore, these constraints on future options are largely defined by historical patterns. Once on a "path"—be it exporting bananas or producing maquila products—a given economic and social structure is set up and maintained. Forces perpetuating the past practices and extending such practices into the future become very strong, often irresistible. Nations on an upward path tend to move forward on that path, at least until declining benefits or stagnation set in. Nations on a declining path also experience the inertial pressures of path dependence, often leading to a deepening entrenchment of the embrace of the downward movement along the given "path." Knowing when and how to "switch" paths is something that some Southeast Asian nations have, but Mexico has certainly not, achieved.

current prognostications suggest weakness in demand in the United States, spelling even more general economic weakness for Mexico. Thus a propitious moment might be seized to strive for what Osvaldo Sunkel has advocated: a shift away from "inward-looking development" fostered by ISI strategies to "development from within," a term first used by Raúl Prebisch (Sunkel 1990: 155). More likely, unfortunately, is that the Bonapartist strategies and dilemmas of President Fox's administration will only create a wider downward spiral of policy nihilism, a sine qua non of neoliberalism. Throughout much of Latin America, neoliberalism is now on the defensive and in precipitous decline. Mexico, the second nation in Latin America to embrace neoliberalism and the one with the closest and deepest embrace of neoliberalism, could well be the last nation of Latin America of any size to abandon neoliberalism. But the slump of 2000–2002 has silenced the triumphalist portrayal of the maquilization model, and the terms of the debate have changed, probably fundamentally and perhaps permanently.

References

Amsden, Alice. 2001. *The Rise of "the Rest."* Oxford: Oxford University Press.
Bacon, David. 2001. "The Border's Growing Labor War," *LaborNet*, www.labornet.org.
Banamex. 2002a. *Review of the Economic Situation of Mexico*, vol. 913 (January).
———. 2002b. *Review of the Economic Situation of Mexico*, vol. 922 (October).
Becerril, Isabel. 2002a. "Los TLC no curan la pobreza," *El Financiero*, November 14.
———. 2002b. "La política económica divide al sector privado," *El Financiero*, August 16.
Boltvinik, Julio. 2002. "Fox, changarros y pobreza," *La Jornada*, November 15. www.jornada.unam.mx.
Buitelaar, Rudolph, and Ramón Padilla Pérez. 2000. "Maquila, Economic Reform and Corporate Strategies," *World Development* 28, no. 9: 1627–42.
Cadena, Guadalupe. 2002. "Urge apoyar al sector productivo nacional," *El Financiero*, November 14.
Carrillo, Jorge. 2001. "Maquila de exportación y empresas mexicanas exitosas." In *Claroscuros: integración exitosa de las pequeñas y medianas empresas en México*, edited by Enrique Dussel Peters. Mexico: Editorial Jus.
Cooney, Paul. 2001. "The Mexican Crisis and the Maquiladora Boom," *Latin American Perspectives* 28, no. 3 (May): 55–83.
Cypher, James. 1990. *State and Capital in Mexico: Development Policy since 1940*. Boulder, Colo.: Westview.

———— 2001a. "Tendencias a la crisis en los noventas ¿obstáculos a la ideología de la globalización?" In *Globalización y alternativas incluyentes para el Siglo XXI*, edited by Jorge Basave et al. Mexico City: Miguel Ángel Porrúa.

————. 2001b. "Developing Disarticulation within the Mexican Economy," *Latin American Perspectives* 28, no. 3 (May): 11–37.

————. 2003. "Recent Tendencies in Development Economics: Bringing Institutions Back In?" In *Institutional Analysis and Economic Policy*, edited by Marc Tool and Paul D. Bush. Boston: Kluwer Academic Publishers.

Durán, José Antonio. 2002a. "Espera industria automotriz exportaciones por 31 mil ddd," *El Financiero*, October 25.

————. 2002b. "Autotips," *El Financiero*, October 15.

Dussel Peters, Enrique. 2002. "Ser maquila o no ser maquila. ¿es esa la pregunta?" Presented at the seminar "Retos y Perspectivas en la Maquiladora Mexicana," Guadalajara, October 30–31.

Fairris, David. 1999. "Lean Production and Workplace Health and Safety." In *Enfrentando el cambio/Confronting Change*, edited by Huberto Juárez and Steve Babson. Puebla, Mexico: Universidad Autónoma de Puebla.

Fleck, Susan. 2001. "A Gender Perspective on *Maquila* Employment and Wages in Mexico." In *The Economics of Gender in Mexico*, edited by Elizabeth Katz and Maria Correia. Washington, D.C.: The World Bank.

Fonte Zenteno, Luis, et al. 1999. "La auténtica contratación colectiva y los 'contratos de protección.'" In *Enfrentando el cambio/Confronting Change*, edited by Huberto Juárez and Steve Babson. Puebla, Mexico: Universidad Autónoma de Puebla.

Gereffi, Gary. 1996. "Mexico's Old and New Maquiladora Industries." In *Neoliberalism Revisited: Economic Restructuring and Mexico's Political Future*, edited by Gerardo Otero. Boulder, Colo.: Westview.

————. 2002. "Globalización, cadenas productivas y paraje de naciones a eslabonamientos superiores." In *Globalización y alternativas incluyentes para el Siglo XXI*, edited by Jorge Basave et al. Mexico City: Miguel Ángel Porrúa.

González Pérez, Lourdes. 2002. "Listo, el plan estratégico de impulso al sector maquilador," *El Financiero*, October 9.

Graaff, J. de V. 1998. "Social Costs." In *The New Palgrave*, edited by John Eatwell et al. Vol. 4. London: Macmillan.

Gruben, William. 2001. "Was NAFTA behind Mexico's Maquiladora Growth?" *Economic and Financial Review, Federal Reserve Bank of Dallas*, third quarter, pp. 11–21.

Guadarrama, José. 2002. "Negro panorama para empresas: Concamin," *El Financiero*, November 11.

Gutiérrez, Elvia. 2002a. "La certificación de la actividad productiva, factor determinante," *El Financiero*, October 17.

————. 2002b. "El apoyo financiero al sector exportador aumentó," *El Financiero*, September 27.

IDB (Interamerican Development Bank). Various years. *Economic and Social Progress in Latin America*. Washington, D.C.: IDB.

INEGI (Instituto Nacional de Estadística, Geografía, e Informática). 2002a. "Sector externo." INEGI, www.dgcnesyp.inegi.gob.mx.

———. 2002b. "Indicadores de competitividad: productividad de la mano de obra en industria manufacturera." INEGI, www.dgcnesyp.inegi.gob.mx/cgi-win/bdi.exe.

Kopinak, Kathryn. 2002. "Environmental Implications of New Mexican Industrial Investment: The Rise of Asian Origin Maquiladoras as Generators of Hazardous Waste," *Asian Journal of Latin American Studies* 15, no. 1: 91–120.

——— 2003. "Maquiladora Industrialization of the Baja California Peninsula: The Coexistence of Thick and Thin Globalization," *International Journal of Urban and Regional Studies*, June, pp. 1–29.

Kourous, George. 1998. "Occupational Health and Safety in the Maquiladoras," *Borderlines* 6, no. 6 (August): 1–4, 11, www.us-mex.org/borderlines.

Macías, Marissa. 2002. "Olvida México inversión en ciencia como palanca de desarrollo," *El Financiero*, September 12.

Malkin, Elisabeth. 2002. "Manufacturing Jobs Are Exiting Mexico," *New York Times*, November 5.

Mortimore, Michael, and Wilson Peres. 2001. "La competitividad empresarial en América Latina," *Revista de la CEPAL* 74 (August): 37–59.

Ramírez, Carlos. 2002. "Fox: continuidad de neoliberalismo, *El Financiero*, November 8.

Ramírez de Aguilar, Fernando. 2002. "México, en el sótano de los niveles de calidad de la OECD," *El Financiero*, October 30.

Reuters. 2002. "Aumentar operaciones en México, planea Maytag," *El Financiero*, October 14.

Rodríguez Gómez, Javier. 2002a. "Lento despegue de la industria maquiladora," *El Financiero*, October 3.

———. 2002b. "Un fracaso el TLCAN," *El Financiero*, October 21.

———. 2002c. "Tocó fondo la crisis en las ensambladoras," *El Financiero*, October 9.

———. 2002d. "Carece México de la infraestructura necesaria para la competencia," *El Financiero*, August 14.

Salas, Carlos. 2002. "Mexico's Haves and Have-Nots: NAFTA Sharpens the Divide," *NACLA Report on the Americas* 35, no. 4 (January–February): 1–4, www.nacla.org.

Salgado, Alicia. 2002. "México aún goza de prestigio económico," *El Financiero*, November 11.

Secretaría del Trabajo y Previsión Social. 2002. "Estadísticas laborales." www.stps.gob.mx.

Silva, Mario Héctor. 2002. "La industria ensambladora, clave para desarrollo del país," *El Financiero*, October 11.

Sunkel, Osvaldo. 1990. "Reflections on Latin American Development." In *Progress toward Technological Autonomy,* edited by James Dietz and Dilmus James. Boulder, Colo.: Lynne Rienner.

UNCTAD (United Nations Conference on Trade and Development). 1999. *World Investment Report 1999.* New York: United Nations.

———. 2001. *World Investment Report 2001.* New York: United Nations.

———. 2002. *Trade and Development Report 2002.* New York: United Nations.

UNDP (United Nations Development Programme). 2001. *Human Development Report 2001.* New York: United Nations.

Vázquez Tercero, Héctor. 2002. "El fisco y las maquiladoras," *El Financiero,* October 28.

Villavicencio, Daniel, and Arturo Lara. 2002. "Learning and Innovation in a Regional Perspective: The Sample of the Industrial Regions on the Mexican-US Border." Presented at the "Seminario Internacional PEKEA," Santiago de Chile, September 10–14.

Wilson, Patricia. 1992. *Exports and Local Development: Mexico's New Maquilas.* Austin: University of Texas Press.

Woo-Cumings, Meredith. 2001. *The Developmental State.* Ithaca, N.Y.: Cornell University Press.

World Bank. 2002. *World Development Report 2002.* New York: Oxford University Press.

Zúñiga, David. 2002. "Gobierno, causante de la pérdida de competitividad," *La Jornada,* November 18, www.lajornada.unam.mx.

Acronyms

ACILS	American Center for International Labor Solidarity
ADEQ	Arizona Department of Environmental Quality
AFL-CIO	American Federation of Labor-Congress of Industrial Organizations
AGEBs	*áreas geoestadísticas básicas* basic geostatistical areas
AIM	Asociación de la Industria Maquiladora Maquiladora Industry Association
AMAC	Asociación de Maquiladoras de Ciudad Juárez Ciudad Juárez Maquiladora Association
AMIGO	Arizona-Mexico International Green Organization
AMM	Asociación de las Maquiladoras Mexicanas Mexican Maquiladora Association
ANAD	Asociación Nacional de Abogados Democráticos National Association of Democratic Attorneys
APSA	Asociación de Profesionales en Seguridad Ambiental Association of Environmental Protection Professionals
ARAN	Asociación de Reforestación en Ambos Nogales Ambos Nogales Revegetation Partnership
ARASA	Asociación Regional Ambiental de Sonora y Arizona Arizona-Sonora Regional Environmental Association
BECC	Border Environment Cooperation Commission
BIP	Border Industrialization Program
BLM	Border Liaison Mechanism

CNA	Comisión Nacional del Agua National Water Commission
Canacintra	Cámara Nacional de la Industria de Transformación National Chamber of the Manufacturing Industry
CANAIVES	Cámara Nacional de la Industria del Vestido National Chamber of Garment Producers
CAT	Comité de Apoyo al Trabajador Worker Support Committee
CCE	Consejo Coordinador Empresarial Business Coordinating Council
CCT	*contrato colectivo de trabajo* collective bargaining contract
CEC	Commission for Environmental Cooperation
CEPAL/ECLAC	Comisión Económica para América Latina y el Caribe Economic Commission for Latin America and the Caribbean
CFO	Comité Fronterizo de Obreros Border Workers' Committee
CILA/IBWC	Comisión Internacional de Límites y Agua International Boundary and Water Commission
CJM	Coalition for Justice in the Maquiladoras
CLR	Campaign for Labor Rights
CNIME	Consejo Nacional de la Industria Maquiladora de Exportación National Council of the Maquiladora Industry
COAPAES	Comisión de Agua Potable y Alcantarillado del Estado de Sonora Sonora State Water and Sewerage Commission
CONACYT	Consejo Nacional de Ciencia y Tecnología National Council of Science and Technology
COPARMEX	Confederación Patronal de la República Mexicana Mexican Employers Council

CROC	Confederación Regional de Obreros y Campesinos
	Revolutionary Confederation of Workers and Peasants
CROM	Confederación Regional de Obreros Mexicanos
	Mexican Regional Labor Confederation
CTK	Coalición de Trabajadores Kukdong
	Kukdong Workers Coalition
CTM	Confederación de Trabajadores de México
	Confederation of Mexican Workers
EAP	economically active population
ECLAC/CEPAL	Economic Commission for Latin America and the Caribbean
	Comisión Económica para América Latina y el Caribe
ENEU	Encuesta Nacional de Empleo Urbano
	National Survey of Urban Employment
EPA	U.S. Environmental Protection Agency
EPZ	export-processing zone
EZLN	Ejército Zapatista de Liberación Nacional
	Zapatista Army of National Liberation
FAT	Frente Auténtico del Trabajo
	Authentic Labor Front
FDI	foreign direct investment
FOSCR	Friends of the Santa Cruz River
GAO	U.S. General Accounting Office
GATT	General Agreement on Tariffs and Trade
GDP	gross domestic product
GIS	geographic information system
GNP	gross national product
IBEP	Integrated Border Environmental Plan
IBWC/CILA	International Boundary and Water Commission
	Comisión Internacional de Límites y Agua

ILO/OIT	International Labour Organization Organización Internacional del Trabajo
ILRF	International Labor Rights Fund
IMF	International Monetary Fund
IMSS	Mexican Social Security Institute

INEGI	Instituto Nacional de Estadística, Geografía e
	    Informática
	National Institute for Statistics, Geography, and
	    Informatics

INFONAVIT	Instituto del Fondo Nacional de la Vivienda para los Trabajadores National Workers' Housing Fund
IRA	individual retirement account
ISI	import-substitution industrialization
ISPT	Impuesto Sobre Productos del Trabajo income tax
ISR	Impuesto Sobre la Renta income tax
IVA	Impuesto Sobre el Valor Agregado value-added tax
JLCAs	Juntas Laborales de Conciliación y Arbitraje Labor Mediation and Arbitration Boards
LFT	Ley Federal del Trabajo federal labor law
MFA	Multifiber Arrangement
MHSSN	Maquiladora Health and Safety Support Network
MNC	multinational corporation
NADB	North American Development Bank
NAFTA	North American Free Trade Agreement
NAO	U.S. National Administrative Office
NGO	nongovernmental organization

NIWTP	Nogales International Wastewater Treatment Plant
OECD	Organisation for Economic Co-operation and Development
OSHA	U.S. Occupational Safety and Health Administration
P3	Partnership for Pollution Prevention
PAFEF	Programa de Apoyo para el Fortalecimiento de las Entidades Federativas Program of Supports to Strengthen Federal Entities
PAN	Partido Acción Nacional National Action Party
PCBs	polychlorinated biphenyls
PRI	Partido Revolucionario Institucional Institutional Revolutionary Party
PROSEC	Programa Promoción Sectorial Sectoral Promotion Program
SCMW	Support Committee for Maquiladora Workers
SE	Secretaría de Economía Economic Ministry
SECOFI	Secretaría de Comercio y Fomento Industrial Trade Ministry
SEMARNAP	Secretaría de Medio Ambiente, Recursos Naturales y Pesca Environment Ministry
SEMARNAT	Secretaría de Medio Ambiente y Recursos Naturales Environment Ministry
SITEKIM	Sindicato Independiente de Trabajadores de la Empresa Kukdong Kukdong Workers Independent Labor Syndicate
SITEMEX	Sindicato Independiente de Trabajadores de la Empresa Mexmode Mexmode Workers Independent Labor Syndicate

SIUE	Secretaría de Infraestructura Urbana y Ecología Urban Infrastructure and Ecology Ministry
SJOIIM	Sindicato de Jornaleros y Obreros Industriales de la Industria Maquiladora Union of Industrial Maquiladora Workers
SNIFF	Sistema Nacional de Información de Fuentes Fijas National Information System for Fixed Sources
SPRNCA	San Pedro Riparian National Conservation Area
SS	Secretaría de Salud Health Ministry
STIMAHCS	Sindicato de Trabajadores de la Industria Metálica, Acero Hierro, Conexos y Similares Metal Workers Union
STPS	Secretaría del Trabajo y Previsíon Social Labor Ministry
SUTRCA	Sindicato Único de Trabajadores de la RCA RCA Workers Union
TNC	transnational corporation
UE	United Electrical Workers
UNCTAD	United Nations Conference on Trade and Development
UNIDO	United Nations Industrial Development Organization
UNT	Unión Nacional de Trabajadores National Workers Union
USAS	United Students Against Sweatshops
USPB	Upper San Pedro basin
USPP	Upper San Pedro Partnership
WRC	Worker Rights Consortium
WTO	World Trade Organization
WTP	willingness to pay

The Contributors

Diane Austin is an assistant research anthropologist with the Bureau of Applied Research in Anthropology at the University of Arizona. Her principal research interests include environmental aspects of community development and participatory research methods. Among her recent publications are "Public-Private Partnerships as Catalysts for Community-based Water Infrastructure Development: The Border WaterWorks Program in Texas and New Mexico Colonias," *Environment and Planning C: Government and Policy* (coauthor, 2002) and "Community-Based Collaborative Team Ethnography: A Community-University-Agency Partnership," *Human Organization* (2003).

Joe Bandy is a sociologist in the Department of Sociology/Anthropology at Bowdoin College. Among his recent publications are the following: "Bordering the Future: Resisting Neoliberalism in the Borderlands," *Critical Sociology* (2000) and "Reterritorializing Borders: Transnational Environmental Justice Movements on the US-Mexico Border," *Race, Gender, and Class* (1997).

Allen Blackman is a fellow in the Quality of the Environment Division of Resources for the Future, a nonprofit, nonpartisan environmental policy research institute in Washington, D.C. He holds a PhD in Economics from the University of Texas at Austin. His recent research focuses on industrial pollution and forestry in Mexico. Related publications include: "Informal Sector Pollution Control: What Policy Options Do We Have?" *World Development* (2000) and "Scrap Tires in Ciudad Juárez and El Paso: Ranking the Risks," *Journal of Environment and Development* (coauthor, 2002).

Leonor A. Cedillo, an independent consultant, formerly served as deputy director of environmental health in Mexico City and was a visiting professor in the Industrial Relations Program of El Colegio de Sonora. An industrial hygienist, her research focuses on the work environment and psychosocial risks among women working in the maquiladoras. Her publications include "Establishing Priorities for Occupational Health Research among Women Working in the Maquiladora Industry," *International Journal of Occupational and Environmental Health* (coauthor, 1997) and "The Prevalence of Musculoskeletal Complaints among Women in Tijuana: Demographic and Occupational Risk Factors," *International Journal of Environmental and Occupational Health* (coauthor, 1999).

James M. Cypher is professor of economics at California State University, Fresno. His principal research focus is on the role of the state in the process of economic development, with an emphasis on Latin American macro-policy issues. He is the author of *State and Capital in Mexico: Development Policy since 1940* (1990) and numerous articles on Mexico, including, most recently, "El modelo de desarrollo exportador: el caso de México," in *Mundialización, transnacionalización y subdesarrollo*, edited by Gregorio Vidal (2001) and "Nafta's Lessons: From Economic Mythology to Current Realities," *Labor Studies Journal* (Spring 2001).

María Eugenia de la O Martínez is a researcher and professor at the Centro de Investigaciones y Estudios Superiores en Antropología Social (CIESAS) in Guadalajara, Mexico. Her doctoral thesis, "... y por eso se llaman maquilas: la configuración de las relaciones laborales en la modernización," was chosen by the Academia de la Investigación Científica as the best doctoral dissertation in sociology of 1997. Her recent publications include: *Historia regional de Baja California: perfil socioeconómica* (coauthor, 2000) and *Globalización, trabajo y maquilas: las nuevas y viejas fronteras en México* (coeditor, 2002).

Catalina A. Denman is rector of El Colegio de Sonora, in Hermosillo, Mexico. An anthropologist, she has conducted research on issues in women's health, with an emphasis on working women, border health, and reproductive health. She is currently co-coordinator of the Transborder Consortium for Research and Action on Women and Health at the United States–Mexico Border and is a founding member of the Red Fronteriza de Salud y Ambiente, a nongovernmental organization initiated in 1992 to deal with improving environmental and health conditions in northern Mexico. Among her publications are *Por los rincones: una antología de métodos cualitativos en la investigación social* (coeditor, 2000) and "Design and Results of the USA-Mexico Border Human Papillomavirus (HPV), Cervical Dysplasia, and *Chlamydia trachomatis* Study," *Pan American Journal of Public Health* (coauthor, 2001).

Siobán D. Harlow is professor in the Department of Epidemiology and associate director of the International Institute, at the University of Michigan. Her research focuses on women's health, reproductive health, and occupational health in developing countries. Her publications include: "Risk Factors for Pre-Eclampsia among Working Women in Mexico," *Paediatric and Perinatal Epidemiology* (coauthor, 2001) and "Self-defined Menopausal Status in a Multi-ethnic Sample of Midlife Women," *Maturitas* (coauthor, 2000).

Alfredo Hualde is director of the Department of Social Studies at El Colegio de la Frontera Norte in Tijuana. His current research examines industrial learning, employment, and skill training in the maquiladora industry and the linkages between educational profiles and development needs in the border region. He has published widely; among his recent titles are *Aprendizaje industrial en la frontera norte de México* (2001) and *Formación educativa y formación en la empresa* (2001).

Alba Jaramillo is a recent graduate of the University of Arizona's Department of Anthropology. Her senior research project investigated maquiladora participation in the Ambos Nogales revegetation partnership.

Michèle Kimpel Guzmán is the air outreach coordinator for the Arizona Department of Environmental Quality. She helped organize and develop the Border Liaison Mechanism Social and Economic Development Subgroup in Ambos Nogales.

Kathryn Kopinak is professor of sociology at King's University College at the University of Western Ontario in London Ontario, Canada. Her current research interests include the environmental impact of Mexican maquiladora industries and their role in shaping regional economies. She is the author of *Desert Capitalism* (1996) and several articles on Mexican maquiladoras, including "Maquiladora Industrialization of the Baja California Peninsula: The Coexistence of Thick and Thin Globalization with Economic Regionalism," *Journal of Urban and Regional Research* (June 2003).

Edna Mendoza is the border hazardous waste coordinator for the Arizona Department of Environmental Quality. She established the AMIGO program.

Barbara Morehouse is associate research scientist at the Climate Assessment for the Southwest (CLIMAS) project at the Institute for the Study of Planet Earth, and adjunct assistant professor of geography at the University of Arizona.

Cirila Ramírez Quintero is a researcher and professor at the Matamoros Regional Office of El Colegio de la Frontera Norte. Her recent publications include: "Unions and Working Conditions in Maquiladoras: Effects on the Family," in *Common Origins, Segmented Futures: Mexican Origin Families in Transnational and Borderland Context*, edited by Peter Ward (in press), and "Experiencias organizativas en la maquiladora," *Revista Nueva Antropología* (2001).

María Eugenia Trejos, a Costa Rican, holds a master's degree from the University of Massachusetts in Amherst and is currently completing a doctoral dissertation in labor studies at the Universidad Autónoma Metropolitana de México. Among her recent published works are: "El solidarismo en Costa Rica: eje de una estrategia antisindical," *Cuadernos del CENDES* (2001) and "Compromisos de gestión y transformaciones laborales en el sector salud de Costa Rica," *Revista de Ciencias Sociales* (Universidad de Costa Rica, 2000–2001).

Robert Varady is deputy director of the Udall Center for Studies in Public Policy, research professor of environmental policy, and adjunct professor of hydrology and water resources—all at the University of Arizona. Varady's PhD is in the history of colonial infrastructure. Since the mid-1980s, he has studied the U.S.-Mexico border, publishing on water management, environmental health, hazardous materials, and protected areas.